An Introduction to Voice Computing in Python

Jim Schwoebel

Boston · Seattle · Atlanta   neuroLex

An Introduction to Voice Computing in Python
By Jim Schwoebel

Copyright © 2018 Jim Schwoebel. All rights reserved.

Printed in the United States of America.

Published by NeuroLex Laboratories Inc. https://www.neurolex.ai

Cover Designer: Faaizah Ali

October 2018:   First Edition

Revision History for the First Edition
2018-10-01:   First release

The NeuroLex logo is a registered trademark of NeuroLex Laboratories, Inc. *An Introduction to Voice Computing in Python,* the cover image, and related trade dress are trademarks of NeuroLex Laboratories, Inc.

While the publisher and author have used good faith efforts to ensure the information and instructions contained in this work are accurate, the publisher and author disclaim all responsibility for errors or omissions, including without limitation responsibility for damages resulting from the use of or reliance on this work. Use of the information and instructions contained in this work is at your own risk. If any code samples or other technology this work contains or describes is subject to open source licenses or the intellectual property rights of others, it is your responsibility to ensure that your use thereof complies with such licenses and/or rights.

ISBN-13: 978-1725656659
ISBN-10: 1725656655

Schwoebel, J. (2018). *An Introduction to Voice Computing in Python.* Boston; Seattle; Atlanta: NeuroLex Laboratories. https://github.com/jim-schwoebel/voicebook

Table of Contents

Acknowledgements……………………………………………………..7

Frequently Asked Questions……………………………………….9-12

0. Introduction……………………………………………………..13-40
- **I.1** - Defining voice computing………………………………………….15
- **I.2** - The history of voice computing………………………………..16-35
- **I.3** - Economic outlook…………………………………………………36-38
- **I.4** - Educational opportunities………………………………………….39
- **I.5** - Conclusion and rest of book ………………………………………40

1. Fundamentals ………………………………………………….41-68
- **1.1** - Basic principles of voice computing…………………………..43-49
- **1.2** - Installation of required dependencies…………………………….50
- **1.3** - How to read and write audio files………………………………50-51
- **1.4** - Manipulating audio files…………………………………………51-54
- **1.5** - Playing audio files………………………………………………54-55
- **1.6** - Recording streaming audio……………………………………..56-58
- **1.7** - Converting audio formats………………………………………58-60
- **1.8** - Transcribing audio………………………………………………60-64
- **1.9** - Text-to-speech systems………………………………………..65-67

2. Collection …………………………………………………….69-106
- **2.1** - Common mistakes……………………………………………….71-74
- **2.2** - Microphone arrays……………………………………………….74-76
- **2.3** - Mixers………………………………………………………………..77
- **2.4** - Recording modes……………………………………………….78-84
- **2.5** - Cleaning audio files…………………………………………….84-90
- **2.6** - Speaker diarization………………………………………………90-92
- **2.7** - Storing voice files……………………………………………….93-98
- **2.8** - Publishing voice content……………………………………….99-102
- **2.9** - MEMUPPS voice controls……………………………………103-105

3. Featurization ………………………………………………….107-148
- **3.1** - What are features?……………………………………………109-111
- **3.2** - Audio features…………………………………………………111-121
- **3.3** - Text features……………………………………………………122-134

3.4 - Mixed features..134-135
3.5 - Meta features...135-138
3.6 - Dimensionality reduction..139-143
3.7 - Feature selection..143-147

4. Data Modeling 149-186

4.1 - What is machine learning?..151-153
4.2 - Obtaining training data...154-156
4.3 - Labeling training data...157-160
4.4 - Classification models..161-167
4.5 - Regression models..167-171
4.6 - Deep learning models..172-179
4.7 - AutoML techniques...180-185

5. Generation 187-202

5.1 - Machine-generated voice data..189-190
5.2 - Generating text 190-197
5.3 - Generating audio data...197-199
5.4 - Generating mixed data..199-201

6. Visualizations 203-230

6.1 - Visualization libraries..205-207
6.2 - Visualizing audio features..207-216
6.3 - Visualizing text features...216-223
6.4 - Visualizing mixed features...223-225
6.5 - Visualizing meta features...226-228

7. Designing Voice Computers 231-302

7.1 - Defining voice computers...233-235
7.2 - Selecting hardware...236-264
7.3 - Building software..264-275
7.4 - Nala: a voice assistant...276-299

8. Server Architectures 303-350

8.1 - Server architectures...305-319
8.2 - Python web frameworks...319-324
8.3 - MongoDB databases...324-328
8.4 - Building Kafka microservices..328-330
8.5 - Minio as a wrapper for GCP/AWS..331-332
8.6 - Authentication with Auth0...332-334
8.7 - Working with Docker containers..334-337

8.8 - Unit tests and integration tests..337-339
8.9 - Code deployment with GitHub/Heroku..340-343
8.10 - Code deployment with Kubernetes on GCP 344-347

9. Security, Legal, and Ethical Considerations 351-378

9.1 - Security considerations 353-363
9.2 - Legal considerations 363-371
9.3 - Ethical considerations 371-377

10. Getting Involved 379-396

10.1 - NeuroLex's story..381-384
10.2 - The Innovation Fellows Program...384-385
10.3 - Building open source software..385-388
10.4 - Conferences...388-390
10.5 - Graduate schools..390-392
10.6 - Finding a job...392-393
10.7 - Launching a startup...394
10.8 - Teaching opportunities..394

Copyright Permissions..397

References..399

Index..401-406

About the Author..408

Acknowledgments

To my entire team @ NeuroLex. Thanks for making the last 2 years so special. Without your insight and conversations, this book would have never been possible. I've learned so much from you and I'm looking forward to learning so much more in the journey that lies ahead:

- **Product Team:** Drew Morris (CTO), James Fairey, Scott Dunbar, Jared Trotter, Russell Ingram, Austin New, Paul Prae, Rohit Nambisan, Marsal Gavalda, and Brian McDonald.
- **Research Team:** Reza Hosseini Ghomi (CMO), Grace Powers, and many research assistants at UW.
- **Marketing/Sales Team:** Elizabeth Jennings, Hermann Spicker, Doug Graham, Rob Wheeler, and Tom Lamar.
- **Innovation Fellows:** Ryan Dunn, Radhika Duvvuri, Aditya Muralidhar, Peter Tang, Alice Romanov, Brittany Wheeler, Shadab Hassan, Jake Peacock, Neel Atawala, Yahia Ali, Timothy Wroge, Larry Zhang, Audrey Wagner, Dylan Pitulski, Wendy Nguyen, Hannah Gersch, Allison Pei, Alyssa Naritoku, and Mugdha Apte.

To the investors that backed NeuroLex: Betaworks, Lightspeed Venture Partners, GGV Capital, and Launch Capital. You all believed in our vision and backed us when no one else did; there is no greater compliment that you could have given us. I'm looking forward to growing NeuroLex alongside you into the future.

To my Colleagues at CyberLaunch - Chris Klaus, Mark Wasiele, Kyle Grossman and all the startups we funded: C3 Security, Cinchapi, CyberDot, DiaScan, LinkSquares, iTreatMD, Ople, Realfactor, Securolytics, Vyrill, and Yaxa. You have greatly shaped my life's journey with the time we shared. I am incredibly thankful for your continued mentorship.

To my wonderful girlfriend, Jess Tsai. Each day you inspire me to be a better person with how hard you work and the amazing patients that you serve. Our conversations about the STEM Advocacy Institute and implicit bias have greatly shaped my views as a CEO. Thanks so much for inspiring me to continue writing and finishing this book.

To my my amazing family - Mom, Dad, Tim, Mike, Andrea, Emmett, Avery, and Ensley. You've taught me to live life to the fullest and have supported me in my highs and lows.

Lastly, for all the developers who have worked tirelessly to open source voice software: Guido van Rossum (Python), Brian McFee (LibROSA), Google Brain (TensorFlow), François Chollet (Keras), David Cournapeau (scikit-learn), Fabrice Bellard (FFmpeg), Chris Bagwell (SoX), Daniel Povey (Kaldi), Xuedong Huang (Sphinx), and Theodoros Giannakopoulos (pyAudioAnalysis) to name a few. Through this book and your continued initiatives, I hope we can foster a friendly and inviting environment for new faces entering the voice computing field.

Frequently Asked Questions

Q.1 How do I get started?

First, clone the repository with the following statement:

```
cd ~
git clone --recurse-submodules -j8 https://github.com/jim-schwoebel/voicebook
```

Next, run the setup.py script to install all required dependencies:

```
cd ~
cd voicebook
python3 setup.py
```

Now you're ready to go to follow all the examples in this book![1]

Q.2 Who is the target audience for this book?

Anyone who is interested to begin learning how to program voice applications in Python. It helps to know some Python, though this is not necessary.[2]

Specifically, this book will help you:

- Understand how to read/write, record, clean, encrypt, playback, transcode, transcribe, compress, publish, featurize, model, and visualize voice files
- Build your own voice computer and voice assistant from scratch
- Design cutting-edge microservice server architectures on top of Docker and Kubernetes
- Get access to 200+ starter scripts in a GitHub repository
- Become involved in the larger open source voice community

Q.3 Why are you writing this book?

Simply, there are relatively few resources to learn how to write voice-enabled software that are straightforward and easy to understand.[3]

---

[1] **Chapter 9** requires custom installation of Postman, Heroku, Docker, Robot 3T, and MongoDB.

[2] **Book recommendations** – If you're looking for another book to start learning Python before you read this book, I would recommend Automating the Boring Stuff or the NLTK book. Both are quite well-written and freely accessible.

[3] **When I first started programming,** Python seemed like the best language to get started. It was simple, had a rich set of libraries for audio processing and manipulation, and had a thriving community. I learned by doing, and in doing I struggled connecting all the various libraries in Python to start a few projects.

Throughout the past 6 months, I have had repeated requests (mostly by the TRIBE members in NeuroLex) for resources to learn voice computing. There are a few great places to start - like sharing documentation of a few modules (e.g. LibROSA); however, this is often not enough to get through the activation energy necessary to build good software. I would find myself taking some breakout sessions with TRIBE members to hack code together to model voice files. Soon, my time became limited as a CEO and I could not help many eager developers wanting to enter into this field.

This book is therefore a first attempt to scale this knowledge in a more repeatable way.

Q.4   How can I provide feedback on the book?

I welcome any feedback on this book. The best way to give feedback is through adding an issue on the GitHub repository. If you could follow these best practices for providing feedback, it would greatly help with resolving any issues:

- Go to 'issues tab': https://github.com/jim-schwoebel/voicebook/issues
- Select 'new issue' to provide feedback, assign this to jim-schwoebel, label the issue as an enhancement, and assign it to the project book feedback.
- Add in the chapter and page number that you're commenting about in the title and the issue (e.g. Chapter 1 - Page 35 - Table 1.1.1 mis-labeled).
- In the description, add in what you think should be fixed (e.g. The table is not labeled properly. The proper label should be Table 1.3.4. Also, the description is a bit unclear. You may want to eliminate the last sentence).

Once you submit your feedback, it should look something like this (Figure Q.4.1):

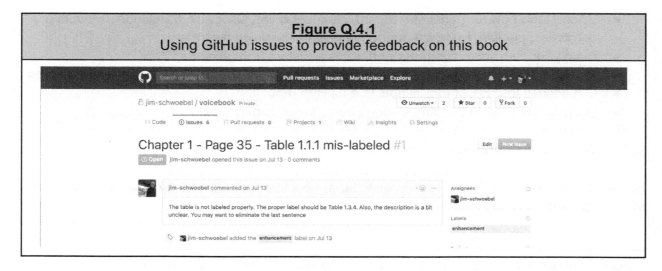

Figure Q.4.1
Using GitHub issues to provide feedback on this book

I'll try my best to reach back out to you within a week, and I take all feedback seriously. Thanks beforehand for any feedback!

Q.5   How can I get involved in the voice community?

See Chapter 10: Getting Involved. This chapter goes through how to become more deeply involved in the voice community through the Innovation Fellows program, building open source software, going to conferences, completing a graduate degree, getting a job, and/or launching a startup.

Q.6   How do I start learning how to build machine learning models?

Check out Chapter 4: Data Modeling. This chapter overviews how to explicitly build a voice-based machine learning model.

If you're just want to learn how to make predictions from pre-trained machine learning models, check out Chapter 3: Featurization. This chapter has over 20 machine learning models that you can use right now in the meta features section (pages 135-138).

Q.7   What is the Innovation Fellows program?

NeuroLex Laboratories ("NeuroLex") is a company with the goal to make voice computing accessible to everyone. Over the past year, we have expanded our team to over 15 people, launched 7 research pilots, built a pipeline of over 80 startup and research collaborators, and have been featured in various press outlets such as the Atlantic and PsychNews.

The Innovation Fellows Program is a competition to engage outstanding individuals with NeuroLex. Specifically, you propose a demo project alongside a mentor in one of three categories: research, data science, or software. You then execute this demo project over a 3-month period either individually or in a group. The program culminates in a Demo Day where you present your project to a panel of judges.[4] Through this structure, you can gain hands-on experience and be part of a sustainable, life-long community.[5]

If you're interested, you can apply for the program @ http://innovate.neurolex.co.

Q.8   How do I cite this book?

Please use this information:

Schwoebel, J. (2018). *An Introduction to Voice Computing in Python.* Boston; Seattle; Atlanta: NeuroLex Laboratories. https://github.com/jim-schwoebel/voicebook

---

[4] **Innovation Fellows Prize** – 1st, 2nd, and 3rd place winners are awarded cash prizes and/or t-shirts.
[5] **Apache license** – Any code you write in the Innovation Fellows program is licensed under an Apache 2.0 license.

Introduction:
Defining Voice Computing

"I always try to write on the principle of the iceberg. There is seven-eighths of it underwater for every part that shows."

-**Ernest Hemingway**
(American Author)

Overview

When I first started programming voice applications I felt like I only saw "the tip of the iceberg." I did not know how transcription models were built or how to build text-to-speech systems through formant additive synthesis methods.[6] It felt as if voice computing knowledge was stored in vaults of training data and code bases that weren't publicly accessible, leading to an air of mystery of how it all worked.[7,8] I felt quite intimidated; I wasn't sure if I could make a contribution that was worthwhile to the voice community at large.[9]

Moreover, the whole discipline of voice computing was quite fragmented and ill-defined. There were fiefdoms of specialists in the areas of speech recognition, text-to-speech synthesis, linguistics, natural language understanding, and deep learning all trying to define voice computing from different angles. As a result, I often had to create new definitions and foster intersections between existing disciplines to build and document innovative software.

This introduction is a first attempt to define voice computing through its disciplinary, historical, economic, and educational components:

- **I.1** - Defining voice computing
- **I.2** - The history of voice computing[10]
- **I.3** - Economic outlook
- **I.4** - Educational opportunities
- **I.5** - Conclusion and rest of book

Through this structure, I hope to inspire you to see the entire iceberg - above and below the water - and feel less intimidated starting voice computing projects.

---

[6] **Instead,** I just knew that Google had an application programming interface (API) that can do all that, and I sought to apply this API for useful purposes.

[7] **In other words,** I felt as though the voice computing community at large intentionally kept "seven-eights of [their voice computing knowledge] underwater for every part [of software] that shows [to generate economic profit]." To play on the quotation by Ernest Hemingway at the beginning of the chapter.

[8] **At the time, big players like Nuance and Google** dominated the transcription market. Now there is much more competition (e.g. IBM/Microsoft/etc.) and a lot of work in deep learning to open-source transcription models :)

[9] **This feeling was intensified because I'm not a PhD-trained speech scientist**, but rather a self-learned software engineer. And almost all jobs out there that seem interesting require a PhD.

[10] **Why voice computing history is important** - It was not until I looked back at history that I felt inspired to *understand* voice computing principles "underneath the iceberg." I found that the human body (e.g. inner ear and vocal chords) inspired many scientists to understand how to build technologies to record and playback voice data (e.g. 1789 - the speaking machine). Like most economic endeavors, there were just as many failures (e.g. HD-DVDs vs. Blue-Rays) as there were successes (e.g. 1970s - Sony - digital sound encoding). There were also many paradigm shifts when new innovations displaced old technologies (e.g. replacement of CDs by .MP3 players).

I.1 Defining voice computing

Let's start out with a few definitions.

Computing is *"any goal-oriented activity requiring, benefiting from, or creating computers."* [11]

Sound computing ('SC'), then, aims to apply computing principles to sound. **Music Computing ('MC')**, applies computing principles to music.[12] **Affective computing** aims to model and simulate human emotions within computers. **Ubiquitous computing ('ubicomp')** is the principle that computing is 'everywhere' with so many sensors, computers, and actuators in the world. **Hands-free computing ('HFC')** occurs when users can interact with computing interfaces without their hands.

With these definitions, we can now define **voice computing ('VC')** as a discipline that *aims to develop hardware or software to process voice inputs*:

- **Voice computing software** can read/write, record, clean, encrypt/decrypt, playback, transcode, transcribe, compress, publish,[13] featurize, model, and visualize voice files.[14]

- **Voice computing hardware** can include a motherboard, microphones, sound cards (with D/A and A/D converters), central processing units (CPUs), graphics cards, storage devices (e.g. hard disks), computer monitors, WiFi chips, Bluetooth chips, radio transmitters, speakers, and a power supply.

A **voice computer**, then, is *any computerized system (assembled hardware and software) that can process voice inputs*. This could include a personal computer (PC), a voice assistant smart speaker (e.g. Amazon Echo), open-source hardware devices (e.g. a Raspberry Pi device), and many other embodiments.[15][16]

This book focuses on voice computing generally to equip you with the foundations necessary to build robust voice-enabled applications in Python.[17]

---

[11] **Computing** - The discipline of computing, as laid out by the Association for Computer Machinery (ACM) in 2005, includes five main disciplines: computer science, computer engineering, information systems, information technology, and software engineering.

[12] **Sound and Music Computing (SMC)** – This term was coined around 1995.

[13] **For example,** software on Facebook could publish voice media on a profile.

[14] **Therefore,** voice computing intersects with the fields of natural language processing, speech recognition, speech synthesis.

[15] **Surprisingly, voice computing has really not had a formal definition** (at least on Wikipedia). It's often loosely used by the media to be associated with new voice interfaces, such as Amazon Alexa or Google Assistant. However, I believe it's necessary to more clearly define and coin this term for the purposes of this book.

[16] **Voice computers** can exhibit a screen or monitor, but this is not not necessary. This means that voice computing is quite different than hands-free computing.

[17] **I believe voice computing (VC)** is a generally more useful definition than speech recognition to help guide the content of this book.

I.2 The history of voice computing

Voice computing has a rich history. A quick way to think about it is in terms of seven historical time periods: the Language period, the Music period, the Scientific period, the Analog period, the Digital period, the Internet period, and the Voice-first period (Figure I.2.1).[18]

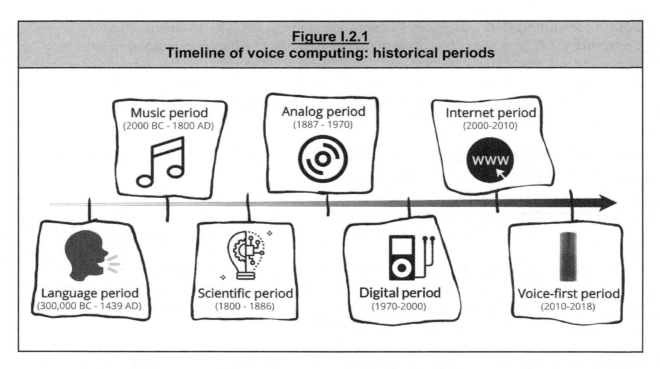

Language period (300,000 BC - 2000 BC) - It all began when humans first evolved the ability to speak and form languages around 300,000 BC.[19] After years of formalizing human speech into words, humans created written languages as the first forms of sound recordings and playback (e.g. phonemes, words, and phrases).[20] This information was often stored on media such as stone tablets or papyrus. It was not until 1439 until printing presses enabled mass distribution of books and newspapers across the world, leading to a revolution in the way languages could be transferred across cultures and geographies.

Music period (2000 BC - 1800 AD) - Like phonemes and written languages, music was one of the earliest forms of sound to be recorded. Ancient cultures inscribed music on cuneiform tablets to store melodies and notes (starting in 2000 BC in modern day Iraq).[21] Then, in a similar manner of how printing presses enabled the mass distribution of written languages, music

---

[18] **If you hate history,** feel free to jump and skim through this introduction if you don't feel like reading.

[19] **Hyoid bone** - The evolution of the hyoid bone led to allowed humans to produce speech vocalizations, which later formed the basis for language systems (e.g. through phonemes).

[20] **Language first appeared in 2690 BC** with the Egyptians as hieroglyphs and morphed into many other forms (e.g. Proto-Indo-European) until the modern day (e.g. English). Language was mostly written down by scribes manually (e.g. monks transcribed the Bible).

[21] **Music notation** – Music inscriptions inspired many iterations and forms of music theory (through Greek times all the way up to the modern day).

boxes were invented to mass distribute melodies to households through music box disks (1800s). Later, other inventions followed to record and playback music, such as player pianos and player organs (1880), revolutionizing the way composers wrote and distributed music.

Scientific period (1800 - 1886) - Next came the era of scientific exploration to record analog sounds in air and reproduce them through mechanical instruments. In 1827, the English scientist Sir Charles Wheatstone coined the word "microphone" to hypothesize how human sound waves could propagate and be captured in air. This led to the invention of the phonautograph in 1857 by Édouard-Léon Scott de Martinville, which was the first device to record sounds as they pass through air through lines etched on paper or glass.[22] This greatly inspired other engineers and scientists to invent devices to capture and playback sound waves, such as Alexander Graham Bell (e.g. 1876 - acoustic telegraph) and Thomas Edison (e.g. 1877 - phonograph). In 1880s, Ramón y Cajal made accurate drawings of the human inner ear, showing how nerve cells propagate auditory information through electrical signals - inspiring scientists to build electrically-driven microphones.

Analog period (1887-1970) - Scientific explorations then led to commercial innovations to record, store, and replay sounds within analog (mechanical and electrical) mediums. The dictaphone (1879) was the first invention that could record speech reliably; however, it was limited to a small corporate community. The gramophone (1887) opened up the ability to record and playback analog sound recordings that could be mass-produced through records, or disks.[23] This invention inspired a wave of other innovations around analog recording devices such as magnetic wire recording devices (1898), the liquid microphone (1903), and the condenser microphone (1916). It was not until magnetic tape recordings (1928-1950s) that analog recordings could be recorded for longer lengths and have relatively high quality.

Moreover, analog playback devices spawned during this period. The first headphones were invented by Nathaniel Baldwin for the Navy in his garage in 1910. For a long time, headphones were only used by the Navy and telephone operators; it was not until John C. Koss invented the first pair of stereo headphones in 1958 that consumers widely adopted this form of playback technology. Moreover, loudspeaker technology was invented in 1924 by Chester W. Rice and Edward W. Kellogg, spawning a wave of innovation of loudspeakers in the years to come.

Around the time of the 1950s, speech recognition technology emerged and became relevant. Early systems for recognizing speech from analog recordings were quite coarse, only being able to recognize spoken digits (e.g. 1952 - IBM Audrey). It was not until Hidden Markov Models (HMMs) were integrated into speech recognition systems that automated transcription software became useful for a variety of industries (e.g. 1985 – could recognize 1,000 words via Kurzweil Applied Intelligence).[24]

---

[22] **Human ear** - Edouard was inspired by the human ear and designed the phonautograph around the ear canal.
[23] **The gramophone** led to a proliferation of music albums in American households and is still used today as record players.
[24] **Speech recognition today** - Now, state-of-the-art speech recognition systems have achieved roughly a 5% error rate, which is roughly equivalent to human comprehension (e.g. 2015 - Google Speech API).

Digital period (1970-2000) - Digital sound encoding (DSE) was then invented by Sony in the 1970s, allowing for analog sound (e.g. amps) recorded through a range of types of microphones (e.g. a condenser microphone) to be converted into digital representations (e.g. numbers). Analog-to-digital converters (A/D converters)[25] and digital-to-analog converters (D/A converters)[26] led to a range of compressed audio formats to emerge (e.g. .WAV file format). These advances led to many more voice recordings to be possible across an array of consumer hardware.

Shortly thereafter, personal computers (~1981) made voice computing accessible to consumers. Particularly, consumers for the first time were able to hear primitive text-to-speech systems from text typed into their keyboards (e.g. iMac - TTS license).[27] The advent of the Internet (1989) allowed for voice media to be played back through web browsers (e.g.1995 - Internet Explorer). Storage media on personal computers (PCs), like CD and DVD writers (1990s), also greatly contributed to adoption and distribution of digital file formats. Moreover, PCs allowed for the development of new programming languages, such as Python, which later became quite significant for processing voice data.

Internet period (2000-2010) - The 2000s was the golden era to record and publish high-quality digital voice recordings on the Internet.[28] Lossless speech codecs (e.g. 2001 - .FLAC) were invented, significantly reducing audio file sizes without sacrificing their overall quality. The adoption of high-fidelity microphones (e.g. MEMS mics) and sound cards on PCs led to podcasting communities to emerge (e.g. iTunes / YouTube), allowing for voice and video content to be distributed and monetized worldwide.[29] Google Chrome was also released in 2008, which created new experiences to record and playback audio within the web browser (e.g. through embedded audio and video codecs). Smartphones (e.g. iPhones) also became widely available, creating new opportunities to record and transmit voice content (e.g. through VoIP networks like Skype).

Moreover, software packages like FFmpeg[30] and SoX[31] allowed for developers with personal computers to generate and manipulate sounds from the command line. Many Python libraries emerged (e.g. LibROSA, NLTK, scikit-learn) to featurize and model text and speech data. Taken together, these shifts made Python a great choice for voice computing projects.

---

[25] **Analog-to-digital converters (A/D converters)** convert analog sound (amps/sec) into samples (numbers).

[26] **Digital-to-analog converters (D/A converters)** convert digital representations of sound back into analog sound.

[27] **Consumers** also heard TTS systems during this time through interfaces like Atari or video games. It's interesting to view such consoles as voice computers, as they were one of the first interfaces for voice computing.

[28] **History of interfaces** - First, we had keyboards to start and stop commands. Then, as applications became more sophisticated, the mouse was invented to help navigate through these applications more seamlessly (e.g. save files on computers and navigate through various applications). New interfaces then emerged as computers became miniaturized: CD players (walkmans, etc.), ipods, and blackberries. It was not until the iPhone that the interface for smartphones became optimal: phones became pocket computers [screen/cpu] loaded with applications enabled with "touchscreen interfaces." [mouse/keyboard]

[29] **iTunes -** I listened to the Brain Science Podcast (hosted by Ginger Campbell) and the Stanford Entrepreneurial Thought Leaders Seminars (hosted by Tina Seelig / Stanford) during this time.

[30] **FFmpeg** is a powerful program for transducing one file format or another.

[31] **SoX** is another program to manipulate audio files to do things like silence removal and automatic generation of sounds.

Voice-first period (2010-2018) - Around 2011, Siri emerged on Apple iPhones as the first voice assistant accessible to consumers. This innovation led to a dramatic shift to building voice-first computing architectures. PS4 was released by Sony in North America (2013 - 70+ million devices), Amazon has released Amazon Echo (2014 - 30M devices), Microsoft released Cortana (2015 - 400 million Windows 10 users), Google released Google Assistant (2016 - 2 billion active monthly users on Android phones), and Apple released HomePod (2018 - 500,000 devices sold, 1 billion devices active with iOS for Siri).[32] These shifts, along with advancements in cloud infrastructure (e.g. AWS/GCP) and codecs[33] have solidified the voice computing field and made it widely relevant to the public at large.

---

[32] **We've now entered** into the era of 'voice-first computing' where users do not even need to use their hands to initiate computing commands. Voice interfaces have become like the new mouse or the new smartphone. Like when the first smartphones emerged (e.g. BlackBerry smartphones), we're still trying to understand the best configuration to interact with voice interfaces (e.g. Amazon Echo and Google Assistant). This ambiguity creates a tremendous opportunity for you as a developer to create new applications and interfaces for voice assistants.

[33] **Wikipedia** - "Opus replaces both Vorbis and Speex for new applications, and several blind listening tests have ranked it higher-quality than any other standard audio format at any given bitrate until transparency is reached, including MP3, AAC, and HE-AAC."

Table I.2.1: The history of voice computing		
Year	Description	Significance to Voice Computing
300000 BC	Humans adapt to have a hyoid bone.	Allowed humans to speak.
2690 BC	The first language is invented around 2690 BC as Egyptian hieroglyphs in the tomb of Seth-Peribsen (2nd Dynasty), Umm el-Qa'ab.	Allowed humans to transmit speech information across generations.
2000 BC	The earliest form of music notation is invented and written on a cuneiform tablet in Sumer (modern-day Iraq).	Led to the reproduction of music through written modes (and modern-day music notation).
1439	Printing press is invented by Johannes Gutenberg.	Allowed for mass distribution of knowledge through language.

1784	Wolfgang Kempelen invents the acoustic-mechanical speech machine modeled from the human vocal tract.	Gave rise to future work in the study of phonetics and speech recognition; much of this work was continued only decades later.
1791	Luigi Galvani (Italy) demonstrates that electricity is the medium by which signals passed to and from the muscles in frogs.	Led to further interest to look at biology for inspiration for voice innovations; specifically, with the muscles of the throat and the electrical patterns that activated them to play back sound media.
~1800	Music boxes are manufactured to replay simple melodies from music box disks.	Led to widespread interest of common households in music playback technology in home.
1827	Sir Charles Wheatsone, an English scientist, coins the term 'microphone.'	Led to a greater scientific interest in the area of how sound waves propagate in air.
1857	The phonautograph is invented as the first device that could record sounds as they pass through air by Parisian inventor Édouard-Léon Scott de Martinville. The first sound recorded ("phonautogram") was a person singing.	Spurred further work in voice recording instruments.

1876	The world's first player piano is invented which could record and playback music with sheets of paper.	Encouraged commercial and scientific work to refine ways to automate music playback.
1876	Alexander Graham Bell invents an acoustic telegraph to transmit audio frequencies through electrical wires.	Led to Bell Telephone Company, which provided telephone access to more than 150,000 in the USA.
1877	The phonograph is invented by Thomas Edison, which can record sound and play it back. It used a grooved metal cylinder wrapped in tinfoil, producing "hill-and-dale recordings."[34]	Led to further work in audio recording. This invention, however, was not commercially viable.
1878	The carbon microphone is invented by David Edward Hughes (later improved in 1920).	Provided another option and medium to record and replay audio.

---

[34] **The first recorded words** were "Mary had a little lamb."

1879	Thomas Edison invents the dictation machine.	Gave rise to the first analog devices to record voices in corporate settings.
1887	Emile Berliner patents a system for sound recording based on flat disks, spiral grooves, and special materials (e.g. glass, zinc, and plastic). These were the first sound recordings that could be mass-produced; however, they only captured a narrow segment of the audible sound spectrum (250 Hz up to about 2,500 Hz).	Led to commercial interest in microphone designs.
1888	Ramón y Cajal (Spain) draws some of the earliest anatomical drawings of the human ear (outer, middle, inner ear), proposing that hair cell motion causes electric potentials to cascade and send auditory information back to the brain's cortex via the auditory nerve.	Stimulated scientists to further explore how the inner ear is a transducer of electricity; led to the use the human body as inspiration for voice computing devices (e.g. microphones).
1898	The first analog magnetic wire recording device is invented by Valdemar Poulsen.	Allowed for longer audio recordings; for the first time, multiple recordings could be made from the same device.

Year	Event	Impact
1900	The first sound film (a video with synchronized sound) is released in Paris.	Made sound films popular, leading to filmmakers becoming more innovative in their use of sound in movies.
1903	Alexander Graham Bell invents the liquid microphone, which uses sulfuric acid and displaced water to produce electrical signals.	Led to further commercial work in the area of microphone design; this was the first working microphone.
1910	The first pair of mono headphones is developed by Nathaniel Baldwin in his kitchen and was purchased by the US Navy.	Spawned a movement for private playback devices and many other headphone designs in the years that followed.
1916	The condenser microphone is invented by E.C. Wente (Western Electric).	Alllowed for low-cost, high-fidelity audio recordings. Condenser microphones are the standard microphones present in most PCs today.
1925	*Western Electric* Record labels adopt Western Electric's condenser microphones, electrical signal amplifiers, and electromechanical recorders.	Opened up the opportunity for a wider range of sounds to be etched onto disks for playback (e.g. electric organs).
1925	Chester W. Rice and Edward W. Kellogg invent the first moving-coil loudspeaker.	Created a cost-effective way to playback sound; moving-coil loudspeakers are commonly used today to playback sound on PCs.

1927	The first feature-length sound film (also known as a "talkie"), the *Jazz Singer,* is released. After great success, sound-on-film becomes a standard in the movie-making business.	Led to a burst of other "talkie" films throughout the late 1920s and early 1930s across America and internationally.
1928	Magnetic tape is invented by Germany in 1928, which allowed for devices to record and playback audio (tape recorders) and video (video tape recorders).[35]	Led to far longer, higher fidelity, and and more editable sound recordings (compared to disk recordings).
1942	The ribbon microphone is invented for radio broadcasting.	Spread broadcast radio virally across America, leading with a fascination with the voice medium to absorb news and other types of information.
1950s	Magnetic tape becomes the standard medium to master audio recordings in the radio and music industries, replacing the disk.	Led to far longer, higher fidelity, and and more editable sound recordings (compared to disk recordings).

---

[35] **Magnetic tape** transformed how sounds were recorded; however, it was kept secret until after the World War II ended.

1952	Bell Labs releases Audrey to recognize spoken digits.[36]	Recognized spoken digits with 90% accuracy (only with inventor), which was state-of-the-art. Led to further work in speech recognition technology.
1958	John C. Koss (jazz musician) produces the first pair of stereo headphones, leading to Koss Corporation (HQ in Milwaukee, WI).	Made headphones accessible to the masses and commercial interest in the area.
1962	IBM Shoebox is invented to understand words.	Understood 16 English words, which broke all previous records. Led to further work in speech recognition technology.
1963	The compact cassette is invented by Phillips.	Helped to facilitate adoption of analog-based recording formats (e.g. ~30-40 minutes per cassette).
1964	The electret microphone[37] (or foil electric microphone) is invented by Gerhard Sessler (Germany) and Jim West (Virginia) at Bell Laboratories with patent no. 3,118,022.	Led to low-cost microphones that could be put into electronic devices. Nearly all modern cell phone and headset microphones are electret microphones (e.g. ~ 1 billion are produced globally each year).

---

[36] **The Audey device**, although accurate, forced the speaker to pause for 350 milliseconds between words and only understood the numbers 1 to 9.

[37] **Electret microphones** use ferroelectric materials to permanently polarize surfaces and generate current.

1970s	The dynamic microphone is invented.	Allowed for lower sound sensitivities and clearer sound recordings.
1970s	SONY Digital sound encoding is invented by Sony.	Facilitated rapid adoption of digital audio formats (e.g. .WAV format).
1979	The first all-digitally recorded album, Ry Cooder's Bop 'Til You Drop, is released. The label was recorded on a 32-track machine built by 3M.	Made digital music albums accessible as a part of mainstream culture.
1981	The personal computer (PC) is released as a product produced by IBM and Microsoft.	Allowed for mass adoption of audio recording and playback technologies through PC-enabled sound cards, microphones, and speakers.
1980s	Compact Disks (CDs) are invented by Sony and Philips, using a laser beam to playback music. CDs could be played back many times without losing fidelity; recordings could be up to 80 minutes long (previously 50 minutes).	Allowed for new voice content to be created and distributed portably, as the CD format was considerably smaller than the predecessor LP format.

Year	Event	Impact
1983	The silicon microphone, or MEMS microphone, is invented by Gerhard Sessler (Germany) and D. Hohm.	Provided more options to record high-fidelity audio (high SNR and high sensitivity) and low power consumption.
1984	Apple integrates text-to-speech (MacInTalk) into their personal computers, licensed from Joseph Katz and Mark Barton.	Brought forth a foray of new innovations in the text-to-speech space, cultivating a culture for other tech companies (e.g. Microsoft) to build or license TTS technologies.
1985	Kurzweil Applied Intelligence (acquired by Lernout & Hauspie) releases the first speech-to-text program built with a Hidden Markov Model (HMM).	Led to transcription models that could recognize up to 1,000 words, making voice applications relevant across a range of industries.
1986	IBM Tangora is released by IBM that uses HMMs to predict phonemes in speech.	Accelerated the use of HMM-based speech recognition models by corporate customers.
1986	Parallel Distributed Processing (a book) is published by James L. McClelland, David E. Rumelhart and the PDP Research Group.	Outlined the framework for a neural-network approach to build speech recognition models (alongside other use cases).

1987	The World of Wonder's Julie Doll, a toy that children could train to respond to their voices, is released publicly.	Brought speech recognition technology to the home and to a new generation.
1988	Digital compact cassettes are invented by Philips and Matsushita.	Facilitated the shift between from analog recording to digital recordings, replacing analog cassettes.
1989	The Internet becomes accessible to the public for the first time.	Led to infrastructure that enabled commercial use for voice technology (e.g. voice-over-IP). Also, led to development of publishing communities for voice media (e.g. iTunes / podcasts).
1990	Dragon (now Nuance) releases Dragon Dictate, the first offline speech recognition system for consumers.	Made speech recognition technology available to the mass market (for home use on PCs).
1990	The Python programming language is invented by Guido van Rossum.	Made it easy to build voice computing applications on personal computers.
1990	The first web browser (the WorldWideWeb) is released as an interface to the Internet by Tim Berners-Lee.	Created an interface for consumers to view voice content posted online; led to web browsers made by commercial entities (e.g. Microsoft - Internet Explorer).

Year	Event	Impact
1991	Sound Exchange (SoX) software is released by Chris Bagwell.	Enabled developers to flexibly manipulate audio files with command line interfaces (CLIs).
1993	The .WAV digital audio file format is invented by Microsoft and IBM.	Allowed for greatly reduced file sizes through audio codecs and compression; spurred on a range of other audio codecs to be invented.
1993	CMUSphinx — The Sphinx package is developed and released by the Sphinx Group at Carnegie Mellon University.[38]	Developed into PocketSphinx, which is a widely used open source transcription library in Python.
1997	DVD format is invented by Phillips and Sony.	Allowed for the storage of more data on a disk drive (replacing CDs); technology was accessible to anyone with a DVD burner.
2000	The .FLAC lossless audio codec is invented.	Reduced file sizes (½) without sacrificing audio quality.
2000	FFmpeg is released as open-source software.	Made a powerful tool for audio file conversion and manipulation open to Python developers.
2001	Natural Language Toolkit (NLTK) library is released by Steven Bird, Edward Loper, Ewan Klein.	Allowed Python developers to build open applications related to natural language processing.

---

[38] **Sphinx** is a continuous-speech, speaker-independent recognition system making use of hidden Markov acoustic models (HMMs) and an n-gram statistical language model. It was developed by Kai-Fu Lee at Carnegie Mellon University as a part of his doctoral dissertation.

2002	Modern sound cards[39] on laptops and desktops allow for analog sound to be recorded through a microphone and produced into a digital file format (e.g. .WAV).	Allowed for anyone with a PC to record and playback audio easily with microphones and speakers.
2003	The iTunes store opens up publicly.	Enabled many DIY enthusiasts to publish their own podcasts and monetize them, greatly helping to facilitate adoption of digital-based voice recording formats (e.g. .MP3).
2003	Skype (acq. Microsoft) announces the release of the first version of its software.	Made voice-over-IP (VoIP) relevant for international calls.
2006	Blue ray disks are invented by Sony.	Put high-definition video and audio in the hands of consumers (~50GB / disk).
2006	Google translate launches as a commercial machine translation product.	Made deep learning models for translation available to the public. Now has 200 million active daily users.

---

[39] **Specifically,** these sound cards contain digital-to-analog converters, audio codecs, and analog-to-digital converts (discussed in greater detail in Chapter 1).

Year	Event	Impact
2006	NSA starts using speech recognition to isolate keywords in speech.	Spawned new research funding into speech recognition technology, leading to further advances.
2007	Google introduces GOOG-411, a telephone-based directory service. This will serve as a foundation for the company's future Voice Search product.	Created a rich dataset for Google's voice applications.
2007	Scikit-learn library is released by David Cournapeau.	Made it very simple to build machine learning models (e.g. SVM models) in Python.
2007	Apple releases the first iPhone model with quad-band GSM cellular connectivity with GPRS and EDGE support for data transfer.	Ushered in a new era of using smartphones for transmitting voice data across cellular and VoIP networks (e.g. Skype).
2008	Micro-SD cards are used as storage media for audio content.	Allowed for Arduinos and other devices (e.g. cameras) to have significant storage capacity (e.g. 32-64 GB). Now can write at 90 MB/sec.
2008	Google releases Chrome, a new web browser.	Enabled more seamless collection of voice data through browsers, with built-in audio and video codecs.

Year	Event	Impact
2008	Google launches the Voice Search app.	Started the process of building transcription models and voice search.
2009	Kaldi software is released by Daniel Povey and others.	Made it easier to develop open source speech recognition projects.
2011	Apple launches Siri, a personal voice assistant for iPhones.	Introduced voice assistants to the public at large. Siri is the most widely used voice assistant by American households.
2012	The .OPUS file format is released as the most modern form of speech codec, replacing .VORBIS and .SPEEX as the gold standard for recording speech-based audio files.	Facilitated more efficient transmission of speech data across cellular and VoIP networks.
2013	PS4 is released to the public through Sony.	Made voice computing relevant for gaming consoles (74 million units sold).
2014	Amazon releases Alexa, a voice-controlled speaker.	Brought voice assistants into mainstream culture - much like early smartphones (e.g. Apple – iPhones).

Year	Event	Impact
2014	Microsoft announces Cortana, a voice assistant for Microsoft Windows.	Opened up the voice computing field to billions of Windows users.
2015	TensorFlow is open-sourced by Google.	Made it possible to quickly build deep learning models; sped up innovations in speech recognition, translation, and text-to-speech (e.g. WaveNet models).
2015	CLOUD SPEECH-TO-TEXT — Google Speech API enters Beta mode, priced at $0.024/minute of transcribed audio and priced per 15 seconds recorded.	Achieved a word error rate of roughly 5% as of 2018, which is approximately the same as human hearing / understanding.
2015	LibROSA library is released at the SciPy conference by Brian McFee.	Made available open source tools for audio featurization, manipulation, self-similarity, filtering, and dynamic time warping.
2015	The pyAudioAnalysis Python library is released by Theodoros Giannakopoulos in a PloS One publication (Greece).	Made available open source tools for audio featurization, speaker diarization, audio file annotation, and HMM modeling.
2015	The Keras library is released in Python by François Chollet.	Made it easy to deploy deep learning models with TensorFlow as a back-end.

Year	Event	Impact
2015	Apple releases AirPods, wireless earbuds, for use with smartphones.	Consumerized the adoption of Bluetooth-based earbuds, opening up new interfaces for voice computers to record and playback audio.
2016	Google Assistant is formally released.	Made Google a significant player in the voice assistant market.
2016	The WaveNet model is published by DeepMind (acquired by Google in 2014).	Produced text-to-speech content with nearly human-level accuracy.
2018	Apple releases HomePod.	Expanded upon Apple's dominance in voice computing (e.g. with Siri embedded in smartphones / laptops).

I.3   Economic outlook

It's an exciting time to be a developer in the voice computing space. As of 2017, 1 in 4 searches on Google are now voice-enabled, Amazon Alexa just passed 10,000 skills, and 100 million calls are completed on WhatsApp daily. The smart speaker market is clearly dominated by Amazon, but it's still unclear who the winner will be in the long-run, as Google Home is expected to make up some of this market share into the future.[40] These trends thus make it attractive to build and monetize voice-based applications.

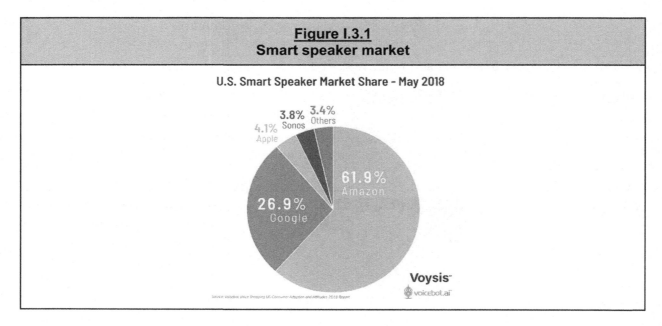

Beyond these trends, voice computing is having a potent effect on the global economy ($104.6B/year).[41] In particular, voice technology is projected to grow at a CAGR of 19-25% by 2025.[42] This is driving innovation across a range of industries including machine learning infrastructure, voice assistants, connected cars, call centers, speech recognition, biometrics, digital health, personal messaging, text-to-speech software, connected home applications, smart agriculture, cloud computing, digital logistics, recruiting, interactive voice response systems, market research, broadcast radio, and many others (Table I.4.1). When viewed in sum-total, machine learning (40% CAGR) and voice assistants (39% CAGR) seem like the most attractive industries to apply voice-based applications currently and into the future.

---

[40] **It seems like smart speakers** are much like early smartphones; we still don't know what the best interface will be. For this reason, expect much variation in the smark speaker market over the next few years, especially as Sonos and Bose enter the market (Figure I.4.1).

[41] **$104.6B market size** – This is estimated from market sizes for voice assistants ($2B), IVR systems ($3.5B), speech recognition ($6B), voice biometrics ($10B), voice messaging ($1.5B), TTS software ($1.5B), broadcast radio advertising ($18B), and 10% of the following markets: machine learning ($100MM), connected cars ($5B), call centers ($800MM), digital health ($2.1B), connected home ($2.5B), smart agriculture ($700MM), cloud computing infrastructure ($30.5B), digital logistics ($1B), digital recruiting ($15B), and market research ($4.4B).

[42] **Statistic taken from** 4-traders and Businesswire.

Table I.3.1 Industries affected by voice computing			
Industry	**Estimated CAGR over next 5 years**	**Factors that impact growth in voice computing field**	**Example company**
Machine learning	40% (~$1B)	Adoption of cloud infrastructure (e.g. AWS/GCP) and creation of new training datasets within enterprises.	H20.ai
Voice assistants	39% ($2B)	Market share by Google Assistant (Google), Alexa (Amazon), Cortana (Microsoft), and Siri (Apple). Consumer reaction to privacy dramatically affects adoption.	Amazon
Connected Cars	31% (~$50B)	Automobile manufacturers like Tesla, BMW, and others investing to develop and release connected cars on market in the consumer price range (adoption of cloud-based technologies).	Tesla
Call centers	25.2% (~$8B)	Time to resolve calls, clauses built into the contracts of call centers.	Cogito
Speech Recognition	19-25% ($6B).	Consumer adoption of voice assistants (e.g. Echo) and enterprise adoption of cloud-based video and speech tools (e.g. Zoom Meetings).	TranscribeMe
Voice Biometrics	19.0% ($10B)	Convenience in authentication and number/scale of cyber breaches.	Yobe
Digital health (Healthcare)	18.0% ($21B)	Adoption of mobile health tools, telehealth tools, electronic medical records (4% CAGR), HIPAA compliant policies (security), and development of new reimbursement codes (diagnostics).	Suki
Voice Messaging	~17.0% ($1.5B)	Mobile enablement, cloud consumption, and a strategic priority by businesses in all sectors to create differentiated customer experiences.	Twilio
Text-to-Speech software	15.92% ($1.5B)	Emergence of smartphones with text-to-speech capabilities.	Lyrebird

Smart Agriculture	13.09% (~$7B).	Growing global population increasing need for food, rise in the need of livestock health and performance monitoring, increasing support of the government in the adoption of modern agriculture techniques.	AgVoice
Cloud computing infrastructure	12.9% ($305B)	AWS, GCP, Azure, and IBM Bluemix cloud offerings and corporate adoption.	Google Cloud Platform
Connected home	11.0% (~$25B)	Rise of consumer adoption of connected devices in the home, such as smart thermostats or smart locks. Many of these things can be tied to voice assistants.	August smart lock
Digital logistics	11.0% ($10B)	Investment in innovation initiatives in the logistic industry.	Oracle
Recruiting / job interviews	8.50% ($150B)	Adoption of tools by recruiters to automate the screening process.	HireVue
Interactive Voice Response (IVR)	7% ($3.5B)	Cloud infrastructure to lower costs and of self-service applications.	Genesys
Market research	3.2% ($44B)	CMOs adopting more data-centric market research initiatives (e.g. budgets).	SurveyLex
Radio broadcast advertising	1.2% ($18B)	Shift from broadcast radio companies (e.g. Entercom) to monetize digital content.	Entercom

I.4 Educational opportunities

Despite great economic growth, it's of note that there will likely be a shortage of data scientists and data engineers capable of analyzing voice data over the next 10 years, following the trend of a shortage of data scientists in general.[43] Therefore, there is a huge need to educate and train the next-generation data scientist that is capable to analyze voice data and apply their work in production environments (Table I.4.1).[44] *This book is but a first attempt to address this shortage.*[45] [46]

The best ways to learn voice computing seem to be through completing a graduate degree in computing (MS/PhD) or as a self-learned individual. If you're into the academic route, check out the list of graduate schools listed in Chapter 10. If you're interested in self-learning, continue reading this book![47]

Note you typically don't need a graduate degree if you're interested in being a voice decision maker, functional analyst, developer, data analyst, or analytics manager (Table I.4.1).

Table I.4.1: Voice job degree requirements		
DSA Framework category	**Postings requesting experienced workers**	**Postings requiring Master's or higher**
All	81%	6%
Data-driven decision makers	88%[48]	5%
Functional analysts	71%	6%
Data systems developers	84%	3%
Data analysts	76%	6%
Data scientists	78%	39%
Analytics managers	94%	11%

---

[43] **There will also be a shortage of engineers that are capable of applying their machine learning models into production environments.** It's one thing to build a machine learning model, and it's quite another thing to put it into production (in an NGINX-based, Kafka distributed microservices architecture). For this reason, I have added an explicit section of this book (Chapter 8) dedicated to help you build production-ready code.

[44] **I have generally found there is an abundance of people** who can analyze natural language data (e.g. text using libraries such as NLTK in Python), but there are few people who can analyze voice files.

[45] **Chapter 10 of the book** is all about how to get involved in the voice community. I hope you are inspired to help build this community.

[46] **There's a need to design new voice computing curricula** - I hope this book leads to more formalized curricula / courses within universities in the area of voice computing.

[47] **I'm biased toward self-learned engineers** because that's the path that I took (☺).

[48] **Note** that although certain managerial jobs are classified as entry level, these numbers typically reflect the years of managerial experience required, as opposed to the overall years of work experience required.

I.5 Conclusion and rest of the book

👋 Way to go! You now know why voice computing is important.

The rest of the book will go through concrete examples of code to help get you started to program voice applications in Python. The fundamentals of voice computing are laid out (Chapter 1). Then you learn how to collect, featurize, model, generate, and visualize voice data (Chapters 2-6). Thereafter, various voice computer designs (Chapter 7) are proposed to guide you in selecting the optimal voice computer for your project. After this, voice computing server architectures (Chapter 8) are outlined to help interface your voice projects with the Internet and reach thousands of users. Legal and security implications of voice computing are then discussed (Chapter 9) to future-proof your software. Lastly, we discuss ways that you can get involved in the voice community (Chapter 10).

If you have not done so yet, make sure you have cloned the Voicebook repo and installed all the dependencies. This will help you not run into any issues in the chapters that follow. To do this, just type this in the terminal:

```
cd ~
git clone --recurse-submodules -j8 https://github.com/jim-schwoebel/voicebook
cd voicebook
python3 setup.py
```

I hope you're excited as I am to start programming! 🤖

Chapter 1:
Voice Computing Fundamentals

"Remember that basketball is a game of habits. If you make the other guy deviate from his habits, you've got him"
-Bill Russell
(Retired NBA basketball player)

Chapter Overview

When I grew up I played basketball pretty much everyday. My coaches always stressed that *fundamentals* were important. Things like how consistently you shot the ball, hedged on defense, turned the ball over, and boxed out to grab rebounds dramatically affected the outcome of most games we played. It was often something simple - like turning the ball over too many times or getting dramatically out-rebounded by the other team - that caused us to lose games. In other words, we "deviated from our habits" and the other team "got us."[49]

Voice computing is very much like basketball. It's quite important to understand the fundamentals: microphone selection, saving and manipulating audio files, using audio codecs to compress audio, etc.[50] It's often something simple (e.g. choice of a microphone) which leads to poor or good voice quality.[51] If you understand and stick to these voice computing fundamentals you can compete with corporate giants like Google, Nuance, IBM, or Amazon (in terms of the software and datasets that you make).[52]

The goal of this chapter is to help get you up-to-speed with how to develop tools in this Voice-first period. Specifically, we will overview:

- **1.1** - Basic principles of voice computing
- **1.2** - Installing dependencies
- **1.3** - How to read and write audio files
- **1.4** - Manipulating audio files
- **1.5** - Playing audio files
- **1.6** - Recording streaming audio
- **1.7** - Converting audio formats
- **1.8** - Transcribing audio
- **1.9** - Text-to-speech systems

In this way, you will have the foundations necessary to thrive and build interesting voice applications in Python.

---

[49] **Bill Russell.** This is from the quote at the beginning of the chapter. Bill Russell is one of my all-time favorite human beings because he is quite humble despite all of his external success (11 NBA championships). He leads by doing and inspires all who surround him to win.

[50] **Like basketball,** it does take some time to refine your craft when programming voice applications. After about a year or so of coding in voice computing you'll be quite comfortable and can usefully contribute to the field at large.

[51] **If you don't stick to these voice computing fundamentals, larger companies will likely out-compete you.** This is mostly due to the engineers at these companies. Most of the people in the voice divisions at Google, for example, have PhDs and are classically trained to know how to build speech-recognition based machine learning models. They may know how to code HMMs or similar algorithms without making mistakes.

[52] **You can offer fresh new approaches** and perspectives to voice computing. Don't be intimidated by the big players. You can get them to deviate from their habits by building a new algorithm or more efficient software than they use internally, which could perhaps lead them to buy your company :-)

1.1 Basic principles of voice computing

To begin, let's review a few simple concepts so you know what is going on behind the scenes on your computer when you collect, transcode, and analyze audio data in your Python code.[53]

One of the most important voice computing concepts to grasp is the importance of the microphone in collecting audio samples. Simply, a **microphone** is a transducer that converts sound (e.g. pressure waves in air) into an electrical signal (e.g. amps - C/s). The most common microphone used for audio applications is the condenser microphone, which uses a diaphragm to produce changes in distance over capacitor plates to produce electrical current (Table 1.1.1).[54] This electrical current generated (C/s) thus is proportional to and represents the analog pressure signal exerted on the area of the diaphragm of the condenser microphone (e.g. pressure = Force / Area).

The **choice of microphone** and **how you use a microphone** dramatically affect audio sample quality (Table 1.1.1). For example, most MacBook Air computers contain condenser microphones that were designed with speech in mind and are inadequate for music recording applications.[55] The further you are away from the microphone the more attenuation there will be in the recorded signal.[56] Also, if you are outdoors there may be noise, such as cars going by or wind, which can reduce sample quality.[57][58] Therefore, you should keep microphone type, distance, and environment constant when recording voice samples to ensure sample quality (e.g. use a MacBook air condenser microphone indoors within 1 meter of computer).

There has also been a trend recently towards using **wireless microphones** - for example, using your iPhone's electret microphone to record and store voice samples.[59] This has made it simpler for end users to interact with voice computers over the last few years.

---

[53] **Why this section exists.** I was really confused with some of these ideas when I first started to code, even as an engineer. Therefore, I think by providing some context it will positively affect the quality of the audio data you collect as well as your overall strategy for writing code.

[54] **The voltage maintained across the capacitor** plates changes with the vibrations in the air, according to the capacitance equation ($C = Q/V$), where Q = charge in coulombs, C = capacitance in farads and V = potential difference in volts. Or, expressed differently, $C = I/R$, I=current (amps) and R=resistance (ohms). Q is constant, so you can rewrite the equation $I = Q * 1/CR$, so as capacitance or resistance changes current changes. The capacitance (5-100 pF) and resistance (1100 MΩ to tens of GΩ) are thus used as high/low pass filters to get good audio signals.

[55] **You can adjust the settings** on your Mac computer using System Preferences > Sound > Input to adjust the microphone gain and also select ambient noise reduction to reduce high-pitched sounds. Note that this may not work for music recording applications.

[56] **Via the equation** $L_{p2} = L_{p1} + 20 \log_{10}(r_1/r_2)$ dB, where L_{p2} is the log pressure at distance 2 (r_2) and L_{p1} is the log pressure at distance 1 (r_1). To calculate a logarithmic pressure all you need to do is $L_p = 20*\log_{10}(p/p_0)$ dB where p is the root mean square sound pressure and p_0 is the reference sound pressure.

[57] **Podcasting equipment** - You can also buy audio interfaces, mixers, windshields, headphones, headphone amplifiers, mic stands, shock mounts, microphone cables, soundproofing material for rooms, digital recorder software (on your phone), and SD cards for storage.

[58] **Use noise-cancelling microphones in noisy environments** - If you are recording in these noisy environments, noise-cancelling lavalier microphones may be a good option to make sure samples can be transcribed properly.

[59] **Wired vs. wireless headphones** - Note that there has been a wave of new wireless microphones emerge in the last few years. This has been a shift from prior wired versions. Specifically, there is a trend to combine microphones with headphones in the ear - known as ear buds (e.g. Apple AirPod).

Table 1.1.1
List of microphones and their utility

Type of microphone	How they work	Utility
Condenser microphone	Uses two capacitor plates and a diaphragm to produce electric current. Capacitance and resistance allow for filtering of current in a way that produces an audio signal.	Wide variety of types; can get low-, moderate-, and high-quality microphones for home or commercial uses.
Dynamic microphone	Uses induction coils attached to a diaphragm to produce sound via electromagnetic induction.	Can customize microphone to various parts of the audio spectrum (e.g. bases); useful for music performances or lecture halls.
Ribbon microphone	Uses corrugated metal ribbon suspended in a magnetic field to produce sound via electromagnetic induction.	Useful for radio broadcasting applications.
Condenser MEMS microphone	A miniaturized version of the condenser microphone etched on silicon wafers.	Small size, high sound quality, reliable and affordable.
Piezoelectric MEMS microphone	Uses a piezoelectric material to on a silicon wafer to produce electrical current when applied to mechanical stress.	Low-power and can be used in tough environments (waterproof, dustproof, particle-resistant, and shockproof). Quite high reliability.
Electret microphone	Uses a permanently charged material (e.g. PTFE plastic film) to produce voltage when subjected to pressure.	Useful for low-cost manufacturing in smartphones or personal computers.

| Noise-cancelling microphone | Many types, but a common type uses two ports as a condenser microphone to subtract noise out from the sample. | Useful to filter out noise in noisy environments and increase transcription accuracy. |

Most computers (e.g. an iMac) come equipped with **sound cards**[60] that support audio data going in and out. The audio data can be sent in either an analog format[61] (e.g. amps = C/s) or in a digital format (e.g. linear PCM data, 10101) through buses (e.g. AC-Link). When a new audio sample is recorded through your selected microphone,[62] the analog data must be converted into a digital format using an analog-to-digital converter (A/D converter) on the sound card (Figure 1.1.1).[63][64] To playback sound through **speakers** and/or **headphones**, sound cards must convert digital data to analog data using a digital-to-analog converter (D/A converter). *Note that sound cards dramatically affect the quality of recording and playing back voice content.*

Once converted to a digital stream, an **audio codec**[65] is a software program used to encode and decode digital audio data to and from a digital audio coding format (Figure 1.1.1 - e.g. linear PCM data → .WAV → linear PCM data).[66][67] An **audio coding format,** then, is the output file type of a digital signal that has been manipulated by an audio codec program (e.g. .WAV). **Audio transcoding** is the process of converting one audio coding format to another (e.g. .MP3 → .WAV). When you transcode audio formats you can lose some of the signal if you convert between lossless format to a lossy format.[68] For example, conversion of speech codecs to music codecs leads to irreversible signal loss (e.g. .WAV → .OPUS → .WAV). A list of common audio coding formats is provided in the following table (Table 1.1.3).

---

[60] **Audio interfaces** - Professional sound cards are also known as audio interfaces; They often have multi-channel sound recording and playback capabilities.

[61] **Analog data for sound from microphones** is represented here as current measurements (A) from a pressure sensor. Amps are a measure of how much current is transmitted through a wire. Thus, as more pressure is exerted on a microphone, the more current that will flow through the wires and thus be converted this way.

[62] **Note that microphone choice is important.** Also, the distance you speak from the microphone is an important factor in high vs. low-quality samples. Keep this in mind when you record audio samples.

[63] **Why do we use digital signals?** The primary disadvantage of analog signals compared to digital transmission is that any system has noise. Digital signals help the data to be stored with less noise and, often, higher quality. Also, these signals are much easier to manipulate and add filters - e.g. low/high pass filters - to eliminate unwanted noise.

[64] **What affects signal quality?** The most important factor relating to signal quality is the sampling rate. Aliasing can occur if the input is sampled below the Nyquist rate, or twice the highest frequency of interest. Higher sampling rates often result in better signal quality but also larger file sizes.

[65] **What CODEC stands for** - Audio codecs get their name from (audio en**CO**der/**DEC**oder).

[66] **Speech codecs** (e.g. .OPUS) are audio codecs that look for sound and language patterns. In addition, since the human voice falls into a much more limited audio range than music, a speech codec is able to achieve the highest voice compression.

[67] **In other words**, codecs compress and decompress digital audio data, allowing for more efficient and standardized data transmission (e.g. through cell networks)

[68] **This is known as generation loss.** From Wikipedia: "The process of transcoding into a lossy format introduces varying degrees of generation loss, while the transcoding from lossy to lossless or uncompressed is technically a lossless conversion because no information is lost; however, the process is irreversible and is more correctly known as destructive."

Figure 1.1.1:
Sample figure illustrating how a codec works

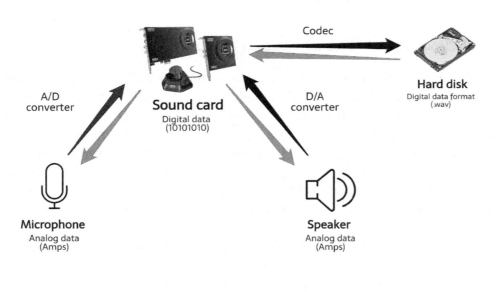

Description: First, an audio sample is collected through a microphone, then an A/D converter converts the analog audio into digital audio (e.g. PCM format, 10101). Then a codec compresses the audio into an audio format (e.g. .WAV format). This audio format then can be decompressed through the codec back into a digital file format to send analog data back to speakers for playback.

Table 1.1.3:
Common audio coding formats

Coding format	Pros	Cons
.MP3	Very small file sizes.	Compression results in some signal loss.
.WAV	Works well to load in .wav files in many Python libraries.	Larger file sizes.
.AAC	Achieves better sound quality than MP3 at the same bit rate.	Proprietary format.
.FLAC	Very small file size and little signal loss.	Must be converted before analyzing .FLAC files.
.OPUS	Focuses on human voice range, so very small file type. Open-source audio codec.	Lossy format; quality is permanently altered to reduce file size.

Audio channels represent the number of audio inputs or outputs of a recorded audio signal. Sound cards can generate various audio channel configurations; however, the most important configurations are ***stereo*** (e.g. 2 channels) and ***mono*** (e.g. 1 channel).[69] Stereo signals can be converted into mono signals - often by averaging the amplitudes of both channels into a signal channel. Mono signals can be converted into stereo signals by cloning the same content from one channel to another, or by adding some effects to the other channel. Therefore, it's important to realize that sound cards can process and output multiple independent sounds simultaneously, as this dramatically affects how you record and playback audio (Figure 1.1.2).

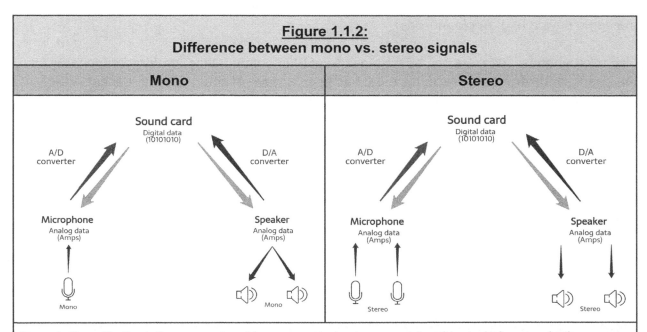

Figure 1.1.2:
Difference between mono vs. stereo signals

Description: On the left a mono signal is represented, where one signal is copied across both speakers. One the right there is a stereo system represented with two channels, where one signal is sent to the left speaker channel and the other signal is sent to the right speaker channel. This is an important concept to grasp, as you can make the right speaker louder than the left speaker to emphasize certain sounds. Stereo sounds often create directionality in sound in space.

To playback mono or stereo audio data, ***a speaker*** is necessary (Table 1.1.4). Speakers operate in the reverse way as a microphone, where analog sound is transduced from an electrical signal (e.g. current - amps). First, the electrical signal is amplified with an **audio power amplifier** and sent to a speaker, which then makes a magnet move to produce pressure waves. Mono audio is played back as the same signal across all speakers, whereas stereo audio is played back on speakers independently in each channel (Figure 1.1.2).

To achieve higher fidelity sound, a speaker can be customized with an enclosure with many sub-speakers, known as ***drivers***. Each driver represents different parts of the audio spectrum. Specifically, **tweeters** are drivers that reproduce high audio frequencies (2000-20000 Hz), **mid-range drivers** reproduce middle frequencies (250-2000 Hz), **woofers** are drivers reproduce low

---

[69] **Sound cards are also capable** of other configurations such as 2.1 (stereo and subwoofer) and 5.1 (surround).

frequencies (40-500 Hz). All of these drivers assembled together in an enclosure is known as a **loudspeaker** (Table 1.1.4). Optionally, **subwoofers** are drivers added separately from the loudspeaker enclosure to reproduce ultra low frequencies (<200 Hz).

Headphones are a specialized version of speakers designed for private use. There are many headphone designs including in-ear headphones, earphones, and headsets (which include a microphone). Headphones can be used with noise isolation or cancellation technology to reduce environmental noise and focus on signal of interest. Headphones have become increasingly used with microphones in tandem, allowing for both recording and playback to happen within the same device (e.g. Apple AirPods).[70]

Like microphones, speakers can be **wireless** (e.g. Bluetooth-enabled) or **wired** depending on the needs of the end user. Recently, there has been a wave of smart speaker designs which allow for speakers to wirelessly connect as peripherals to voice computers.

Table 1.1.4: Speaker types and their utility		
Speaker type	**Description**	**Utility**
Headphones	Headphones play sound to the ears while being muted in the exterior environment. Many types exist including in-ear, earphones, headsets, and noise-reduction headphones.	Allows for playback of sound without disturbing others around you.
Dynamic Speaker	Composed of a 1) magnet; 2) cooler; 3) voice coil; 4) suspension; and 5) membrane. A diaphragm moves back and forth to create pressure waves. The diaphragm is a cone for low and mid frequencies and a dome for high frequencies. A full-range driver is usually 3-8 inches, a specialized driver that can cover the entire frequency range.	The most common type of loudspeaker. Can playback the entire audio frequency range. Typically in televisions, computer speakers, etc.

---

[70] **Apple AirPods** - A trend recently has been to combine microphones and headphones together through an in-ear device, allowing for always-on voice applications. The first mainstream earbud to capture this trend is Apple AirPods, which was released in 2016 (uses Bluetooth).

Piezoelectric speaker	Uses a piezoelectric material to generate sound.	Can produce a high-frequency 'buzzing' sound (1-5kHz).
Electrostatic loudspeaker	Sound is generated by force exerted on membrane suspended in an electrostatic field.	Has a good frequency response, low distortion, and light weight; however, has a bad base response and sensitivity to humidity levels.
Loudspeaker	Composed of (1) mid-range driver; (2) a tweeter; and (3) woofers assembled together with an enclosure. Sometimes, (4) subwoofers are used for sounds in the lowest part of the audio spectrum (below 200 Hz). Drivers are sub-speakers and represent different parts of the audio spectrum.	Mid-range drivers reproduce middle frequencies of sound (250-2000 Hz); tweeters reproduce high audio frequencies (2000-20000 Hz); woofers reproduce low frequencies (40-500 Hz); and subwoofers reproduce ultra low frequencies (20-200 Hz).
Ribbon loudspeaker	Uses a thin diaphragm and a planar coil suspended in a magnetic field to produce sound; the reverse of the ribbon microphone configuration.	Ribbon tweeters are useful to produce high frequencies; often have directionality in the output speaker.

Okay, great! Now we're ready to start writing code.

1.2 Installation of required dependencies

To begin, make sure that you have run the setup.py script in the book folder to make sure you have all the required dependencies for this chapter (Figure 1.2.1). If you have already done this, you can skip this section. To do this, you can run:

**Figure 1.2.1
How to run setup.py script from terminal**

```
cd ~
git clone git@github.com:jim-schwoebel/voicebook.git
cd ~
cd voicebook
python3 setup.py
```

Now you have all the dependencies necessary to follow along with the chapters in the book. You don't need to worry about any other installations. ☺

1.3 How to read and write audio files

Let's get started with just reading and writing a sample audio file.

There are quite a few libraries to read audio files including pydub, wave, LibROSA, SciPy, and SoundFile. Note that some of these libraries require certain audio formats to read properly. For example, LibROSA can read both .WAV (mono or stereo) and .MP3 files (mono or stereo); however, the wave library can only read .WAV file formats (mono or stereo). The most flexible library for reading audio files is pydub, which can read in files in .WAV, .MP3, .OGG, and many other formats. Depending on the application, each of these libraries have pros and cons (Table 1.3.1).

Note that most of these libraries give back the sample rate (samples/sec) as well as the raw data samples as numeric value frames. These raw data samples often reflect the power amplitude of the signal in each frame.

Table 1.3.1: How to read/write audio files: *read_write_audio.py*			
Library	**File formats**	**Channels accepted**	**Example code implementation:** *read_write_audio.py* *Assume 'test.wav' is in current directory*
| **Pydub** | .WAV, .MP3, .OGG, .FLV, .MP4, .WMA, .AAC, | mono or stereo | ```python
from pydub import AudioSegment
# read/write data
data = AudioSegment.from_wav("test.wav")
data.export("new_test.wav")
``` |
| **Wave** [71] | .WAV | mono or stereo | ```python
import wave
# read/write data
data=wave.open('test.wav', mode='rb')
params=data.getparams()
# _wave_params(nchannels=1, sampwidth=2,
framerate=16000, nframes=47104, comptype='NONE',
compname='not compressed')
``` |
| **LibROSA** | .WAV, .MP3 | mono or stereo | ```python
import librosa
# read/write data
y, sr = librosa.load('test.wav')
librosa.output.write_wav('new_test.wav', y, sr)
``` |
| **SciPy** | .WAV | mono or stereo | ```python
from scipy.io import wavfile
# read/write data
fs, data = wavfile.read('test.wav')
wavfile.write('new_test.wav',fs, data)
``` |
| **SoundFile** | .WAV, .FLAC, .OGG, .MAT | mono or stereo | ```python
import soundfile as sf
# read/write data
data, fs = sf.read('test.wav')
sf.write('new_test.ogg', data, fs)
``` |

1.4 Manipulating audio files

Now that we know how to read and write audio files, you may be wondering how to manipulate audio files - like removing silence from the beginning and ends of files or merging two audio files together. Luckily, there are quite a few Python libraries to help with these tasks (Table 1.4.1).

---

[71] **Note I did not write files with wave library.** It's a bit more complicated to write files with the wave library, as this requires the struct module to compile frames in a certain way to write to audio files. The wave library is is often useful to generate periodic-sounding audio files from cosine/sine functions.
```

Table 1.4.1:	
Libraries for manipulating audio files	
Library	**How it's useful for audio manipulation**
Pydub	Good for simple audio file manipulation - like file stitching, making songs louder, repeating, or fading in/out.
Pysox	Good for things like adding a chorus, adjust gains and volumes, pad silence to the end of files, remove silence, and remove noise. I prefer to use SoX from the command line with the os module in Python.
Wave	Useful for adding filters (e.g. high or low pass filters) for manipulating audio data.
LibROSA	Rich audio engineering library of filterbanks, dynamic time warping libraries, self-similarity, and audio featurization (discussed later in modeling chapter).
SciPy	Useful for reading audio files and manipulating with with filters (digital signal processing applications) and connecting Python code to MATLAB / Fortran.

The most significant library for audio manipulation is probably SoX (Table 1.4.2).[72][73] It can add tone/filter effects like adding base, production effects like adding a chorus, adjust gains and volumes, pad silence to the end of files, remove silence, and remove noise. Although there is a wrapper for SoX in Python (pysox), I prefer to use SoX from the command line with the os module in Python (e.g. using os.system('')) because there is better documentation around SoX in general.

Table 1.4.2:	
Useful sox commands in terminal	
For all commands, assume files 'one.wav' and 'two.wav' are in current directory. Most of these commands are taken from this tutorial.	
Goal	**Python code:** *sox_commands.py*
| **Combine files** | ```
import os
# take in one.wav and two.wav to make three.wav
os.system('sox one.wav two.wav three.wav')
``` |
| **Trim** | ```
# take first second of one.wav and output to output.wav
os.system('sox one.wav output.wav trim 0 1')
``` |

---

[72] **SoX** stands for **SO**und e**X**change. SoX is a quite powerful library and is important enough to have a dedicated Wikipedia page.

[73] **The first version of SoX** was released in July 1991 by Chris Bagwell et al. SoX's software has gone through a series of revisions and has quite a lot of features.

Increase volume	`# make volume 2x in one.wav and output to volup.wav` `os.system('sox -v 2.0 one.wav volup.wav')`
Decreasing volume	`# make volume ½ in one.wav and output to voldown.wav` `os.system('sox -v -0.5 one.wav volup.wav')`
Reverse	`# reverse one.wav and output to reverse.wav` `os.system('sox one.wav reverse.wav reverse')`
Change sampling rate	`# change sample rate of one.wav to 16000 Hz` `os.system('sox one.wav -r 16000 sr.wav')`
Changing audio quality	`# change audio file to 16 bit quality` `os.system('sox -b 16 one.wav 16bit.wav')`
Convert mono file to stereo	`# convert mono file to stereo by cloning channels` `os.system('sox one.wav -c 2 stereo.wav')`
Convert stereo file to mono	`# make stereo file mono by averaging out the channels` `os.system('sox stereo.wav -c 1 mono.wav')`
Change audio file speed	`# double speed of file` `os.system('sox one.wav 2x.wav speed 2.0')`

Of course, you can always use other libraries in Python to manipulate audio files besides SoX. If you're trying to use another library that is more secure for production settings (e.g. not relying on os module), I'd recommend using pydub (Figure 1.4.3). In my opinion, it has the easiest-to-use syntax to quickly manipulate audio files and has great documentation.

Table 1.4.3:
Useful pydub commands
This is taken directly from the pydub documentation.

Goal	Python code: *pydub_commands.py*
Load audio file	`from pydub import AudioSegment` `song = AudioSegment.from_wav("never_gonna_give_you_up.wav")`

Slice audio	`# pydub does things in milliseconds`
	`ten_seconds = 10 * 1000`
	`first_10_seconds = song[:ten_seconds]`
	`last_5_seconds = song[-5000:]`

| Make beginning louder and end quieter | ```
# boost volume by 6dB
beginning = first_10_seconds + 6
# reduce volume by 3dB
end = last_5_seconds - 3
``` |
| Concatenate audio | ```
# combine segments
without_the_middle = beginning + end
``` |
| Crossfade | ```
# 1.5 second crossfade
with_style = beginning.append(end, crossfade=1500)
``` |
| Repeat | ```
# repeat the clip twice
do_it_over = with_style * 2
``` |
| Fading in and out | ```
# 2 sec fade in, 3 sec fade out
awesome = do_it_over.fade_in(2000).fade_out(3000)
``` |
| Output results as .MP3 | ```
# export .mp3
awesome.export("mashup.mp3", format="mp3")
``` |

1.5 Playing audio files

Once you have an audio file, you may want to play it back to users. This is especially useful if you have pre-recorded something like a greeting or message. Or, you may have generated a tone that you would like to play back to users to prompt a response in voice assistants.

Something to think about is whether you want the playback to occur synchronously or asynchronously. **Synchronous playback** means that the audio file will play back within the Python code and block other code from running while the playback is occuring. **Asynchronous playback** allows you to execute code in the background while this audio file is playing.

For **synchronous playback** but I prefer using the pygame module, as it's blocking by default and fairly simple to execute (Figure 1.5.1):

Figure 1.5.1
How to playback audio files synchronously: *play_sync.py*

```
import pygame
def sync_playback(filename):
    # takes in a file and plays it back
    pygame.mixer.init()
    pygame.mixer.music.load(filename)
    pygame.mixer.music.play()
sync_playback('one.wav')
```

For **_asynchronous playback_** the best Python library to use is soundevice (Figure 1.5.2). You can play a file back with a certain sample rate and numpy array of values and stop it at any time while executing code. This is useful for things like playing music in the background and keeping the script running (e.g. like a voice assistant). In the example below, a file named 'play.wav' in the current directory is loaded in and played and then some code is run printing text on the screen, and then it is stopped after 1 second using the time.sleep() function. This script thus gives you the power to have flexible code that can run asynchronously while playing back audio.

Figure 1.5.2
How to playback audio files asynchronously: *play_async.py*

```python
import sounddevice as sd
import soundfile as sf
import time

def async_playback(filename):
    data, fs = sf.read(filename)
    sd.play(data, fs)
    return data, fs

# playback file
data, fs = async_playback('play.wav')

# can execute commands
print('able to execute this before finishing')
print('hi, this is cool!')

# can stop after 1 second playing back
time.sleep(1)
sd.stop()
print('stopped')
```

There are many other ways to play back audio, such as using SoX from the command line,[74] the simpleaudio library, through ffmpeg,[75] etc., but I have left them out here because you really only need to master synchronous and asynchronous playback techniques to write high-quality Python code. I've found that the two libraries above to be quite compatible with almost any Python-based voice application that I end up writing.

---

[74] **SoX** - You can playback audio using SoX with os.system('play one.wav')
[75] **FFmpeg** - You can playback audio using ffmpeg with subprocess.call(["ffplay", "-nodisp", "-autoexit", audio_file_path])

1.6 Recording streaming audio

It's also important to understand how to customize the **_default recording microphone_** on your computer. Often, the default microphone is properly set up; however, if you have multiple mics it may not be on the right setting. You can use the sounddevice library to check for and set default microphone settings (Figure 1.6.1).

Figure 1.6.1
How to check available microphones: *mic_check.py*

```python
import sounddevice as sd

mics=sd.query_devices()
default_devices=sd.default.device
default_input=default_devices[0]
default_output=default_devices[1]

# prints all available devices
for i in range(len(mics)):
    print(mics[i])
# can set default device easily with
sounddevice.default.device = 0

# recording mic - {'name': 'Built-in Microphone', 'hostapi': 0,
'max_input_channels': 2, 'max_output_channels': 0, 'default_low_input_latency':
0.0029478458049886623, 'default_low_output_latency': 0.01,
'default_high_input_latency': 0.01310657596371882, 'default_high_output_latency':
0.1, 'default_samplerate': 44100.0}

# recording output - {'name': 'Built-in Output', 'hostapi': 0,
'max_input_channels': 0, 'max_output_channels': 2, 'default_low_input_latency':
0.01, 'default_low_output_latency': 0.008798185941043084,
'default_high_input_latency': 0.1, 'default_high_output_latency':
0.018956916099773242, 'default_samplerate': 44100.0}
```

As you can see, on my iMac computer I have 1 microphone with default sample rates of 44100 Hz and a max number of channels of 2. I also have an output speaker system that has similar settings to play back audio. In this scenario, my default microphone and speaker settings are set up properly and I do not need to make any changes.

Just like playing back audio, it's important to think about whether or not you want to record files *synchronously* or *asynchronously.* Recall that synchronous recording disallows you to run Python code while an audio file is recording, whereas asynchronous recording allows you to record data from the microphone while Python code is running in the background.

It's quite easy to *synchronously* record audio files in Python. Here is a quick function to do this (Figure 1.6.2). In this code, the script records a mono, 16000Hz file named 'async_record.wav' in the current directory. This function makes it quite easy to modify the duration of recording (in seconds), the sample rate (fs), and the number of channels (channels) in the function itself. *Feel free to experiment with this script before moving on.*

Figure 1.6.2
How to record audio files synchronously: *sync_record.py*

```python
import sounddevice as sd
import soundfile as sf
import time

def sync_record(filename, duration, fs, channels):
    print('recording')
    myrecording = sd.rec(int(duration * fs), samplerate=fs, channels=channels)
    sd.wait()
    sf.write(filename, myrecording, fs)
    print('done recording')

# playback file
sync_record('sync_record.wav', 10, 16000, 1)
```

For *asynchronous audio recording*, it's not much different. All we need to do is execute code before the sd.wait() function. Here we can print a few things out before outputting the file 'async_record.wav' as a 16000 Hz mono file (Figure 1.6.3).

Figure 1.6.3
How to record audio files asynchronously: *async_record.py*

```python
import sounddevice as sd
import soundfile as sf
import time

# make some helper functions
def printstuff(number):
    for i in range(number):
        print(i)
```

```python
def async_record(filename, duration, fs, channels):
    print('recording')
    myrecording = sd.rec(int(duration * fs), samplerate=fs, channels=channels)
    # can execute commands
    print('able to execute this before finishing')
    printstuff(30)
    # now wait until done before writing to file
    sd.wait()
    sf.write(filename, myrecording, fs)
    print('done recording')

# playback file
async_record('async_record.wav', 10, 16000, 1)
```

These two short examples should give you an idea of the power of synchronous and asynchronous recordings. Of course, there are also a lot of other ways to record audio files with the PyAudio and wave libraries; however, I find these to overcomplicated for beginners. I think the sounddevice and SoundFile libraries together make a powerful combination with very simple syntax that is quite elegant to read and follow.

1.7 Converting audio formats

There's often a need to convert audio from one format to another, also known as **transcoding**. For example, many transcription engines require audio samples collected to be in a certain format for them to be interpreted properly. You may have collected some files that were not this format; for example, most audio samples are collected at 44100 Hz and have 2 channels. If you don't know how to convert the data you recorded into the right format, you may get errors when using the Google Speech API to transcribe audio.[76] Therefore, this section will get you up-to-speed on how to convert audio files from one format to another.

The gold standard for converting one file format to another is through a program called FFmpeg. FFmpeg, like SoX, is important enough to have its own Wikipedia page. Pretty much every large company uses this software in some way or another.[77] You can easily call FFmpeg through the ffmpy module, which is a wrapper for FFmpeg (Figure 1.7.1).

---

[76] **The Google Speech API** requires that all audio samples be 16000 Hz mono .WAV file format for optimal interpretation. If you don't have it in this format, the API will respond with an error.
[77] **You should already have this installed** if you have run the setup.py script at the beginning of this chapter.

Figure 1.7.1
How to convert audio files using ffmpy module: *convert_file.py*

```python
import ffmpy

def convert_wav(filename):
    #take in an audio file and convert with ffpeg file type
    #types of input files: .mp3
    #output file type: .wav

    if filename[-4:] in ['.mp3','.m4a','.ogg']:
        ff = ffmpy.FFmpeg(
            inputs={filename:None},
            outputs={filename[0:-4]+'.wav': None}
            )
        ff.run()

convert_wav('test.mp3')
```

Alternatively, you can just call FFmpeg directly through the os.system() method. I prefer to use the os.system() method for ffmpeg because it's often fewer lines of code, though using the os.system() method could be a security threat when used in production settings (Figure 1.7.2).

Figure 1.7.2
How to convert audio files using FFmpeg: *ffmpeg_commands.py*
Assume all these files referenced are in the current directory.

```python
import os

# convert audio from one file format to another
os.system('ffmpeg -i input.mp3 output.ogg')

# extract audio from a video
os.system('ffmpeg -i video.mp4 -vn -ab 256 audio.mp3')

# merge audio and video files
os.system('ffmpeg -i video.mp4 -i audio.mp3 -c:v copy -c:a aac -strict experimental output.mp4')

# add a cover image to audio file
os.system('ffmpeg -loop 1 -i image.jpg -i audio.mp3 -c:v libx264 -c:a aac -strict experimental -b:a 192k -shortest output.mp4')

# crop an audio file (second 90 to second 120)
os.system('ffmpeg -ss 00:01:30 -t 30 -acodec copy -i inputfile.mp3 outputfile.mp3')
```

One thing also to know is that the *.FLAC format is a lossless audio format* can save space if you are storing a large volume of audio files in cloud architecture. For example, to record 1 minute of a .WAV file is [3.5 MB]. If you converted it to .FLAC and stored it in storage the file would reduce to [1.5 MB]. This is something you should consider if you're building a large-scale system, as this is what Google and larger tech companies do on their servers to save money.

For more advanced use cases, check out the FFmpeg documentation @ https://www.ffmpeg.org/.

1.8 Transcribing audio

You may have just recorded a few voice notes through your recently implemented sync_record() function and now you are wondering how to convert these recordings into text. This process of converting audio files to text is known as *transcription.*

Fundamentally, transcription is broken up into automated and manual methods. **Automated transcription methods** use language models and acoustic models to represent phonemes into numbers and in turn produce meaningful lexical representations from known dictionaries.[78] In contrast, *manual transcription methods* use humans-in-the-loop to manually listen to audio files and transcribe them.[79] Although automated transcription techniques have become much more accurate in recent years (reaching word error rates as low as 5%), there are still some scenarios where manual transcription is better, such as in professions with advanced vocabularies (e.g. medical transcription).

I'm assuming you don't care much about the manual transcription. If you're like me, you really hate listening to audio and trying to make sense out if it! ☺

So, let's talk a bit more about automated transcription methods.

Automated transcription can be classified as either **open source** or **proprietary**. Open source transcription methods are free and can be used in offline settings.[80] Proprietary transcription methods are cloud-based and require the use of ReST-enabled application programming interfaces (APIs) to transcribe audio (e.g. often require access tokens).[81]

---

[78] **You can build your own transcription models** using a library known as Kaldi. It's quite complicated, but with persistence you can definitely build your own acoustic and language model. There is even a wrapper in Python for Kaldi in a module known as pyKaldi.

[79] **One great manual transcription service is a company called TranscribeMe.** They charge roughly $0.80/minute of audio processed. Note they do charge a bit more if the audio is noisy.

[80] **If you have a limited vocabulary (<200 words)**, I'd highly recommend using an open source platform with a custom language model. The easiest open-source transcription tool for this is PocketSphinx, developed by Carnegie Mellon University.

[81] **If you have a fairly large vocabulary,** I'd recommend using a proprietary system like the Google Speech API. Note that the Google Speech API requires that all audio samples be 16000 Hz mono files, so take this into account and convert files as necessary.

Each of these automated transcription methods have their pros/cons. Proprietary transcription methods often have high accuracy (95% accuracy) but can be costly ($0.024/min). Open source transcription methods often have lower accuracy (70-80% accuracy) but are generally free and more customizable (e.g. easy to make custom transcription models). Depending on your needs, you may want to go with a proprietary or open source method (Table 1.8.1).

Table 1.8.1: Comparison between open source and proprietary transcription engines			
Transcription type	Pros	Cons	Examples
Open source	More customizable Offline capability Free	Low-accuracy (70-80%) Complicated documentation	PocketSphinx DeepSpeech
Proprietary	High accuracy (>95%) Low-latency; generally reliable.	Expensive ($0.024/min) Only cloud-capability Not customizable	Google Speech API IBM Speech API Microsoft Speech API

Luckily, in Python there is a module called SpeechRecognition that bundles many of the commonly used transcription engines without much initial setup.

PocketSphinx is perhaps the most widely used open source transcription method used in Python. Made by researchers at Carnegie Mellon University, it's 100% open source and quite easy to implement in Python. Here is a quick bit of code to implement PocketSphinx with the SpeechRecognition library (Figure 1.8.1). *Feel free to mess around with this for a little bit before moving on.*

Figure 1.8.1:
How to transcribe with PocketSphinx: *sphinx_transcribe.py*

```python
import speech_recognition as sr_audio
import sounddevice as sd
import soundfile as sf
import os, json, datetime

def sync_record(filename, duration, fs, channels):
    print('recording')
    myrecording = sd.rec(int(duration * fs), samplerate=fs, channels=channels)
    sd.wait()
    sf.write(filename, myrecording, fs)
    print('done recording')

def transcribe_audio_sphinx(filename):
    r=sr_audio.Recognizer()
    with sr_audio.AudioFile(filename) as source:
        audio = r.record(source)
    text=r.recognize_sphinx(audio)
    print('transcript: '+text)
    return text

def store_transcript(filename, transcript):
    jsonfilename=filename[0:-4]+'.json'
    print('saving %s to current directory'%(jsonfilename))
    data = {
        'date': str(datetime.datetime.now()),
        'filename':filename,
        'transcript':transcript,
        }
    print(data)
    jsonfile=open(jsonfilename,'w')
    json.dump(data,jsonfile)
    jsonfile.close()

# record file and print transcript
filename='sync_record.wav'
sync_record(filename, 10, 16000, 1)
transcript=transcribe_audio_sphinx(filename)

# now write the transcript into a .json file
store_transcript(filename, transcript)
```

After you run this code, you should get an output like in the figure below (Figure 1.8.2). If you are having trouble, make sure you have all the required dependencies installed.

Figure 1.8.2:
Output from Figure 1.8.1 *(sphinx_transcribe.py)*

```
>> recording
>> done recording
>> transcript: "as they want a great isn't ours is what is he is as works in a site in this meeting's works
>> saving sync_record.json to current directory"
>> {'date': '2018-07-10 15:57:41.441517', 'filename': 'sync_record.wav', 'transcript': "as they want a great isn't ours is what is he is as works in a site in this meeting's works"}
```

Now let's move on to implementing a proprietary automated transcription method. For the sake of simplicity, let's use the **Google Speech API**.

Before continuing, you will need to follow the instructions to install Google Cloud Client Libraries.[82] By the end of the process you will receive a Google Application Credentials .JSON file that give you the access key to your Google Cloud Platform account.

To continue, you need to set up a path to that environment variable in the Mac terminal. To do this, open up your terminal and type in open .bash_profile in the /Users/ directory (Figure 1.8.3). Once you do this, you will see a .TXT file pop up with various environment variables that you can edit. The **environment variables** are just variables that can be accessed by Python outside of your program so that it makes it easy to share variables across code bases. In this case, we're interested in setting an environment variable to the GOOGLE_APPLICATION_CREDENTIALS path so that the Google Speech API client library knows where to look to authenticate that you have access to the Google Speech API. To do this, go to a new line and type in the environment variable path where your .JSON file is located.

Figure 1.8.3:
How to setup environment variables for the Google Speech API

```
cd ~
open .bash_profile

# now put the Google environment variable into .bash_profile and save it
export GOOGLE_APPLICATION_CREDENTIALS='/Users/jim/desktop/GOOGLEFILENAME.json'
```

Now that you have this setup, we can now build a simple script to transcribe audio using the Google Speech API (Figure 1.8.4).

---

[82] **Google Cloud Speech-to-Text docs** - Check out the website (https://cloud.google.com/speech-to-text/docs/) to make sure you have the most up-to-date instructions on how to do this.

Figure 1.8.4:
How to transcribe with Google Speech API: *google_transcribe.py*

```python
import speech_recognition as sr_audio
import sounddevice as sd
import soundfile as sf
import os, json, datetime

def transcribe_audio_google(filename):
    # transcribe the audio (note this is only done if a voice sample)
    r=sr_audio.Recognizer()
    with sr_audio.AudioFile(filename) as source:
        audio = r.record(source)
    text=r.recognize_google_cloud(audio)

    return text

def sync_record(filename, duration, fs, channels):
    print('recording')
    myrecording = sd.rec(int(duration * fs), samplerate=fs, channels=channels)
    sd.wait()
    sf.write(filename, myrecording, fs)
    print('done recording')

def store_transcript(filename, transcript):
    jsonfilename=filename[0:-4]+'.json'
    print('saving %s to current directory'%(jsonfilename))
    data = {
        'date': str(datetime.datetime.now()),
        'filename':filename,
        'transcript':transcript,
        }
    print(data)
    jsonfile=open(jsonfilename,'w')
    json.dump(data,jsonfile)
    jsonfile.close()

# record file and print transcript
filename='google_record.wav'
sync_record(filename, 10, 16000, 1)
transcript=transcribe_audio_google(filename)
# now write the transcript into a .json file
# e.g. google_record.wav transcript will be stored in google_record.json
store_transcript(filename, transcript)
```

Great! Now you're really ready to make some sophisticated voice applications.

1.9 Text-to-speech systems

The last section of this chapter focuses on **text-to-speech systems** (TTS systems), or systems that automatically transform written text into speech.

You may first ask, "why are text-to-speech systems important?"

There are many applications where converting a string of text like "the weather is 95 degrees outside"[83] into speech could be useful. You may be wanting to broadcast an emergency message to a large number of people and it could be faster to do it through an automated system. Or, you may just have too much text to summarize at any one time for a human being to record everything (e.g. all the street names across New York City). Suffice it to say there are many scenarios where TTS systems are useful.

Like transcription engines, there are **proprietary TTS** and **open source TTS systems**. Honestly, though, I can't tell much of a difference between an open source and proprietary system, so I'd stick with the open source libraries if you can.

My favorite library in Python for implementing a TTS system is the pyttsx3 library. It has great documentation and is 100% open source. The pros are that there are many voices that you can customize in the library (upwards of 30-40 voices). The con is that you cannot actually save the files that are played back.[84]

Let's get started with a simple function to play back audio from a string (Figure 1.9.1).

Figure 1.9.1:
How to play back text with default settings: *speak.py*

```
import pyttsx3

def speak_text(text):
    engine = pyttsx3.init()
    engine.say(text)
    engine.runAndWait()

# change text as necessary
text=input('type text to speak here: \n')

# speak output text
spoken_time=speak_text(text)
```

---

[83] **Personally,** I really like getting the weather through a text-to-speech system as opposed to reading it on weather.com or a similar site.
[84] **There are some hacks here** to get beyond this, though, like recording a TTS in real-time or using Apple's TTS system to make recorded voices in the opensource world.

Well that is fun; however, you may want to configure the voice and speed to your needs. I wrote a quick script (speak_custom.py) to do this and output the default settings in a defaults.json file. This script allows you to select a voice that you like from the 30+ voices available with the pyttsx3 library (Figure 1.9.2). This script iterates through various speaking speeds and voices so that you can pick a voice that you like. Once a voice is played you type in the terminal a 'y' if you like the voice or a 'n' if you don't like the voice. In this way, you can make a voicebank that is relevant to you for future Python projects.[85]

Figure 1.9.2:
How to play back text with default settings in CLI: *speak_custom.py*

```
# run this in the terminal
cd ~
cd voicebook
cd chapter_1
python3 speak_custom.py

# this will now guide you in setting up your own custom voice and save it in a
defaults.json file
```

If you are in more of a production setting, you can go with Google's WaveNet voice models. Google does not charge you until you reach 1 million characters/month (that's like 164,000 words); after that, it's fairly affordable only charging $16/mo for every 1 million additional characters that you speak. [86] [87] The main benefit of using Google's WaveNet models is that you can save the files easily and reuse them after you do use the API; that makes the process of generating speech and reuse much easier by caching some of the commonly used TTS phrases to end users. The con is really the cost; though it seems insignificant, I'm sure it could add up if you are sending billions of characters a month to Google Cloud Platform (GCP).

Assuming you still have the GOOGLE_APPLICATION_CREDENTIALS environment variable setup in your .bash_profile, all you need to do to play back text with a Google WaveNet model is to follow their documentation (Figure 1.8.3).

---

[85] **Select a voice you like!** We're going to revisit this in future chapters, so I'd get comfortable with the voice you select for your peojcts!! Otherwise, you (or your significant other) may get annoyed with the voice.
[86] Calculated on Wolfram Alpha! :)
[87] **Although you can use proprietary TTS systems** like Google's Wavenet models, I don't think it's really necessary. I believe in the open-source community when it comes to TTS tools and they will only get better. So I'd try to use an open-source solution and if you really need to go with a proprietary one follow this tutorial to set up google TTS here.

Figure 1.9.3:
How to play back text using Google Text-to-Speech: *speak_google.py*

```python
def speak_google(text, filename, model):
    """Synthesizes speech from the input string of text."""
    from google.cloud import texttospeech
    client = texttospeech.TextToSpeechClient()
    input_text = texttospeech.types.SynthesisInput(text=text)
    # Note: the voice can also be specified by name.
    # Names of voices can be retrieved with client.list_voices().
    voice = texttospeech.types.VoiceSelectionParams(
        language_code='en-US',
        ssml_gender=texttospeech.enums.SsmlVoiceGender.FEMALE,
        name=model)
    audio_config = texttospeech.types.AudioConfig(
        audio_encoding=texttospeech.enums.AudioEncoding.MP3)
    response = client.synthesize_speech(input_text, voice, audio_config)
    # The response's audio_content is binary.
    with open(filename, 'wb') as out:
        out.write(response.audio_content)
        print('Audio content written to file %s'%(filename))

# experiment with various voices
base='output'
models=['en-US-Wavenet-A','en-US-Wavenet-B','en-US-Wavenet-C','en-US-Wavenet-D',
'en-US-Wavenet-E','en-US-Wavenet-F']
text='hey I am testing out google TTS'

# Loop through various voices
# now all these files will be in the current directory
for i in range(len(models)):
    speak_google(text, base+'_'+models[i]+'.mp3', models[i])
```

Although you can use proprietary TTS systems like Google's WaveNet models, I don't think it's really necessary. I believe in the open source community when it comes to TTS tools, as they will only get better over time. So I'd try to use an open source solution first. If you really need to go with a proprietary TTS system I'd use Google because their models seem to be the best-in-class and most cost-effective.

1.10 Conclusion

👏 Are you excited yet? You learned a lot in this chapter. By now you should feel more comfortable with the fundamentals of voice computing: reading/writing audio files, manipulating audio files, playing back audio through speakers, saving streaming audio, converting audio formats with codecs, transcribing audio, and implementing TTS systems.

If you are interested to read more on any of these topics, check out some of the Python modules and/or software packages below:

- Reading/writing voice files
    - SoundFile. https://github.com/bastibe/SoundFile
- Manipulating voice files
    - SoX. http://sox.sourceforge.net/
    - Pydub. https://github.com/jiaaro/pydub
- Audio file playback
    - Pygame. https://www.pygame.org/docs/ref/mixer.html
    - Sounddevice. https://python-sounddevice.readthedocs.io/en/0.3.11/
- Recording audio files
    - Sounddevice. https://python-sounddevice.readthedocs.io/en/0.3.11/
- Audio file conversion
    - FFmpeg. https://www.ffmpeg.org/
    - FFmpy module. http://ffmpy.readthedocs.io/en/latest/
- Transcription
    - SpeechRecognition. https://pypi.org/project/SpeechRecognition/
    - Pocketsphinx. https://github.com/cmusphinx/pocketsphinx-python
    - Google Speech API. https://cloud.google.com/speech-to-text/
- Text-to-speech systems (TTS)
    - Pyttsx3. https://github.com/nateshmbhat/pyttsx3
    - Google TTS. https://cloud.google.com/text-to-speech/

The next chapter focuses on how to best collect voice files. Specifically, it lays out some best practices to ensure that you are collecting high-quality samples. This is very important to get right before we go on and discuss how to analyze the data that you collect. 🎤

Chapter 2:
Collection

"One cannot collect all the beautiful shells on the beach. One can collect only a few, and they are more beautiful if they are few."
   -**Anne Morrow Lindberg**
   (Author and Aviator)

Chapter Overview

When you were little, did you ever go to the ocean and pick up and collect sea shells? I would go around and pick up every single shell that I could find, clean them in the water, and put them in a jar. Rarely, I'd find a sand dollar. In these situations, I became super excited and often shared my findings with my brother and family. When I got back home, I would have so many shells that I would have to take them all out of the jar in order to find the sand dollar again and show it to my friends.

Collecting voice files is much like collecting seashells along the ocean.[88] You can't collect sand dollars from far away because you can't see them, and you can't collect high-fidelity vocalizations far away from a microphone because the audio would be attenuated and low volume. After you collect a sand dollar, you often want to wash off all the sand to make sure it looks aesthetically pleasing; similarly, after you collect a voice file you often want to filter out all the noise (e.g. air conditioning noise in the background) to make sure it can be appropriately understood when played back. After you clean a sand dollar, you must store it in a separate place (e.g. in your backpack) in order to access it efficiently; otherwise, it gets cluttered in with all the other shells if placed in a container like a jar. In a similar manner, if you store high-signal audio files with a bunch of audio files that are noise it's quite hard to access these high-signal audio files; therefore, it's often best to put high-quality audio files in a separate place (e.g. in a separate folder on a computer). Lastly, after you have the sand dollar in your backpack you often like to showcase it to friends. Likewise, high-quality audio, if accessible, is often able to be published on mediums like SoundCloud or YouTube.

This chapter will overview:

- **2.1** - Common mistakes
- **2.2** - Microphone arrays
- **2.3** - Mixers
- **2.4** - Recording modes
- **2.5** - Cleaning audio files
- **2.6** - Speaker diarization
- **2.7** - Storing voice files
- **2.8** - Publishing voice content
- **2.9** - MEMUPPS voice controls

In this way, you can collect, clean, and store 'sand dollar audio.'

---

[88] **Why this chapter exists** - How you collect, clean, and store audio is often important. For example, audio samples can be high or low quality based on the distance you are away from a microphone. Or, you may be recording a sample outdoors in a noisy environment and then try to compare these samples to silent samples indoors. Moreover, you may have recorded an analog audio file and stored it on an old cassette tape; as a result, the files you have recorded are practically useless for modeling later because it's hard to get them to a .WAV format.

2.1 Common mistakes

I wanted to start off this chapter going over some common mistakes I've seen over-and-over again when building voice collection software in Python.

The choice of a microphone (Table 2.1.1), the distance from the microphone (Table 2.1.2), the environment (Table 2.1.3), the sample rate (Table 2.1.4), the number of channels (Table 2.1.4), and the type of transcoding methodology (Table 2.1.4) strongly affect audio quality. In general, it's okay to have a bit of noise as long as that noise is consistent. *Please keep this mind when you design voice recording protocols or you'll regret it later!*

The first common mistake in recording audio is **changing microphones** halfway through generating a dataset. For example, you may record some of your samples with an iPhone and then use another computer, which has poorer audio quality. You thus need to now clean the laptop-collected samples to be of similar quality as the iPhone-collected samples otherwise the dataset is unsuitable for modeling purposes. *Therefore, always remember to keep the microphone constant when generating new datasets. If multiple mics are necessary, make a dataset with a mixture of microphones representative of your use case*[89] (Table 2.1.1).

Table 2.1.1 **List of microphones and their utility**		
Type of microphone	**How they work**	**Utility**
Condenser microphone	Uses two capacitor plates and a diaphragm to produce electric current. Capacitance and resistance allow for filtering of current in a way that produces an audio signal.	Wide variety of types; can get low-, moderate-, and high-quality microphones for home or commercial uses.
Dynamic microphone	Uses induction coils attached to a diaphragm to produce sound via electromagnetic induction.	Can customize microphone to various parts of the audio spectrum (e.g. bases); useful for music performances or lecture halls.
Ribbon microphone	Uses corrugated metal ribbon suspended in a magnetic field to produce sound via electromagnetic induction.	Useful for radio broadcasting applications.

---

[89] **For example,** a 50% laptop iPhone microphone and 50% Mac computer microphone mixture could be used to represent users that may be 50% of the time in front of their laptops and 50% of the time in front of their phones.

Condenser MEMS microphone	A miniaturized version of the condenser microphone etched on silicon wafers.	Small size, high sound quality, reliable and affordable.
Piezoelectric MEMS microphone	Uses a piezoelectric material to on a silicon wafer to produce electrical current when applied to mechanical stress.	Low-power and can be used in tough environments (waterproof, dustproof, particle-resistant, and shockproof). Quite high reliability.
Electret microphone	Uses a permanently charged material (e.g. PTFE plastic film) to produce voltage when subjected to pressure.	Useful for low-cost manufacturing in smartphones or personal computers.
Noise-cancelling microphone	Many types, but a common type uses two ports as a condenser microphone to subtract noise out from the sample.	Useful to filter out noise in noisy environments and increase transcription accuracy.

Another common mistake in collecting audio data is not keeping the ***distance*** a user speaks from the microphone constant. You don't want to speak too close to the mic, as it could lead to clipping[90] and an irrecoverable signal. Also, you don't want to change the distance you speak from the mic, as this leads to incredible variability in output RMS power and volume.[91] *Thus, keep distance-away-from-the-microphone in mind when building voice collection protocols* (Table 2.1.2).

---

[90] **Clipping** occurs when a signal on a pressure sensor reaches maximum volume.
[91] **Data cleaning -** Although this is solvable (as shown in the cleaning section later on), it can lead to signal distortion and take up a lot of time that you don't have.

Table 2.1.2: Distance from microphone and volume drop		
Distance from microphone	**Volume drop**	**Ways to overcome**
1 inch	Too close to the mic and speaking loudly; leads to clipping.	Called a plosive or clipping - cannot fix it; signal loss.
<1 foot	n/a	n/a - good signal
1 meter	~1-2x drop in volume.	If necessary, volume increase by 1-2x.
2 meters	~2x drop in volume.	SoX volume increase by 2x.
4 meters	~4x drop in volume.	SoX volume increase by 4x.
8 meters	~8x drop in volume.	SoX volume increase by 8x.

Another common mistake that people make in recording audio is to **change environments** during a voice recording session. You may be in indoors where it is quiet for the first half of the recording and then go walk outside where it is noisy halfway during the second half of a recording (e.g. honking car ambient noise). The data recorded now is quite messy, as you have to determine the time points when the environment shift happened and only use part of the data that is not noisy (e.g. the first half). If you keep the environment constant it becomes much easier to clean the data; for example, if you remain indoors and there is an ambient air conditioner in your room that is on, you can then remove that noise from almost all the files that you had recorded by using a noise floor and SoX (covered later on in this chapter). *Therefore, always try to keep the environment as constant as you can when you develop voice recording software* (Table 2.1.3).

Table 2.1.3 Recording environments and noise profiles		
Environment type	**Noise level**	**Ways to overcome**
Airplane or car	High	SoX noise floor
Indoor room	Little to none	N/A
Outside (wind)	Variable	Use windshield on microphone or filter using SoX.
Air conditioner	Low	Subtraction of noise from sample.
Two speakers	High	Use speaker diarization to separate voices.

The last common mistake is in *inconsistent sampling, channel definitions*, or *audio formats*. A common standard is to sample stereo (2 channel) audio sample at 44100 Hz as a .WAV file. Another common standard is to sample a mono (1 channel) audio sample at 16000 Hz as a .WAV file. You should also try to avoid transcoding between lossless and lossy codecs (e.g. .WAV→ .OPUS → .WAV), as this will cause the sample to lose some information.[92] *I'd try to pick one of these types of recording settings and stick to it for your voice protocol; these recording settings are fairly standard in the speech industry and using them allows for near-perfect reconstruction of speech signals* (Table 2.1.4).

Table 2.1.4:
Common audio recording settings

Channels	Sampling rate	Audio format(s)	Utility
Stereo (2 channels)	44100 Hz	.WAV	44100 Hz is a common sampling rate for audio applications to perfectly reconstruct sound.[93]
Mono (1 channel)	16000 Hz	.WAV	Most vocalizations happen between 250 Hz and 8000 Hz, so 16000 Hz satisfies the Nyquist condition.[94] Note that the Google Speech API requires 16000 Hz, mono, .WAV to function properly.

Now that you know all these common mistakes, we can now progress on and talk about more advanced microphone configurations.

2.2 Microphone arrays

A *microphone array* (mic array) is a group of microphones that can record audio into separate channels.[95] Mic arrays take many different forms; however, they most commonly have between 2-8 channels and are configured with various forms of pre-loaded digital signal processing software (Table 2.1). This is useful for a variety of purposes; for example, you may want to understand the directionality of an audio signal. You may also want to filter noise out of an audio signal from channels that do not contain the signal of interest.[96] You also may want to customize audio recordings and the ways they are played back (e.g. record from only certain channels).

---

[92] **When to use lossy codecs** - There are some use cases where lossy codecs can make sense; for example, when you are broadcasting terabytes (TB) of audio data per second.
[93] **From Wikipedia:** "The 44.1 kHz audio sampling rate is widely used due to the compact disc (CD) format, dating back to its use by Sony from 1979."
[94] **Nyquist rate** - This is because human hearing has a max frequency of 20000 Hz and sound must be sampled at 2x the max frequency, known as the Nyquist rate, in order to perfectly reconstruct the signal.
[95] **Another example:** You may have a microphone array (N=2) composed of 1) a condenser microphone on the MacBook Pro and 2) a wireless lavalier microphone.
[96] **For example**, if I have a circular array of 8 microphones, I can weight the 2 microphones closest to me more than the ones in the back, as the RMS power of the microphones closest to me most likely contain the signal of interest. This is known as beamforming, which is further discussed on page 76.

Table 2.2.1 Types of microphone arrays		
Microphone array	**Specifications**	**Price**
UMA-8 Microphone Array	<ul><li>Circular USB microphone array</li><li>DSP processing for Beamforming</li><li>AEC</li><li>Noise reduction</li><li>2 channel and 8 channel mode.</li><li>Powered by XMOS XVF3000 new chipset.</li></ul>	$98
Respeaker	<ul><li>Four microphones array / 12 programmable RGB LED indicators</li><li>Speech algorithms/features for voice activity detection (VAD)</li><li>Direction of arrival and noise suppression</li><li>De-reverberation/acoustic echo cancellation</li></ul>	$79
Matrix creator	<ul><li>8 microphones with beamforming and echo cancellation</li><li>Contains temperature, pressure, UV, motion, and orientation sensors</li><li>Has Spartan-6 FPGA board - re-configurable for machine learning-on-a-chip and CPU-intensive tasks</li><li>Zigbee and Z-wave wireless device capability</li><li>Near-field communication (NFC) capability to interact with smartphones.</li></ul>	$99
Blue Yeti microphone	<ul><li>3 condenser microphones</li><li>Can customize pattern selection - cardioid, bidirectional, omnidirectional & stereo</li><li>Gain control, mute button, zero-latency headphone output</li><li>Can be used for podcasting, voice-overs, interviews, and conference calls</li></ul>	$89

To elaborate, mic arrays are useful to help enhance audio collected within the voice range. **Beamforming** is a signal processing technique that allows for directional reception of audio signals to enhance audio quality. For example, in a circular array of 8 microphones you may weight the microphone with the highest RMS energy more when recombining signals.[97] In this way, you can have a higher fidelity recording than configurations with only one microphone.

In addition, ***acoustic echo suppression (AES)***[98] and ***acoustic echo cancellation (AEC)***[99] ***algorithms*** improve voice quality by suppressing acoustic echo (e.g. sounds played back through loudspeaker) and line echo (e.g. electrical impulses in wires and impedance mismatches). Together, these techniques greatly enhance audio files to achieve a ***higher signal-to-noise*** (SNR) ratio.

Lastly, mic arrays are also useful because they can be used to customize sound recording and playback. For example, there are techniques to produce and replay sound recordings in 3-dimensions - as if you are in the same room as when the recording took place - through **binaural recording** and **binaural playback.**[100] Moreover, the Blue Yeti microphone (Table 2.1.1) has 3 condenser microphones which can customize the pattern of recording through the array as cardioid, bidirectional, omnidirectional or stereo. Microphone arrays thus allow for more precise control of voice recordings.

Note that most modern voice interfaces (e.g. Amazon Echo) use microphone arrays with adaptive beamforming technology to capture audio within the voice range; however, most playback techniques in these devices are mono sound spread across a loudspeaker.

---

[97] **Adaptive vs. conventional beamforming algorithms -** In adaptive beamforming, the weights adjust to a desired signal and are not fixed whereas conventional beamforming has a fixed weight set to focus on a signal of interest. Most modern echo devices use adaptive beamforming algorithms.

[98] **From Wikipedia:** "Echo suppressors work by detecting a voice signal going in one direction on a circuit, and then muting or attenuating the signal in other direction."

[99] **From Wikipedia:** "Echo cancellation involves first recognizing the originally transmitted signal that re-appears, with some delay, in the transmitted or received signal. Once the echo is recognized, it can be removed by subtracting it from the transmitted or received signal."

[100] **Binaural recording -** In this technique of sound recording, there are usually two microphones placed in a mannequin's ear as if it were listening to a live sound recording. In this way, you can playback audio in separate channels (L / R) to make it sound like the sound is being produced in real-time.

2.3 Mixers

A *mixer* (or mixing console) is a peripheral device capable of recording audio *simultaneously* and in *separate channels*.[101][102] For voice applications, mixers are useful to *source separate speakers*. For example, if someone is calling in from a radio station and has a mobile phone as a source of audio, it should be on a separate channel from the radio station (e.g. on a ribbon microphone) so that the two can be easily separated.[103] This can be done with a *telephone balance unit,* which allows for a telephone line and another microphone to be connected on a mixer.[104] Then, audio can be sent to a computer and processed on a sound card, as would be done through a typical microphone jack (Figure 2.3.1).

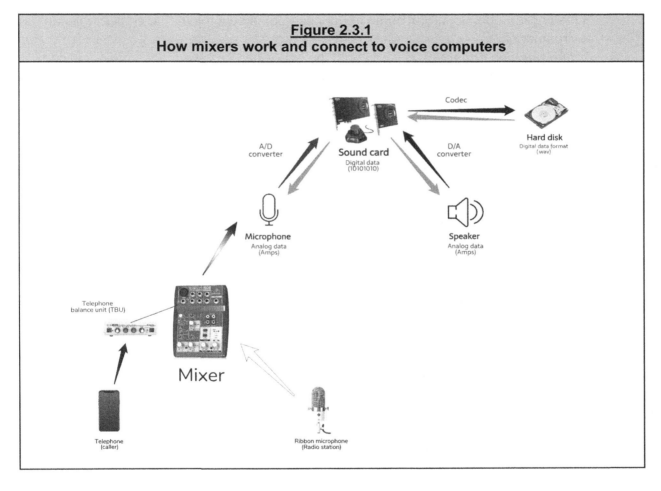

**Figure 2.3.1
How mixers work and connect to voice computers**

---

[101] **From Wikipedia:** "A mixer can control analog or digital signals. The modified signals are summed to produce the combined output signals, which can then be broadcast, amplified through a sound reinforcement system or recorded."

[102] **Mixers are also capable** of playing back stereo sound through a speaker array, or a group of speakers that has capability of playing back in separate channels. Mixers thus allow for advanced customization for voice recordings and can be used to add effects to voice media.

[103] **Otherwise,** you would have to do some sophisticated post-collection modeling techniques (e.g. PCA speaker diarization) to source-separate the speakers if they were mixed together.

[104] **Muting sounds** - You may want to mute the phone call coming in before going live on the radio so that it is not broadcasted. This can be easily done on a mixer.

2.4 Recording modes

When writing audio recording scripts, it's often useful to think in terms of modes as this helps you plan how best to write your code (e.g. with default scripts / modules).[105]

In this vein, there are 3 main modes to collect audio samples:

1. **Active collection** means that an audio sample is collected and there is some response from the program as a result of collecting the audio.[106]
2. **Passive collection** means that an audio sample is collected and there is no response from the program as a result of collecting audio; in other words, audio files are collected in the background, usually at some frequency (e.g. once a minute) to characterize an environment.[107]
3. **Active-passive collection** is when both the active and passive modes are combined, meaning there are some parts of your program that collect audio samples and have responses from end users and other parts of your program that passively collect data.[108]

Also, Python scripts can be run synchronously or asynchronously, as mentioned in the previous chapter. **Synchronous audio collection** is **blocking**, meaning Python cannot run any other code while collecting audio files. In contrast, **asynchronous audio collection** is **nonblocking**, meaning that Python can run additional code while the audio sample is being collected.

Therefore, there are really 6 audio collection modes:

1. **Active-synchronous (AS) mode** - record audio synchronously, prompting a user action;
2. **Active-asynchronous (AA) mode** - record audio asynchronously, prompting a user action;
3. **Passive-synchronous (PS) mode** - record audio in the background synchronously, prompting no user action;
4. **Passive-asynchronous (PA) mode** - record audio in the background asynchronously, prompting no user action;

---

[105] **For example,** if you're trying to run survey that requires fetching the weather from a user input, it may make sense to pursue an active-asynchronous strategy to fetch the weather of the last location of the user before the sample is done recording as opposed to an active-synchronous strategy that fetches weather serially after a user input is provided so that the weather results can propagate quickly,.

[106] **Active collection example** - A user may be prompted to answer the question - 'Are you from New York, yes or no' and if the user says yes the weather is retrieved from weather.com.

[107] **Passive collection example** - You may be sampling audio in your house to build a model to detect when doors open and close. To do this, you sample audio every 1 minute or so for a few days. Then you can sort out samples later to detect which ones are door opens vs. silence and build a model for door opens.

[108] **Active-passive example** - In the case of a voice assistant there may be an 'always-on' mode to listen for certain hotwords, known as wake words. This is listening passively until a wake word is detected on a microphone (passive). As soon as a wake word is detected, the voice assistant then guides users with prompts (e.g. how can I help you?), which leads to an action like ordering a pizza (active).

5. ***Active-Passive synchronous (APS) mode*** - record audio actively - prompting a user action, followed by recording an audio sample passively - all in a synchronous manner.
6. ***Active-Passive asynchronous (APA) mode*** - record audio actively - prompting a user action, followed by recording an audio sample passively - all in an asynchronous manner.

Let's quickly go through each of these examples quickly by writing some code.

In the first case, ***active-synchronous (AS) mode***, all we have is a simple script that collects audio from a user and prompts an action. A good example could be to build a voice chatbot that asks a user a very simple question like "do you want to fetch the weather?" If the user responds yes, then the weather is fetched. If the user does not say yes, then the weather is not fetched. Note that we can use os.system('open [url]') to open up a web browser and PocketSphinx for transcribing audio files to determine whether or not the user said yes or no (Figure 2.4.1).

Figure 2.4.1:
Active-synchronous (AS) mode: *as_record.py*

```python
import sounddevice as sd
import soundfile as sf
from bs4 import BeautifulSoup
import speech_recognition as sr_audio
import os, pyttsx3, pygame, time

def sync_record(filename, duration, fs, channels):
    print('recording')
    myrecording = sd.rec(int(duration * fs), samplerate=fs, channels=channels)
    sd.wait()
    sf.write(filename, myrecording, fs)
    print('done recording')

def sync_playback(filename):
    # takes in a file and plays it back
    pygame.mixer.init()
    pygame.mixer.music.load(filename)
    pygame.mixer.music.play()

def speak_text(text):
    engine=pyttsx3.init()
    engine.say(text)
    engine.runAndWait()

def transcribe_audio_sphinx(filename):
    # transcribe the audio (note this is only done if a voice sample)
    r=sr_audio.Recognizer()
    with sr_audio.AudioFile(filename) as source:
        audio = r.record(source)
    text=r.recognize_sphinx(audio)
    print('transcript: '+text)
```

```python
    return text

def fetch_weather():
    os.system('open https://www.yahoo.com/news/weather')

speak_text('would you like to get the weather?')
sync_playback('beep.mp3')
time.sleep(2)
sync_record('response.wav',2,16000,1)
transcript=transcribe_audio_sphinx('response.wav')
if transcript.lower().find('yes') >= 0 or transcript.lower().find('yeah') >= 0:
    fetch_weather()
```

In the second case, ***active-asynchronous (AA) mode***, we can rearrange the script to fetch the weather before the user is done speaking (Figure 2.4.2). We can store the weather page (fetched on yahoo.com) in a .PDF using the pdfkit module in Python. This makes it easy to fetch the weather again in the same day from a .PDF so we don't have to make repeated requests.

Figure 2.4.2:
Active-asynchronous (AA) mode: *aa_record.py*

```python
import sounddevice as sd
import soundfile as sf
from bs4 import BeautifulSoup
import speech_recognition as sr_audio
import os, pyttsx3, pdfkit, pygame

def sync_record(filename, duration, fs, channels):
    print('recording')
    myrecording = sd.rec(int(duration * fs), samplerate=fs, channels=channels)
    try:
        fetch_weather()
    except:
        pass
    sd.wait()
    sf.write(filename, myrecording, fs)
    print('done recording')

def sync_playback(filename):
    # takes in a file and plays it back
    pygame.mixer.init()
    pygame.mixer.music.load(filename)
    pygame.mixer.music.play()

def speak_text(text):
    engine=pyttsx3.init()
    engine.say(text)
    engine.runAndWait()
```

```python
def transcribe_audio_sphinx(filename):
    # transcribe the audio (note this is only done if a voice sample)
    r=sr_audio.Recognizer()
    with sr_audio.AudioFile(filename) as source:
        audio = r.record(source)
    text=r.recognize_sphinx(audio)
    print('transcript: '+text)
    return text

def fetch_weather():
    link='https://www.yahoo.com/news/weather'
    pdfkit.from_url(link, 'out.pdf')

speak_text('would you like to get the weather?')
sync_playback('beep.mp3')
time.sleep(1.2)
sync_record('response.wav',5,16000,1)
transcript=transcribe_audio_sphinx('response.wav')
if transcript.lower().find('yes') >= 0 or transcript.lower().find('yeah')>=0:
    speak_text('ok, great here it is.')
    os.system('open out.pdf')
```

In the third case, **passive-synchronous (PS) mode**, we can collect audio files in the background in a blocking manner fairly simply through a while loop (e.g. with 10 iterations sleeping every 10 seconds). These files can be stored in a new folder called 'recordings.' *Feel free to modify and play with these settings to fit your desired use case* (Figure 2.4.3).

Figure 2.4.3:
Short script demonstrating passive synchronous (PS) mode: *ps_record.py*

```python
import sounddevice as sd
import soundfile as sf
import time, os, shutil

def sync_record(filename, duration, fs, channels):
    print('recording')
    myrecording = sd.rec(int(duration * fs), samplerate=fs, channels=channels)
    sd.wait()
    sf.write(filename, myrecording, fs)
    print('done recording')

# make a folder to put recordings in
try:
    os.mkdir('recordings')
    os.chdir(os.getcwd()+'/recordings')
except:
    shutil.rmtree('recordings')
    os.mkdir('recordings')
    os.chdir(os.getcwd()+'/recordings')
```

```
i=0
# loop through 10 times recording a 2 second sample
# can change to infinite loop ==> while i > -1:
while i<10:
    # record a mono file synchronously
    filename=str(i+1)+'.wav'
    print('recording %s'%(filename))
    sync_record(filename, 2, 16000, 1)
    time.sleep(10)
    i=i+1
```

In the fourth case, ***passive-asynchronous (PA) mode,*** all we need to do is switch a few things around to do some other things while the audio files are recording. For example, we may want to fetch battery information with the psutil module while a user is querying to speed up the process of analysis (Figure 2.4.4).[109]

Figure 2.4.4:
Passive-asynchronous (PA) mode: *pa_record.py*

```
import sounddevice as sd
import soundfile as sf
import time, os, shutil, psutil
# define synchronous recording function (did this is Chapter 1)
def get_battery():
    battery = psutil.sensors_battery()
    plugged = battery.power_plugged
    percent = str(battery.percent)
    return percent

def sync_record(filename, duration, fs, channels):
    print('recording')
    myrecording = sd.rec(int(duration * fs), samplerate=fs, channels=channels)
    print('battery is currently at %s'%get_battery())
    sd.wait()
    sf.write(filename, myrecording, fs)
    print('done recording')
# make a folder to put recordings in
try:
    os.mkdir('recordings')
    os.chdir(os.getcwd()+'/recordings')
except:
    shutil.rmtree('recordings')
    os.mkdir('recordings')
    os.chdir(os.getcwd()+'/recordings')
```

---

[109] **Note** this is one of many things that you could do while the sample is being recorded.

```
i=0

# loop through 10 times recoridng a 2 second sample
# can change to infinite loop ==> while i > -1:
while i<10:
    # record a mono file synchronously
    filename=str(i+1)+'.wav'
    print('recording %s'%(filename))
    sync_record(filename, 2, 16000, 1)
    time.sleep(10)
    i=i+1
```

In the fifth case, **active-passive synchronous (APS) mode**, we can just combine the active synchronous (AS) mode (*as_record.py*) with the passive synchronous (PS) mode (*ps_record.py*), executed in series. This is easily done using the os module in Python and the scripts we wrote previously (Figure 2.4.5).[110]

Figure 2.4.5:
Active-passive-asynchronous (APS) mode: *aps_record.py*

```
import os

# ONLY 1 CONFIGURATION
# active-synchronous (AS)
os.system('python3 as_record.py')
# passive-synchronous (PS)
os.system('python3 ps_record.py')
```

We can then change a few lines of code to make this example *active-passive asynchronous (APA) mode*. Again, we can just combine the active asynchronous (AS) mode (*aa_record.py*) with the passive asynchronous (PS) mode (*pa_record.py*), executed in series. Note there are many more options for writing code in APA mode, as only one of the scripts executed needs to be asynchronous. All of these combinations are listed below (Figure 2.4.6).

---

[110] **Note that** APS mode requires that the entire Python script contains synchronous code.

Figure 2.4.6:
Active-passive-asynchronous (APA) mode: *record_apa.py*

```
import os

# APA CONFIG 1 (AA → PA)
os.system('python3 aa_record.py')
os.system('python3 pa_record.py')

# APA CONFIG 2 (AS→ PA)
# os.system('python3 as_record.py')
# os.system('python3 pa_record.py')

# APA CONFIG 3 (AA→ PS)
# os.system('python3 aa_record.py')
# os.system('python3 ps_record.py')
```

Great! I hope these concrete examples helped you better understand the various recording modes.

2.5 Cleaning audio files

Sometimes noise is unavoidable. In these cases, there are ways to clean audio files.

Recall from the prior chapter the **SoX (SOund eXchange)** software package. We can use this package to eliminate noise, increase or decrease volume, clip audio files to certain lengths, combine or multiplex audio files, transcode audio files, change sampling rates, change number of channels, and remix audio files.

2.5.1 Noise reduction or cancellation - One of the most common problems when recording audio is having a 'hummm..' sound from an air conditioning unit in the background that interferes with the voice signal of interest. SoX contains a *noiseprof* feature to use a sample to delete noise from the entire sample. Therefore, we can clip a small portion of the audio (say the first 100 milliseconds) and use this as a noise cancellation throughout the rest of the file to delete noise. If this is something that is affecting your audio, you can clean the audio with the *remove_noise.py* script (Figure 2.5.1):

Figure 2.5.1
How to remove noise from file: *remove_noise.py*

```python
import soundfile as sf
import os

def remove_noise(filename):
    #now use sox to denoise using the noise profile
    data, samplerate =sf.read(filename)
    duration=data/samplerate
    first_data=samplerate/10
    filter_data=list()
    for i in range(int(first_data)):
        filter_data.append(data[i])
    noisefile='noiseprof.wav'
    sf.write(noisefile, filter_data, samplerate)
    os.system('sox %s -n noiseprof noise.prof'%(noisefile))
    filename2='tempfile.wav'
    filename3='tempfile2.wav'
    noisereduction="sox %s %s noisered noise.prof 0.21 "%(filename,filename2)
    command=noisereduction
    #run command
    os.system(command)
    print(command)
    #reduce silence again
    #os.system(silenceremove)
    #print(silenceremove)
    #rename and remove files
    os.remove(filename)
    os.rename(filename2,filename)
    #os.remove(filename2)
    os.remove(noisefile)
    os.remove('noise.prof')

    return filename

remove_noise('test.wav')
```

2.5.2 Changing volume - Another common problem with collected audio is having too low or high volume in the sample. If a volume is too high, clipping may occur, making the data unusable; there's nothing you can do here. If the volume is still high and no clipping has occured, you can lower the volume (Figure 2.5.2). If the volume is too low, you can increase the audio volume (Figure 2.5.2). *Note that volume edits are perhaps the most widely used forms of voice editing, as people often speak too far away or too close from microphones.*

Figure 2.5.2
How to change volume: *change_volume.py*

```python
import os

def change_volume(filename, vol):
    # rename file
    if vol > 1:
        new_file=filename[0:-4]+'_increase_'+str(vol)+'.wav'
    else:
        new_file=filename[0:-4]+'_decrease_'+str(vol)+'.wav'
    # changes volume, vol, by input
    os.system('sox -v %s %s %s'%(str(vol),filename,new_file))

    return new_file
# increase volume by 2x
new_file=change_volume('5.wav', 2)
# decrease volume by 1/2
new_file=change_volume('5.wav', 0.5)
```

2.5.3 Trimming audio files – Noise may occur halfway through a session. In these cases, you may want to clip the audio file (e.g. obtain the first 10 seconds). You can easily do this with the *trim_audio.py* script (Figure 2.5.3):

Figure 2.5.3
How to trim audio files: *trim_audio.py*

```python
import os

def trim_audio(filename, start, end):
    clip_duration=end-start
    new_filename=filename[0:-4]+'_trimmed_'+str(start)+'_'+str(end)+'.wav'
    command='sox %s %s trim %s %s'%(filename,new_filename,str(start),str(clip_duration))
    os.system(command)
    return new_filename

# trim from second 30 to 40 => (test_trimmed_30_40.wav)
trim_audio('test.wav', 30, 40)
```

2.5.4 Combining audio files in series - You also may have recorded multiple audio files in series that may need to be combined. Or, you may want to repeat the same audio file again and again. These things can easily be done with the *combine.py* script (Figure 2.6.4).

Figure 2.5.4
How to combine audio files: *combine.py*

```python
import os

def combine_files(one,two):
    three=one[0:-4]+'_'+two[0:-4]+'.wav'
    os.system('sox %s %s %s'%(one,two,three))
    return three

combine_files('test1.wav','test2.wav')
```

2.5.5 Transcoding - You also may have to transcode the audio from one audio format to another (e.g. .WAV→ .MP3). This can be done with the ffmpy module (*transcode.py*), a Python wrapper for FFmpeg (Figure 2.5.5).

Figure 2.5.5
How to transcode audio files: *transcode.py*

```python
import ffmpy

def convert_wav(input_file, output_file):
    #take in an audio file and convert with ffmpeg to proper file type
    try:
        ff = ffmpy.FFmpeg(
            inputs={input_file: None},
            outputs={output_file: None}
            )
        ff.run()
    except:
        print('error')

# output to test.wav
convert_wav('test.mp3', 'test.wav')
```

2.5.6 Changing sample rates - You also may need to change the audio sample rate. This can be done using the *change_samplerate.py* script. Note this command uses a sample rate that has to be converted in terms of kHz instead of Hz, so we have to divide the sample rate by 1000 before executing the command in the terminal (Figure 2.5.6).

Figure 2.5.6
How to convert sample rates: *change_samplerate.py*

```python
import os

def change_samplerate(filename, samplerate):
    new_filename=filename[0:-4]+'_sr'+str(samplerate)+'.wav'
    new_samplerate=str(int(samplerate/1000))
    os.system('sox %s -r %sk %s'%(filename, new_samplerate, new_filename))
    return new_filename

change_samplerate('test.wav',48000)
```

2.5.7   Channel manipulation - You also may need to mix down an audio file from stereo to mono, combine two mono audio files into a stereo file, or extract two mono channels (L/R) independently from a stereo file. You can do these things with the functions defined in the *change_channels.py* script (Figure 2.5.7):

Figure 2.5.7
How to change number of channels: *change_channels.py*

```python
import os

def stereo2mono(filename):
    #Change stereo to mono
    new_filename=filename[0:-4]+'_mono.wav'
    os.system('sox %s %s remix 1-2'%(filename,new_filename))
    return new_filename
def separate_channels(filename):
    #Change stereo to two mono files (mix-down)
    channel_1=filename[0:-4]+'_1.wav'
    channel_2=filename[0:-4]+'_2.wav'
    os.system('sox %s %s remix 1'%(filename, channel_1))
    os.system('sox %s %s remix 2'%(filename, channel_2))
    return channel_1, channel_2
def multiplex(channel_1, channel_2):
    #Convert two mono files into one stereo file (multiplexing)
    output=channel_1[0:-4]+'_'+channel_2[0:-4]+'.wav'
    os.system('sox -M %s %s %s'%(channel_1,channel_2,output))
    return output

stereo2mono('stereo.wav')
separate_channels('stereo.wav')
multiplex('stereo_1.wav','stereo_2.wav')
```

2.5.8 Silence removal - You may have recorded an audio file that is too long. In these scenarios, you may want to clip the audio file to remove the leading or trailing silence. This can easily be done with the *trim_silence.py* script (Figure 2.5.8).

Figure 2.5.8
How to trim silence: *trim_silence.py*

```
import os

def trim_silence(filename):
        new_filename=filename[0:-4]+'_trimmed.wav'
        command='sox %s %s silence -1 1 0.1 1'%(filename, new_filename)+"% -1 2.0 1%"
        os.system(command)
        return new_filename

# trim the leading and trailing silence => (test_trimmed.wav)
trim_silence('test.wav')
```

2.5.9 Custom cleaning software - If none of the above options work to clean your data, there are intuitive software programs that you can use to manipulate sounds (Table 2.5.9). These software programs can add in effects (e.g. background drums if music), add filters (e.g. high or low-pass filters), combine audio streams from separate channels into a single channel, or adjust an audio file's volume.[111] I find using such software is good for one-off projects but often is inefficient for editing a large number of files.[112]

---

[111] **Audacity** - If you're looking for a free package to get started, Audacity is definitely the way to go.
[112] **Paid products** - Adobe Audition, Zoom, and Pro Tools are great paid products to do music editing. Although they are not on Table 2.6.9, I do use some of these tools in my free time.

Table 2.5.9 List of software packages that can help analyzing audio files					
Product	Price	Overall	Interface	Filters	Support
WavePad	$39.95	9.5/10		10/10	10/10
Audacity	$0.00	9.5/10		10/10	5/10
RecordPad Home	$59.99	9.2/10		10/10	9/10
GoldWave	$45.00	8.4/10		10/10	8/10
Blaze Media Pro	$50.00	8.3/10		8.5/10	6.3/10
Mixcraft 8	$179.00	7.8/10		8.5/10	8/10
i-Sound Recorder 7	$29.95	7.5/10		2.8/10	10/10

2.6 Speaker diarization

You may need to separate multiple speakers from a recorded voice sample, something known as ***speaker diarization.*** We can do this using the PyAudioAnalysis library,[113] which uses Fisher Linear Semi-Discriminant Analysis for speaker diarization.[114]

Say we have two speakers who are in the same conversation, speaker A and speaker B. To diarize and annotate a transcription when conversation shifts between the two speakers, you can run the *diarize.py* script (Figure 2.6.1).

---

[113] **To get this to work** I had to port PyAudioAnalysis to Python3. You can read more about this library here: https://github.com/tyiannak/pyAudioAnalysis/wiki/5.-Segmentation

[114] **Note** there are many other ways to diarize speakers, and almost all of these techniques use some form of unsupervised machine learning technique.

Figure 2.6.1
How to implement speaker diarization in terminal: *diarize.py*

```
cd ~
cd voicebook/chapter_2_collection
python3 diarize.py
```

Now there will be 2 folders made in the current directory: *diarize_incoming* and *diarize_processed*. If you put in the file that needs to be diarized in the *diarize_incoming* folder the file will automatically be diarized into Speaker A and Speaker B.[115] Then, each speaker is transcribed using Google Speech API (if available) or PocketSphinx.[116] The output is then saved as a .zip file in the *diarize_processed* folder (e.g. test.wav → test_diarization.zip). After unzipping the output folder, the diarization contains the raw audio ('test.wav'), some metadata ('test.json'), all the speaking elements of speaker 1 (folder='1'), all the speaking elements of speaker 2 (folder='2'), and a transcript of the entire session segmented by each speaker (Figure 2.6.2 and Figure 2.6.3):

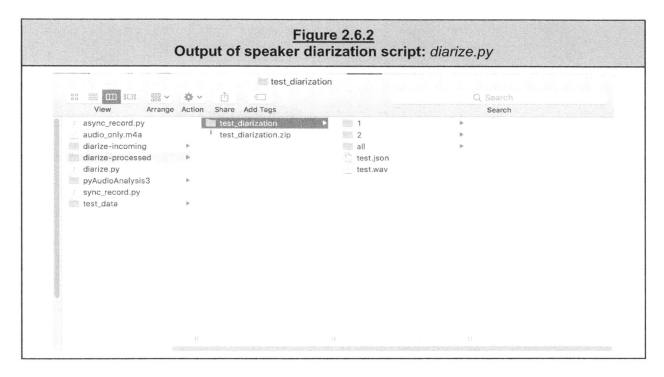

Figure 2.6.2
Output of speaker diarization script: *diarize.py*

---

[115] **Note** that this script can handle any file format (.M4A, .WAV, etc.) that FFmpeg can analyze.
[116] **Note** that this can take a long time for any recording that is over 30 minutes.

Figure 2.6.3
Transcript output from speaker diarization script:
diarize_processed/test_diarization/all/transcript.txt (top) and
diarize_processed/test_diarization/test.json (bottom)

speaker 1: we're here and you know so yes only a cookie

speaker 0: in our own

speaker 1: for today wrong can

speaker 0: there you didn't sell

speaker 1: by the or mine is also is road map

speaker 0: directly on the

…[this continues to the end of the transcript]

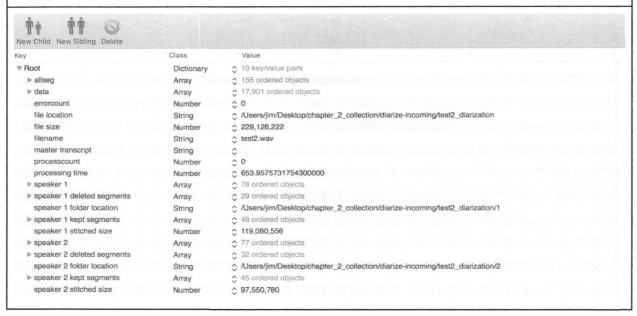

There are multiple benefits of running the *diarize.py* script as a while loop. If you are trying to analyze a large number of files, all you need to do is drag and drop them in the *diarize-incoming* folder and let the script finish (e.g. you can let it run overnight to process many audio recordings). Also, you can create a pipeline of while loops to process this data in series; for example, once a diarization is made it could then be streamed in the *diarize-processed* folder and another script (e.g. *featurize.py*) *could* then featurize this sample by moving it into a *featurize-incoming folder*. Lastly, you can apply machine learning models (e.g. age or gender) to further label the samples using a similar folder structure (e.g. *models-incoming / models-processed*).

2.7 Storing voice files

If you are storing a large number of .WAV files on your computer, you could compress the audio files to the *.FLAC audio format.* Recall that the the .FLAC audio codec is lossless, meaning that it can store the audio data at roughly half the size of .WAV files without sacrificing audio quality. Here is a short script to help you record some audio data (in .WAV format), convert the recorded .WAV files into .FLAC format using FFmpeg, and then compress all the recorded files into a .ZIP file (Figure 2.7.1). *I highly recommend using .FLAC if you're storing a large number of files on a server.*[117]

Figure 2.7.1
Converting voice files to .FLAC format: *convert_flac.py*

```python
import shutil, os, ffmpy

def zipdir(folder, delete):
    # ziph is zipfile handle
    shutil.make_archive(folder, 'zip', folder)
    if delete == True:
        shutil.rmtree(folder)

def convert_flac():
    listdir=os.listdir()
    removedfiles=list()
    for i in range(len(listdir)):
        if listdir[i][-4:]!='flac':
            file=listdir[i]
            newfile=file[0:-4]+'.flac'
            os.system('ffmpeg -i %s %s'%(file,newfile))
            os.remove(file)
            removedfiles.append(file)
    return removedfiles

# get 10 files recorded in 'recordings' folder in current directory
# record them if the folder doesn't exist
hostdir=os.getcwd()
if 'recordings' not in os.listdir():
    os.system('python3 ps_record.py')

# change to directory of recordings to compress all files in directory
os.chdir(hostdir+'/recordings')
convert_flac()

# change back to main directory and compress files, delete main folder
os.chdir(hostdir)
zipdir('recordings', True)
```

---

[117] **You can play back .FLAC files** with VLC media player (on Mac operating systems).

If you are 100% positive that all the files are voice or music files, you can save additional space by converting the .WAV file to **.*OPUS audio format*** for storage. Recall that .OPUS is a lossy audio codec, meaning that audio files only encode information within the voice range (e.g. usually 20 Hz-20kHz). You can compress .WAV files into .OPUS files with the *convert_opus.py* script (Figure 2.7.2). *Note that this script uses the opus-tools package conveniently located in the voicebook cloned repository (chapter_1_collection/opustools).*[118]

Figure 2.7.2
Converting voice files to .OPUS format: *convert_opus.py*

```python
import shutil, os, ffmpy

def zipdir(folder, delete):
    # ziph is zipfile handle
    shutil.make_archive(folder, 'zip', folder)
    if delete == True:
        shutil.rmtree(folder)


def convert_opus(opusdir):
    curdir=os.getcwd()
    listdir=os.listdir()
    removedfiles=list()
    for i in range(len(listdir)):
        if listdir[i][-4:]!='opus':
            # get new file names
            file=listdir[i]
            newfile=file[0:-4]+'.opus'
            # copy file to opus encoding folder
            shutil.copy(curdir+'/'+file, opusdir+'/'+file)
            os.chdir(opusdir)
            # encode with opus codec
            os.system('opusenc %s %s'%(file,newfile))
            shutil.copy(opusdir+'/'+newfile, curdir+'/'+newfile)
            # delete files in opus folder
            os.remove(file)
            os.remove(newfile)
            # delete .wav file in original dir
            os.chdir(curdir)
            os.remove(file)
            removedfiles.append(file)
    return removedfiles

# get 10 files recorded in 'recordings' folder in current directory
# record them if the folder doesn't exist
hostdir=os.getcwd()
opusdir=hostdir+'/opustools'
```

---

[118] **Installing from source code** - you can also compile .OPUS conversion tools from source separately. Note I took this package and put it in the voicebook repository to make it easier for you to convert between .WAV and .OPUS formats.

```python
if 'recordings' not in os.listdir():
    os.system('python3 ps_record.py')

# change to directory of recordings to compress all files in directory
os.chdir(hostdir+'/recordings')
convert_opus(opusdir)
# change back to main directory and compress files, delete main folder
os.chdir(hostdir)
zipdir('recordings', True)
```

You can also easily convert your .ZIP files back to .WAV format after implementing either of the two prior scripts (*convert_flac.py* or *convert_opus.py*). Specifically, the *unpack_files.py* script unpacks a .ZIP file, checks for an audio format (.FLAC and .OPUS), and then transcodes the files back to .WAV format. The transcoding process uses FFmpeg for .FLAC audio formats or the opustools package for .OPUS audio formats (Figure 2.7.3). *Note that if you convert a .WAV file to .OPUS and then back to .WAV there will be some signal loss.*

Figure 2.7.3
Unpacking compressed .FLAC or .OPUS files: *unpack_files.py*

```python
import zipfile, os, shutil

def unzip(file):
    filepath=os.getcwd()+'/'+file
    folderpath=os.getcwd()+'/'+file[0:-4]
    zip = zipfile.ZipFile(filepath)
    zip.extractall(path=folderpath)
def convert_wav(opusdir):
    curdir=os.getcwd()
    listdir=os.listdir()
    removedfiles=list()
    for i in range(len(listdir)):
        file=listdir[i]
        newfile=file[0:-5]+'.wav'
        if file[-5:] in ['.opus','.flac']:
            if file[-5:]=='.flac':
                os.system('ffmpeg -i %s %s'%(file, newfile))
                os.remove(file)
            elif file[-5:]=='.opus':
                # copy file to opus encoding folder
                print(file)
                shutil.copy(curdir+'/'+file, opusdir+'/'+file)
                os.chdir(opusdir)
                # encode with opus codec
                os.system('opusdec %s %s'%(file,newfile))
                shutil.copy(opusdir+'/'+newfile, curdir+'/'+newfile)
                # delete files in opus folder
                os.remove(file)
                os.remove(newfile)
```

```python
                # delete .wav file in original dir
                os.chdir(curdir)
                os.remove(file)
# extract zip file into 'recordings' folder
unzip('recordings.zip')
# now cd into this folder and convert files to wav format
opusdir=os.getcwd()+'/opustools'
os.chdir('recordings')
print(os.listdir())
convert_wav(opusdir)
```

Moreover, there are many **storage mediums** for audio files (Table 2.7.1).[119] In order of cost-effectiveness, these include: hard disks ($0.029/GB) > USB flash drives ($0.242/GB) > cloud providers/FTP servers ($0.276/GB/year) > SD cards ($0.586/GB). *If you're trying to store over 6TB of files, a cloud provider (e.g. AWS) is probably the best option to ensure data portability and integrity.*

Table 2.7.1
List of storage mediums and cost

Storage medium	Storage capacity	Rough costs
USB Flash drive	16GB - 256GB	$6.99 - $61.99[120]
SD Card	8GB - 512GB	$20.88 - $299.99.[121]
Hard disk	500GB - 6TB	$44.50 - 173.99.[122]
FTP Server	Virtually unlimited	Varies.[123]
Cloud provider	Virtually unlimited	$0.023/GB per month for AWS.

Up to this point we've only been storing data to the hard disk on your computer because this has been most convenient. However, there are scenarios when local storage is not ideal; for example, when you use a Raspberry Pi with little RAM memory and storage capacity. In these scenarios, it's best to just upload the files directly to a server and delete the files locally after they have been collected. Here is a short script to save a .WAV file, upload this .WAV file to a FTP server, and then the .WAV file is deleted locally (Figure 2.7.4). Alternatively, you can upload samples to a cloud provider, like Google Storage Buckets and remove the file locally (Figure 2.7.5). In this way, you flexibly collect and store audio files on lightweight devices.

---

[119] **Don't use DVDs or CDs!** They're totally obsolete.
[120] **Cost of USB Flash drive storage -** $61.99 (256GB), $27.99 (128GB), $13.99 (64GB), $7.99 (32GB), $6.99 (16GB).
[121] **Cost of SD card storage -** $299.99 (512GB), $124.99 (256GB), $58.95 (128GB), $34.50 (64GB), $20.88 (32GB).
[122] **Cost of hard disk storage -** $173.99 (6TB), $99.99 (4TB), $87.99 (3TB), $59.99 (2TB), $44.99 (1TB), $44.50 (500GB).
[123] **Cost of FTP server storage –** This depends on the hosting service and plan (~$11/mo for unlimited storage).

Figure 2.7.4
Uploading files to FTP servers: *store_ftp.py*

```python
import sounddevice as sd
import soundfile as sf
import time, os, shutil
from ftplib import FTP


def sync_record(filename, duration, fs, channels):
    print('recording')
    myrecording = sd.rec(int(duration * fs), samplerate=fs, channels=channels)
    sd.wait()
    sf.write(filename, myrecording, fs)
    print('done recording')
    return filename

def upload_file(file, session)
    uploadfile = open(file,'rb')
    session.storbinary('STOR %s'%(file),uploadfile,1024)
    uploadfile.close()

# get environment variables
domain=os.environ['DOMAIN_NAME']
username=os.environ['DOMAIN_USER']
password=os.environ['DOMAIN_PASSWORD']

# log into session
session = ftplib.FTP(domain,username,password)

# record sample (note, could loop through and record samples with while loop)
file = sync_record('test.wav',10,16000,1)

# upload to server / remove file
upload_file(file, session)
os.remove(file)

# log off server
session.quit()
```

Figure 2.7.5
Uploading files to Google storage: *store_gcp.py*

```python
import sounddevice as sd
import soundfile as sf
import time, os, shutil
from google.cloud import storage

def sync_record(filename, duration, fs, channels):
    print('recording')
    myrecording = sd.rec(int(duration * fs), samplerate=fs, channels=channels)
    sd.wait()
    sf.write(filename, myrecording, fs)
    print('done recording')
    return filename


def upload_gcp(bucket_name, source_file_name):
    destination_blob_name=source_file_name
    """Uploads a file to the bucket."""
    storage_client = storage.Client()
    bucket = storage_client.get_bucket(bucket_name)
    blob = bucket.blob(destination_blob_name)

    blob.upload_from_filename(source_file_name)

    print('File {} uploaded to {}.'.format(
        source_file_name,
        destination_blob_name))

# Instantiates a client
storage_client = storage.Client()

# The name for the new bucket
bucket_name = 'test-bucket'

# Creates the new bucket
bucket = storage_client.create_bucket(bucket_name)
print('Bucket {} created.'.format(bucket.name))

# get a recording (can loop here too)
file=syn_record('test.wav', 10, 16000, 1)
# upload this recording to gcp
upload_gcp(bucket_name, file)
# delete file after the recording has been uploaded
os.remove(file)
```

2.8   Publishing voice content[124]

Publishing recorded voice content is now easier than ever (Table 2.8.1). You can email or text message voice notes to someone with smartphones (3B+ users). You can also interact with a voice interface: Siri (1B+ users), Cortana (1B+ users), Google Assistant (500M+ users), Amazon Echo (30M+ users). You can also post voice recordings on social networks: Facebook (2B+ users), YouTube (1B+ users), LinkedIn (562M+ users), or Twitter (330M+ users). You can also post voice content on podcasting networks: iTunes (1B+ users) or SoundCloud (40M+ users). Digital radio stations are another way to publish voice content through radio ads: Spotify (170M+ users) or Pandora (81M+ users). Lastly, storage websites are a great way to share voice media through shareable links: Google Drive (800M+ users) and Dropbox (500M+ users).

In general, it seems like the most convenient way to share recorded voice content is through the **web browser** (e.g. Google Chrome) and **shareable links**. In some cases, external services may need to host your voice content in order for it to be published (e.g. to send a voice message and/or generate a radio ad). Also, you can publish your content **privately** or **publicly**. Some publishing services are **paid** (e.g. publishing on Dropbox, >500GB) and other are **free** (e.g. sending an email) depending on the features and functionality desired.

Table 2.8.1: Ways to publish non-streaming voice content

Publisher	Media type	Audience	Reach (users)
Email users	Voice as attached media to email	Private (link url share)	3B+ users (1B+ gmail, 400M+ outlook)
Text message	Voice note or media	Private (voice message or link url share)	1:1 or 1:many (2.5 billion smartphone users across the world).
facebook	Recorded voice note posted on timeline or in private message	Public or private (voice message or link url share)	2B+ users.
YouTube	Blogs or recorded conference meetings	Public (link url share)	1B+ users.

---

[124] **Why this section is important** – It is important to know what mediums to publish voice content so that it has the most impact. This often takes the form of back-end API-to-API connections to other services, as will be discussed later in Chapter 8 - designing voice computers. This also could increase the monetary value of copyrighted voice samples in terms of their net reach.

Voice interfaces	Voice content played back through skills and/or actions.	Private (through interaction with voice interface).	Cortana (1B+), Siri (1B+), Google Assistant (>500M+ devices), Amazon Echo (>30 million units).
iTunes	Podcasts	Public (link url share)	1.2 billion iPhone units sold.
Cloud storage sites (Dropbox)	Recorded meetings (e.g. zoom meetings)	Public or private (link url share)	800M+ users (Google Drive) 500M+ users (Dropbox)
LinkedIn	Professional voice-related content	Public or private (message)	562M+ users
Twitter	Any voice file through a URL	Public or private (message)	330M+ active users.
Digital radio (Spotify, Pandora)	Broadcast radio advertising	Private (radio ad)	170M+ users (Spotify) 81M+ users (Pandora)
SoundCloud	Podcasts, music, and other media.	Public (link URL share)	40 million registered users.
Slack	A link to an audio file on a channel (#social).	Public or private (url with link)	2.7 million active users

| kaggle | Publish voice dataset online (for ML community to use for modeling). | Public (dataset shared with link) | 536,000 registered users |

In *streaming applications*, voice content may be published and recorded through the cellular network (e.g. AT&T) or the Internet (e.g. Voice-over-IP - VoIP - systems). Cellular networks have long dominated phone and conference calls; however, VoIP systems have driven down costs and are being rapidly adopted by consumers through new hardware interfaces (e.g. FaceTime). In general, most of the streaming applications are for private use and/or business applications (e.g. conference calls or screen sharing). Streaming voice infrastructure is thus becoming more significant and will likely grow in the years ahead (Table 2.8.2).

<u>**Table 2.8.2**
Publishing streaming voice media</u>

VoIP system	Media type	Public or private	Size
Phone call	Audio	Private	2.5B+ people with a smartphone.
skype (conference call)	Video or audio	Private	1B+ users. (microsoft put skype natively in Windows 10)
YouTube (live stream)	Video	Public or private	1B+ users.
(Apple FaceTime)	Video	Private	1.2 billion iPhone units sold.
npr (public radio stations)	Broadcast radio advertising or call-ins	Public (AM/FM radio)	230+ million adults

CNN (broadcast television networks)	Video	Public	200M+ people daily.
facebook (live stream)	Video	Public or private	2B+ users.
(Hangouts on air)	Video or audio	Private	~500M+ users
slack (calling features)	Audio	Private	2.7 million active users
GoToMeeting	Video or audio	Private	N/A
amazon Chime	Video	Private	N/A
Google Duo	Video	Private	N/A
zoom	Video or audio	Private	N/A
UberConference	Audio and screen sharing.	Private	N/A

Taken together, the publishing landscape for voice computing seems quite fragmented. Voice content also competes directly with video content for publishing, and it is still unclear which use cases consumers prefer to be delivered through video versus voice (e.g. FaceTime vs. UberConference). Also, many of the tech giants seem to be progressing toward building and distributing voice infrastructure through streaming video VoIP systems, which will lead to a large volume of voice data collected through videos. As a result, there will likely be more waves of innovation before standards emerge for publishing, distributing, and monetizing voice content.

2.9 MEMUPPS voice controls

There are many factors that affect the quality of audio recordings including the **M**icrophone, recording **E**nvironment, recording **M**ode, **U**ser operation, cleaning **P**rocess, **P**ublishing medium, and **S**torage method.

If you use different microphones, machine learning models may be picking up differences in microphones as opposed to the signals that you are trying to measure or separate.[125] Recording environments also may have noise (e.g. cars passing by outside vs. being indoors in a room), thereby distorting audio signals. In addition, the mode of recording matters because it may elicit different voice responses in the end user. In terms of user operation, the distance from the microphone matters to control volume (e.g. if you are too far away from the mic samples may be collected at low volume). If you clean the audio inconsistently, it may throw off any models that you try to build (e.g. removing noise).[126] Controlling the publishing medium helps you to understand the net reach of the audio files collected (e.g. number of listens). Lastly, if you store audio files in different audio formats or many locations, it may be difficult to build models and/or create interoperable datasets.

We keep all these principles, known as ***MEMUPPS voice controls***, in mind in this book:

1) **M**icrophone control - assume a mono microphone signal as the source input.
2) **E**nvironment control - stay indoors so that the audio is not affected by external background noise.
3) **M**ode – record samples in synchronous-active (SA) recording mode; keep duration of all recordings 20 seconds.
4) **U**ser control - assume a distance of 3 feet away from the microphone.
5) **P**rocess control – assume no processing (e.g. noise removal) on the raw audio, uses .WAV codec for digital encoding/decoding.
6) **P**ublishing control – publish data samples locally (intended to be private with little reach).
7) **S**torage control – store data locally on a hard disk in the .WAV format.

---

[125] **For this reason,** make sure that you control for microphones before recording data and it is representative of your user base. For example - if many of your users use 40% windows computers and 60% Mac computers, you probably want to make a dataset that consists of 40% windows audio recordings and 60% Mac audio recordings with different mixtures of microphones.

[126] **Noise removal affects transcription accuracies -** If you remove noise before sending a voice file to google transcription, you actually get poorer transcription accuracy than if you did no filtering because Google's models are trained on noisy data.

To help log MEMUPPS controls in your code base, you can tag voice files manually with the *pytaglib* module.[127] In the example below, I tag the microphone type, environment, recording mode, sample type, distance from microphone, processing labels, and storage location (Figure 2.9.1). I did not add in any publishing controls because the file is intended to be kept locally. In this way, you can make sure that you can detect variations in your data and filter the data appropriately for modeling later on. *Feel free to add in additional tags as you see fit!* ☺

Figure 2.9.1:
Using the MEMUPPS mindset to label audio files: *label_memupps.py*

```python
import os, taglib, json
import sounddevice as sd
import soundfile as sf

def get_defaults():
    if 'label.json' in os.listdir():
        data=json.load('label.json')
    else:
        mic=input('what is the microphone?')
        env=input('what is the environment?')
        mode=input('what is the mode?')
        sampletype=input('sample type? (e.g. voice)')
        distance=input('what is the distance from mic?')
        process=input('do you use any processing (e.g. SoX noisefloor, .wav--> .opus --> .wav)? if so what?')
        storage=input('where are you storing files?')
        data={
            'microphone':mic,
            'environment':env,
            'mode':mode,
            'sample type': sampletype,
            'distance':distance,
            'processing':process,
            'storage':storage,
        }

        jsonfile=open('label.json','w')
        json.dump(data,jsonfile)
        jsonfile.close()
    return data

def label_sample(file):
    data=get_defaults()
    audio=taglib.File(os.getcwd()+'/'+file)
    print(audio)
    audio.tags['microphone']=data['microphone']
    audio.tags['environment']=data['environment']
    audio.tags['mode']=data['mode']
```

---

[127] **Musicians often do this** by tagging the name of the artist on .MP3 files, etc.

```python
        audio.tags['sample type']=data['sample type']
        audio.tags['distance']=data['distance']
        audio.tags['processing']=data['processing']
        audio.tags['storage']=data['storage']
        audio.save()

def sync_record(filename, duration, fs, channels):
    print('recording')
    myrecording = sd.rec(int(duration * fs), samplerate=fs, channels=channels)
    sd.wait()
    sf.write(filename, myrecording, fs)
    print('done recording')
    label_sample(filename)

file='test.wav'
sync_record(file,10,18000,1)
```

2.10 Conclusion

👋 Well done! You now have all the knowledge necessary to collect 'sand dollar audio.' Be sure to keep in mind MEMUPPS voice controls to make sure audio is collected consistently;

- **M**icrophone control
- **E**nvironment control
- **M**ode control
- **U**ser controls
- **P**rocessing controls
- **P**ublishing controls
- **S**torage controls

Here are some links for additional documentation if you'd like to go deeper on anything related to data collection:

- Data collection
    - PySoundFile. https://pysoundfile.readthedocs.io/en/0.9.0/
    - Sounddevice. https://python-sounddevice.readthedocs.io/en/0.3.11/
    - Os. https://docs.python.org/3/library/os.html
- Cleaning audio
    - SoX. http://sox.sourceforge.net/
- Speaker diarization
    - pyAudioAnalysis. https://github.com/tyiannak/pyAudioAnalysis/wiki/5.-Segmentation
- Transcoding
    - FFmpeg. https://www.ffmpeg.org/
    - .OPUS codec. http://opus-codec.org/
    - .FLAC codec. https://xiph.org/flac/
- Storage
    - Google Cloud Storage Client Library. https://cloud.google.com/storage/docs/reference/libraries
    - Ftplib. https://docs.python.org/3/library/ftplib.html
    - Shutil. https://docs.python.org/3/library/shutil.html
    - Zipfile. https://docs.python.org/3/library/zipfile.html
- MEMUPPS voice controls
    - Pytaglib. https://pypi.org/project/pytaglib/

The next chapter is all about fingerprinting voice files with features, which will help with modeling later on. ✍

Chapter 3:
Featurization

"Voices are like fingerprints, from Cagney to Bogart. They never lost it. My voice is instrumental in categorizing me."
-**Sylvester Stallone**
(American actor, producer and filmmaker)

Chapter Overview

Voices are like fingerprints. Fingerprints have very distinct patterns - loops, arches, and whorls - that persist throughout someone's life. In a similar way, voices have very distinct patterns - acoustic, text, mixed, and meta features- that are "instrumental in categorizing you."

Like DNA, we can sequence the voice. DNA is composed of genes, which are fundamentally composed from adenine, thymine, guanine, and cytosine base pairs arranged in a double helix structure. Speech, on the other hand, is composed of words, which are fundamentally composed from phonemes (e.g. 'a', 'b', etc.) exerted at varying powers and speaking rates.

Although we have made some advances, we still don't know all the information that is contained within voice data. We know that vocal productions are typically between 250 Hz and 8000 Hz, males have a lower voice (85-180 Hz) than females (165-255 Hz), and RMS power is a good feature for detecting age. But we're discovering new things everyday; for example, specific voice features can be used with machine learning models to detect early-stage psychosis (~80% accurately) or depression (89% accurately). What else will we find?

This chapter is all about building automated frameworks to sequence voice data with features.[128] Specifically, we'll cover:

- **3.1** - What are features?
- **3.2** - Audio features
- **3.3** - Text features
- **3.4** - Mixed features
- **3.5** - Meta features
- **3.6** - Dimensionality reduction
- **3.7** - Feature selection

In this way, we can discover what features in the voice matter the most for problems that you are trying to solve.

---

[128] **DNA sequencing analogy** – You can think of this chapter laying automated frameworks to sequence voice samples like when Craig Venter developed shotgun sequencing to sequence DNA.

3.1 What are features?

If you are new to machine learning, you may ask, "what are features?"

Simply, **features** are descriptive numerical representations to describe something.[129] The process of tagging features to an object is known as **data labeling.** There are an infinite number of features that can describe an object, but some features are more relevant than others. The process of selecting the ideal feature configuration to describe an object is known as **feature selection.**

Voice features, therefore, are features that describe information contained within the original audio file format (e.g. MFCC coefficients in a recorded 20 second .WAV file).

The process of feature selection is often goal-oriented; it's often a means to help build a **machine learning model** to classify two or more groups from each other. In other words, features help to **reduce dimensionality** and simplify the representations of objects so that they can be processed with less computational power.

Note that *too few features* or *irrelevant features* can lead to inaccurate model representations, or **overfitting**. For example, you may notice that the intensity of light outside is lower whenever it is raining outside. Then, you may then make a mental model (stereotype) that associates light intensity with rain and believe it is raining when it is just cloudy outside - something known as a **false positive.** You'd need additional features to complete the picture to reduce false positives, such as relative humidity and water volume on the ground surface. Therefore, you often can **reduce overfitting** by selecting **appropriate features** for a given modeling task.

The process of assessing the accuracy of a machine learning model is known as **cross-validation.** There are many types of cross-validation; however, the most common forms are leave-one-out analysis or k-folds. In general, cross-validation uses a **training set,** or a subset of data with extracted features that is used to train a machine learning model, and a **testing set,** or a subset of data with extracted features that is used to test the performance of a machine learning model.[130]

As a concrete example, let's try to describe features that may classify 50 males from 50 females. Some features are more descriptive than others; for example, there are features in the voice - like the fundamental frequency - that clearly separate most males from females. Also, males tend to have lower essential body fat[131] than females. Males also typically have more facial hair than females (e.g. beards). On the other hand, things like knee shape or waist size may not really be that useful to separate out males or females. The fundamental frequency,

---

[129] **Feature example** - A human being has features of 1 face, 2 ears, 2 eyes, 2 hands, a nose, etc.
[130] **Validation set** - A validation set is often used when building deep learning models. Simply validation sets are subsets of data with extracted features that is used to optimize model hyperparameters (e.g. learning rate).
[131] **Essential body fat** - Essential body fat is the amount of fat you need to function normally, accounts for 10 to 13 percent of a woman's total body fat; men have just 2 to 5 percent of essential body fat.

facial hair density, and essential body fat could then all be relevant features; however, knee shape and waist size may be irrelevant features to separate genders.[132]

Fortunately, Python has a rich set of modules for feature creation, manipulation, and selection. The most important library in Python for dealing with features and vectors is **numpy**.[133] Let's go through some quick coding examples to get you up-to-speed with the basic functionality of this library for this chapter and the chapters that follow (Table 3.1.1). *If you are already comfortable working with numpy, feel free to skip the rest of this section.*

colspan="2"	Table 3.1.1 Useful numpy commands: *numpy_commands.py*
Goal	**How to implement in IDLE3 python interpreter**[134]
| **Convert a list into a numpy array**<br>(can make lists first then convert lists into numpy arrays) | ```
import numpy as np
>>> g=[5,2,61,1]
>>> type(g)
<class 'list'>
>>> g=np.array(g)
>>> type(g)
<class 'numpy.ndarray'>
``` |
| **Indexing numpy arrays**<br>(same as lists in Python) | ```
>>> g[0]
5
``` |
| **Serializing numpy data to database**<br>(.JSON database) | ```
>>> import json
>>> data={
        'data':g.tolist(),
        }
>>> jsonfile=open('test.json','w')
>>> json.dump(data,jsonfile)
>>> jsonfile.close()
``` |
| **Loading numpy data from database**<br>(.JSON database) | ```
>>> newdata=json.load(open('test.json'))
>>> numpydata=np.array(newdata['data'])
>>> type(numpydata)
<class 'numpy.ndarray'>
>>> numpydata
array([ 5,  2, 61,  1])
``` |

---

[132] **Model training from features** - Note we can then train a model on 40 males and 40 females (training set) and leave out 10 males and 10 females (testing set) using the features [fundamental frequency, facial hair density, BMI]. A machine learning model, such as a support vector machine algorithm, can then can be made to separate out the groups (males vs. females). The process of building and optimizing machine learning models is covered in the next chapter.

[133] **Note** - You should definitely get comfortable with the numpy module, as this probably the most important library in Python for data science related tasks.

[134] **To load the IDLE3 Python interpreter,** go to the terminal and type in 'idle3' and then enter. There are better IDEs to write Python code (e.g. Sublime); however, IDLE3 has important features to debug your code.

| **Get basic data** (shape, size) | ```
>>> numpydata.shape
(4,)
>>> numpydata.size
4
``` |
| **Get statistical features from an array** (calculate mean, standard deviation, min, max) | ```
>>> np.mean(numpydata)
17.25
>>> np.std(numpydata)
25.301926804099327
>>> np.amin(numpydata)
1
>>> np.amax(numpydata)
61
``` |
| **Initialize new empty array with zeros** (shape is customizable) | ```
>>> makezeros=np.zeros(5)
>>> makezeros
array([0., 0., 0., 0., 0.])
``` |
| **Array operations** (add arrays, subtract arrays, and multiply array by scalar) | ```
>>> A=np.zeros(4)
>>> A+numpydata
array([ 5.,   2.,  61.,   1.])
>>> A-np.array([2,-1,5,8])
array([-2.,   1.,  -5.,  -8.])
>>> 5*numpydata
array([ 25,  10, 305,   5])
``` |

Now that you know how to use numpy arrays, we're ready to start extracting features from voice files. :)

3.2 Audio features

Audio features are features that are derived from encoded audio collected through a microphone (e.g. a .WAV file).[135] These could be things like the fundamental frequency, the RMS power, mel-frequency spectrogram coefficients ('MFCC coefficients'),[136] or the zero-crossing rate to name a few (Table 3.1.1).[137] In order to extract audio features, you often have to break up an audio file into segments, known as ***windows*** (often between 20-100 milliseconds), which then can be used to average activity throughout the length of the audio file. Commonly, audio features are used for phoneme classification (e.g. to build acoustic transcription models), emotion labeling (e.g. happy/sad), speaker recognition (e.g. speaker A vs. speaker B), gender detection (e.g. male/female), and/or age detection (e.g. 20s vs. 30s).

---

[135] **Acoustic features** – Audio features are also commonly known as acoustic features. I use the term audio features because I think it's clearer and is easier to differentiate from text or other types of features based on the data input.

[136] **Wikipedia:** "mel-frequency cepstrum (MFC) is a representation of the short-term power spectrum of a sound, based on a linear cosine transform of a log power spectrum on a nonlinear mel scale of frequency."

[137] **Note:** I only could put the most relevant features i could find on this table; this is not an exhaustive list. There are many research groups right now making new audio features for noise classification and signal enhancement; definitely do you own research to find the most ideal features for your use case.

Table 3.2.1:
List of common audio features

Feature	Description	Use case
Mel spectrogram frequency coefficients (MFCC coefficients)	Frequency bands that narrow in on the human voice range (usually 13 types).	Classifying phonemes.
Mel spectrogram frequency delta coefficients	A variation of the MFCC coefficients above; MFCC delta coefficients are commonly combined with MFCC coefficients in audio feature embeddings.	Classifying phonemes.
Fundamental frequency	The lowest frequency of a periodic voice waveform.	Useful for classifying genders.
Jitter	Deviation of periodicity in a periodic signal. $$Jitter(absolute) = \frac{1}{N-1}\sum_{i=1}^{N-1}|T_i - T_{i+1}|$$	Useful for speaker recognition and pathological voice quality.
Shimmer	Cycle-to-cycle variations in the amplitude. $$Shimmer(dB) = \frac{1}{N-1}\sum_{i=1}^{N-1}|20\log(A_{i+1}/A_i)|$$	Useful for speaker recognition and pathological voice quality.
Formant frequencies	$$F_1 = \frac{c}{4L}$$ Higher frequency resonances can be calculated by determining all odd multiples of the first formant.	Detecting intratracheal lengths.
File duration	The overall length of the audio file.	Detecting speaking rates.

Root mean squared (RMS) energy	The mean of the energy emitted into the microphone over a span of time. $$f_{\text{rms}} = \lim_{T \to \infty} \sqrt{\frac{1}{T} \int_0^T [f(t)]^2 \, dt}.$$	Detecting stress or new environments.
Spectral centroid	Center of mass of an audio spectrum, or the weighted mean of the frequencies present in the signal. $$\text{Centroid} = \frac{\sum_{n=0}^{N-1} f(n) x(n)}{\sum_{n=0}^{N-1} x(n)}$$ where x(n) represents the weighted frequency value, or magnitude, of bin number n, and f(n) represents the center frequency of that bin.	Characterizes 'brightness' of sound (timbre).
Spectral flux	How quickly the power spectrum of an audio signal is changing from one frame to the next.	Characterizes environments.
Onset strength	A measurement of the power which a voice recording begins and stops.	Helps localize sound sources.
Spectral contrast	The decibel difference between peaks and valleys in the spectrum.	Helps to detect noise in samples.
Spectral flatness	Entropy measure that helps assess self-similarity in an audio signal. $$\text{Flatness} = \frac{\sqrt[N]{\prod_{n=0}^{N-1} x(n)}}{\frac{\sum_{n=0}^{N-1} x(n)}{N}} = \frac{\exp\left(\frac{1}{N} \sum_{n=0}^{N-1} \ln x(n)\right)}{\frac{1}{N} \sum_{n=0}^{N-1} x(n)}$$	Useful for noise detection (1) compared to tone-signals (0).
Spectral rolloff	Frequency below which the total energy is typically concentrated.	Speech bandwidth characterization and segmentation (diarization).
Zero-crossing rate	The rate of sign changes in a sample of audio. (+/-) or (-/+). $$zcr = \frac{1}{T-1} \sum_{t=1}^{T-1} \mathbb{1}_{\mathbb{R}_{<0}}(s_t s_{t-1})$$	Useful to measure periodicity and detect voices.

For the purposes of this section, let's assume that you have collected high-quality audio samples and you know how to read audio data. If you're having trouble reading audio data, check back in Chapter 1 (e.g. in read/writing audio files section). If you need to manipulate and clean your data, check back in Chapter 2 (e.g. how to use SoX to enhance audio files).

My favorite library to extract acoustic features is **LibROSA**. Note that LibROSA captures audio features in 20 millisecond windows and numpy feature arrays can get quite large.[138] Therefore, it's often useful to take the mean, standard deviation, minimum, maximum, and median of these features and embed them into an array for further analysis. Here is a short script to help you extract 187 acoustic features with this library (Figure 3.2.1).

Figure 3.2.1:
Extracting audio features with LibROSA library: *librosa_features.py*

```python
import librosa
import numpy as np

# get statistical features in numpy
def stats(matrix):
    mean=np.mean(matrix)
    std=np.std(matrix)
    maxv=np.amax(matrix)
    minv=np.amin(matrix)
    median=np.median(matrix)

    output=np.array([mean,std,maxv,minv,median])

    return output

# featurize with librosa following documentation
# https://librosa.github.io/librosa/feature.html
def librosa_featurize(filename, categorize):
    # if categorize == True, output feature categories
    print('librosa featurizing: %s'%(filename))

    y, sr = librosa.load(filename)

    # FEATURE EXTRACTION
    ######################################################
    # extract major features using librosa
    mfcc=librosa.feature.mfcc(y)
    poly_features=librosa.feature.poly_features(y)
    chroma_cens=librosa.feature.chroma_cens(y)
    chroma_cqt=librosa.feature.chroma_cqt(y)
    chroma_stft=librosa.feature.chroma_stft(y)
    tempogram=librosa.feature.tempogram(y)

    spectral_centroid=librosa.feature.spectral_centroid(y)[0]
    spectral_bandwidth=librosa.feature.spectral_bandwidth(y)[0]
    spectral_contrast=librosa.feature.spectral_contrast(y)[0]
    spectral_flatness=librosa.feature.spectral_flatness(y)[0]
    spectral_rolloff=librosa.feature.spectral_rolloff(y)[0]
```

---

[138] **The 20-millisecond window** - This window is quite standard for speech-related applications and was pioneered mostly in the speech recognition community.

```python
onset=librosa.onset.onset_detect(y)
onset=np.append(len(onset),stats(onset))
tempo=librosa.beat.tempo(y)[0]
onset_features=np.append(onset,tempo)
onset_strength=librosa.onset.onset_strength(y)
zero_crossings=librosa.feature.zero_crossing_rate(y)[0]
rmse=librosa.feature.rmse(y)[0]

# FEATURE CLEANING
###########################################################

# onset detection features
onset_features=np.append(onset_features,stats(onset_strength))

# rhythm features (384) - take the first 13
rhythm_features=np.concatenate(np.array([stats(tempogram[0]),
                                stats(tempogram[1]),
                                stats(tempogram[2]),
                                stats(tempogram[3]),
                                stats(tempogram[4]),
                                stats(tempogram[5]),
                                stats(tempogram[6]),
                                stats(tempogram[7]),
                                stats(tempogram[8]),
                                stats(tempogram[9]),
                                stats(tempogram[10]),
                                stats(tempogram[11]),
                                stats(tempogram[12])]))

# spectral features (first 13 mfccs)
spectral_features=np.concatenate(np.array([stats(mfcc[0]),
                                  stats(mfcc[1]),
                                  stats(mfcc[2]),
                                  stats(mfcc[3]),
                                  stats(mfcc[4]),
                                  stats(mfcc[5]),
                                  stats(mfcc[6]),
                                  stats(mfcc[7]),
                                  stats(mfcc[8]),
                                  stats(mfcc[9]),
                                  stats(mfcc[10]),
                                  stats(mfcc[11]),
                                  stats(mfcc[12]),
                                  stats(poly_features[0]),
                                  stats(poly_features[1]),
                                  stats(spectral_centroid),
                                  stats(spectral_bandwidth),
                                  stats(spectral_contrast),
                                  stats(spectral_flatness),
                                  stats(spectral_rolloff)]))
```

```python
        # power features
        power_features=np.concatenate(np.array([stats(zero_crossings),
                                                stats(rmse)]))
        # you can also concatenate the features
        if categorize == True:
            # can output feature categories if true
            features={'onset':onset_features,
                      'rhythm':rhythm_features,
                      'spectral':spectral_features,
                      'power':power_features}
        else:
            # can output numpy array of everything if we don't need categorizations
            features = np.concatenate(np.array([onset_features,
                                                rhythm_features,
                                                spectral_features,
                                                power_features]))

        return features

features=librosa_featurize('test.wav', False)
```

Another library to extract audio features is **PyAudioAnalysis**. PyAudioAnalysis can extract 34 audio features: the zero-crossing rate (1), energy (2), entropy of energy (3), spectral centroid (4), spectral spread (5), spectral entropy (6), spectral flux (7), spectral rolloff (8), MFCCs (9-21), chroma vectors (22-33), and chroma deviations. Unfortunately, the PyAudioAnalysis library is written in Python2; however, I provide a script in Python3 so that it's easier for you (Figure 3.2.2). *Note that this script extracts 170 features in total, as each of these individual features is reduced to means, standard deviations, maxes, mins, and medians with the stats() function.*

Figure 3.2.2:
Extracting audio features with PyAudioAnalysis: *pyaudio_features.py*

```python
import os,json
import numpy as np

def stats(matrix):
    mean=np.mean(matrix)
    std=np.std(matrix)
    maxv=np.amax(matrix)
    minv=np.amin(matrix)
    median=np.median(matrix)
    output=np.array([mean,std,maxv,minv,median])
    return output

def pyaudio_featurize(file):
    # use pyaudioanalysis library to export features
    # exported as file[0:-4].json
    os.system('python pyaudio_help.py %s'%(file))
```

```python
    jsonfile=file[0:-4]+'.json'
    g=json.load(open(jsonfile))
    features=np.array(g['features'])
    # now go through all the features and get statistical features for array
    new_features=list()
    all_labels=['zero crossing rate','energy','entropy of energy','spectral centroid',
                'spectral spread', 'spectral entropy', 'spectral flux', 'spectral rolloff',
                'mfcc1','mfcc2','mfcc3','mfcc4',
                'mfcc5','mfcc6','mfcc7','mfcc8',
                'mfcc9','mfcc10','mfcc11','mfcc12',
                'mfcc13','chroma1','chroma2','chroma3',
                'chroma4','chroma5','chroma6','chroma7',
                'chroma8','chroma9','chroma10','chroma11',
                'chroma12','chroma deviation']
    labels=list()

    for i in range(len(features)):
        tfeature=stats(features[i])
        for j in range(len(tfeature)):
            new_features.append(tfeature[j])
            if j==0:
                labels.append('mean '+all_labels[i])
            elif j==1:
                labels.append('std '+all_labels[i])
            elif j==2:
                labels.append('max '+all_labels[i])
            elif j==3:
                labels.append('min '+all_labels[i])
            elif j==4:
                labels.append('median '+all_labels[i])

    new_features=np.array(new_features)
    os.remove(jsonfile)

    return new_features, labels

features, labels =pyaudio_featurize('test.wav')
```

Alternatively, **SoX** is good at extracting various audio features related to amplitudes and frequencies. I typically use this library to add-on metadata on top of features extracted from PyAudioAnalysis and/or LibROSA. Although painful,[139] the features can be extracted with some text manipulation and put into a numpy array with the *sox_features.py* script (Figure 3.2.3).

---

[139] **It's difficult to extract SoX features with Python -** This is because SoX outputs the data to sterror instead of stdout; it took me a while to figure out what command was necessary to output the SoX stat command into a text file.

Figure 3.2.3:
Extracting audio features with SoX CLI: *sox_features.py*

```python
import os
import numpy as np

def clean_text(text):
    text=text.lower()
    chars=['a','b','c','d','e','f','g','h','i','j','k','l','m',
           'o','p','q','r','s','t','u','v','w','x','y','z',' ',
           ':', '(',')','-','=','"','.']
    for i in range(len(chars)):
        text=text.replace(chars[i],'')

    text=text.split('\n')
    new_text=list()
    # now get new text
    for i in range(len(text)):
        try:
            new_text.append(float(text[i].replace('\n','').replace('n','')))
        except:
            pass
            #print(text[i].replace('\n','').replace('n',''))

    return new_text

def sox_featurize(filename):
    # soxi and stats files
    soxifile=filename[0:-4]+'_soxi.txt'
    statfile=filename[0:-4]+'_stats.txt'
    os.system('soxi %s > %s'%(filename, soxifile))
    os.system('sox %s -n stat > %s 2>&1'%(filename, statfile))
    # get basic info
    s1=open(soxifile).read()
    s1_labels=['channels','samplerate','precision',
               'duration','filesize','bitrate','sample encoding']
    s1=clean_text(s1)

    s2=open(statfile).read()
    s2_labels=['samples read','length','scaled by','maximum amplitude',
               'minimum amplitude','midline amplitude','mean norm','mean amplitude',
               'rms amplitude','max delta','min delta','mean delta',
               'rms delta','rough freq','vol adj']

    s2=clean_text(s2)

    labels=s1_labels+s2_labels
    features=np.array(s1+s2)
    return features, labels

features, labels = sox_featurize('test.wav')
```

If you are currently doing academic research and plan to publish, it may be important to test a custom audio embedding (e.g. with LibROSA) against audio embeddings widely used in research. Important audio embeddings to keep in mind are the **AudioSet embedding** (Google) and **OpenSMILE embeddings** (Table 3.1.2).

	Table 3.1.2 Standardized audio research feature embeddings	
Feature array	Description	Size
AudioSet embedding	Used by Google research for audio modeling of YouTube data; uses the VGGish model as a feature extractor.	128 features (per second of audio)
OpenSMILE embeddings	GeMAPS embedding (52 features), the AVEC feature set (2,268 features), and the Interspeech Emotion Challenge feature set (384 features) are commonly used to validate work in research. Note that commercial licenses are available, but it's free for education and research use.	Varies (52-2,268 features)

In 2017, Google Research proposed a 128-dimension VGGish AudioSet embedding per second of audio to help classify various events on YouTube videos. Since then, this embedding has become widely adopted and the original paper has been cited over 150 times by other research groups. Therefore, it seems as if Google has been making some strides recently to standardize audio and video arrays for deep learning applications.

To make it easy to extract AudioSet features, I've made the *audioset_features.py script* Figure 3.2.4).[140] Note 128 dimensions are generating for every second of audio, so this can get quite high-dimensional quickly. Therefore, it's likely best to take the means and standard deviations of these windows to reduce dimensionality to a 256-dimensional representation of an audio file of N length. Note that this script requires you to download the Vggish model files (vggish_model.ckpt and vggish_pca_params.npz), which can take a bit of time; however, after these files have been downloaded you can use the script as a general-purpose feature extractor.

---

[140] **The 256-dimensional representation** is in new_features in the Figure 3.2.4. Note that this figure skips down to the bottom of the audioset_features.py script because it's quite long and complex to setup AudioSet if you're unfamiliar with TensorFlow. However, this script should make these features much more accessible to you.

Figure 3.2.4:
Extracting AudioSet features: *audioset_features.py*

```python
# ^^ ... (down to main script in audioset_features.py)
# get current directory
curdir=os.getcwd()

# download audioset files if audioset not in current directory
if 'audioset' not in os.listdir():
    try:
        setup_audioset(curdir)
    except:
        print('there was an error installing audioset')

# record a 10 second, mono 16k Hz audio file in the current directory
filename='test.wav'
sync_record(filename,10,16000,1)

# now let's featurize an audio sample in the current directory, test.wav
features, new_features =audioset_featurize(filename)
# print('new features')
# print(new_features)
# print(len(new_features))
```

OpenSMILE is another powerful C library useful to extract acoustic features for research purposes.[141] For example, the **GeMAPs embedding** has been put forth by researchers as a standard for featurizing audio files for use in health diagnosis research with this library.[142] Like the other libraries in this chapter, OpenSMILE can extract 1) chroma features; 2) MFCC features; 3) PLP features (PLP cepstral coefficients); 4) prosodic features (fundamental frequency, voicing probability, and loudness contours); and many more. *Since the library is written in C, extracting features with OpenSMILE is beyond the scope of this book.*[143]

Typically, I'd pick one of these embeddings (LibROSA, PyAudioAnalysis, SoX, or AudioSet) and go with it for some initial modeling. However, if you have the flexibility you can also just capture all of these features quite easily using *audio_features.py* script (Figure 3.2.7). Although a bit more computationally intensive for your computer, capturing all the features gives you the most flexibility for modeling later on. It also helps to provide exhaustive metadata if you can't keep the raw audio file (e.g. for legal / security purposes).

---

[141] **Proprietary** - Unfortunately, the OpenSMILE library is proprietary; though, the creators allow for the use of the library for free for research and educational use.

[142] **GeMAPs** - The Geneva minimalistic acoustic parameter set (GeMAPS) is used by many researchers to assess the accuracy of voice models.

[143] **OpenSMILE book** – If you'd like to explore OpenSMILE embeddings further, you can read the book that they released on their website.

Figure 3.2.7
Extracting all audio features: *audio_features.py*

```python
import librosa_features as lf
import pyaudio_features as pf
import sox_features as sf
import audioset_features as af
import numpy as np

def audio_featurize(filename, jsondump):
    # extract features, go back to this directory everytime
    curdir=os.getcwd()
    pyaudio_features, pyaudio_labels = pf.pyaudio_featurize(filename)
    os.chdir(curdir)
    librosa_features=lf.librosa_featurize(filename, False)
    os.chdir(curdir)
    sox_features, sox_labels = sf.sox_featurize(filename)
    os.chdir(curdir)
    audioset_allfeatures, audioset_features =audioset_featurize(filename)
    os.chdir(curdir)

    features={
        'pyaudio':pyaudio_features.tolist(),
        'librosa':librosa_features.tolist(),
        'sox':sox_features.tolist(),
        'audioset':audioset_features.tolist(),
        }
    # now make an array with all these features
    data={
        'filename':filename,
        'features':features,
        }

    # dump to .json database
    if jsondump==True:
        jsonfilename=filename[0:-4]+'.json'
        jsonfile=open(jsonfilename,'w')
        jsonfile.write(data, jsonfile)
        jsonfile.close()

    return data

data=audio_featurize('test.wav')
```

3.3 Text features

Text features*[144]** are any features that are derived from an output transcript from a speech-to-text model, or ***transcription model. Some example features include things like keyword frequencies (e.g. count of words 'basketball'), part-of-speech tags (e.g. noun frequency), letter frequencies (e.g. 'a'), and sentiment polarity (e.g. positive or negative) to name a few (Table 3.3.1). Commonly, text features are used for topic classification, emotion detection, and document classification.

Table 3.3.1: List of common text features		
Text feature	**Example**	**Use case**
Keyword frequency	Count of word 'basketball' relative to the total number of words.	Useful to determine topics.
Character frequencies	Count of the letter 'a' relative to all characters.	Letter frequencies represent phonemes in speech and sometimes enrich model accuracies. A standard list of phonemes in English is provided by the International Phonetic Alphabet.
Part-of-speech tags	Number of nouns in the entire transcript.	Can be used to infer the type of speech production - for example, whether it's descriptive, interjectory, or free speech.
Sentiment polarity	Positive, negative, or neutral.	Can detect whether the content of the transcript is positive, negative, or neutral; helps to detect emotional content.
Brunet's index	A measure of the richness of text; a complexity measure.	Can measure cognitive impairment associated with Alzheimer's disease.
Morphological features	Past, present, or future tense of a verb (lemma and surface forms).	Useful to see time-based content in a conversation.
Syntactic features	Dependencies between tokens and parts of speech (e.g. noun-verb-noun frequency throughout entire text).	Useful for biometric identification; people have unique syntaxes which describe their interactions.

---

[144] **Linguistic vs. text features** - Text features are also known as linguistic features; I prefer the term 'text features' because it's a bit clearer to communicate and everyone knows what text is. Otherwise, you may be confused.

Named entity recognition	The frequency of a specific person, Jim, being used in a transcript. Base phrases for topic analysis - like all the words relating to the word car.	Useful to determine the relevance of certain things in a conversation. Also, useful for topic labeling.

The choice of transcription model matters when extracting text features, as transcription accuracy varies across different models. For example, a transcription model may be really good at picking up numerical digits but bad at complex vocabularies. Some transcription models may perform well in noisy environments (e.g. Google) while others may be optimized for less noisy environments (e.g. PocketSphinx). *Therefore, try to keep the method of transcription consistent when featurizing text data.*[145]

Now let's transcribe some voice data. You can use an imported python script (*transcribe.py*) to transcribe audio with the **Google Speech API**, **PocketSphinx**, or the open-source **DeepSpeech model** (Figure 3.3.1).[146] Conveniently, you can use the transcribe_all() function to easily transcribe an audio file with all these methods and output the data to a .JSON file named like the audio file (e.g. 'test.wav' → 'test.json').

Figure 3.3.1:
Various ways to transcribe audio data: *record_transcribe.py*

```python
import transcribe as ts
import sounddevice as sd
import soundfile as sf

def sync_record(filename, duration, fs, channels):
    print('recording')
    myrecording = sd.rec(int(duration * fs), samplerate=fs, channels=channels)
    sd.wait()
    sf.write(filename, myrecording, fs)
    print('done recording')

# record a test file
sync_record('test.wav', 10, 44100, 2)

# fetch a google transcript (note: you need environment vars setup)
try:
    google_transcript=ts.transcribe_google('test.wav')
except:
    print('do not have proper environment variables setup')
```

---

[145] **MEMUPPS** - Recall the MEMUPPS voice controls; transcription would be a form of auditory processing.

[146] **DeepSpeech** - Note that if you don't have the DeepSpeech model already installed on your machine it will auto-setup and install this for you. Also, the DeepSpeech model can be computationally intensive, so if it does not work well for your machine I would recommend using PocketSphinx.

```
# transcribe with pocketsphinx
sphinx_transcript=ts.transcribe_sphinx('test.wav')

# transcribe with deepspeech (can be CPU intensive)
sphinx_transcript=ts.transcribe_deepspeech('test.wav')

# record a sample file and transcribe using all transcription methods
# then, output all the transcripts into a jsonfile ('test.json')
jsonfile=ts.transcribe_all('test.wav')
```

Sometimes transcriptions can be messy - for example, there may be multiple spaces and/or odd spellings. Also, you may want to parse through transcripts to engineer new text features; for example, you may want to count the number of times 'the' is used within the first two sentences of a transcript. In these situations, it's useful to learn how to manipulate strings in Python so that you can appropriately clean and featurize text data (Table 3.3.1).

<div align="center">**Table 3.3.1** **Common ways to manipulate strings in Python:** *string_commands.py*</div>	
Goal	**How to implement in IDLE3 Python interpreter**
Break up the string into individual words in a list.	```>>> transcript='I am having a happy jolly day today writing this chapter. I ran across Boston this morning and just had my morning coffee shipped from Heart Coffee in portland, Oregon.'
>>> transcript.split()
['I', 'am', 'having', 'a', 'happy', 'jolly', 'day', 'today', 'writing', 'this', 'chapter.', 'I', 'ran', 'across', 'Boston', 'this', 'morning', 'and', 'just', 'had', 'my', 'morning', 'coffee', 'shipped', 'from', 'Heart', 'Coffee', 'in', 'portland,', 'Oregon.']```
Break up a string into individual sentences.	```>>> transcript.split('.')
['I am having a happy jolly day today writing this chapter', ' I ran across Boston this morning and just had my morning coffee shipped from Heart Coffee in portland, Oregon', '']
>>> sentences=transcript.split('.')
>>> len(sentences)
3
>>> sentences[0]
'I am having a happy jolly day today writing this chapter'
>>> sentences[1]
' I ran across Boston this morning and just had my morning coffee shipped from Heart Coffee in portland, Oregon'
>>> sentences[2]
''```

| **Replace certain elements in a string** | ```
>>> transcript.replace('Oregon','OR')
'I am having a happy jolly day today writing this chapter. I ran across Boston this morning and just had my morning coffee shipped from Heart Coffee in portland, OR.'
``` |
| **Find the index of certain elements in a string** | ```
>>> transcript.find('I')
0
>>> transcript.find('jolly')
20
``` |
| **Slicing a string** | ```
>>> transcript[0:20]
'I am having a happy '
``` |
| **Counting the number of occurrences of a word or a part of a string (e.g. letter).** | ```
>>> transcript.count('I')
2
>>> transcript.count('hello')
0
>>> transcript.count('a')
13
``` |
| **Concatenating strings** | ```
>>> transcript+' This is additional stuff...'
'I am having a happy jolly day today writing this chapter. I ran across Boston this morning and just had my morning coffee shipped from Heart Coffee in portland, Oregon. This is additional stuff...'
``` |
| **Repeating strings** | ```
>>> transcript*2
'I am having a happy jolly day today writing this chapter. I ran across Boston this morning and just had my morning coffee shipped from Heart Coffee in portland, Oregon.I am having a happy jolly day today writing this chapter. I ran across Boston this morning and just had my morning coffee shipped from Heart Coffee in portland, Oregon.'
``` |
| **Manipulating cases of the string** (upper, lower, title) | ```
>>> transcript.upper()
'I AM HAVING A HAPPY JOLLY DAY TODAY WRITING THIS CHAPTER. I RAN ACROSS BOSTON THIS MORNING AND JUST HAD MY MORNING COFFEE SHIPPED FROM HEART COFFEE IN PORTLAND, OREGON.'
>>> transcript.lower()
'i am having a happy jolly day today writing this chapter. i ran across boston this morning and just had my morning coffee shipped from heart coffee in portland, oregon.'
>>> transcript.title()
'I Am Having A Happy Jolly Day Today Writing This Chapter. I Ran Across Boston This Morning And Just Had My Morning Coffee Shipped From Heart Coffee In Portland, Oregon.'
``` |
```

Now that you know some basic string manipulation techniques, we can now extract some text features.[147] The best starter library to do this is **natural language toolkit**, or **NLTK**. I prefer NLTK for prototyping because there is great documentation and even a whole book written on it by the library authors.[148] Here is a short script to extract 63 features using the NLTK library, the TextBlob library (e.g. to extract sentiment), and various text processing techniques laid out in Table 3.3.1 (Figure 3.3.2):

Figure 3.3.2
Extracting text features using NLTK: *nltk_features.py*

```python
import nltk
from nltk import word_tokenize
import speech_recognition as sr_audio
import numpy as np
from textblob import TextBlob
import transcribe as ts

def nltk_featurize(file):
    # get transcript
    transcript=ts.transcribe_sphinx('test.wav')
    #alphabetical features
    a=transcript.count('a')
    b=transcript.count('b')
    c=transcript.count('c')
    d=transcript.count('d')
    e=transcript.count('e')
    f=transcript.count('f')
    g_=transcript.count('g')
    h=transcript.count('h')
    i=transcript.count('i')
    j=transcript.count('j')
    k=transcript.count('k')
    l=transcript.count('l')
    m=transcript.count('m')
    n=transcript.count('n')
    o=transcript.count('o')
    p=transcript.count('p')
    q=transcript.count('q')
    r=transcript.count('r')
    s=transcript.count('s')
    t=transcript.count('t')
    u=transcript.count('u')
    v=transcript.count('v')
    w=transcript.count('w')
```

---

[147] **Natural language processing (NLP)** - The computing discipline associated with manipulating and transforming text data. I find most developers are more familiar with NLP than speech processing, so this naturally may be an easier place to start if you're learning how to manipulate and featurize voice data.

[148] **NLTK book and my journey learning Python -** I actually started programming in Python by reading the NLTK book, as have many other programmers.

```python
    x=transcript.count('x')
    y=transcript.count('y')
    z=transcript.count('z')
    space=transcript.count(' ')

    #numerical features and capital letters
    num1=transcript.count('0')+transcript.count('1')+transcript.count('2')+transcript.count('3')+transcript.count('4')+transcript.count('5')+transcript.count('6')+transcript.count('7')+transcript.count('8')+transcript.count('9')
    num2=transcript.count('zero')+transcript.count('one')+transcript.count('two')+transcript.count('three')+transcript.count('four')+transcript.count('five')+transcript.count('six')+transcript.count('seven')+transcript.count('eight')+transcript.count('nine')+transcript.count('ten')
    number=num1+num2
    capletter=sum(1 for c in transcript if c.isupper())

    #part of speech
    text=word_tokenize(transcript)
    g=nltk.pos_tag(transcript)
    cc=0
    cd=0
    dt=0
    ex=0
    in_=0
    jj=0
    jjr=0
    jjs=0
    ls=0
    md=0
    nn=0
    nnp=0
    nns=0
    pdt=0
    pos=0
    prp=0
    prp2=0
    rb=0
    rbr=0
    rbs=0
    rp=0
    to=0
    uh=0
    vb=0
    vbd=0
    vbg=0
    vbn=0
    vbp=0
    vbp=0
    vbz=0
    wdt=0
    wp=0
```

```python
wrb=0

for i in range(len(g)):
    if g[i][1] == 'CC':
        cc=cc+1
    elif g[i][1] == 'CD':
        cd=cd+1
    elif g[i][1] == 'DT':
        dt=dt+1
    elif g[i][1] == 'EX':
        ex=ex+1
    elif g[i][1] == 'IN':
        in_=in_+1
    elif g[i][1] == 'JJ':
        jj=jj+1
    elif g[i][1] == 'JJR':
        jjr=jjr+1
    elif g[i][1] == 'JJS':
        jjs=jjs+1
    elif g[i][1] == 'LS':
        ls=ls+1
    elif g[i][1] == 'MD':
        md=md+1
    elif g[i][1] == 'NN':
        nn=nn+1
    elif g[i][1] == 'NNP':
        nnp=nnp+1
    elif g[i][1] == 'NNS':
        nns=nns+1
    elif g[i][1] == 'PDT':
        pdt=pdt+1
    elif g[i][1] == 'POS':
        pos=pos+1
    elif g[i][1] == 'PRP':
        prp=prp+1
    elif g[i][1] == 'PRP$':
        prp2=prp2+1
    elif g[i][1] == 'RB':
        rb=rb+1
    elif g[i][1] == 'RBR':
        rbr=rbr+1
    elif g[i][1] == 'RBS':
        rbs=rbs+1
    elif g[i][1] == 'RP':
        rp=rp+1
    elif g[i][1] == 'TO':
        to=to+1
    elif g[i][1] == 'UH':
        uh=uh+1
    elif g[i][1] == 'VB':
        vb=vb+1
```

```python
        elif g[i][1] == 'VBD':
            vbd=vbd+1
        elif g[i][1] == 'VBG':
            vbg=vbg+1
        elif g[i][1] == 'VBN':
            vbn=vbn+1
        elif g[i][1] == 'VBP':
            vbp=vbp+1
        elif g[i][1] == 'VBZ':
            vbz=vbz+1
        elif g[i][1] == 'WDT':
            wdt=wdt+1
        elif g[i][1] == 'WP':
            wp=wp+1
        elif g[i][1] == 'WRB':
            wrb=wrb+1

#sentiment
tblob=TextBlob(transcript)
polarity=float(tblob.sentiment[0])
subjectivity=float(tblob.sentiment[1])

#word repeats
words=transcript.split()
newlist=transcript.split()
repeat=0
for i in range(len(words)):
        newlist.remove(words[i])
        if words[i] in newlist:
                repeat=repeat+1

features=np.array([a,b,c,d,
e,f,g_,h,
i,j,k,l,
m,n,o,p,
q,r,s,t,
u,v,w,x,
y,z,space,number,
capletter,cc,cd,dt,
ex,in_,jj,jjr,
jjs,ls,md,nn,
nnp,nns,pdt,pos,
prp,prp2,rbr,rbs,
rp,to,uh,vb,
vbd,vbg,vbn,vbp,
vbz,wdt,wp,wrb,
polarity,subjectivity,repeat])

labels=['a', 'b', 'c', 'd',
        'e','f','g','h',
        'i', 'j', 'k', 'l',
```

```
                    'm','n','o', 'p',
                    'q','r','s','t',
                    'u','v','w','x',
                    'y','z','space', 'numbers',
                    'capletters','cc','cd','dt',
                    'ex','in','jj','jjr',
                    'jjs','ls','md','nn',
                    'nnp','nns','pdt','pos',
                    'prp','prp2','rbr','rbs',
                    'rp','to','uh','vb',
                    'vbd','vbg','vbn','vbp',
                    'vbz', 'wdt', 'wp','wrb',
                    'polarity', 'subjectivity','repeat']

        return features, labels


# transcribe with pocketsphinx
features, labels = nltk_featurize('test.wav')
```

The **spaCy library,** on the other hand, is better at extracting text features that relate to syntax (e.g. pronoun-to-noun ratio per sentence) and named entities (e.g. places).[149] SpaCy is also a bit faster and more accurate at parsing transcripts than NLTK, so it's often better to use spaCy in production settings. This library also has great documentation and follow-through tutorials if you get stuck. Here is a short script to extract roughly 315 text features with spaCy:

Figure 3.3.3
Extracting linguistic features using spaCy: *spacy_features.py*

```
import spacy_features

# Alice's Adventures in Wonderland = text
transcript=open('alice.txt').read()
features, labels = spacy_featurize(transcript)

# shows feature array with labels = 315 features total
print(features)
print(labels)
print(len(features))
print(len(labels))
```

---

[149] **SpaCy feature extraction -** SpaCy is useful for extracting parts of speech, rule-based morphological features, syntactic dependency parsing features (e.g. base phrases for topic analysis), and named entities (e.g. a person). Note it's often better to use spaCy for production settings because it's a faster and more accurate text parser.

Lastly, **gensim** can extract vocabulary-sensitive text features. Particularly, it comes built with a **Word2vec model maker**, which can be used to make word embeddings for a particular group of text corpuses.[150] Transcriptions can be used to train Word2vec models, which then it could be used to featurize new text arrays of N size (e.g. 100).[151] Here is a quick example on how to make and use a Word2vec model to featurize text (Figure 3.3.4).[152]

Figure 3.3.4
Using Word2vec models for featurization with gensim: *gensim_features.py*

```python
import os
import numpy as np
from gensim.models import Word2Vec

def w2v_train(textlist,size,modelname):
    sentences=list()

    #split into individual word embeddings
    for i in range(len(textlist)):
        if len(textlist[i].split())==0:
            pass
        else:
            sentences.append(textlist[i].split())

    #test (for small samples)
    #print(sentences)
    model = Word2Vec(sentences, size=size, window=5, min_count=1, workers=4)

    if modelname in os.listdir():
        #do not save if already file in folder with same name
        pass
    else:
        print('saving %s to disk...'%(modelname))
        model.save(modelname)

    return model
```

---

[150] **Word2vec - From Wikipedia:** "Word2vec is a group of related models that are used to produce word embeddings. These models are shallow, two-layer neural networks that are trained to reconstruct linguistic contexts of words. Word2vec takes as its input a large corpus of text and produces a vector space, typically of several hundred dimensions, with each unique word in the corpus being assigned a corresponding vector in the space. Word vectors are positioned in the vector space such that words that share common contexts in the corpus are located in close proximity to one another in the space."

[151] **As shown in the next chapter,** it's often useful to create multiple Word2vec models and then use the independent Word2vec arrays for modeling

[152] **Note once you train the model with w2v_train**, you do not need to train the model again on the training corpus. It can be used to featurize any sentence into the future.

```python
def sentence_embedding(sentence,size,modelname):
    # Load model
    model=Word2Vec.load(modelname)
    
    sentences2=sentence.split()
    
    w2v_embed=list()
    for i in range(len(sentences2)):
        try:
            #print(sentences2[i])
            w2v_embed.append(model[sentences2[i]])
            #print(model[sentences2[i]])
        except:
            #pass if there is an error to not distort averages... :)
            pass
    
    out_embed=np.zeros(size)
    for j in range(len(w2v_embed)):
        out_embed=out_embed+w2v_embed[j]
    
    out_embed=(1/size)*out_embed
    
    return out_embed

# load alice and wonderland corpus and build w2v model
text=open('alice.txt').read()
transcript='I had a great time at the bar today.'
modelname='alice.pickle'
w2v_train(text,100,modelname)
features=sentence_embedding(transcript, 100,modelname)
print(features)
print(len(features))
```

Following what we did with audio features, let's now extract all possible text features using the things we've discussed in this section (Figure 3.3.5). It's quite easy to just import all the text featurization scripts we wrote (*nltk_features.py, spacy_features.py, gensim_features.py*) as modules and extract all these features with a text_featurize() function. *Note that it's often a good practice to state the transcription method that you use explicitly so you don't make any mistakes cleaning data later on (e.g. combining google transcripts with sphinx transcripts).*

Figure 3.3.5
Extracting all text features: *text_features.py*

```python
import transcribe as ts
import sounddevice as sd
import soundfile as sf
import nltk_features as nf
import spacy_features as spf
import gensim_features as gf
import numpy as np
import os, json

def sync_record(filename, duration, fs, channels):
    print('recording')
    myrecording = sd.rec(int(duration * fs), samplerate=fs, channels=channels)
    sd.wait()
    sf.write(filename, myrecording, fs)
    print('done recording')

def text_featurize(filename,jsondump):
    # transcribe with sphinx
    transcript=ts.transcribe_sphinx('test.wav')
    # now put transcript through various feature engines
    nltk_featureset, nltk_labels=nf.nltk_featurize(transcript)
    spacy_featureset, spacy_labels=spf.spacy_featurize(transcript)
    # make gensim embedding on alice and wonderland text
    # (or any text corpus you'd like)
    modelname='alice.pickle'
    if modelname not in os.listdir():
        text=open('alice.txt').read()
        gf.w2v_train(text,100,modelname)
    gensim_featureset=gf.sentence_embedding(transcript,100,modelname)

    data={
        'transcript':transcript,
        'transcript type':'sphinx',
        'nltk':np.array(nltk_featureset).tolist(),
        'spacy':np.array(spacy_featureset).tolist(),
        'gensim':np.array(gensim_featureset).tolist(),
        }

    if jsondump == True:
        jsonfilename=filename[0:-4]+'.json'
        jsonfile=open(jsonfilename,'w')
        json.dump(data,jsonfile)
        jsonfile.close()

    return data
```

```python
# record and get transcript
if 'test.wav' not in os.listdir():
    sync_record('test.wav', 10, 44100, 2)

# now extract all text features
data=text_featurize('test.wav', True)
```

3.4 Mixed features

Mixed features relate audio features to text features through some relationship. This often takes the form of ratios (e.g. speaking rate = total word count : total time in seconds). Since it's not necessarily very intuitive, I prefer to make mixed features through random combinations of text features with audio features (Figure 3.4.1). Note that mixed features are quite a new data type in the voice computing world; thus, you may not see much published about them.

<u>**Figure 3.4.1**</u>
Building mixed features: *make_mixed_features.py*

```python
import pyaudio_features as pf
import spacy_features as sf
import transcribe as ts
import random

# get features
pyaudio_features, pyaudio_labels=pf.pyaudio_featurize('test.wav')
transcript=ts.transcribe_sphinx('test.wav')
spacy_features, spacy_labels=sf.spacy_featurize(transcript)

# relate some features to each other
# engineer 10 random features by dividing them and making new labels
mixed_features=list()
mixed_labels=list()
for i in range(10):
    # get some random features from both text and audio
    i1=random.randint(0,len(pyaudio_features)-1)
    label_1=pyaudio_labels[i1]
    feature_1=pyaudio_features[i1]
    i2=random.randint(0,len(spacy_features)-1)
    label_2=spacy_labels[i2]
    feature_2=spacy_features[i2]
    # make new label
    mixed_label=label_2+' (spacy) ' + '| / | '+label_1 + ' (pyaudio)'
    print(mixed_label)
    mixed_labels.append(mixed_label)
    # make new feature from labels
    mixed_feature=feature_2/feature_1
    print(mixed_feature)
    mixed_features.append(mixed_feature)
```

As you can imagine, this concept can be applied quite endlessly using combinatorics (Table 3.4.1). I've only included a few features here, but feel free to engineer some mixed features yourself and add them into this script (*make_mixed_features.py*). This process of making new features is known as **feature engineering**.[153]

Table 3.4.1 List of random mixed features from executing make_mixed_features.py	
Feature definition	Output value
Xxx (spacy) | / | median chroma3 (pyaudio)	0.0
! (spacy) | / | min chroma2 (pyaudio)	0.0
INTJ (spacy) | / | max chroma10 (pyaudio)	0.0
# (spacy) | / | max spectral entropy (pyaudio)	0.0
Xxxxx'x (spacy) | / | std mfcc12 (pyaudio)	0.0
std sentence polarity (spacy) | / | mean chroma3 (pyaudio)	0.0
Xx'xxxx (spacy) | / | min chroma2 (pyaudio)	0.0
xxx"--xxx (spacy) | / | std mfcc5 (pyaudio)	0.0
prt (spacy) | / | median spectral centroid (pyaudio)	6.730238582160183
! (spacy) | / | min chroma deviation (pyaudio)	0.0

3.5   Meta features

Meta features are features outputted from classification or regression-based machine learning models that are trained on audio, text, or mixed features (Table 3.5.1).[154][155] In other words, they can compress extracted features further into sub-features - for example, the gender can be detected from the MFCC coefficients extracted from LibROSA and a support vector machine learning model, leading to a feature, 1 or 0 - 1 for male and 0 for female. You may also have an array of accent models that you can use to classify a user's location or use emotional models to

---

[153] **Audio time series and mixed features -** We can also break up speech samples into windows and build mixed features this way. For example, let's assume we recorded a sample that is 5 minutes long. We could break up this file into fifteen 20 second chunks - [0-20 seconds, 20-40, 40-60, 60-80, 80-100, 100-120, 120-140, 140-160, 160-180, 180-200, 200-220, 220-240, 240-260, 260-280, 280-300]. Each of these chunks can then be transcribed and compared throughout the entire session with specific auditory features. For example, the number of nouns and the RMS power can have a ratio in every window.

[154] **This may seem a bit weird at first,** but it makes a bit more sense through some concrete examples - like in the example of race detection or gender detection. :)

[155] **Lack of standardization!** Note there is really no standard for these ML model feature pipelines and most of this research has been brought to attention by competitions like AVEC for emotional or depression recognition.

model things like customer frustrations during call center applications (to predict churn rates).[156] Thus, meta features can be useful for labeling audio samples and can be seamlessly combined with audio, text, and mixed features.[157]

	Table 3.5.1 Table of meta voice features		
Meta feature(s) (# features)	**Feature array (training data)**	**Accuracy ranges, winning model type**	**Output from model**
Ages (7)	Modified LibROSA audio embedding (common voice, N=1000+)	70-77% (+/- 0.6%), k-nearest neighbors (knn).	Teens, twenties, thirties, forties, fifties, sixties, and seventies
Gender (1)	Modified LibROSA audio embedding (common voice, N=1000+)	~87-88% (+/- 6.0%), k-nearest neighbors (knn).	Male or female.
Ethnicity (1)	Modified LibROSA audio embedding (internal data, N= ~150)	88.7% (+/- 5.2%), support vector machines (svm).	African American or Caucasian.
Accents (19)	Modified LibROSA audio embedding (Kaggle, N=~35)	51-82% (+/- 6-8%), various model types.	French, Japanese, Cantonese, Romanian, Korean, Turkish, Macedonian, Dutch, English Italian, Swedish, Amharic, Vietnamese, Russian, Mandarin, Portuguese, Polish, Spanish, and German.
Diseases (15)[158]	Modified LibROSA audio embedding (YouTube, N=~30)	~60-80% (+/-10-15%), various model types.	Addiction, ADHD, ALS, Anxiety, Autism, Colds, Depression, Dyslexia, Glioblastoma, Graves Disease, Multiple Sclerosis, Parkinson's disease, Postpartum Depression, Schizophrenia, and Sleep Apnea.

---

[156] **Cogito** - A company called Cogito (Boston, MA) is killing it with this business model.

[157] **Linear independence vs. dependence** – Note that some machine learning models work better on independent vs. dependent variables. Since meta features often share information with existing feature embeddings, they can sometimes affect the accuracy of machine learning models adversely.

[158] **Note high risk here** for false positives due to small datasets.

Emotions (6)	Modified LibROSA audio embedding (YouTube, N=~100)	55-80% (+/- 15%), various model types.	Happy, sad, neutral, disgust, angry, and surprised.
Audio quality (1)	Modified LibROSA audio embedding (internal, manually tagged, N=~70)	75.6% (+/- 8.2%), logistic regression.	Highquality or lowquality.
Fatigue level (1)	Modified LibROSA audio embedding (internal, manually tagged, N=~80)[159]	77.2% (+/- 8.4%), gaussian naïve bayes (NB).	Fatigued or awake.
Stress level (1)	Modified LibROSA embedding (internal, manually tagged, N=~80)	78.9% (+/- 9.3%), logistic regression.	Stressed or calm.
Speaking type (1)	Modified LibROSA audio embedding (internal, manually tagged, N=~60)	79.6% (+/- 8.0%), adaboost.	Natural or not natural (abnormal) speech.
Music genres (15)	Modified LibROSA embedding (YouTube data, N=~30)	~70-90% (+/- 10-12.0%), support vector machines (svm).	Alternative, Christian, country, edm, folk, holiday, indie, jazz, latin, newage, pop, rap, reggae, rock, soundtrack.

To help guide you, I've made it quite simple to create meta feature arrays through the *meta_features.py* script. This script extracts acoustic features as we normally would and then applies pre-trained machine learning models to estimate features like age, gender, ethnicity, accent, disease status, emotions, music type, and audio quality (Figure 3.5.1).[160] All you need to do is run the script one time and it will create a folder, *load_dir*, in the current directory. Then, place any audio files you'd like to process in this *load_dir* directory (e.g. 20 sec .WAV files). If you run the script again (e.g. python3 *meta_features.py*), all the audio files will then be featurized with the script and put into a .JSON file (e.g. 'test.wav' → 'test.json'). In this way, all you need are the model files (.PICKLE format) in the *meta_models* folder and new features will be loaded into the array (71 features in total).[161]

---

[159] **Manual labeling / overfitting** - We used an audio engineer on our team (James Fairey) to label 1000 samples manually by hand. This likely induced some error in the labeling process and overfitting of models to one person's intuition. A better way to make these models into the future would get some crowd-sourced pool of people to label these samples (N=30 per sample averaged out value).

[160] **English language** - Note the language is assumed to be english, so these models may all fail if you switch languages.

[161] **Note that this is something** we will further discuss in the next chapter when we build these machine learning models. For now, you can just trust they work.

Figure 3.5.1
Extracting meta features (71): *meta_features.py*

```
>> META FEATURES

[1, 0, 0, 1, 0, 0, 0, 0, 1, 1, 1, 0, 0, 1, 0, 0, 0, 0, 1, 0, 0, 0, 0, 0, 0, 0, 0, 0, 0, 1,
1, 0, 0, 0, 0, 0, 0, 0, 0, 0, 0, 0, 0, 0, 0, 1, 0, 0, 0, 1, 0, 0, 0, 0, 0, 0, 0, 1, 0, 0, 1,
0, 0, 0, 0, 0, 0, 0, 0, 0, 0]


>> META CLASSES:

['controls', 'adhd', 'africanamerican', 'controls', 'alternativecontrolbalanced',
'amharic_controls', 'angry_controls', 'anxiety', 'controls', 'controls', 'controls',
'cantonese', 'christian', 'controls', 'country', 'depression', 'disgust_controls',
'dutch_controls', 'controls', 'edmcontrolbalanced', 'english', 'awake', 'fear_controls',
'fifties_controls', 'folkcontrolbalanced', 'fourties_controls', 'french_controls', 'male',
'german', 'controls', 'controls', 'happy_controls', 'holiday', 'indiecontrolbalanced',
'italian', 'japanese', 'jazzcontrolbalanced', 'korean', 'latin', 'macedonian_controls',
'mandarin_controls', 'multiple_sclerosis', 'natural', 'neutral_controls',
'newagecontrolbalanced', 'controls', 'polish', 'popcontrolbalanced', 'portuguese_controls',
'controls', 'badquality', 'rapcontrolbalanced', 'reggae', 'rock', 'romanian',
'russian_controls', 'sad', 'controls', 'seventies_controls', 'sixties', 'controls',
'soundtrackcontrolbalanced', 'spanish_controls', 'stressed', 'surprise_controls', 'swedish',
'teens', 'thirties', 'turkish', 'twenties', 'vietnamese_controls']
```

The list goes on… there's an infinite number of meta models and meta features that you could add to this. Like mixed features, this is quite an active area for feature engineering research. Feel free to use the models for whatever you'd like to; they are released under an Apache 2.0 license.

3.6 Dimensionality reduction

There still remains many features that we extracted (>1000 audio, text, mixed, and meta features). ***Dimensionality reduction techniques (DRTs)***[162] can compress existing feature sets into smaller sizes without changing the data dramatically (Table 3.6.1).[163]

DRTs are either ***supervised*** or ***unsupervised,*** depending on how they are implemented. Supervised techniques use some training data to learn the features that are most representative of a given dataset (e.g. have labels). Unsupervised techniques, on the other hand, do not use any prior knowledge about the dataset (e.g. have no labels). In general, unsupervised techniques are good at prototyping and understanding data *as a first pass*. Then, as you get more refined and granular, you can progress to supervised techniques (e.g. LDA representations) to reduce dimensions even further, if necessary.

<div align="center">Table 3.6.1 List of automated feature selection methods</div>			
Technique	**Supervised or unsupervised?**	**Pros**	**Cons**
Principal Component Analysis (PCA)	Unsupervised	Easy to execute in scikit-learn library. Can be used as a pre-processing step in many machine learning pipelines.	Highly sensitive to outliers in the dataset. Does not scale well to large datasets. Does not capture local structures.
Independent component analysis (ICA)	Unsupervised	Works for non-Gaussian signals and that they are statistically independent from each other.	Does not work for Gaussian signals very well; for these cases use PCA.

---

[162] **Dimensionality reduction methods** can thus be used as feature extractors themselves; in fact, many speech recognition models use use LDA and/or PCA - including the AudioSet embedding discussed previously. Meta features also are a form and subset of dimensionality reduction; however, this section extends dimensionality reduction into methods you can apply to any feature set.

[163] **Featurization as a form of dimensionality reduction** - We have already thought about this in prior sections when we built feature arrays; for example, instead of taking thousands of MFCC features in PyAudioAnalysis we have instead taken the means, standard deviations, minimums, maximums, and median value for every MFCC coefficient (1-13) throughout the entire duration of a speech sample (Assuming 44.1kHz and 10 seconds - 44100 samples/sec * 10 seconds).. This reduced the dimensionality from 882,000 to 170 features. Similarly, we reduced dimensionality with meta features, from 882,000 samples to 71 features extracted with machine learning models.

K-means clustering (vector quantization)	Unsupervised	Low computational cost burden.	Does not consider temporal evolution of signals.
Canonical correlation analysis	Unsupervised	Good for datasets with high correlation.	Not very robust in datasets with high variance.
Partial least squares regression	Unsupervised	Good for linear datasets.	Not good for nonlinear datasets.
Manifold learning	Unsupervised	No good framework for handling missing data. Few people know how to actually implement these techniques.	More generalizable to nonlinear datasets (representative of real-world data). Computationally-intensive.
Supervised dictionary learning (SDL)	Supervised	Simple representation as weighted sum of features.	N/A.
Linear discriminant analysis or Correspondence analysis	Supervised (continuous data)	Good for when the class means and variances are known.	Not robust when class centroids coincide or class covariances vary. Sensitive to sampling rates (e.g. undersampling).
Variational Autoencoders (VA)[164]	Supervised	Neural network. Powerful and accurate.	Prone to overfitting. Doesn't work well on small datasets. CPU/GPU intensive.

---

[164] **I get asked all the time from data scientists,** "why don't you just use deep learning to learn the features that are relevant?' Oftentimes, there is not enough training data (need >1000 samples in each class for this to be accurate). We're currently working on some work within NeuroLex with variational autoencoders to learn which features best represent a given set of classes (e.g. depressed vs. not depressed).

Common unsupervised techniques include ***principal component analysis*** (PCA), ***independent component analysis*** (ICA), ***k-means clustering*** (also known as *vector quantization*), ***canonical correlation analysis, PLS regression,*** and ***manifold learning***. PCA is often used to reduce dimensionality of MFCC feature arrays and spectrograms (e.g. the the Google AudioSet embedding described earlier is PCA-whitened). ICA often is used for noise reduction (e.g. the "cocktail party problem" of listening in on one person's speech in a noisy room). Vector quantization is used quite frequently when building acoustic transcription models (e.g. phoneme detection). Canonical correlation analysis is good for datasets with features that are highly correlated to each other. PLS regression is good for linear datasets. Lastly, manifold learning is useful in situations where there are nonlinear relationships in multi-dimensional data (e.g. many noises in environment with voices). These techniques can easily be implemented with the scikit-learn library on some sample audio data (Figure 3.6.1).

<u>**Figure 3.6.1**</u>
Implementing unsupervised techniques: *dimensionality_reduction.py*

```python
import numpy as np
import json, os

# load data (149 in each class)
data = json.load(open(os.getcwd()+'/data/africanamerican_controls.json'))
X= np.array(data['africanamerican'])
Y= np.array(data['controls'])


##################################################################
##                    UNSUPERVISED TECHNIQUES                   ##
##################################################################
# Principal Component Analysis
from sklearn.decomposition import PCA

# calculate PCA for 50 components
pca = PCA(n_components=50)
pca.fit(X)
X_pca = pca.transform(X)

# Independent component analysis
from sklearn.decomposition import FastICA

ica = FastICA(n_components=50)
S_ = ica.fit_transform(X)   # Reconstruct signals

# K-means clustering
from sklearn.cluster import KMeans
kmeans = KMeans(n_clusters=50, random_state=0).fit_transform(X)
```

```
# Canonical correlation analysis
from sklearn.cross_decomposition import CCA
cca = CCA(n_components=50).fit(X, Y).transform(X, Y)
new_X=cca[0]
new_Y=cca[1]

# PLS regression
from sklearn.cross_decomposition import PLSRegression
pls = PLSRegression(n_components=50).fit(X, Y).transform(X, Y)
pls_X=pls[0]
pls_Y=pls[1]

# manifold learning
from sklearn import manifold
manifold_X = manifold.Isomap(10, 50).fit_transform(X)
manifold_Y = manifold.Isomap(10,50).fit_transform(Y)
```

Supervised techniques include **supervised dictionary learning** (SDL), **linear discriminant analysis** (LDA), and **variational autoencoders** (e.g. via neural networks). As the name implies, supervised dictionary learning techniques construct dictionaries and pick a few elements in the dictionary ("representatives") to reproduce the original signal. In contrast, LDA models are great for tasks where the mean and variances are known - for example, in cases of speech recognition (e.g. phoneme classification) and MFCC coefficients. Variational autoencoders, on the other hand, apply neural networks to describe how to weight features.[165] All of these techniques are quite powerful, and variational autoencoders are becoming increasingly used as an alternative to PCA and other techniques (on large datasets).

Figure 3.6.2
Implementing supervised techniques: *dimensionality_reduction.py*

```
import numpy as np
import json, os

# load data (149 in each class)
data = json.load(open(os.getcwd()+'/data/africanamerican_controls.json'))
X= np.array(data['africanamerican'])
Y= np.array(data['controls'])

################################################################
##                    SUPERVISED TECHNIQUES                   ##
################################################################
```

---

[165] **Autoencoder / codec analogy -** An autoencoder is something that simply encodes and decodes information. Think of codecs - they encode and decode digital audio data; this is just the same idea applied to features.

```python
# supervised dictionary learning
from sklearn.decomposition import MiniBatchDictionaryLearning
dico_X = MiniBatchDictionaryLearning(n_components=50, alpha=1,
n_iter=500).fit_transform(X)
dico_Y = MiniBatchDictionaryLearning(n_components=50, alpha=1,
n_iter=500).fit_transform(Y)

# linear discriminant analysis
from sklearn.discriminant_analysis import LinearDiscriminantAnalysis as LDA
from sklearn.discriminant_analysis import QuadraticDiscriminantAnalysis as QDA
from sklearn.model_selection import train_test_split

# make a train set and train labels
Z=np.array(list(X)+list(Y))
newlabels=list()
for i in range(len(X)):
    newlabels.append('1')
for i in range(len(Y)):
    newlabels.append('0')

X_train, X_test, y_train, y_test = train_test_split(Z, newlabels, test_size=0.33,
random_state=42)

lda = LDA(n_components=50).fit(X_train, y_train).transform(X)
```

3.7 Feature selection

Now that you know how to compress features down to smaller sizes without losing much information, you may now ask - "how do I know what features I should keep or remove?"

This is known as the process of **feature selection,** which helps to set priorities as to what features are most important for a given machine learning problem. It often involves removing features that are not necessary (e.g. sparse features that do not contain any signal).[166]

There are three main ways to automate feature selection: 1) filler methods, 2) wrapper methods, and 3) embedded methods (Table 3.6.1).[167] In general, filter methods use some sort of ranking algorithm to keep or remove features, wrapper methods use machine learning models to rank feature importances, and embedded methods learn what features are important while building machine learning models. The most frequently used feature selection techniques are embedded methods (e.g. LASSO) or wrapper methods (e.g. recursive feature elimination).

---

[166] **Sparsity -** A high-dimensional dataset can make it difficult to apply certain machine learning techniques. Data that have many 0 values (e.g. blank data) is known as the problem of sparsity.

[167] **Automation** is often necessary for speech modeling, as many speech features are not intuitive; for example, MFCC coefficients aren't really something that we think about everyday.

Table 3.6.1
Feature selection methods

Method	Description	Examples
Filter method	The features are ranked by the score and either selected to be kept or removed from the dataset. Set of all Features → Selecting the Best Subset → Learning Algorithm → Performance	Chi squared test, information gain, and correlation coefficient scores.
Wrapper method	Wrapper methods consider the selection of a set of features as a search problem, where different combinations are prepared, evaluated and compared to other combinations. Set of all Features → [Generate a Subset → Learning Algorithm] (Selecting the Best Subset loop) → Performance	Recursive feature elimination algorithm.
Embedded methods	Embedded methods learn which features best contribute to the accuracy of the model while the model is being created. Set of all Features → [Generate the Subset → Learning Algorithm + Performance] (Selecting the best subset loop)	LASSO, elastic net, and ridge regression.

There are many Python libraries to help with the feature selection process (Table 3.7.1). My favorite libraries to assist with this process are MLpy, scikit-feature, yellowbrick, and scikit-learn. To be consistent, though, I'll execute all the scripts with scikit-learn (Figure 3.7.1).

Figure 3.7.1
How to select features: *select_features.py*

```python
import os, json
import numpy as np

# Load data
data = json.load(open('africanamerican_controls.json'))
X=np.array(data['africanamerican'])
Y=np.array(data['controls'])
training=list()
for i in range(len(X)):
    training.append(X[i])
for i in range(len(Y)):
    training.append(Y[i])

# get labels (as binary class outputs)
labels=list()
for i in range(len(X)):
    labels.append(1)
for i in range(len(Y)):
    labels.append(0)


############################################################
##                    Chi Square test                     ##
############################################################
from sklearn import preprocessing
from sklearn.feature_selection import SelectKBest, chi2
from sklearn.model_selection import train_test_split

X_train, X_test, y_train, y_test = train_test_split(training, labels,
test_size=0.20, random_state=42)
X_train=np.array(X_train)
X_test=np.array(X_test)
y_train=np.array(y_train).astype(int)
y_test=np.array(y_test).astype(int)

# normalize features so they are non-negative [0,1], or chi squared test will fail
# it assumes all values are positive
min_max_scaler = preprocessing.MinMaxScaler()
chi_train = min_max_scaler.fit_transform(X_train)
chi_labels = y_train

# Select 50 features with highest chi-squared statistics
chi2_selector = SelectKBest(chi2, k=50)
X_kbest = chi2_selector.fit_transform(chi_train, chi_labels)
```

```python
##############################################################
##              Recursive feature elimination              ##
##############################################################
from sklearn.linear_model import LogisticRegression
from sklearn.feature_selection import RFE
from sklearn.svm import SVR

model = LogisticRegression()
rfe = RFE(model, 50)
fit = rfe.fit(X_train, y_train)

# List out number of features and selected features
print("Num Features: %d"% fit.n_features_)
print("Selected Features: %s"% fit.support_)
print("Feature Ranking: %s"% fit.ranking_)


##############################################################
##                     LASSO technique                     ##
##############################################################
from sklearn.svm import LinearSVC
from sklearn.feature_selection import SelectFromModel

lsvc = LinearSVC(C=0.01, penalty="l1", dual=False).fit(X_train, y_train)
model = SelectFromModel(lsvc, prefit=True)
X_new = model.transform(X_train)
print(X_new.shape)
# (238, 208) --> (238, 22), draamtic reduction of features using LASSO
```

The topic of feature selection is quite complex; however, hopefully these three examples provided you some tools to begin selecting features on your own. I encourage you to read the scikit-learn documentation or look into additional modules for feature selection (Table 3.7.1). Most answers to the questions you have are likely googleable or found on Stack Overflow.

Table 3.7.1
Python libraries for feature selection

Library	Documentation quality	Use cases
Scikit-learn (recommended)	Best	Many.
MLpy	Great	Dimensionality reduction techniques.
Scikit-feature	Great	40 feature selection algorithms.
Yellowbrick	Great	Useful for visualization of features.
MIxtend	Great	Sequential feature selector, column selector, exhaustive feature selector.
Scikit-rebate	Great	RBAs: ReliefF, SURF, SURF, MultiSURF, and MultiSURF algorithms.
ELI5	Great	Black-box estimator.
ML featureselection	Okay	Greedy algorithm, feature importance, correlation coefficient, feature combinations.
Feature selectionGA	Poor	Genetic algorithms.
Bortua	Poor	Various.
ReliefF	Poor	Supervised learning feature selection, where feature interactions are important.

3.8 Conclusion

👏 Way to go! You now know how to extract features from voice samples (audio features, text features, mixed features, and meta features). You also now know how to reduce dimensionality and optimize feature embeddings for your given use case. Here is some additional material on the topics covered in case you'd like to go deeper on anything:

- Audio features
    - LibROSA. https://librosa.github.io/librosa/core.html
    - PyAudioAnalysis. https://github.com/tyiannak/pyAudioAnalysis
    - SoX. http://sox.sourceforge.net/
    - OpenSMILE. https://audeering.com/technology/opensmile/
    - AudioSet. https://github.com/tensorflow/models/tree/master/research/audioset
- Text features
    - NLTK. https://www.nltk.org/
    - SpaCy. https://spacy.io/
    - Gensim. https://radimrehurek.com/gensim/
    - Textblob. https://textblob.readthedocs.io/en/dev/
- Mixed features
    - PyAudioAnalysis. https://github.com/tyiannak/pyAudioAnalysis
    - SpaCy. https://spacy.io/
- Meta features
    - Scikit-learn. http://scikit-learn.org/
    - Keras. https://keras.io/
    - TensorFlow. https://www.tensorflow.org/
- Dimensionality reduction
    - Scikit-learn. http://scikit-learn.org/
    - Megaman. https://github.com/mmp2/megaman
    - TensorFlow. https://www.tensorflow.org/install/
- Feature selection
    - Scikit-learn. http://scikit-learn.org/
    - MLpy. http://mlpy.sourceforge.net/
    - Scikit-feature. http://featureselection.asu.edu/
    - Yellowbrick. http://www.scikit-yb.org/en/latest/

By the end of the next chapter you will be able to make your own machine learning models and thus make your own meta feature embeddings. Brace yourself - as you'll be able to contribute to the era of Deep Learning! 😊

Chapter 4:
Data modeling

"Just as electricity transformed almost everything 100 years ago, today I actually have a hard time thinking of an industry that I don't think AI will transform in the next several years."
-Andrew Ng
(Chief Scientist, Baidu)

Chapter Overview

Have you ever imagined what it was like when humans first saw lightening? If you were the scientific type, you may have been curious and wondered how to harness that power.[168] If you're the cautious type, you may have been frightened and wanted to run away. Or, if you're more of an artist you may have just stood back in awe - looking at lightning from a more aesthetic perspective.

In a similar way, we've seen powerful machine learning techniques become practically accessible for the first time in history. You may feel afraid of what machine learning can do, be in awe of its potential, or become more curious to learn it at a deeper level.[169] [170]

Hopefully you're the curious type, as this chapter focuses all about how to build voice-based machine learning models. You'll use libraries like scikit-learn and Keras and the features you extracted in Chapter 3 to solve various machine learning problems, like classifying someone's gender from a voice sample.

Specifically, we'll overview:

- 4.1 - What is machine learning?
- 4.2 - Obtaining training data
- 4.3 - Labeling training data
- 4.4 - Classification models
- 4.5 - Regression models
- 4.6 - Deep learning models
- 4.7 - AutoML approaches

In this way, you'll be equipped with some some practical examples to get started building and deploying machine learning models.

Happy modeling!

---

[168] **In June 1752** Ben Franklin attached a metal key to the bottom of a dampened kite string and flew a kite into lightning to see if it could be harnessed.

[169] **Weaponized machine learning -** Some of us are afraid to see weaponized machine learning used by governments to attack power grids. Many of us are sitting back and watching the industry emerge in awe, not knowing exactly how to implement it in their enterprise.

[170] **WaveNet models -** We have machines that can generate near-human-like voices with WaveNet models. Although these models are still recognizable as machines, we're close to being able to generate voices where you cannot tell the difference.

4.1 What is machine learning?

Simply, ***machine learning*** (ML) is the process of teaching a machine something that is useful.[171] Machines are fed ***training data***[172] in the form of ***feature arrays*** and compress patterns in these feature arrays into ***models*** through ***algorithms.*** These models can then be used practically to label new forms of data.

ML models are ***classification models*** or ***regression models*** depending on the goal. If the goal is to separate out into classes (e.g. male or female), then this is known as a classification problem.[173] Alternatively, if the end goal is to measure some correlation and the output is more a numerical range (e.g. often between 0 and 1), then this is more of a regression problem (Figure 4.1.1).[174] *Note that understanding both of these types of models is very important to grasp the power of machine learning.*

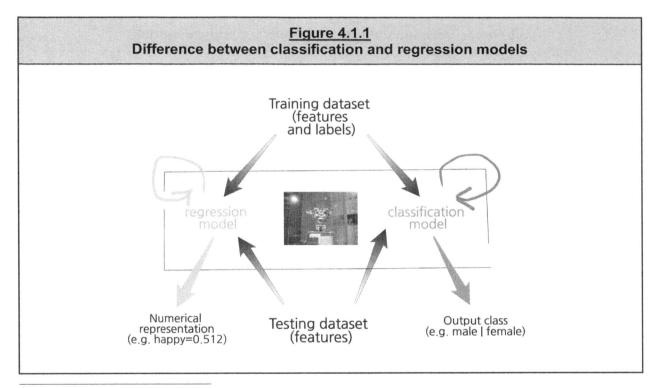

**Figure 4.1.1
Difference between classification and regression models**

---

[171] **Data science definition** - Machine learning is only one part of the toolkit in data science. Data science is the sum-total knowledge of knowing how to model data - from data cleaning to featurization to modeling to visualization, to even model deployment on server architectures. By the end of this book I hope you become better as a data scientist, not just as a devops machine learning engineer.

[172] **Training set** - Training data is also known as the training set, which is the set of examples used to train a machine learning algorithm.

[173] **Classification model example** - You may give a machine 50 images of cars and manually label the colors of cars - green, blue, and red. From featurizing these images in terms of the net pixel color RGB value, the machine then can estimate what color future cars are if they are given similar representations.

[174] **Regression model example** - An example could be measuring the average emotion in a face in terms of happiness, sadness, neutrality, anger, disgust, and/or surprise. Microsoft actually has an emotion model API for this exact use case. This API outputs a regression score for each emotion like this: { "anger": 9.29041E-06, "contempt": 0.000118981574,"disgust": 3.15619363E-05, "fear": 0.000589638,"happiness": 0.06630674, "neutral": 0.00555004273, "sadness": 7.44669524E-06, "surprise": 0.9273863}.

Moreover, machine learning models can be *unsupervised* or *supervised,*[175] depending on how they are trained (Figure 4.1.2). If machines do not require labels (e.g. just need features), this is known as an unsupervised learning problem. Alternatively, if machines require *labels* (e.g. male or female in addition to features), this is known as a supervised learning problem. Thus, supervised learning problems require labels and unsupervised learning problems do not require labels.[176]

The performance of ML models is assessed through *cross-validation techniques (CVTs).* CVTs throw *testing data*[177] at the model to see how it performs and sometimes (but not always) require a third type of data known as *validation data* in order to *optimize the hyperparameters* of machine learning models (Figure 4.1.1).[178] Therefore, it's important to leave some data out during the process of training a machine learning model so that it can be properly tested.[179]

Figure 4.1.2
Difference between unsupervised and supervised models

Supervised learning	Unsupervised learning
In supervised learning, machines take in features and labels to then build a model. In this way, it can look for a new feature and attach that label to it into the future.	In unsupervised learning, machines take in raw features and make labels based on a number of classes. In this way, machines can sort the data without any sort of label.

---

[175] **Semi-supervised learning** - Semi-supervised algorithms are a mix of both unsupervised and supervised techniques, and they require less labeled data than typical supervised algorithms.

[176] **Labeling speech data** - Labeling speech data (e.g. phonemes) is quite tedious; however, this is how many speech recognition models are made. Hopefully in the future we'll have easier ways to label speech data. This means that unsupervised techniques are increasingly important for speech processing applications.

[177] **Testing set** - Testing data is also known as the testing set, or the set of examples left out that are used for testing the performance of the machine learning algorithm. This is often done through some form of cross-validation (e.g. k-folds: 5-fold cross-validation).

[178] **Hyperparameters** - Hyperparameters are simply configurations of variables that help refine the scope of machine learning models - such as alpha, network layers (in deep learning), loss functions, etc.

[179] **Size of cross-validation dataset** - Usually somewhere between 5-33% of the data is used for cross-validation, depending on the size of the dataset; generally, the larger the dataset, less data is necessary for cross-validation.

If a machine is trained using a neural network, this is known as a ***deep learning model.***[180] [181] [182] Neural networks use ***weights***, ***layers***, and ***loss functions*** to optimize a feature representation for a given problem (Figure 4.1.3). Typically, these layers compress features to lower and lower feature sizes and output the desired class and/or regression representation. Through these methods, deep learning models often (but not always) yield higher accuracy on very large datasets than classical machine learning techniques (e.g. support vector machines).

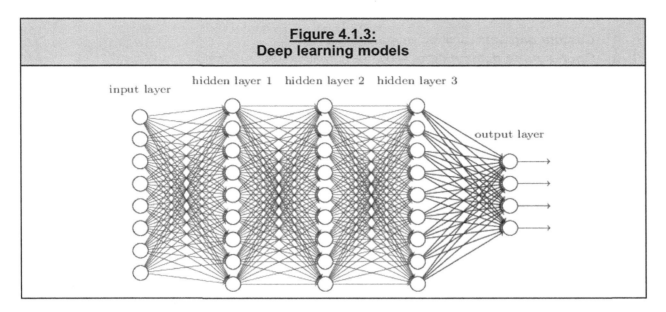

**Figure 4.1.3:
Deep learning models**

The process of picking and optimizing machine learning models is quite ad-hoc and varies from data scientist to data scientist. There's really no best standard on how to do things in this field; it's best to use intuition and judgement. Therefore, it's sometimes better to build machine learning models without a human-in-the-loop, something known as ***automated machine learning (AutoML).***[183]

This chapter is thus all about making the feature arrays that you built in the prior chapter useful. By the end of this chapter you should have a much better grasp of what machine learning can do and its practical use cases to build models from audio, text, mixed, and/or meta features.

---

[180] **History of deep learning** - Deep learning has been around for quite some time. It was not until a few years ago that it became powerful enough to apply practically - with the advent of GPU architectures and low-cost, high performance computers. Also, libraries like TensorFlow and Keras have opened up deep learning techniques to be accessible to everyone, making it much easier to build ML-enabled software.

[181] **Simple classification vs. deep learning** - For the purposes of this book, I name anything other than a deep learning algorithm a 'simple machine learning algorithm.'

[182] **Reinforcement learning** - Deep learning models are capable of *reinforcement learning or* optimizing a machine learning model to achieve some goal (e.g. win a video game). Otherwise, deep learning models can be supervised, semi-supervised, or unsupervised, as discussed previously.

[183] **Automated machine learning** - There has been great progress in this area, and this is something we will go over in this chapter. I expect many data scientists to perform less poorly than automated approaches in the years to come because machines can iterate models over a larger dimensional space; they are just limited in time and computational power.

4.2 Obtaining training data

As AI is the new electricity, data is the new oil that is needed to power such electricity. Therefore, it's often useful to take a step back and think about strategies to obtain large amounts of labeled voice data.

There are three main ways to obtain training datasets:[184]

1) *Custom datasets* (built by you privately);
2) *Open source dataset* (free, allow for unrestricted use); or
3) *Proprietary datasets* (paid, restricted use).

4.2.1 - Custom datasets - To build a custom dataset, you can follow the tutorials in *Chapter 1* on how to collect voice data synchronously or asynchronously.[185] However, this often has some limitations; for example, you may overfit a dataset to a particular microphone or environment. In other words, custom models may not generalize well across many users.

Therefore, I've found that *YouTube* is a great alternative to build custom datasets quickly. Since YouTube has a wide range of microphones and environments, you are much less likely to overfit the model to one particular environment and can create more general-purpose models.[186]

You can use the **youtube_scrape repository**[187] to build YouTube playlists and associated labels (Figure 4.2.1).[188] First, you need to create a playlist from a list of playlist IDs and/or URLs using the *make_playlist.py* script (e.g. yc podcasts). You can then download the files with the *download_playlist.py* script (e.g. yc_podcast.json). In this way, you can create a large list of videos and convert these files using FFmpeg to the proper format (e.g. .WAV files), featurize these audio files, and then use these featurized audio files to train machine learning models.

---

[184] **History of voice datasets -** Unfortunately, many companies have closed voice datasets over the years. SRI International and Nuance are well-known for being protective of voice patents, suing others over infringement and claiming as much possible intellectual property (IP) as possible.[184] Despite this bad reputation, the climate has shifted greatly to be more open with new initiatives to open source voice datasets to the public (e.g. the Common Voice Dataset released by the Mozilla Foundation).

[185] **Custom datasets** can be quite useful voice-controlled applications for building custom language models and/or hotword detectors, as will be shown later. If you do build a custom dataset with your own recordings, *make sure you label the data you collect correctly - either between [0,1] for a desired regression problem or into classes (e.g. male/female) if you're solving a classification problem.*

[186] **Number of videos on YouTube -** YouTube has 7 billion videos available, so it most certainly has some sort of data that you're trying to model. It's also good for future content; 300 hours of new content are uploaded per minute on YouTube.

[187] **This repo is** available at https://github.com/jim-schwoebel/youtube_scrape

[188] **An alternative** is using a yscrape.py script. You can clone the repository below to get access to templates: https://github.com/NeuroLexDiagnostics/train-diseases

Figure 4.2.1
How to build YouTube speech datasets: *make_playlist.py | download_playlist.py*

```
cd ~
cd voicebook/chapter_4_modeling/youtube_scrape
python3 make_playlist.py
what is the name of this playlist? -> CNN
what is the playlist id or URL? -> PL6XRrncXkMaVn1uL6rdocyTfn7mcALdMS
# input 'n' or blank '' to stop making your playlist
python3 download_playlist.py
what is the name of the playlist to download? -> CNN.json
```

4.2.2 - Open source datasets - Moreover, some valuable open source datasets have been released over the past few years (Table 4.2.1). The Common Voice (2017) dataset contains over 150,000 voices labeled with age, gender, and accent information (428 validated hours of audio recordings).[189] Moreover, Google AudioSet (2017) contains over 2 million ten second sound recordings with 600+ classes of labeled audio (1 million speech samples).[190] The Urban Sound dataset has 1,302 sound recordings labeled with 10 environmental classes to help with adding noise to datasets. The NeuroLex Voice Dataset contains over 500 voice samples across 10+ disease indications (2018) and can be used to prototype simple classification models for diseases (e.g. depression). The Mivia Audio Events Dataset can be used to include emergency sounds into your speech data (e.g. gunshots). Lastly, the Karoldvl dataset is a rich dataset of animal sounds (e.g. cats).

Table 4.2.2
List of open source voice datasets

Dataset (link)	Description
Common Voice Dataset	150k recordings, open sourced by Mozilla Foundation. Useful for building models on age, accent, and gender.
Google AudioSet	2 million recordings over 600+ classes of audio (contains over 1 million speech samples). Some example classes include: music, speech, vehicle, and musical instrument.
Urban Sound dataset	1302 files of different urban related sounds. Specifically, each file is labeled with air_conditioner, car_horn, children_playing, dog_bark, drilling, enginge_idling, gun_shot, jackhammer, siren, and street_music.

---

[189] **Note** - This is perhaps the most important dataset was recently released by Mozilla Firefox.
[190] **Note** - These sounds often require significant cleaning to focus in on the sound of interest.

NeuroLex Disease Dataset	This dataset contains over 500 YouTube samples labeled with addiction, adhd, als, anxiety, autism, cold, controls, depression, dyslexia, glioblastoma, graves disease, multiple_sclerosis, parkinsons, postpartum_depression, schizophrenia, sleep_apnea, and stressed. As of right now, it is the most diverse dataset for disease-related research across a range of diseases. We hope to expand it into the future.
NeuroLex Emotion Dataset	This dataset contains >2000 labeled emotions with 20 second voice files: happy, sad, neutral, angry, disgust, and fear. These were all extracted from YouTube videos.
Mivia audio events dataset	6,000 recordings. Classes mostly include emergency related events like glass breaking, gunshots and screams. The 6000 events are divided into a training set (composed of 4200 events) and a test set (composed of 1800 events).
Karoldvl	2000 recordings of various animals sounds including dogs, rooster, pigs, cows, and frogs.

4.2.3 - Proprietary datasets - There are also a few proprietary datasets that you must pay to access. The most significant one seems to be the Linguistic Data Consortium out of UPenn, which is free for educational use and costs $24k/year to use commercially (Table 4.2.3).[191]

<div align="center">**Table 4.3.3** **Proprietary voice datasets**</div>		
Dataset link)	**Description**	**Cost**
Linguistic data consortium	UPenn-based dataset (led by Dr. Mark Lieberman). Datasets for accented English, emotional speech, and custom transcription datasets.	~$24k/year subscription to use commercially; free for research and educational use.

In summary, I would first suggest checking out the open source datasets above. If you can't find an open source dataset to fit your modeling needs, I'd go about trying to collect and label data on YouTube or another large website. If that doesn't work, you can collect data through some structured protocol (e.g. an IRB), making sure to follow the *MEMUPPS* voice protocols. Lastly, if you need to you can pay for datasets through some sort of license or annualized subscription.

---

[191] **Generally,** I'm not a huge fan of pay-to-play datasets (P2P), so I'd try to prototype using free and/or collected datasets yourself before going on to P2P datasets (we'll be using free datasets in this book).

4.3 Labeling training data

Labeling is the process of tagging training datasets with useful information.

For example, you may have 1,000 twenty-second voice files in your training dataset. The problem you may be going after is background noise classification, but all you have right now are the raw files.

You could go about labeling this dataset in multiple ways; however, the most common technique for labeling voice data is still through ***manual labeling.*** This means it may make sense to get a human observer label each sample as (3) high, (2) moderate, or (1) low noise and then use these labels to build supervised machine learning classifiers.

To help guide you, I've made a template ('template.xlsx') for tagging voice datasets collected on YouTube.[192] As a general rule-of-thumb, it's a good practice to label the video URL,[193] the clip length,[194] the start/stop times,[195] the master label (e.g. noise),[196] the speaker's age (e.g. twenties),[197] the speaker's gender (e.g. male),[198] the speaker's accent (e.g. French accent),[199] the audio quality (e.g. 3/4), and the environment (e.g. indoors/outdoors). All of these things can affect the performance of the machine learning models that you build so these labels can help you better understand how and why a model becomes overfitted.

Figure 4.3.1
How to consistently label speech samples manually: *label_samples.py*

```
python3 label_samples.py
what is the master label (e.g. stressed)?
-> noise
>> sample number: 0
what is the URL of the video?
-> https://www.youtube.com/watch?v=47HLiAxHgdo
how long is the audio sample in seconds? (e.g. 20)
-> 20
what are the stop and start times of the video (e.g. 0:13-0:33)
-> 0:05-0:25
is this person stressed? 1 for yes, 0 for no
-> 1
is this person a child (c, <13) or adolescent (d, 13-18) or adult (a, >18 <70) or
```

---

[192] **Although** this has been customized for YouTube, it can be used to label many other audio datasets.
[193] **YouTube URL** - For example, https://m.youtube.com/watch?v=PZi38gUFTaw
[194] **Clip length** - For example, 20 seconds.
[195] **Clip start/stop times** - For example, 0:13-0:33.
[196] **Master label** - For example, noise or control.
[197] **Age label** - Child (<13) or adolescent (13-18) or adult (>18 <70) or elderly (>70).
[198] **Gender label** - For example, male or female.
[199] **Accent label** - For example, American or Foreign.

```
elderly (e, >70)?
-> a
is this person male (m) or female (f)?
-> m
does this person have an American (a) or foreign (f) accent?
-> a
what is the audio quality? (1 - poor, 2 - moderate, 3 - good quality, 4 - high
quality)
-> 3
is the environment indoors (i) or outdoors (o)?
-> i
sample number: 1
what is the URL of the video?
# ...After entering [''] here, it ends the script and outputs excel sheet below.
```

>> Output: noise.xlsx

URL	Clip Lengt	Start and	Label: is t	Age	Gender	Accent	Audio qual	Environme
https://w	20	0:05-0:25	1	adult (>18	male	american	3	indoors

Now that we have this spreadsheet, we can now easily download the videos online with the *y-scrape.py* script (Figure 4.3.2). This script takes in the spreadsheet generated above in Figure 4.3.1 and downloads the videos. Then, all the videos are converted into audio files (.WAV files), making sure they are clipped at the appropriate places. This script also keeps the labels in a .JSON database in case they need to be later referenced.[200] In this way, you can consistently label speech data for featurization and modeling.

---

[200] **Labels** - These labels are url, clip length, start/stop, main label, ages, genders, accents, audio quality, and environment type.

> **Figure 4.3.2:**
> **Downloading YouTube videos from spreadsheet:** *y_scrape.py*
>
> ```
> python3 y_scrape.py
> what is the file name?
> -> Stressed_1.xlsx
> # All the files are then downloaded and converted to .WAV format with FFmpeg ...
> ```
>
> snipped0_s...end_25.json
> snipped0_s...end_25.wav
> stressed_1.xlsx
>
> | Root | Dictionary | 9 key/value pairs |
> |---|---|---|
> | Accent | String | american |
> | Age | String | adult (>18 years old) |
> | Clipped points | String | 0:05-0:25 |
> | Date | String | 2018-07-23 14:33:43.592518 |
> | Environment | String | indoors |
> | Gender | String | male |
> | Label | String | 1 |
> | Length | String | 20 |
> | URL | String | https://www.youtube.com/watch?v=47HLiAxHgdo |
>
> ^ the output contains clipped wav files named like snipped[i]_start_end.wav. This allows for you to use these files for machine learning purposes.

If you have a very large dataset (e.g. 100,000 files), it may not be practical to label these files manually. Therefore, ***automated labeling techniques*** are necessary.

For example, you may have collected a video stream which contains both audio and video content. Since the audio and video were collected in series at the same time, you may be able to use some of the video features to label the audio file to determine the desired class label.[201]

To make this more concrete, let's look at an emotion detection problem where we are trying to determine the emotion of a 20 second sample of audio. Emotions are quite hard to label within audio files. In fact, we've had a trained audio engineer tag over 1000 files and label things like stress level, happy, sad, neutrality, anger, etc. In contrast, features extracted from videos can be a bit more intuitive than audio features for labeling classes.[202] [203] You can tell when someone

---

[201] **Video/image libraries** - I find the best way to label audio files with meta models is often with video or images. There are a few video and imaging editing libraries that are important to know about for these purposes - like opencv or scikit-video. Feel free to look at their documentation and starter examples if you'd like to get better at video or image featurization and automated data labeling.

[202] **Meta features are a little harder to extract** - Meta features can be a bit more difficult to extract than the other feature types (audio features, text features, and mixed features), mostly because it takes a bit of knowledge of how to featurize and deploy machine learning models.

[203] **Race detection with meta features** - It may be quite hard to determine race from an audio file explicitly; however, it is much easier to determine race from images. Say you have a video of a subject speaking for 1 minute in front of the camera. You could extract audio files from these videos and then take roughly 120 images of the video in series (e.g. take 1 image of a video every 0.5 seconds). Then, we can do some facial detection cleaning on the images to narrow in purely on faces. We may want to then look at these images a bit more deeply - like look at the intensity of certain pixels or something else to define what 'race is.' As soon as we have a definition for race, we can then make an image-based *meta model* to label races. This can then be used to tag audio features into different classes - for example, caucasian, african american, etc.

is smiling that they are happy, and these things likely correlate to emotion. However, it may be hard to tell if someone is authentically happy over the phone.

Perhaps we can find an emotional dataset (e.g. CNN videos on YouTube involving the Trump election) that we can train models on for emotion. Once we download such videos (e.g. through the prior described *y-scrape.py* script), we can then segment the videos into audio .WAV files or muted .MP4 video files (Figure 3.5.1). The video and audio files can then be spliced in equal intervals - say every 20 seconds - and off-the-shelf facial recognition models can be used to tag faces in the videos.[204] If there are faces, we can then extract the net emotion using another off-the-shelf emotion model from the muted video stream and label the audio files from the most probable emotion detected in these images. In this way, we can segment various audio files into categories - happy, sad, disgusted, neutral, angry, or surprised - without really knowing anything else other than off-the-shelf (video-fed) machine learning models and how to parallelize audio and video streams.

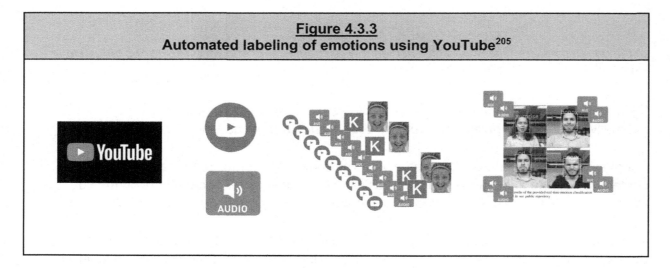

Figure 4.3.3
Automated labeling of emotions using YouTube[205]

Video and image-based automated labeling methods for voice files is beyond the scope of this book, as it often requires an introduction to image and video processing. However, if this is something that interest you check out the documentation for like opencv or scikit-video.

---

[204] **Haar cascade** - It's often useful to extract faces from these images and use these for labeling using a model known as a haar_cascade. Many of these models are provided in the OpenCV base package and are open-source. https://docs.opencv.org/3.3.1/d7/d8b/tutorial_py_face_detection.html

[205] **Research on automated labeling of emotions** - Automated voice labeling techniques on emotion labeling is an active area of research for our company.If this is an area that you'd like to explore deeper, feel free to reach out to me @ js@neurolex.co and we can get you involved in a research project.

4.4 Classification models

Now that we can collect, label, and featurize training data, we can build some machine learning classification algorithms. Before we do this, though, let's get you up-to-speed on the different types of *supervised* machine learning algorithms.

There are many types of **supervised machine learning algorithms** - k-nearest neighbors (KNN), naive bayes (NB), decision trees/random forests, support vector machines (SVM), neural networks, hard voting, soft voting, adaboost, and gradient boosting (Table 4.4.1). As discussed previously (section 4.3), supervised algorithms require labels and features.[206] All of these algorithms can be useful for speech applications, depending on the problem that you are trying to solve.[207] [208]

<u>Table 4.4.1</u>
Various machine learning algorithms and their biases

Algorithm	Learning type	Class	Restriction bias[209]	Preference bias
K-nearest neighbors	Supervised	Instance-based	Suffers the curse of dimensionality	Prefers problems that are distance-based.
Naive Bayes	Supervised	Probabilistic	Works well when inputs are independent variables	Prefers problems where probability will be always greater than 0 in each class.
Decision trees or Random Forests	Supervised	Tree	Less useful on problems with low covariance	Prefers problems with categorical data.
Support vector machines	Supervised	Decision boundary	Works when there is a clear distinction between two classes.	Prefers binary classification problems.

---

[206] **Unsupervised vs. supervised learning** – Supervised learning requires labels and features. In contrast, unsupervised algorithms do not require any labels only features and specified number of clusters.

[207] **Speaker diarization** – Speaker diarization is almost always unsupervised in nature (requires i-vectors and clusters to separate groups, but no training labels).

[208] **Supervised learning** - Most problems you will encounter will likely be supervised and require training labels.

[209] **If you're new to machine learning,** I wouldn't get too wrapped up in things like restriction biases or preference biases. If you're the type that likes to go deeper on these sorts of things, you'd read Thoughtful Machine Learning with Python; I thought this was a great start book on the topic.

Neural networks	Supervised	Nonlinear functional approximation	Little restriction bias.	Prefers binary inputs.
Hard or soft voting	Supervised	Ensemble	Variable, depends on voting type.	Variable, depends on voting type.
Adaboost	Supervised	Ensemble	Sensitive to noisy data and outliers.	Prefers less noisy data.
Gradient Boosting	Supervised	Ensemble	Prone to overfitting.	Prefers high bias, low variance.

Now that you know various machine learning classification techniques at a surface level, let's dive into an example. Let's first get some data in the train_diseases folder, which has some spreadsheets that match with the excel sheet labeling format discussed in section 4.3. Specifically, we can get some training data from individuals who have schizophrenia-related symptoms and control data from regular YouTube video bloggers (Figure 4.4.2). 😌 *Note, downloading this data could take up to 3 hours, depending on your internet connection; therefore, it may be a good time to take a break and then come back!*

Figure 4.4.2
Downloading training data using train_diseases repo: *terminal commands*

```
cd ~
cd voicebook/chapter_4_modeling/train_diseases
python3 yscrape.py
'what is the file name?'
-> schizophrenia.xlsx
python3 yscrape.py
'what is the file name?'
-> controls.xlsx
```

Now that we have the schizophrenia (N=35) and control groups (N=38), we can now build some machine learning algorithms. To make things easy for you, I've created the *train_audioclassify.py* script to audio featurize[210] and subsequently model the datasets using the scikit-learn library. All you thus need are the audio files separated in folders and the script can make models for you (e.g. the folders act as labels).

---

[210] **Audio feature embedding** - These features include MFCC and MFCC delta features over different windows (208 features total). There is no PCA dimensionality reduction or anything, just means, standard deviations, max, min, and medians.

Figure 4.4.3
Building machine learning algorithms in terminal: *train_audioclassify.py*

```
cd ~
cd voicebook/chapter_4_modeling
python3 train_audioclassify.py
# insert number of classes and class names
how many classes are you training? -> 2
what is the folder name for class 1? -> schizophrenia
what is the folder name for class 2? -> controls
# now all the classes will featurize
>> SCHIZOPHRENIA - featurizing snipped38_start_2_end_22.wav
>> making 0.wav
>> [-4.51487917e+02  1.32250653e+02 -6.48964827e+02 -2.16927909e+02...
   9.57062705e-04  4.54699943e-02 -5.85259705e-02  5.74577384e-02]
>> ...
>> Decision tree accuracy (+/-) 0.20779263167344933
>> 0.5733333333333334
>> Gaussian NB accuracy (+/-) 0.1305543735171076
>> 0.7866666666666667
>> SKlearn classifier accuracy (+/-) 0.039999999999999994
>> 0.48
>> Adaboost classifier accuracy (+/-) 0.22666666666666668
>> 0.6366666666666667
>> Gradient boosting accuracy (+/-) 0.1319090595827292
>> 0.6599999999999999
>> Logistic regression accuracy (+/-) 0.07557189365836424
>> 0.7366666666666667
>> Hard voting accuracy (+/-) 0.2341889076033373
>> 0.6766666666666666
>> K Nearest Neighbors accuracy (+/-) 0.12666666666666668
>> 0.5633333333333332
>> Random forest accuracy (+/-) 0.2758824226207808
>> 0.7333333333333333
>> svm accuracy (+/-) 0.13556466271775172
>> 0.7533333333333333
>>
>> most accurate classifier is Gaussian NB with audio features (mfcc coefficients).
saving classifier to disk.
>>
>> Summarizing session...
>> GaussianNB(priors=None)
>>
>> ['gaussian-nb', 0.7866666666666667, 0.1305543735171076]
```

As you can see, this script tests 11 model types: decision trees, naive bayes, soft voting classifier (SVC), adaboost, gradient boosting, logistic regression, hard voting, k-nearest neighbors (KNN), random forest, and support vector machines (SVM). The script then picks and saves the best performing model (in this case, gaussian naive bayes) as a .PICKLE file (*schizophrenia_controls_sc_audio.pickle*). The script also outputs a text file (*schizophrenia_controls_sc_audio.txt*) summarizing the session file in the /models directory.[211] In this way, it's quite easy to build and optimize audio models.

Figure 4.4.4
Text output of the training session: *schizophrenia_controls.txt**
* This file is available in the cd voicebook/chapter_4_modeling/models/ directory

SUMMARY OF MODEL SELECTION

WINNING MODEL:

gaussian-nb: 0.7866666666666667 (+/- 0.1305543735171076)

MODEL FILE NAME:

schizophrenia_controls_sc_audio.pickle

DATE CREATED:

2018-07-23 19:59:09.854434

EXECUTION TIME:

2.0662899017333984

GROUPS:

['schizophrenia', 'controls']
(34 in each class, 33% used for testing)

TRAINING SUMMARY:

train labels

['schizophrenia', 'controls', 'schizophrenia', 'schizophrenia', 'controls', 'controls', 'schizophrenia', 'schizophrenia', 'controls', 'schizophrenia', 'controls', 'schizophrenia', 'controls', 'controls', 'schizophrenia', 'schizophrenia', 'schizophrenia', 'schizophrenia', 'controls', 'schizophrenia', 'schizophrenia', 'controls', 'controls', 'controls', 'schizophrenia', 'controls', 'controls', 'schizophrenia', 'schizophrenia', 'schizophrenia', 'controls', 'controls', 'controls', 'controls', 'schizophrenia', 'controls', 'schizophrenia', 'schizophrenia', 'schizophrenia', 'controls', 'controls', 'schizophrenia', 'controls', 'schizophrenia', 'controls']

---

[211] **Some quick notes** - Note that the script uses 33% of the data for testing and 67% of the data for training via scikit-learn's train-test-split function. Also, a *k-fold cross-validation (cv=5)* technique was used (Figure 4.4.4). The datasets were also auto-balanced (e.g. only 34 in each class were used, as opposed to 34 in schizophrenia and 39 in controls).

> test labels
>
> ['controls', 'schizophrenia', 'schizophrenia', 'schizophrenia', 'schizophrenia', 'controls', 'controls', 'schizophrenia', 'controls', 'schizophrenia', 'schizophrenia', 'controls', 'controls', 'schizophrenia', 'controls', 'controls', 'controls', 'schizophrenia', 'controls', 'schizophrenia', 'controls', 'schizophrenia', 'controls']
>
> **FEATURES:**
>
> audio features (mfcc coefficients).
>
> **MODELS, ACCURACIES, AND STANDARD DEVIATIONS:**
>
> sk: 0.48 (+/- 0.039999999999999994)
> knn: 0.5633333333333332 (+/- 0.12666666666666668)
> decision-tree: 0.5733333333333334 (+/- 0.20779263167344933)
> adaboost: 0.6366666666666667 (+/- 0.22666666666666668)
> gradient boosting: 0.6599999999999999 (+/- 0.1319090595827292)
> hard voting: 0.6766666666666666 (+/- 0.2341889076033373)
> random forest: 0.7333333333333333 (+/- 0.2758824226207808)
> logistic regression: 0.7366666666666667 (+/- 0.07557189365836424)
> svm: 0.7533333333333333 (+/- 0.13556466271775172)
> gaussian-nb: 0.7866666666666667 (+/- 0.1305543735171076)
>
> (C) 2018, NeuroLex Laboratories

You can repeat the same process for text features (*train_textclassify.py*), audio-text features (*train_audiotextclassify.py*), and Word2vec model features (*train_w2vclassify.py*). In the end, the most accurate feature array seems to be, in general, the w2vclassify feature array (Table 4.4.2).[212] This probably means that the dataset is sensitive to specific vocabularies, and that specific words can be used to separate out controls from those who exhibit psychotic symptoms. *Note, however, that the standard deviation of accuracy is quite high - meaning a larger sample size is necessary to fully validate these conclusions.*[213]

Table 4.4.2 Performance of various machine learning models and feature embeddings			
Script	**Best model**	**Accuracy (+/-)**
train_audioclassify.py	Gaussian Naive Bayes	78.7% accuracy (+/- 13.1%)
train_textclassify.py	Support Vector Machines	77.7% accuracy (+/- 3.0%)
train_audiotextclassify.py	Decision tree	62.0% accuracy (+/- 11.2%)
train_w2vclassify.py	Gaussian Naive Bayes	86.7% accuracy (+/- 19.4%)

---

[212] **Visualizemodels.py** - Note that you can visualize all trained models with the *visualizemodels.py* script.

[213] **Selecting sample size** - N=100 is a good size typically as a minimum for these types of models.

Now that we have built these algorithms, we can now load them with new audio samples to make some predictions (Figure 4.4.5). To make this easy, I've built a *load_classify* script to featurize new audio files and apply these models to predict new class labels. It works by looking for audio files in the */load_dir* folder.[214] These audio files are then featurized according to the types of models that are present in the */models* folder.[215] What results is a .JSON file output with predicted classes and estimated model accuracies. For example, if you have a file 348.wav put into the */load_dir*, then the files would be *348_audio.json* if you ran the *load_audioclassify.py* script.[216] [217]

Figure 4.4.5
Applying model to predict new classes: *load_audioclassify.py, ./load_dir/348_audio.json*

```
python3 load_audioclassify.py
# assume 348.wav is in ./load_dir, outputs ./load_dir/348_audio.json (shown below)
```

{"filename": "348.wav", "filetype": "audio file", "class": ["controls"], "model": ["schizophrenia_controls_sc_audio.pickle"], "model accuracies": [0.7866666666666667], "model deviations": [0.1305543735171076], "model types": ["gaussian-nb"], "features": [[-322.9664360980726, 59.53868288968913, -462.5294083924505, -166.3993076206564, 131.38738649438437, 52.44671783868567, -33.74398658437562, 227.8102207133376, 9.52738149362727, 28.505927165579884, -90.65927286414657, 71.52976680142815, 9.73530102063688, 25.62432182324615, -66.02663398503707, 73.87513246074612, -1.596002360610912, 22.81632350096357, -87.30807566263049, 41.72876898633217, 0.8865486997595385, 17.735652130525168, -65.99456073539176, 52.43567091641821, -14.286216477070838, 14.128449781073533, -59.836804831757654, 18.175026917411316, -9.131276510645463, 13.701302570519355, -57.44541029310883, 25.74622598177111, -4.545971824836885, 10.899138142787697, -42.116927063121395, 29.536967420470695, -3.4558647963609186, 10.31513522815575, -36.17230935229129, 26.551369428146693, -3.6667095757279236, 10.079488079876286, -33.78123311320836, 26.14112294381864, 5.366060779304841, 8.570956061981061, -19.248854886451802, 38.20513572569962, -5.458667628428172, 7.490745204714798, -31.338790159786562, 12.539046082339311, 0.024288590342538358, 10.584946850085212, -34.52340818393254, 38.15078289969128, -0.156898762979172, 11.158828455811786, -34.10403400345244, 30.973152153233336, 0.020648845552068328, 5.827064754672902, -22.052042500906857, 16.81872640844321, -0.06170338085832314, 5.229174923928, -14.518978383592026, 14.845857302315114, -0.049626077796690964, 4.521180649402735, -14.998074177634704, 12.378100326632655, 0.07415513595268168, 3.724070455888158, -9.939566189661432, 10.85577098792062, -0.017072005372266726, 2.7463908847692204, -6.600475000502117, 6.524786791283427, -0.02310274039018664, 2.7092557498939636, -7.467322311111723, 7.481090337383571, 0.04464197716713606, 2.198722832501255, -6.884387758311641, 7.844106037059699, 0.045382707259550105, 2.0580935158253872, -6.638462605186588, 5.991186816663746, -0.013702557713332408, 1.9496130791163644, -6.458246324901151, 5.7716202748695, -0.007340250450717803, 1.640910358611695, -5.380714141939734, 5.539025057788075, 0.011411587050311969, 1.3949062816882583, -4.390308824019425, 4.13132941219398, -291.2947346432915, 49.04737058565422, -381.6816501283554, -222.9638855557117, 158.3460978309033, 23.15415034729552, 99.62697329203677, 189.70121020164896, 7.287058326977949, 30.77474443760493, -38.71228832828984, 56.208286170618955, -1.0950341842073796, 21.3498811006992, -34.41685805740065, 31.926254848624147, -9.172025861857653, 11.511454213511039, -29.874153138705573, 8.203596981294625, 2.6663941698626865, 6.753684660513026, -5.9061357505887955, 19.305474480034082, -14.088225581455214, 17.47630600064678, -49.8886801840349, 8.935818425975743, -13.521963272886959, 8.25999525518404, -24.851695100203774, -0.11752456737790722, -12.762992506945213, 8.598616338770906, -29.72115313687536, 0.05275012294025435, -4.531403069755177, 11.8713757531457, -24.376936764599744, 12.207624665298002, -2.6914750628989266,

---

[214] **The ./load_dir folder is automatically generated** - Note that if this folder does not exist it is automatically created.
[215] **For example,** if there is one model (trained with the train_audioclassify script), then new samples will be featurized with an audio feature embedding; or, if there are two models (one with train_audioclassify and one with train_textclassify), the new samples will be featurized with an audio feature embedding and text embedding separately.
[216] **Likewise,** the files would be 348_text.json, 348_audiotext.json, and 348_w2v.json for models trained with the train_textclassify.py, train_audiotextclassify.py, and train_w2vclassify.py scripts, respectively.
[217] **Labeled vs. unlabeled data value** - This section should show you how easy it is to make and load machine learning models. The bottleneck is often just creating a clean dataset with proper labels. Therefore, it's important to make and label datasets properly, as laid out in Section 4.3.

```
14.673164819510685, -22.308447521294887, 17.767626038347583, 11.80700932417913, 10.516802160193405, -
13.092759032892214, 24.963056992755536, -10.390953114902164, 6.1887066403103965, -20.39253124562046,
2.7941268719402848, -4.41480192601625, 7.0550461587501, -15.045545852884578, 5.8468320221431656,
0.22555437964894862, 4.881477566532211, -4.990490269946867, 8.519079155558249, 3.4745028409138827,
2.7045163211953187, 0.5391937155699558, 8.988399905874912, 0.45051536549204274, 4.824805683998831, -
4.424922867740668, 9.67554223394205, -0.8502687288362012, 3.135194132853677, -4.844124443962841,
4.754766492721427, 0.870140923131266, 1.1137966493666094, -1.4131441258277446, 2.418345086057676,
2.4254793474500635, 1.2058772715931956, 0.5825294849801214, 4.536777131050609, 0.10251353649615984,
1.51146113365032, -1.4592806547585204, 3.291502702928505, -1.075428938064348, 1.0559521971759946, -
2.4408814841825865, 1.12308565480587, -0.3002420005778045, 2.4751693616737347, -3.6333810904861688,
3.34737386167248, 0.17805269515377548, 3.7250267108754236, -5.189309157660288, 5.579262003298437,
0.24091712079378458, 2.451817967640338, -5.215650064568107, 2.3865116769275567, 0.003640041240486553,
1.4235044885102617, -2.379919268715038, 1.5581599658532437]], "count": 0, "errorcount": 0}
```

4.5 Regression models

Sometimes you face problems where you need to input a feature array and output a range of values - usually from 0 and 1 - to predict a class. For example, you may want to estimate the output class values of all the emotions in a range (e.g. 0.873) instead of as binary classes (e.g. 1 or 0) so you can better fit models to data. These are known as *regression problems.*

These problems are solved by building *regression models*. Regression models often assume a linear combination of input variables and assign weights to these variables to predict the output. Some common types of regression models include ordinary least squares, ridge regression, lasso, multi-task lasso, elastic net, multi-task elastic net, least angle regression (LARS), LARS lasso, orthogonal matching pursuit, bayesian ridge regression, automatic relevance determination, logistic regression, stochastic gradient descent, perceptron, passive aggressive algorithms, robustness regression, random sample consensus, Theil-Sen estimator, Huber regression, and polynomial regression (Table 4.6.1).[218]

<u>Table 4.6.1:</u>
<u>Types of regression models: pros/cons</u>

Model	Short description	Limitations
Ordinary least squares	Works well on linear data that has independent variables.	Does not work well on nonlinear data with outliers; sensitive to random errors.
Ridge regression	Addresses some issues of ordinary least squares; robust to collinearity.	N/A.
Lasso	Estimates sparse coefficients; generally there are fewer parameters to tune.	N/A.
Multi-task Lasso	Can estimate sparse coefficients for multiple regression problems jointly (n_samples, n_tasks).	Selected features are the same for all the regression problems.

---

[218] **Scikit-learn** - You can read more about these regression models in the scikit-learn documentation.

Elastic net	Trained with L1 and L2 as a regularizer, tuned with l1_ratio parameter; kind of in between ridge and lasso regression.	N/A.
Multi-task elastic net	Estimates sparse coefficients for multiple regression problems jointly (n_samples, n_tasks).	N/A.
Least angle regression (LARS)	Works well on high-dimensional data - numerically efficient in context when number of dimensions is significantly greater than number of points.	Sensitive to the effects of noise.
LARS lasso	Implements LASSO with a LARS algorithm.	Sensitive to the effects of noise.
Orthogonal matching pursuit (OMP)	Like least-angle regression, but better.	N/A.
Bayesian ridge regression	Allows for regularization to be tuned to the data at hand with probabilistic models (not hard set).	Inference can be time-consuming.
Automatic relevance determination (ARD)	Like Bayesian ridge regression but can lead to sparser rates.	N/A.
Logistic regression	Good for binary datasets.	N/A.
Stochastic gradient descent (SGD)	Efficient to fit linear models when number of features is very large; useful for regularization deep learning models.	N/A.
Perceptron	Does not require learning rate or be regularized, updates only on mistakes.	Resulting models are sparser.
Passive aggressive algorithms	Does not require learning rate, includes a regularization parameter, c.	N/A.
Robustness regression	Useful to fit a regression model in presence of corrupt data - outliers or errors in the model.	N/A.
Random sample consensus (RANSAC)	Useful for both linear and non-linear regression problems - separates data based on inliers and outliers.	N/A.

Theil-Sen estimator	Fits data to medians in multiple dimensions, robust to multivariate outliers.	Suffers from the curse of dimensionality; higher dimensionality causes the model to be no better than ordinary least squares.
Huber regression	Alternative to TheilSen Regressor and RANSAC Regressor.	More sensitive to outliers than TheilSen and RANSAC.
Polynomial regression	Works well on nonlinear features.	N/A.

Now let's dive into an example. We can use the *train_audioregression.py* to train a regression model on audio features, much like we did in the *train_audioclassify.py* script (Figure 4.6.1).[219] As you can see, the script implements these algorithms: linear regression, ridge regression, LASSO, elastic net, LARS, OMP, logistic regression, stochastic gradient descent, passive-aggressive, RANSAC, Theil-San, Huber regression, and a polynomial.[220] Typically, I look at the R^2 and mean absolute error as the main values to see how well a regression model performs. In this case, the best performing model seems to be logistic regression with a mean absolute error of 0.253, which makes sense because this is binary data and a logistic regression fits a S curve. All of this data is outputted to a .XLSX file in the ./models directory, and the primary model is dumped into a .PICKLE file (Figure 4.6.1).[221]

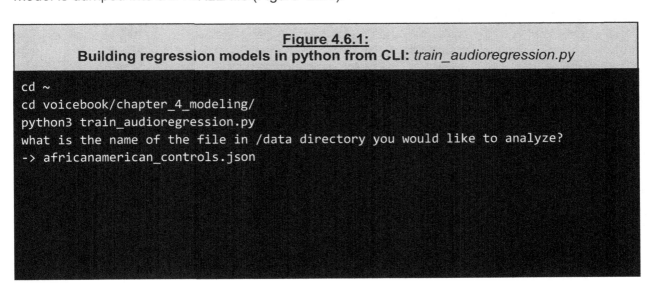

Figure 4.6.1:
Building regression models in python from CLI: *train_audioregression.py*

```
cd ~
cd voicebook/chapter_4_modeling/
python3 train_audioregression.py
what is the name of the file in /data directory you would like to analyze?
-> africanamerican_controls.json
```

---

[219] **Note that** africanamerican_caucasians.json was trained using the train_audioclassify script and we can implement this script as long as you have your desired feature embeddings for each class.

[220] **Note that** just because you have a R^2 value closer to -1 or 1 doesn't necessarily mean you have a good regression model. The best way to evaluate regression models is through stats like the R^2 value, explained variances, mean absolute error, mean squared log error, and median absolute error.

[221] **Named** *africanamerican_controls.xlsx* and *africanamerican_controls_regression.pickle*, respectively.

```
>> RESULTS:

+----------------------------------------+-----------+----------------------+
|                 model type             | R^2 score | Mean Absolute Errors |
+----------------------------------------+-----------+----------------------+
|              linear regression         |   -1.672  |        0.656         |
+----------------------------------------+-----------+----------------------+
|              ridge regression          |    0.047  |        0.367         |
+----------------------------------------+-----------+----------------------+
|                    LASSO               |    0.426  |        0.273         |
+----------------------------------------+-----------+----------------------+
|                 elastic net            |    0.483  |        0.255         |
+----------------------------------------+-----------+----------------------+
|        Least angle regression (LARS)   |    0.065  |        0.478         |
+----------------------------------------+-----------+----------------------+
|                 LARS lasso             |   -0.025  |        0.502         |
+----------------------------------------+-----------+----------------------+
|      orthogonal matching pursuit (OMP) |   -0.032  |        0.39          |
+----------------------------------------+-----------+----------------------+
|             logistic regression        |   -0.019  |        0.253         |
+----------------------------------------+-----------+----------------------+
|      stochastic gradient descent (SGD) |   -0.153  |        0.41          |
+----------------------------------------+-----------+----------------------+
|                 perceptron             |   -7.297  |        1.131         |
+----------------------------------------+-----------+----------------------+
|        passive-agressive algorithm     |    0.316  |        0.329         |
+----------------------------------------+-----------+----------------------+
|                   RANSAC               |    0.316  |        0.329         |
+----------------------------------------+-----------+----------------------+
|                 Theil-Sen              |   -1.672  |        0.674         |
+----------------------------------------+-----------+----------------------+
|              huber regression          |   -0.582  |        0.49          |
+----------------------------------------+-----------+----------------------+
|        polynomial (linear regression)  |   -0.582  |        0.49          |
+----------------------------------------+-----------+----------------------+

>> logistic regression has the lowest mean absolute error (0.25252525252525254)
>> saving file to disk (africanamerican_controls_regression.pickle)...
```

We can now make predictions with this model like we did in the classification section. Using the script load_audioregression.py we can now analyze files in the ./load_dir again. Note that this script features an audio file with audio features (208 features discussed previously), and then applies the logistic regression model. What results is a numerical output; in this case 1.0 - which makes sense because we were doing a binary classification anyways. In this way, we can predict output classes with regression models (Figure 4.6.2).[222]

---

[222] **However,** if you had labeled data that was more of a range [0,1] then this output can change to be something like 0.677. I typically set a threshold for a class; for example, anything above 0.5 would be the 'control' group and anything under 0.5 would be the 'african american' group.

Figure 4.6.2:
Building regression models in Python from CLI: *train_audioregression.py*

```
python3 load_audioregression.py
>> 1.0
>> controls
```

{"filename": "348.wav", "filetype": "audio file", "class": ["controls"], "model": ["africanamerican_controls_regression.pickle"], "model types": ["logistic regression"], "stats": [{"explained_variance": -0.008230452674897082, "mean_absolute_error": 0.25252525252525254, "mean_squared_log_error": 0.12132651866621247, "median_absolute_error": 0.0, "r2_score": -0.03221079873235233}], "features": [[-322.9664360980726, 59.53868288968913, -462.5294083924505, -166.3993076206564, 131.38738649438437, 52.44671783868567, -33.74398658437562, 227.8102207133376, 9.52738149362727, 28.505927165579884, -90.65927286414657, 71.52976680142815, 9.73530102063688, 25.62432182324615, -66.02663398503707, 73.87513246074612, -1.596002360610912, 22.81632350096357, -87.30807566263049, 41.72876898633217, 0.8865486997595385, 17.735652130525168, -65.99456073539176, 52.43567091641821, -14.286216477070838, 14.128449781073533, -59.836804831757654, 18.175026917411316, -9.131276510645463, 13.701302570519355, -57.44541029310883, 25.74622598177111, -4.545971824836885, 10.899138142787697, -42.116927063121395, 29.536967420470695, -3.4558647963609186, 10.31513522815575, -36.17230935229129, 26.551369428146693, -3.6667095757279236, 10.079488079876286, -33.78123311320836, 26.14112294381864, 5.366060779304841, 8.570956061981061, -19.248854886451802, 38.20513572569962, -5.458667628428172, 7.490745204714798, -31.338790159786562, 12.539046082339311, 0.024288590342538358, 10.584946850085212, -34.52340818393254, 38.15078289969128, -0.156898762979172, 11.158828455811786, -34.10403400345244, 30.973152153233336, 0.020648845552068328, 5.827064754672902, -22.052042500906857, 16.81872640844321, -0.061703380858323 14, 5.229174923928, -14.518978383592026, 14.845857302315114, -0.04962607796690964, 4.5211806494022735, -14.998074177634704, 12.378100326632655, 0.07415513595268168, 3.724070455888158, -9.939566189661432, 10.85577098792062, -0.017072005372266726, 2.7463908847692204, -6.600475000502117, 6.524786791283427, -0.02310274039018664, 2.7092557498939636, -7.467322311111723, 7.481090337383571, 0.04464197716713606, 2.198722832501255, -6.88438775831641, 7.844106037059699, 0.045382707259550105, 2.0580935158253872, -6.638462605186588, 5.991186816663746, -0.013702557713332408, 1.9496130791163644, -6.458246324901151, 5.7716202748695, -0.007340250450717803, 1.6409103586116958, -5.380714141939734, 5.539025057788075, 0.01141158705031 1969, 1.3949062816882583, -4.390308824019425, 4.13132941219398, -291.2947346432915, 49.04737058565422, -381.6816501283554, -222.9638855557117, 158.3460978309033, 23.15415034729552, 99.62697329203677, 189.70121020164896, 7.287058326977949, 30.77474443760493, -38.71222832828984, 56.208286170618955, -1.0950341842073796, 21.3498811006992, -34.41685805740065, 31.926254848624147, -9.172025861857653, 11.511454213511039, -29.874153138705573, 8.203596981294625, 2.6663941698626865, 6.753684660513026, -5.9061357505887955, 9.305474480034082, -14.088225581455214, 17.47630600064678, -49.8886801840349, 8.935818425975743, -13.521963272886959, 8.25999525518404, -24.851695100203774, -0.11752456737790722, -12.762992506945213, 8.598616338770906, -29.72115313687536, 0.05275012294025435, -4.531403069755177, 11.8713757531457, -24.376936764599744, 12.207624665298002, -2.6914750628989266, 14.673164819510685, -22.308447521294887, 17.767626038347583, 11.80700932417913, 10.516802160193405, -13.092759032892214, 24.963056992755536, -10.390953114902164, 6.1887066403103965, -20.39253124562046, 2.7941268719402848, -4.41480192601625, 7.0550461587501, -15.045545852884578, 5.8468320221431656, 0.22555437964894862, 4.881477566532211, -4.990490269946867, 8.519079155558249, 3.4745028409138827, 2.7045163211953187, 0.5391937155699558, 8.988399905874912, 0.45051536549204274, 4.824805683998831, -4.424922867740668, 9.67554223394205, -0.8502687288362012, 3.1351941328536777, -4.844124443962841, 4.754766492721427, 0.870140923131266, 1.1137966493666094, -1.4131441258277446, 2.418345086057676, 2.4254793474500635, 1.2058772715931956, 0.5825294849801214, 4.536777131050609, 0.10251353649615984, 1.51146113365032, -1.4592806547585204, 3.291502702928505, -1.075428938064348, 1.0559521971759946, -2.4408814841825865, 1.12308565480587, -0.3002420005778045, 2.4751693616737347, -3.6333810904861688, 3.34737386167248, 0.17805269515377548, 3.7250267108754236, -5.189309157660288, 5.579262003298437, 0.24091712079378458, 2.451817967640338, -5.215650064568107, 2.3865116769275567, 0.003640041240486553, 1.4235044885102617, -2.379919268715038, 1.5581599658532437]], "count": 0, "errorcount": 0}

This short introduction should get you thinking at least how to begin thinking with a regression mindset. *I typically prefer using classification models for speech-related tasks, so I'd start there and use regression if the classification accuracies are not high enough.*

4.7 Deep learning models

If you have sufficient data (e.g. typically >1000 in each class), deep learning models could yield better performance than simple classification or regression models.

Deep learning models use **neural networks, layers, neurons, weights, epochs, batch sizes, regularization, loss functions,** and **backpropagation** to transform input features to output classes (Table 4.7.1). In general, the goal of the network is to minimize some loss function (e.g. binary crossentropy) through various configurations of layers and regularization techniques. In this way, deep learning models can produce powerful representations of information simply through adjusting weights of neurons in each layer.

Table 4.7.1
Deep learning terms and definitions

Term	Definition	Example(s)
Neural network	A combination of neurons that learn patterns through the flow of information into and out of it. Over time, weights can change the learning of these representations, meaning that the more information the network is fed, the better the overall representation.	Multilayer perceptron (MLP). See Figure 4.7.2 for more exhaustive list of examples.
Layers	The number of steps a neural network goes from an input to an output. Layers can increase or decrease in size over time (e.g. autoencoders).	Input layer, output layer, hidden layer.
Neuron	The fundamental unit of each layer that stores weights in and out of the layer.	N/A.
Weights	The internal representations of each neuron - going into and out of each layer.	0.4.
Epoch	The number of times information flows back and forth through a neural network (often through batches).	30.
Batch size	The number of training examples put through the neural network at every epoch. The higher the batch size, the more RAM memory needed.	20.

Regularization	The process of introducing new information to a neural network to reduce overfitting.	Max pooling, dropout, batch normalization, L2 regularization.
Loss functions	Maps a series of variables to a real number representing some cost associated with an event. The goal of neural networks is to minimize these cost functions.	binary crossentropy, categorical, crossentropy.
Backpropagation ("Back prop")	Take partial derivatives (or gradient) of a function. Useful for optimizing paths of the network through stochastic gradient descent (SGD).	N/A.

It's become much easier to apply deep learning with libraries like **Keras**, which have abstracted much of the back-end knowledge of neural networks and made it quite simple to execute into a code base.[223] [224] Let's take building a multilayer perceptron (MLP). It's only a few lines of code to build this neural network with the Keras library (Figure 4.7.1):

---

[223] **Don't be intimidated by deep learning;** you don't need a PhD to practically apply it. However, having a PhD helps to understand it.
[224] **Keras** uses TensorFlow as their back-end and is in process of porting over many other back-ends. It's designed to be agnostic to vendors like Google or Microsoft.

Figure 4.7.1:
Building a simple deep learning model in Keras (MLP): *keras_mlp.py*

```python
from keras.models import Sequential
from keras.layers import Dense, Activation

model = Sequential()
model.add(Dense(32, activation='relu', input_dim=100))
model.add(Dense(1, activation='sigmoid'))
model.compile(optimizer='rmsprop',
              loss='binary_crossentropy',
              metrics=['accuracy'])

# Generate dummy data
import numpy as np
data = np.random.random((1000, 100))
labels = np.random.randint(2, size=(1000, 1))

# Train the model, iterating on the data in batches of 32 samples
model.fit(data, labels, epochs=10, batch_size=32)
```

There are quite a few neural network configurations (Figure 4.7.2).[225][226] These configurations are often engineered around use cases. For example, autoencoders are useful for learning feature representations of datasets (as mentioned in the last chapter) whereas LSTM models are useful to learning time series information present in a feature set. Therefore, it is important to have some underlying knowledge of the problem domain to engineer the best network configuration for a given problem.

A good place to start building a neural network is by looking for research papers published around the problem that you are solving. For example, if I go on Google and search "best neural network for speech recognition" you can quickly find a lot of articles stating that a Long short-term memory (LSTM) recurrent neural networks (RNNs) perform well for speech recognition tasks. Therefore, it may be good to start out with a LSTM RNN based on a research paper in the space. *Note that many of these research papers have GitHub repositories and you can access them to build your architecture and there is a great list of starter models* in the Keras repository.

In general, the two most important algorithms for voice computing are Long Short-term Memory RNNs (LSTM RNNs) models and multilayer perceptrons (MLPs). I often find that it's good to

---

[225] **Some examples include:** perceptrons, feed-forward neural networks, radial basis networks, deep feedforward networks, recurrent neural networks (RNNs), long short-term memory networks (LSTM), gated recurrent units, autoencoders, markov chains, hopfield network, boltzmann machines, deep belief networks (DBNs), deep convolutional networks, generative adversarial networks, liquid state machines (LSMs), and echo state networks (ESNs). See Figure 4.7.1 for visual representations of these networks.

[226] **If you want to get serious about deep learning** you can take a Udacity course called deep learning (by Google). It's completely free.

start out building a multilayer perceptron (MLP) model, and if it seems like it is working then we can go on and build an optimized LSTM model. *Everyone always has a different perspective on modeling though, so feel free to go with whatever intuition you have as a starting point for modeling.*

Before continuing, I want to just let you know that if you're confused right now that is okay! At first, I greatly struggled with some of these concepts. It took about a month or so of trial-and-error network-making before I felt comfortable with a lot of these ideas. You don't really need to understand exactly everything going on in order to code neural networks; you just have to know how to evaluate them in terms of loss functions and build them in terms of layers. For these reasons, I highly encourage you to use Keras (as opposed to TensorFlow or another machine learning library) as a starting point to build neural networks.

Also, note that neural networks aren't necessary for a wide array of modeling tasks. I usually start with a simple classifier (e.g. *train_audioclassify.py*) or regression model (e.g. *train_audioregression.py*). If you have over 1,000 samples and you are not achieving your desired accuracy, you can then progress to [neural network]-based classification or regression models. In thinking this way, you can learn a lot about what families of machine learning classifiers (e.g. KNNs) work and then use these within intermediate layers of neural networks too. This strategy thus allows you to build more innovative and experimental network configurations.

**Figure 4.7.2:
Complete list of neural networks**

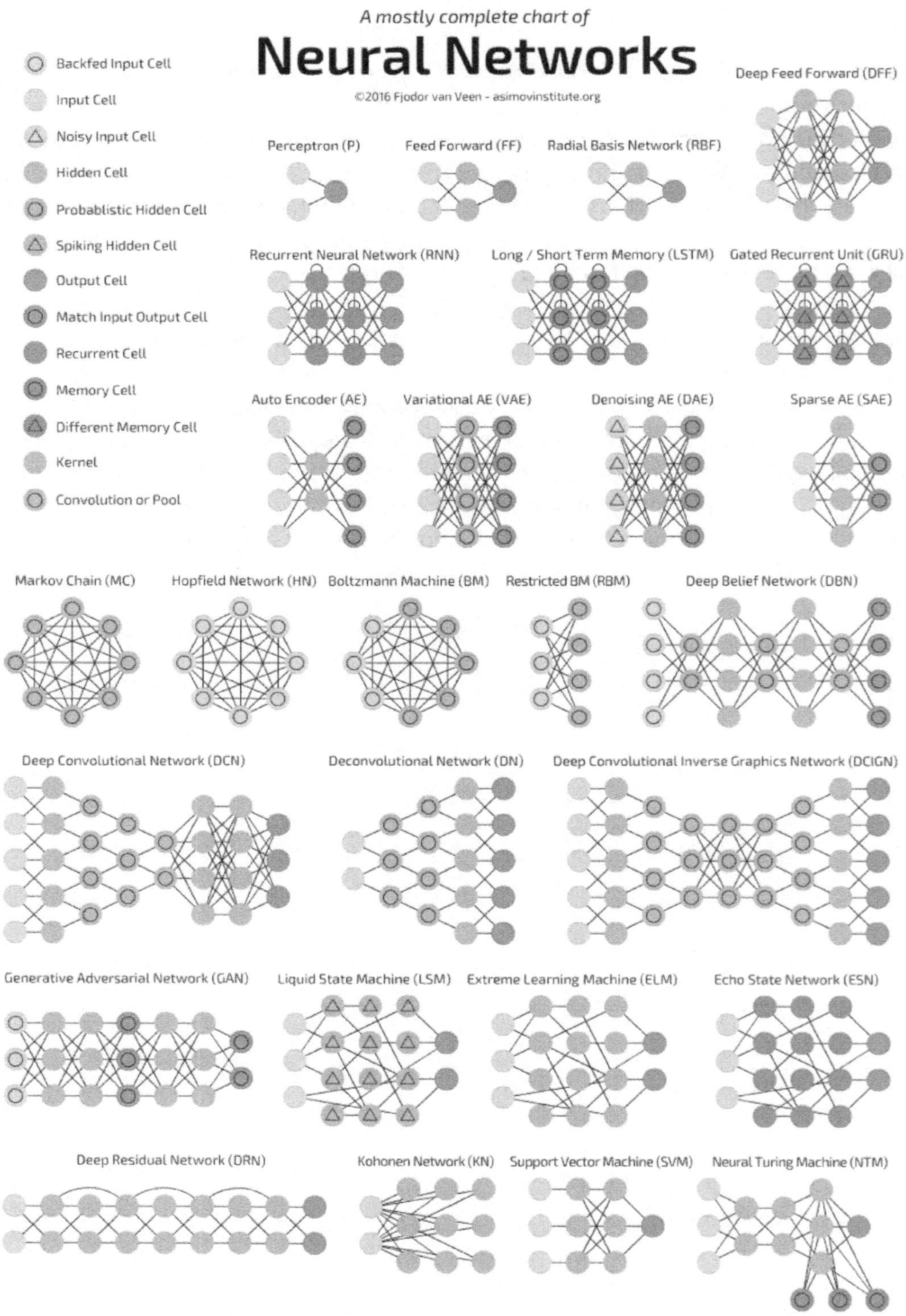

A mostly complete chart of
Neural Networks
©2016 Fjodor van Veen - asimovinstitute.org

- Backfed Input Cell
- Input Cell
- Noisy Input Cell
- Hidden Cell
- Probablistic Hidden Cell
- Spiking Hidden Cell
- Output Cell
- Match Input Output Cell
- Recurrent Cell
- Memory Cell
- Different Memory Cell
- Kernel
- Convolution or Pool

Perceptron (P), Feed Forward (FF), Radial Basis Network (RBF), Deep Feed Forward (DFF)

Recurrent Neural Network (RNN), Long / Short Term Memory (LSTM), Gated Recurrent Unit (GRU)

Auto Encoder (AE), Variational AE (VAE), Denoising AE (DAE), Sparse AE (SAE)

Markov Chain (MC), Hopfield Network (HN), Boltzmann Machine (BM), Restricted BM (RBM), Deep Belief Network (DBN)

Deep Convolutional Network (DCN), Deconvolutional Network (DN), Deep Convolutional Inverse Graphics Network (DCIGN)

Generative Adversarial Network (GAN), Liquid State Machine (LSM), Extreme Learning Machine (ELM), Echo State Network (ESN)

Deep Residual Network (DRN), Kohonen Network (KN), Support Vector Machine (SVM), Neural Turing Machine (NTM)

Now let's progress to building some neural networks with speech data! We can use a convenient *train_audiokeras.py* script to do this (Figure 4.7.3). Note that since the data we are using only has like ~150 training samples, the model overfits quickly, achieving a very high accuracy at predicting the training dataset (99%) but poor accuracy (50%) when applied to the test dataset. For this reason, I usually don't start building deep learning-based models until I have over 1,000 samples in each category.

Figure 4.7.3
Training a Keras model from audio features: *train_audiokeras.py*

```
cd ~
cd voicebook/chapter_4_modeling
python3 train_audiokeras.py
folder name 1
-> africanamerican
folder name 2
-> controls
>> ...
>> [[1.]]
>> Epoch 1/20
149/149 [==============================] - 0s 2ms/step - loss:3.8728 - acc:0.3423
>> Epoch 2/20
149/149 [==============================] - 0s 29us/step - loss:0.3178 - acc:0.3624
>> Epoch 3/20
149/149 [==============================] - 0s 26us/step - loss:-0.0068 - acc:0.4228
>> ...
>> final acc: 50.34%
>> ...
>> Saved africanamerican_controls_dl_audio.json model to disk
>> summarizing data...
>> testing loaded model
>> 'Loaded model from disk'
>> [[1.]]
```

The model that you built also has a nice summary, like when you trained classification models (Figure 4.7.4).

> **Figure 4.7.4**
> **Training a Keras model from audio features:** *train_audiokeras.py*
>
> **SUMMARY OF MODEL**
>
> Keras-based implementation of a neural network, 208 audio input features (mfccs and their deltas), 1 output feature; binary classification, 2 layers (relu | sigmoid activation functions), loss=binary_crossentropy, optimizer=rmsprop
>
> **MODEL FILE NAME:**
>
> africanamerican_controls_dl_audio.json | africanamerican_controls_dl_audio.h5
>
> **DATE CREATED:**
>
> 2018-07-25 12:53:14.936489
>
> **EXECUTION TIME:**
>
> 7.947792053222656
>
> **GROUPS:**
>
> Group 1: africanamerican (74 training, 74 testing)
> Group 2: controls (74 training, 74 testing)
>
> **FEATURES:**
>
> Audio features - mfcc coefficients (200 features)
>
> **MODEL ACCURACY:**
>
> accuracy: 50.335570529803334
>
> (C) 2018, NeuroLex Laboratories

Now that we've built the model (saved as a .H5 and a .JSON file with weights), we can now apply the model like all the others using the *load_audiokeras.py* script. This script features the audio file into the right format and then applies all the Keras models that you put in the ./models directory to the file, saving the result to a _*kerasaudio.json* file in the ./load_dir folder (Figure 4.7.5). This file naming scheme falls in line with the previous classification and regression load scripts.

Figure 4.7.5:
Applying Keras-based deep learning models on new data: *load_audiokeras.py*

```
cd ~
cd voicebook/chapter_4_modeling/
python3 load_audiokeras.py
>> 348.wav
>> making 0.wav
>> making 1.wav
>> …
>> making 38.wav
>> controls
```

{**"filename"**: "348.wav", **"filetype"**: "audio file", **"class"**: ["controls"], **"h5 models"**: ["africanamerican_controls_dl_audio.h5"], **"json models"**: ["africanamerican_controls_dl_audio.json"], **"model types"**: ["mlp"], **"features"**: [-322.9664360980726, 59.53868288968913, -462.5294083924505, -166.3993076206564, 131.38738649438437, 52.44671783868567, -33.74398658437562, 227.8102207133376, 9.52738149362727, 28.505927165579884, -90.65927286414657, 71.52976680142815, 9.73530102063688, 25.62432182324615, -66.02663398503707, 73.87513246074612, -1.596002360610912, 22.81632350096357, -87.30807566263049, 41.72876898633217, 0.8865486997595385, 17.735652130525168, -65.99456073539176, 52.43567091641821, -14.286216477070838, 14.128449781073533, -59.836804831757654, 18.175026917411316, -9.131276510645463, 13.701302570519355, -57.44541029310883, 25.74622598177111, -4.545971824836885, 10.899138142787697, -42.116927063121395, 29.536967420470695, -3.4558647963609186, 10.31513522815575, -36.17230935229129, 26.551369428146693, -3.6667095757279236, 10.079488079876286, -33.78123311320836, 26.14112294381864, 5.366060779304841, 8.570956061981061, -19.248854886451802, 38.20513572569962, -5.458667628428172, 7.490745204714798, -31.338790159786562, 12.539046082339311, 0.024288590342538358, 10.584946850085212, -34.52340818393254, 38.15078289969128, -0.156898762979172, 11.158828455811786, -34.10403400345244, 30.973152153233336, 0.020648845552068328, 5.827064754672902, -22.052042500906857, 16.81872640844321, -0.06170338085832314, 5.229174923928, -14.518978383592026, 14.845857302315114, -0.04962607796690964, 4.5211806494022735, -14.998074177634704, 12.378100326632655, 0.07415513595268168, 3.724070455888158, -9.939566189661432, 10.85577098792062, -0.017072005372266726, 2.7463908847692204, -6.600475000502117, 6.524786791283427, -0.02310274039018664, 2.7092557498939636, -7.467322311111723, 7.481090337383571, 0.04464197716713606, 2.198722832501255, -6.88438775831641, 7.844106037059699, 0.045382707259550105, 2.0580935158253872, -6.638462605186588, 5.991186816663746, -0.013702557713332408, 1.9496130791163644, -6.458246324901151, 5.7716202748695, -0.007340250450717803, 1.6409103586116958, -5.380714141939734, 5.539025057788075, 0.011411587050311969, 1.3949062816882583, -4.390308824019425, 4.13132941219398, -291.2947346432915, 49.04737058565422, -381.6816501283554, -222.9638855557117, 158.3460978309033, 23.15415034729552, 99.62697329203677, 189.70121020164896, 7.287058326977949, 30.77474443760493, -38.71222832828984, 56.208286170618955, -1.0950341842073796, 21.3498811006992, -34.41685805740065, 31.926254848624147, -9.172025861857653, 11.511454213511039, -29.874153138705573, 8.203596981294625, 2.6663941698626865, 6.753684660513026, -5.9061357505887955, 19.305474480034082, -14.088225581455214, 17.47630600064678, -49.8886801840349, 8.935818425975743, -13.521963272886959, 8.25999525518404, -24.851695100203774, -0.11752456737790722, -12.762992506945213, 8.598616338770906, -29.72115313687536, 0.05275012294025435, -4.531403069755177, 11.8713757531457, -24.376936764599744, 12.207624665298002, -2.6914750628989266, 14.673164819510685, -22.308447521294887, 17.767626038347583, 11.80700932417913, 10.516802160193405, -13.092759032892214, 24.963056992755536, -10.390953114902164, 6.1887066403103965, -20.39253124562046, 2.7941268719402848, -4.41480192601625, 7.0550461587501, -15.045545852884578, 5.8468320221431656, 0.22555437964894862, 4.881477566532211, -4.990490269946867, 8.519079155558249, 3.4745028409138827, 2.7045163211953187, 0.5391937155699558, 8.988399905874912, 0.45051536549204274, 4.824805683998831, -4.424922867740668, 9.67554223394205, -0.8502687288362012, 3.1351941328536777, -4.844124443962841, 4.754766492721427, 0.870140923131266, 1.1137966493666094, -1.4131441258277446, 2.418345086057676, 2.4254793474500635, 1.2058772715931956, 0.5825294849801214, 4.536777131050609, 0.10251353649615984, 1.51146113365032, -1.4592806547585204, 3.291502702928505, -1.075428938064348, 1.0559521971759946, -2.4408814841825865, 1.12308565480587, -0.3002420005778045, 2.4751693616737347, -3.6333810904861688, 3.34737386167248, 0.17805269515377548, 3.7250267108754236, -5.189309157660288, 5.579262003298437, 0.24091712079378458, 2.451817967640338, -5.215650064568107, 2.3865116769275567, 0.003640041240486553, 1.4235044885102617, -2.379919268715038, 1.5581599658532437], **"count"**: 0, **"errorcount"**: 0}

The sky's the limit with neural networks. *Take some time now to experiment with different layers and configurations yourself!*

4.8 AutoML approaches

Automated machine learning (AutoML) is a new discipline evolving to help use machines to create and optimize machine learning models. Although we built some models previously, these models are not optimized - meaning that there are certain parameters that you can tune to get more optimal performance of a given family of models.

Let's take the gradient boosting classification algorithm as an example. There are various parameters here - loss, learning_rate, n_estimators, subsample, criterion, min_samples_split, min_samples_leaf, etc. - that affect the model performance (Figure 4.8.1). This often requires some knowledge as to how the model executes its algorithm and can take a long time to become an expert at this for every model. As a result, it is often useful to automatically tune these *hyperparameters* to different values and select a machine learning model that has the best parameters.

Figure 4.8.1   **Tuning parameters for the gradient boosting classifier**
class sklearn.ensemble.**GradientBoostingClassifier**(*loss='deviance', learning_rate=0.1, n_estimators=100, subsample=1.0, criterion='friedman_mse', min_samples_split=2, min_samples_leaf=1, min_weight_fraction_leaf=0.0, max_depth=3, min_impurity_decrease=0.0, min_impurity_split=None, init=None, random_state=None, max_features=None, verbose=0, max_leaf_nodes=None, warm_start=False, presort='auto'*)

This idea can be applied to both simple classification/regression and deep learning problems. We're lucky that there has been a surge of software recently to make it much easier to optimize these hyperparameters.

4.8.1 AutoML techniques for simple classification

The best library I've found for implementing AutoML approaches for simple classification problems is through a library called **TPOT**. The TPOT library uses genetic programming techniques to construct, preprocess, and select feature configurations and models. These models are then tuned with various parameters to get the highest possible accuracy (Figure 4.8.2). The result is an output Python file that you can use to train and validate the model (most of the library is compatible with scikit-learn, which we've been using before). In this way, you don't have to do that much to get quite accurate models.

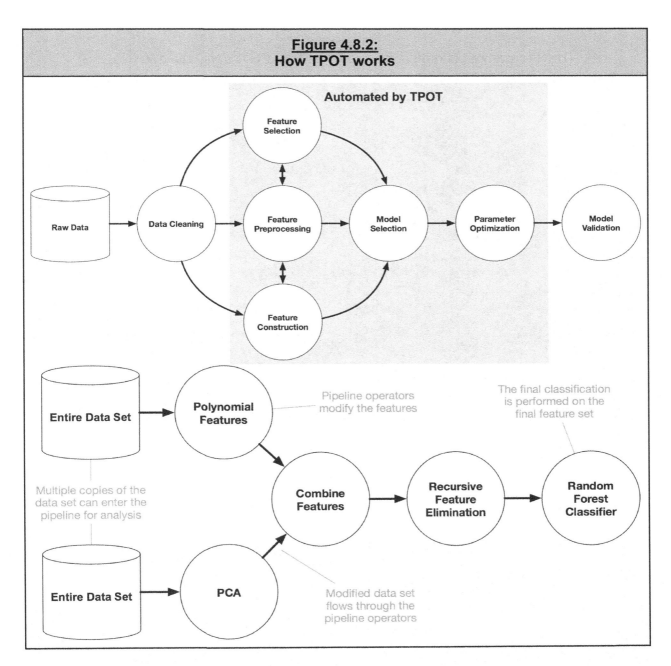

Figure 4.8.2: How TPOT works

We can now obtain an optimized machine learning model by running the TPOT script (*train_audioTPOT.py*). The result will be an output .PICKLE file with the optimized classifier along with a .JSON file with the resulting accuracies and pipeline model type. As you can see, this pipeline achieves a roughly 92.0% accuracy on the data (Figure 4.8.3); not bad!

Figure 4.8.3
How to train a classification model using TPOT: *train_audioTPOT.py*

```
cd ~
cd voicebook/chapter_4_modeling/
python3 train_audioTPOT.py
classification (c) or regression (r) problem?
-> c
what is the name of class 1?
-> africanamerican
what is the name of class 2?
-> controls
>> Generation 1 - Current best internal CV score: 0.9056433904259992
>> Generation 2 - Current best internal CV score: 0.9100878348704435
>> Generation 3 - Current best internal CV score: 0.9100878348704435
>> Generation 4 - Current best internal CV score: 0.9100878348704435
>> Generation 5 - Current best internal CV score: 0.9191787439613526

>> Best pipeline:
LogisticRegression(LogisticRegression(MinMaxScaler(StandardScaler(input_matrix)),
C=1.0, dual=False, penalty=l1), C=5.0, dual=True, penalty=l2)
>> saving classifier to disk
```

We can now load this model as we would any other model with a load script. This time, we use load_audioTPOT.py to run all the TPOT classifiers in the load_dir folder (Figure 4.8.4).

Figure 4.8.4
How to load a TPOT classification model: *load_audioTPOT.py*

```
cd voicebook/chapter_4_modeling
python3 load_audiotpot.py
>> making 0.wav
>> making 1.wav
>> making 2.wav
>> ...
>> making 36.wav
>> making 37.wav
>> making 38.wav
>> controls
```

4.8.2 AutoML techniques for regression

We can also use TPOT for regression-related problems (Figure 4.8.5):

Figure 4.8.5
How to train a regression model using TPOT: *train_audioTPOT.py*

```
cd ~
cd voicebook/chapter_4_modeling/
python3 train_audioTPOT.py

classification (c) or regression (r) problem?
-> r
what is the name of class 1?
-> africanamerican
what is the name of class 2?
-> Controls
>> Generation 1 - Current best internal CV score: -0.06707070707070706
>> Generation 2 - Current best internal CV score: -0.06707070707070706
>> Generation 3 - Current best internal CV score: -0.06707070707070706
>> Generation 4 - Current best internal CV score: -0.062207740346188735
>> Generation 5 - Current best internal CV score: -0.062207740346188735

>> Best pipeline: KNeighborsRegressor(input_matrix, n_neighbors=4, p=1, weights=distance)
>> saving classifier to disk
```

Again, we can use load_audioTPOT.py to run all the TPOT classifiers in the load_dir folder (Figure 4.8.6). This time there is 2 classes output because it will also load the classifier that we trained in the previous section (Section 4.8.1). Note that the *tpotaudio.json* file was deleted before re-running the script so that it could run properly; otherwise, the script would not run because there is already a featurization and TPOT model in the ./load_dir folder.

Figure 4.8.6
How to load a regression model using TPOT: *load_audioTPOT.py*

```
cd voicebook/chapter_4_modeling
python3 load_audiotpot.py
>> making 0.wav
>> making 1.wav
>> making 2.wav
>> ...
>> making 36.wav
>> making 37.wav
>> making 38.wav
>> controls
>> controls
```

4.8.3 AutoML techniques for deep learning

We are only starting to see automated machine learning methods applied to deep learning architectures. Generally, though, the techniques we went through in this chapter should yield pretty good results; *you should only be looking to these solutions if you are trying to get on the range of 1-2% increase in accuracy in a model.*

Specifically, there are companies like H20.AI and DataRobot that help with auto optimizing deep learning hyperparameters for you. Or, you could use cloud-based offering by Google or Amazon. I'd recommend using H20.ai, as they seem like they have the biggest community and they are [cloud provider]-agnostic (Table 4.8.1). Note also there are repositories like Devol or Auto-Keras that you can use for free to optimize Keras deep learning models.[227]

Table 4.8.1
List of AutoML engines and repositories

Library	Pros	Cons
Devol	• Open source (free) • Uses Keras, which is portable to other deep learning frameworks	• Documentation is sparse • Requires a lot of CPU power, may not work for all datasets
Auto-Keras	• 100% open source • Uses Keras, which is portable to other deep learning frameworks	• In alpha mode; some bugs • Optimization is tailored to image-based (as opposed to audio) datasets
clarifai	• Cloud provider agnostic • Free for the first 5,000 operations per month	• Complicated scale-up pricing strategy; unclear of costs • Focuses more on machine vision than speech
H₂O.ai	• Great community; over 155,000 users • Clean interface • Cloud provider agnostic • Rich array of models	• API and documentation could use some work
DataRobot	• Cloud provider agnostic • Drag-and-drop simple interface	• Lack of speech analysis featurization and analysis

---

[227] **Future versions** - I hope to add a tutorial using Auto-Keras and Devol in a future version of this book.

Google Cloud	<ul><li>Can do transfer learning with pre-trained models</li><li>Efficient hardware / TPU performance</li><li>Google is a leader in deep learning with TensorFlow</li></ul>	<ul><li>Relatively high cost</li><li>Dependent on cloud provider (e.g. Google Cloud Platform)</li></ul>
Microsoft Azure	<ul><li>Drag-and-drop interface is very simple</li><li>Can monetize models in the Azure marketplace</li></ul>	<ul><li>Dependent on cloud provider (e.g. Microsoft Azure)</li></ul>

Auto-ML and hyperparameter tuning for deep learning models is a bit beyond the scope of this book. It takes some time to be a veteran deep learning practitioner. However, if you can take multiple classes online for free to refine your knowledge in this area.

4.9 Conclusion

👏 Congrats! You now know how to build machine learning models with voice data. If you're stuck or would like to go deeper than this chapter, check out the documentation for the following datasets and libraries:

- Obtaining training data
    - Common Voice Dataset. https://www.kaggle.com/mozillaorg/common-voice
    - AudioSet. https://research.google.com/audioset/
    - NeuroLex Disease. https://github.com/neurolexdiagnostics/train-diseases
- Data labeling
    - Pandas. http://pandas.pydata.org
    - Xlsxwriter. https://xlsxwriter.readthedocs.io/
    - Pytube. https://github.com/nficano/pytube
- Featurization
    - SpeechRecognition. https://pypi.org/project/SpeechRecognition/
    - LibROSA. https://librosa.github.io
    - PyAudioAnalysis. https://github.com/tyiannak/pyAudioAnalysis
    - SpaCy. https://spacy.io
    - NLTK. http://www.nltk.org
    - Gensim. https://radimrehurek.com/gensim/
- Building machine learning classifiers
    - Numpy. http://www.numpy.org
    - Scikit-learn. https://youtu.be/2kT6QOVSgSg
- Building regression models
    - Statsmodels. https://www.statsmodels.org/stable/index.html
    - Scikit-learn. https://youtu.be/2kT6QOVSgSg
- Deep learning
    - Keras. https://keras.io
    - TensorFlow. https://www.tensorflow.org/
    - Deep learning book. http://neuralnetworksanddeeplearning.com/index.html
    - Udacity class. https://www.udacity.com/course/deep-learning--ud730
- AutoML
    - Auto-Keras. https://autokeras.com/
    - TPOT. https://github.com/EpistasisLab/tpot
    - Devol. https://github.com/joeddav/devol
    - Clarifai. https://clarifai.com/
    - H20.ai. https://www.h2o.ai/
    - DataRobot. https://www.datarobot.com/
    - Google Cloud ML engine. https://cloud.google.com/ml-engine/

In the next chapter we'll delve deep into machine-generated speech samples. Brace yourself for the future of human-machine interactions! 🗣

Chapter 5:
Generation

"Intelligence is the ability to adapt to change."
-Stephen Hawking
(Mathematician and Physicist)

Chapter Overview

The story of Stephen Hawking is perhaps one of the most remarkable stories of all time. A brilliant mathematician, he was diagnosed with Amyolateral Sclerosis (ALS) at just age 21. Having just started graduate school, he was given 2 years to live.

Despite this, he eventually finished his thesis in the area of general relativity and cosmology and went on to be one of the most prolific physicists of our time.

Beyond his incredible willpower, he was able to accomplish all this by embracing novel speech-generating devices.[228] At first, he could generate only a few words. Then he could generate 15 words per minute through a primitive computer program with an American accent. As his condition worsened and older versions became unusable (due to more restrictions in muscle movement), newer versions of speech synthesizers were created using brain waves (EEGs) and facial expressions to communicate speech. These primitive tools allowed for him to continue to contribute to the scientific community up until his death (2018).

This story shows you the power of voice computing. Not only can voice computers help restore functionality to those who have lost their voices, they open up a whole new way for us to augment our own voices as they are now. We can create clones of our own voices, generate new vocabularies and transcription models, and even generate new poems. This allows for voice computers to emit a sense of individuality and creativity in how we interact with others in this ever-changing, IoT-centered world.

This chapter is all about how to use computing platforms to automate the creation of voice content.

Specifically, it will cover:

- **5.1** - Machine-generated voice data
- **5.2** - Generating text data
- **5.3** - Generating audio data
- **5.4** - Generating mixed data

In this way, you can harness the power of large datasets for generative purposes!

---

[228] **As he got older,** he completely lost his voice and resorted to new ways to communicate - for example, with color cards and members of his close family.

5.1 Machine generated voice data

So far, we've discussed how to collect, featurize, and model voice data. What happens when you have collected voice samples from millions of users? Or, even, billions of users?[229]

There are many things you could do with such a dataset. For starters, that's enough data to build highly accurate deep learning models for things like gender detection, accent detection, and/or race detection. But soon you'll solve many of those problems and likely get bored.

Next, you may be thinking about how to monetize such a dataset. Perhaps you could resell this dataset to third parties? Well, maybe; however, doing that could violate some state, national, or international laws. Therefore, you probably want to steer clear of those legal issues.

The next solution may be to generate new, ***machine-generated voice data (MGVD)*** from the existing data. Could you you train a voice computer to have an entire conversation with a human and have the human believe that the computer is a human?[230]

In turns out you can, and you can do much more. For example, this year (2018) Google unveiled **Google Duplex**,[231] a skill on Google Assistant (Figure 5.1.1); this skill can call any restaurant - almost fully understanding the other side (in multiple accents) - and then make a reservation (e.g. schedule haircut appointment). In various demos, the people being called by Duplex thought they were talking to a live person and made the reservation for the machine caller (e.g. 10 am tomorrow). As you can see, machine-generated voice content is becoming increasingly relevant in today's world - bringing forth both an exciting and scary future.

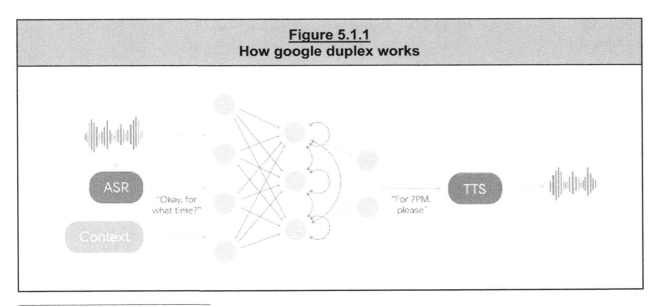

**Figure 5.1.1
How google duplex works**

---

[229] **Big company questions** - These are the questions that companies like Google and others are thinking about.
[230] **The privacy and legal implications** of some of these things are discussed later (Chapter 7), but suffice it to say that we're amid a rapid shift in how people think about privacy and how they license their content. And it's opening up the door for us to have machine be generative mixes of their own minds into technology.
[231] **Google Duplex** – Google Duplex uses natural language understanding, deep learning, and text-to-speech.

The fusion of natural language understanding with text-to-speech systems opens up a window for us to build a machine capable to sustain conversations with humans as if humans cannot tell the difference.[232] Whether good or bad - machine generated voice content is changing and will continue to change the way we interact with technology and the world around us.

There are many other things you can do with a large database of speech samples. For example, you could use the speech transcripts to create a chatbot custom to a specific user, automate a poem around the vocabulary of a unique person, or even summarize a news article in the user's own words. Also, you can generate ultra-realistic voice clones from small snippets of speech and thus build custom text-to-speech models from user-labeled samples in your large repository.[233] [234] The list goes on...

This chapter thus is all about how to generate voice content generally with machines.[235] It's broken up into 3 main types of machine-generated voice data:

- Generating text data (Section 5.2)
- Generating audio data (Section 5.3)
- Generating mixed data (Section 5.4)

Each of these sections will be discussed in the following sections through practical examples.

5.2 Generating text data

Machine-generated text data (MGTD) is text output from machine learning models or software trained on a set of text corpuses.[236] These text corpuses can come from any source - voice transcripts, books, blogs, etc. In this way, we can generate realistic *text samples* from this training data.

There are many types of machine-generated text data (Table 5.2.1). The primary data types include text messages, emails, art pieces, summaries, news articles, or search queries. There are can also be mixes of any of these. Thus, it's powerful to think with this perspective to generate useful text data types for the modern world, especially on publishing platforms like Facebook or smartphones (e.g. text messages/emails).

---

[232] **Voice turing machines** – This is known as a Turing Machine. This has been attempted by large companies - such as through the Amazon's Alexa Prize, a multimillion-dollar competition to build AI that can chat like a human.

[233] **Pros/cons of personal TTS systems** - For example, people may be able to record 30 seconds of your voice and then use it to steal your banking credentials. On the other hand, you may be able to have a "personal AI" that responds with your voice when you are away to augment your workflow.

[234] **Lyrebird** - Check out a company called LyreBird; their mission is to create voice clones (text-to-speech models) from small training sets of speech.

[235] **User vs. group machine-generated generated voice content** - Note could be either at the user-level or group level, depending on the end goal.

[236] **What is a text corpus?** – A text corpus is just a long string of text. For example, a book is a corpus when reduced to a long string in Python.

\multicolumn{2}{c}{**Table 5.2.1**}
\multicolumn{2}{c}{**Types of machine-generated text data**}
Data type	**Description of goal**
Text message	Generate a text message answer from a prior text message (or a random message).
Email	Generate an email response from an incoming email (or a random message).
Text art	Generate a random poem from a list of prior poems.
Summary	Generate a summary of all the emails you have received during the day.
News article	Generate a news article from a list of all the news articles published during the day.
Blog post	Generate a blog post from a list of prior blog posts. (e.g. Wordpress feed or some other feed).
Chatbot queries	Generate a search query response from an input and and intent and then access information as a response.

Let's start out generating some *text messages*. We can use the text message corpus available in the ./chapter_5_generation/data/ folder for this task. All you need to do is unzip this file in the ./data folder and then run the *generate_text.py* script. Since we're training on 54,919 texts, it could take a while (~ 1.25 hours). Note that depending on the temperature you get more or less casual responses (Figure 5.2.1). This is a pretty good result after only 1 training epoch!

Figure 5.2.1
Generating text messages: *generate_text.py*

```
cd ~
cd voicebook/chapter_5_generation/
python3 generate_text.py
>> 54,919 texts collected.
>> Training on 2,887,069 character sequences.
>> Epoch 1/1
  118/22555 [..............................] - ETA: 1:25:28 - loss: 2.3823
11508/22555 [==============>...............] - ETA: 28:44 - loss: 1.8921
19778/22555 [==========================>...] - ETA: 7:32 - loss: 1.8588
22555/22555 [==============================] - 3707s 164ms/step - loss: 1.8509
```

```
####################
Temperature: 0.5
####################
```

Ok i can have the inside to confirm the room to go to meet u all in the place prepare to come to be at hair. Haha. Thanks!

Ehh ok. Thanks! I dunno in the plan profe late to go me to prois already and like the things and my check time lol

Shall see <#> to me true late on the rest time to contell on the class money to reply my mrt reply.

Using a similar strategy, we can generate some **emails**.[237] Let's use a subset of the ENRON email dataset as our training corpus. Specifically, we can use allen-p's sent messages in the ENRON dataset to generate new emails. I've prepared this data as 'emails.txt' in the ./chapter_5_generation/data directory (Figure 5.2.2).

Figure 5.2.2
Generating emails: *generate_email.py (top), terminal (middle), output (bottom)*

```python
import os, json
from textgenrnn import textgenrnn

# now use textgenrnn to train a model (1 epoch = faster)
os.chdir('data')
textgen = textgenrnn()
textgen.train_from_file('emails.txt', num_epochs=1)

# now generate new text messages
newmsgs=list()
for i in range(10):
    newmsg=textgen.generate()
    print(str(i)+': '+newmsg)
    newmsg.append(newmsgs)
```

```
cd ~
cd voicebook/chapter_5_generation
python3 generate_email.py
>> Using TensorFlow backend.
>> 601 texts collected.
>> Training on 521,976 character sequences.
>> Epoch 1/1
   24/4077 [..............................] - ETA: 17:35 - loss: 2.4576
```

---

[237] **Note** - You can download all your emails using Google Takeout (if you are a gmail user). https://takeout.google.com

> Lucy,
>
> I will be on a reviewer on a fund to bring the formation on the Steve Englide with a consummisse for the designards to track on the contracts to computer to out of the description to trade the to the profit state to pay the process.

Now let's generate some ***text art pieces.*** Over the span of my college years, I wrote over 60 poems. Many were quite melancholic and existential, but one structure I really enjoyed building is the ABQBA structure - with the Q representing a question and As and Bs rhyming at the end. Knowing this, we can generate some new poems from prior poems I've written. You can easily restrict a syntactical structure using NLTK or a similar library to parse through all the content of the poems and generate a poem; however, getting things like singular/plural verbs and grammar paths can be sometimes challenging and requires a bit more effort to code properly. Here's a short script in Python on how to do this (*generate_poem.py*).

<u>Figure 5.2.3</u>
Generating poems: *generate_poem.py (top), ./data/voice.txt (bottom)*

```
cd ~
cd voicebook/chapter_5_generation
python3 generate_poem.py
would you like a random poem?
-> n
what is the name of the poem? (noun)
-> voice
what is the description?
-> a short poem about voices.
```

Voice

I seek a religious-emotional Voice
The systems– is approximate
Why is it still to go?
The forces is subjective
The things is a implicitly, transcendence

I seek a fruitful Voice
The Yesterday is illimitable
Why is it about to know?
The year is false
The journey. is a little, disease

I seek a challenging Voice
The tension. is changeable
Why is it only to pursue?
The other. is speculative
The consciousness. is a sensibly. pure

> I seek a happiness Voice
> The towards is stable
> Why is it again to come?
> The hopes is human-machine
> The species; is a divergent game
>
> I seek a estimating Voice
> The acumen is subjective
> Why is it ceaselessly to white,?
> The reliance. is consummate
> The proof is a peripheral house

Text summarization is the discipline of compressing large corpuses of text (e.g. long articles) into shorter summaries.[238] You can think of research papers; they are summarized in terms of abstracts. In a similar way, we can quickly summarize books or large text files through simple manipulations. We can use the **sumy** library to insert a URL (e.g. a Wikipedia URL) and get back a 10-sentence summary (Figure 5.2.3).

Figure 5.2.4
Summarize wikipedia article: *generate_summary.py*

```
cd ~
cd voicebook/chapter_5_generation
python3 generate_summary.py
what file type is this (t) for text, (w) for website.
-> w
what link would you like to summarize on Wikipedia?
-> https://en.wikipedia.org/wiki/Information_technology
```

Humans have been storing, retrieving, manipulating, and communicating information since the Sumerians in Mesopotamia developed writing in about 3000 BC, [3] but the term information technology in its modern sense first appeared in a 1958 article published in the Harvard Business Review ; authors Harold J. Leavitt and Thomas L. Whisler commented that "the new technology does not yet have a single established name. Their definition consists of three categories: techniques for processing, the application of statistical and mathematical methods to decision-making , and the simulation of higher-order thinking through computer programs. Several products or services within an economy are associated with information technology, including computer hardware , software, electronics, semiconductors, internet, telecom equipment , and e-commerce . Based on the storage and processing technologies employed, it is possible to distinguish four distinct phases of IT development: pre-mechanical (3000 BC – 1450 AD), mechanical (1450–1840), electromechanical (1840–1940), and electronic (1940–present). Comparable geared devices did not emerge in Europe until the 16th century, and it was not until 1645 that the first mechanical calculator capable of performing the four basic arithmetical operations was developed. The development of transistors in the late 1940s at Bell Laboratories allowed a new generation of computers to be designed with greatly reduced power consumption. Although XML data can be stored in normal file systems , it is commonly held in relational databases to take advantage of their "robust implementation verified by years of both theoretical and practical effort".
... [continued reference section]

---

[238] **Text summarization** - The field within natural language processing that aims to take a large corpus of text and summarize it into its most important components. You can do this through abstractive (abstracting main ideas and summarizing them) or extractive methods (extracting pieces in document).

Moreover, you may want to generate a ***news article*** or a ***blog post*** automatically (Figure 5.2). If you're like me, I get lazy writing pieces to post on LinkedIn; you could randomly generate a blog post (trained from AI articles, etc.), edit this post for errors, and then publish this online as if it were your own. There's a dataset called the Blog corpus[239] that we can use to generate some blog posts, much like we did earlier with text messages and emails (Figure 5.2.5). You may not even know the difference!

<u>**Figure 5.2.5**</u>
Generate blog posts: *generate_blogpost.py*

```
cd voicebook/chapter_5_generation
python3 generate_blogpost.py
>> 1,850 texts collected.
>> Training on 2,399,298 character sequences.
>> Epoch 1/1
   257/18744 [..........................] - ETA: 1:05:57 - loss: 1.8847
>> I think I am sure if is the care with this is the includes and did I could tell
it in the summer company. You can add out of the taster age and again, the path and
i was the exciting in the swirl that is some inversed to talk to child of summing
at the one... we were because its a bad with my heart
```

Lastly, ***chatbots*** have emerged as an interface for machine-generated text data.[240] Specifically, the goal of chatbots is to engineer an interface where you can submit a query and then receive a response. There often is some vertical goal here - like streamlining customer service queries or acting as a frequently-asked-questions (FAQ) page on a website. Luckily, Python has a well-documented library for building chatbots called ***ChatterBot***. In the example below, we parse through a FAQ page on a website with BeautifulSoup and then train a chatbot on all these questions and answers (Figure 5.2.6).

<u>**Figure 5.2.6**</u>
Generating a chatbot from FAQ training data: *make_chatbot.py*

```
from chatbot.trainers import ListTrainer
from chatterbot import ChatBot
import os, requests
from bs4 import BeautifulSoup

# works on Drupal FAQ forms
page=requests.get('http://cyberlaunch.vc/faq-page')
soup=BeautifulSoup(page.content, 'lxml')
```

---

[239] **Blog Corpus** – this dataset is available at this link: http://u.cs.biu.ac.il/~koppel/BlogCorpus.htm
[240] **Smarterchild** - the earliest chatbot that I recall was Smartchild on AOL's instant messenger (AIM). You can type in a query and you'd get back a response. You could also call people directly with this system and type in speech, which was interesting.

```python
g=soup.find_all(class_="faq-question-answer")
y=list()

# initialize chatbot parameters
chatbot = ChatBot("CyberLaunch")
chatbot.set_trainer(ListTrainer)

# parse through soup and get Q&A
for i in range(len(g)):
    entry=g[i].get_text().replace('\xa0','').split('   \n\n')
    newentry=list()
    for j in range(len(entry)):
        if j==0:
            qa=entry[j].replace('\n','')
            newentry.append(qa)
        else:
            qa=entry[j].replace('\n',' ').replace('   ','')
            newentry.append(qa)

    y.append(newentry)

# train chatbot with Q&A training corpus
for i in range(len(y)):
    question=y[i][0]
    answer=y[i][1]
    print(question)
    print(answer)

    chatbot.train([
        question,
        answer,
        ])

# now ask the user 2 sample questions to get response.
for i in range(2):
    question=input('how can I help you?')
    response = chatbot.get_response(question)
    print(response)
```

Now if we run this chatbot we can query it and get some answers (Figure 5.2.7). In this way, text-generated content can be easily fetched from user queries in a logically consistent way.

Figure 5.2.7
Engaging with a chatbot via CLI

```
cd ~
cd voicebook/chapter_5_generation
python3 make_chatbot.py
how can I help you?
-> when is demo day?
>> Our Summer 16' Demo Day will be on August 25, 2016. Please visit
demoday.cyberlaunch.vc for more information.

how can I help you?
-> where are you located?
>> Our office is located in Technology Square - Georgia's ground zero for
innovation. Visit www.cyberlaunch.vc/contact for the address and directions.
```

In summary, machine-genereated text content is quite powerful. It can be used for an array of purposes in voice computing – from composing poetry to even building chatbots. Hopefully you feel a bit inspired to build upon these ideas to generate text useful to your daily life.

5.3 Generating audio data

Machine-generated audio data (MGAD) is audio data generated from a machine. At first, you may think of MGAD only as speech data generated from a text-to-speech (TTS) model, but this definition goes far beyond that to include filtered voice samples, audio summaries, and even audio art forms (Table 5.3.1). In other words, MGAD creates new raw audio from some training set of audio samples.

Table 5.3.1
Types of machine-generated audio data

Data type	Description of goal
Text-to-speech model	Build a custom text-to-speech model from a few voice snippets.
Filtered audio sample	Add a filter to a voice sample - such as lowering/increasing the voice frequency for voice obfuscation, de-noising for voice enhancement, or manipulating the voice to sound like someone else.
Audio summary	Remix various pieces of audio together.
Audio art forms	Creating new audio pieces that could be perceived as art pieces.

Let's start out with a **text-to-speech (TTS) model**. We can easily save new voice samples generated from a TTS model with Apple's internal voice library[241] (Figure 5.3.1). When you run the *generate_tts.py* script there will be 2 folders created in the current directory: *./tts-incoming* and *./tts-processed*. The script looks for incoming .TXT files (in *./tts-incoming* folder) and makes these .TXT files into .WAV files (in the *./tts-processed* folder). In the following example, I make a TTS file of the machine-generated poem that we created earlier by placing it in the *./tts-incoming* folder ('voice.txt' → 'voice.wav' → 55 seconds). *Feel free to listen to the file (it will be in the ./chapter_5_generation/data directory), or make a few files yourself before moving on.*

Figure 5.3.1
Generating TTS files locally with Python (in terminal): *generate_tts.py*

```
python3 generate_tts.py
>> ['Voice.txt']
>> Voice.txt found, processing...
>> Voice
>> making tts file...
>> Voice.aiff
>> converting Voice.aiff to Voice.wav
>> Voice.wav
>> sleeping..
```

You can also create MGAD by taking an audio input and manipulating it with **audio filters**. These filters can be used to obfuscate the voice sample, enhance the voice sample, or manipulate the voice sample in other ways - such as increasing the pitch. Let's now take the sample we created (*'Voice.wav'*) and manipulate it a few times before moving on. In the following example, we make three manipulations to this voice file; specifically, we make it 1) sound lower ('Voice_slow.wav'); 2) become obfuscated by changing the pitch ('Voice_lowpitch.wav'); 3) sound noisy by adding a beeping sound in the background ('Voice_noise.wav'). In this way, you can customize the playback of audio media to end users. *For a more detailed section on how to use SoX to manipulate audio, check back to Chapter 2 (section 2.5 - pages 84-90).*

Figure 5.3.2
Manipulating audio (in terminal): *generate_filtered.py*

```
cd ~
cd voicebook/chapter_5_generation
python3 generate_filtered.py
what is the name of the wav file (in ./data/ dir) you would like to manipulate?
-> Voice.wav
>> Voice_lowpitch.wav, Voice_noise.wav, and Voice_slow.wav output in current dir
```

---

[241] **Commercial use -** Do not use this software commercially; Apple limits you from doing this with their licenses. You would be better off using WaveNet models built from Google's text-to-speech API.

Lastly, you can stitch various audio files together to summarize a session – something known as ***audio summarization.***[242] Let's assume we have 5 voice samples collected from various people. You can take some random splices of these audio samples and then summarize it with a remixed audio file with the *generate_remix.py* script (Figure 5.3.3).

Figure 5.3.3
Remixing audio (in terminal): *generate_remix.py*

```
cd ~
cd voicebook/chapter_5_generation
python3 generate_splice.py
what folder (in ./data folder) do you want to create splices for?
-> mix
how long (in secs) do you want the splices
-> 2
# generated files >> snipped_Voice_lowpitch.wav, snipped_Voice_noise.wav,
snipped_Voice_slow.wav, snipped_Voice.wav
python3 generate_remix.py
what folder (in ./data directory) would you like to remix?
-> mix_snipped
# generated files >> remix-normalized.wav, remix.wav
```

There's much more you can do with machine-generated audio data; for example, adding noise into datasets may be useful for training machine learning models that are more robust in noisy environments. Also, you may be able to create new audio art pieces by remixing audio together; you may find these remixes more useful than playing back text summaries. Nonetheless, hopefully you've become more interested to learn more and can now practically apply this mindset to your code base.

5.4   Generating mixed data

Machine-generated mixed data (MGMD) is machine-generated text and audio data used together. MGMD often has the end goal of being able to parse through user intents and respond intelligently to user queries.

Voice-enabled chatbots are perhaps the most important use case for MGMD. In this scenario, a chatbot is tied to a user query. Then, user queries are are filtered to identify an intent. This intent drives an action by the chatbot - such as grabbing the weather. In this way, you can embed voice queries into chatbot interfaces.

Let's quickly extend the chatbot we built before to have voice capability (Figure 5.4.1):

---

[242] **Voice art -** You can mix audio summarization methods with random filtering to similarly create voice art. In some cases, the remixes themselves can be perceived as art pieces. Again, this is kind of a new area of research.

Figure 5.4.1
Voice chatbot as a form of mixed data: *make_vchatbot.py*

```python
from chatterbot.trainers import ListTrainer
from chatterbot import ChatBot
import os, requests
from bs4 import BeautifulSoup
import speech_recognition as sr_audio
import sounddevice as sd
import soundfile as sf
import pyttsx3, time

# define some helper functions
def sync_record(filename, duration, fs, channels):
    print('recording')
    myrecording = sd.rec(int(duration * fs), samplerate=fs, channels=channels)
    sd.wait()
    sf.write(filename, myrecording, fs)
    print('done recording')

def transcribe_sphinx(file):
    r=sr_audio.Recognizer()
    with sr_audio.AudioFile(file) as source:
        audio = r.record(source)
    transcript=r.recognize_sphinx(audio)
    print('sphinx transcript: '+transcript)

    return transcript

def speak_text(text):
    engine = pyttsx3.init()
    engine.say(text)
    engine.runAndWait()

# works on Drupal FAQ forms
page=requests.get('http://cyberlaunch.vc/faq-page')
soup=BeautifulSoup(page.content, 'lxml')
g=soup.find_all(class_="faq-question-answer")
y=list()

# initialize chatbot parameters
chatbot = ChatBot("CyberLaunch")
chatbot.set_trainer(ListTrainer)

# parse through soup and get Q&A
for i in range(len(g)):
```

```python
            entry=g[i].get_text().replace('\xa0','').split('   \n\n')
            newentry=list()
            for j in range(len(entry)):
                if j==0:
                    qa=entry[j].replace('\n','')
                    newentry.append(qa)
                else:
                    qa=entry[j].replace('\n',' ').replace('     ','')
                    newentry.append(qa)

            y.append(newentry)

# train chatbot with Q&A training corpus
for i in range(len(y)):
    question=y[i][0]
    answer=y[i][1]
    print(question)
    print(answer)

    chatbot.train([
        question,
        answer,
        ])

# now ask the user 2 sample questions to get response.
for i in range(2):
    speak_text('how can I help you?')
    # record a voice sample
    sync_record('sample.wav', 5, 16000, 1)
    # transcribe this voice sample and remove the audio
    question=transcribe_sphinx('sample.wav')
    os.remove('sample.wav')
    # speak_text('okay, processing...')
    response = chatbot.get_response(question)
    # speak the response instead of playing it on screen
    print(str(response))
    speak_text(str(response))
```

I'm going to skip elaborating on mixed data because we are going to build our own chatbot later - called Nala. If this is something that interests you, feel free to skip to Chapter 8 - designing voice computers. 😊

5.5 Conclusion

👏 Woo hoo! You now know how to generate text, audio, and mixed data with machines.

If you'd like to explore this area further, check out the documentation below:

- Text data
    - Textgenrnn. https://github.com/minimaxir/textgenrnn
    - Sumy. https://github.com/miso-belica/sumy
    - Chatterbot. https://github.com/gunthercox/ChatterBot
    - NLTK. https://www.nltk.org/
    - SpaCy. https://spacy.io/
    - ENRON dataset. https://www.cs.cmu.edu/~./enron/
    - NUS-SMS-corpus. https://github.com/WING-NUS/nus-sms-corpus
    - Blog corpus. http://u.cs.biu.ac.il/~koppel/BlogCorpus.htm
    - 20 newsgroups. http://scikit-learn.org/stable/datasets/twenty_newsgroups.html
- Audio data
    - LibROSA. https://librosa.github.io/librosa/
    - pySoundFile. https://pysoundfile.readthedocs.io/en/0.9.0/
    - Random. https://docs.python.org/2/library/random.html
- Mixed data
    - Chatterbot. https://github.com/gunthercox/ChatterBot
    - Pyttsx3. https://github.com/nateshmbhat/pyttsx3
    - PocketSphinx. https://github.com/cmusphinx/pocketsphinx
- Modeling
    - Keras. https://keras.io/
    - TensorFlow. https://keras.io/

The next chapter focuses on data visualization. In this way, you will be able summarize voice data to non-programmers. ✓

Chapter 6:
Visualizations

"Simple can be harder than complex: you have to work hard to get your thinking clean to make it simple."
-Steve Jobs
(Co-Founder, Apple)

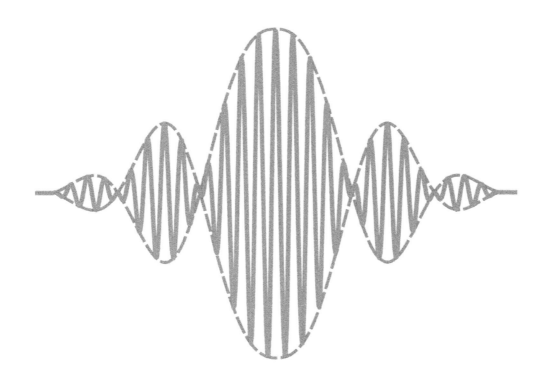

Chapter Overview

Voice data is truly information-rich. It contains audio features (e.g. MFCC coefficients), text features (e.g. sentiment polarity), mixed features (e.g. average the pause length after the word 'the' in the session), and meta features (e.g. age extracted with a machine learning model).[243] [244] Due to the many forms it can take, complicated visualizations permeate throughout the voice computing field.

Making voice data simple to understand for non-scientists is quite difficult.[245] Therefore, this chapter proposes some template scripts to guide you in visualizing voice data.

Specifically, we'll cover:

- **6.1** - Visualization libraries
- **6.2** - Visualizing audio features
- **6.3** - Visualizing text features
- **6.4** - Visualizing mixed features
- **6.5** - Visualizing meta features

In this way, we can *work hard to get your thinking clean* to communicate voice datasets to non-programmers.

---

[243] **I'm a functional type of person**. I buy a computer to code; I buy a small table to eat food on. I often don't make decisions based on design or aesthetics. Therefore, data visualization is not one of my strengths. I often use Matplotlib graphs as long as it can accomplish my goals.

[244] **Feature strategies** - For audio features, I find myself plotting audio data as spectrograms - which try to plot the relationship between frequency, power, and time in one graph. For text features, I often use Matplotlib or other libraries to make simple visualizations to compare text features across groups (e.g. noun frequencies). For mixed features, I often find creative ways to superimpose text on top of spectrograms in ways that make sense.

[245] **Steve Jobs** truly is the pinnacle of someone who has taken something very complex - a smartphone - and made it so simple that even children could use it intuitively. We still have yet to find a Steve Jobs of voice computing, as most of the people who have contributed to the field are formally trained scientists.

6.1 Visualization libraries

There are many libraries you could look into as well as a starting point for data visualization in Python (Table 6.1.1). The libraries I use most to visualize data are Matplotlib, Bokeh, and Missingno. Matplotlib is the legacy library in Python for plotting just about anything; it's often useful for a first pass at the data you are trying to analyze. Bokeh, on the other hand, creates output visualizations for web browsers - which is useful if you're trying to build client-facing applications. Missingno is useful to visualize missing data; I use it to get a quick glance of the dataset at hand to make sure it is complete. Together, this suite of visualization tools can be used to solve most problems that you will likely face.

Table 6.1.1 Visualization libraries in Python		
Library	**Description**	**Example plot**
Matplotlib	Can do pretty much anything - including make line plots, multiple subplots, display background images in graphs, contour graphs, histograms, paths in graphs, 3D plots, streamplots, ellipses, bar charts, pie charts, tables, scatter plots, GUI widgets, filled curves, date graphs, log plots, polar plots, and even make Xkcd-style plots. *Matplotlib is usually my 'go-to' to start with, and if I can't make the visualizations I need with this library I look to alternative libraries.*	
Seaborn	Seaborn is a Python data visualization library based on Matplotlib. It provides a high-level interface for drawing attractive and informative statistical graphics	
Ggplot	A plotting system for Python based on R's ggplot2 and the Grammar of Graphics. It is built for making professional looking, plots quickly with minimal code.	

Bokeh	Bokeh is an interactive visualization library that targets modern web browsers for presentation. Its goal is to provide elegant, concise construction of versatile graphics, and to extend this capability with high-performance interactivity over very large or streaming datasets.	
Pygal	Simple alternative to Matplotlib; ever-growing community with pretty good documentation.	
Plotly Dash	Build beautiful web-based interfaces in Python Dash is a Python framework for building analytical web applications. No JavaScript required. Built on top of Plotly.js, React, and Flask, Dash ties modern UI elements like dropdowns, sliders, and graphs to your analytical Python code.	*Plotly dash was recently released as opensource software!*
Geoplotlib	Useful to plot geographical data.	
Gleam	Good for scatterplots and interactive visualizations.	
Missingno	Useful to visualize which features are missing and build heatmaps for feature visualizations and to discover geographical trends in data.	

| Leather | Simple plots quickly. Useful for bar charts, scatter plots, and line charts. | 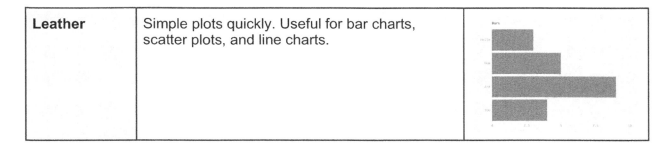 |

Note that depending on your end goal any of the libraries laid out in Table 6.1.1 can be useful to you. I'll leave it to you to look to each library's documentation; most of these libraries are fairly well documented with coding examples to get you started.

6.2 Visualizing audio features

There are two types of audio data that can be visualized: *streaming (real-time) audio data* and *recorded audio data.* **Real-time audio data** is data collected instantaneously and **recorded audio data** is data that has been collected in the past.

For visualizing audio data in real-time, we can record short snippets of audio (e.g. 20 milliseconds) and then use these recordings to extract features in near-real-time. Then we plot these features in the terminal as an output print statement based on the average RMS energy during each 20-millisecond period (Figure 6.2.1). Although primitive, this example quickly shows you how you could tune various acoustic features to sound visualizations. *Note that this script normalizes to the maximum RMS energy so that the plot is relevant to your environment.*

Figure 6.2.1
Visualizing streaming audio data in Python: *audio_stream.py, audio_stream.txt*

```
import sounddevice as sd
import soundfile as sf
import random, time, librosa, os
import numpy as np

def visualize_data(sample, minimum, maximum):
    difference=maximum-minimum
    delta=difference/10
    bar='==.==.' 246
    if sample <= minimum:
        # 1 bar
        output=bar
    elif minimum+delta >= sample > minimum:
```

---

[246] **Manipulate bar** - feel free to manipulate this to whatever bar visualization you'd like - could be '==' or '--' or '=.=.=.' If you do change it, be sure to change the output at end to not be output[0:-1] but rather whatever you'd like to represent.

```python
            # 1 bar
            output=bar
        elif minimum+delta*2 >= sample > minimum+delta:
            # 2 bars
            output=bar*2
        elif minimum+delta*3 >= sample >= minimum+delta*2:
            # 3 bars
            output=bar*3
        elif minimum+delta*4 >= sample > minimum+delta*3:
            # 4 bars
            output=bar*4
        elif minimum+delta*5 >= sample > minimum+delta*4:
            # 5 bars
            output=bar*5
        elif minimum+delta*6 >= sample > minimum+delta*5:
            # 6 bars
            output=bar*6
        elif minimum+delta*7 >= sample > minimum+delta*6:
            # 7 bars
            output=bar*7
        elif minimum+delta*8 >= sample > minimum+delta*7:
            # 8 bards
            output=bar*8
        elif minimum+delta*9 >= sample > minimum+delta*8:
            # 9 bars
            output=bar*9
        elif maximum > sample >= minimum+delta*9:
            # 10 bars
            output=bar*10
        elif sample >= maximum:
            # 10 bars
            output=bar*10
        else:
            print(sample)
            output='error'

    # plot bars based on a min and max
    return output[0:-1]

def record_data(filename, duration, fs, channels):
    # synchronous recording
    myrecording = sd.rec(int(duration * fs), samplerate=fs, channels=channels)
    sd.wait()
    sf.write(filename, myrecording, fs)
    y, sr = librosa.load(filename)
    rmse=np.mean(librosa.feature.rmse(y)[0])
```

```python
    os.remove(filename)

    return rmse*1000

# take a streaming sample and then put that data as it is being recorded
minimum=0
maximum=70
samples=list()

for i in range(100):
    # record 20ms of data
    sample=record_data('sample.wav',0.02, 44100, 1)
    if sample > maximum:
        maximum=sample
        print('new max is %s'%(maximum))
    samples.append(sample)
    #print(sample)
    print(visualize_data(sample,minimum,maximum))

    # other stuff - if you'd like to sleep or generate random samples
    # keep going streaming
    # randomize data
    # sample=random.randint(0,30)
    #time.sleep(0.2)
samples=np.array(samples)
minval=np.amin(samples)
maxval=np.amax(samples)
print('minimum val: %s'%(str(minval)))
print('max val: %s'%(str(maxval)))
```

We can get a bit more creative and also plot paths of the RMS power over time as the streaming samples come in (Figure 6.2.2). **Path plotting** is useful to see how local samples compare to their neighbors (or samples that come before and/or after). In general, I use this technique to see if there are any obvious outliers when recording a sample. If there seem to be some outliers, it may indicate a defective microphone or microphone cable.

Figure 6.2.1
Visualizing streaming audio data paths in Python: *audio_path.py*

```python
import sounddevice as sd
import soundfile as sf
import random, time, librosa, os
import numpy as np
import matplotlib.pyplot as plt
from drawnow import drawnow

def make_fig():
    plt.scatter(x, y)
def record_data(filename, duration, fs, channels):
    # synchronous recording
    myrecording = sd.rec(int(duration * fs), samplerate=fs, channels=channels)
    sd.wait()
    sf.write(filename, myrecording, fs)
    y, sr = librosa.load(filename)
    rmse=np.mean(librosa.feature.rmse(y)[0])
    os.remove(filename)

    return rmse*1000
# initialize plot
plt.ion()  # enable interactivity
fig = plt.figure()  # make a figure
x = list()
y = list()
for i in range(100):
    # record 20ms of data
    sample=record_data('sample.wav',0.02, 44100, 1)
    x.append(i)
    y.append(sample)
    drawnow(make_fig)
plt.savefig('stream.png')
os.system('open stream.png')
```

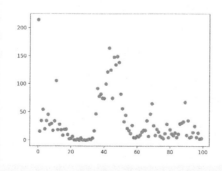

Spectrograms are perhaps the most powerful and universal representation of audio data. Specifically, spectrograms plot the frequency, time, and power together in one graph. This allows you to quickly spot periodic patterns over time. Changes in intensity of colors help to see how power relates to frequency. Often, it's easy to see where there is the most activity.

Let's dive into making some spectrograms with LibROSA (Figure 6.2.2). This script takes in an audio file and plots various spectrograms on different scales (linear-frequency power, log-frequency-power, constant-Q power with notes, constant-Q power in Hz, chromagram, linear power spectrogram, log-power spectrogram, and a tempogram). *Note that sometimes it is better to view spectrograms on logarithmic scales and power in dB, as it's easier to notice frequency and power changes this way.*

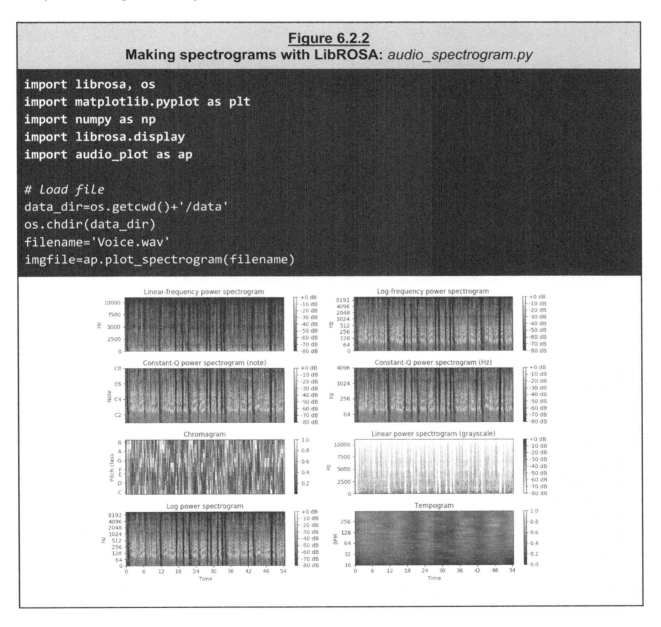

It's also useful to know how to plot many files at once. Here is a short script to plot audio files in a folder in terms of their frequency spectrum and oscillograms (Figure 6.2.3).

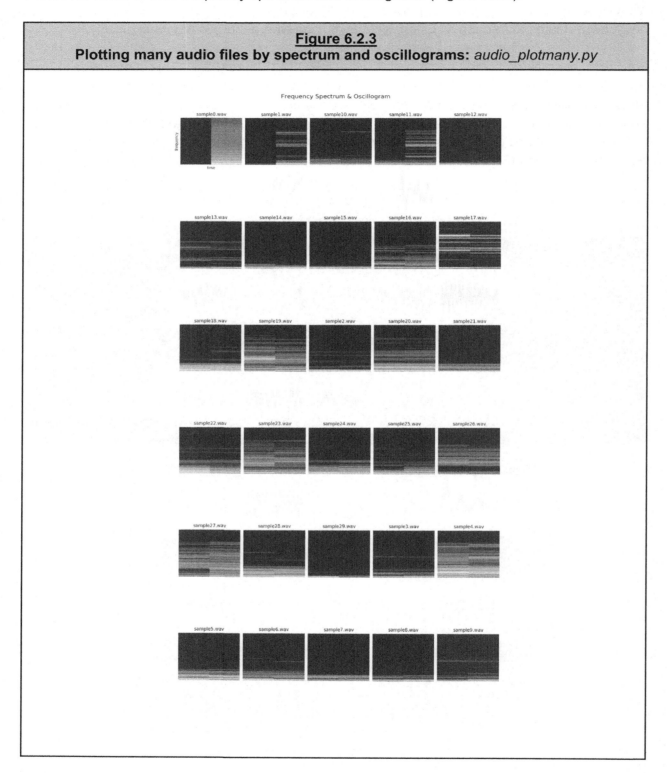

Figure 6.2.3
Plotting many audio files by spectrum and oscillograms: *audio_plotmany.py*

You can similarly plot the ***spectral power densities*** in Matplotlib (Figure 6.2.4). The spectral power density is a useful measure to determine the net power of a signal over various frequencies. Spectral power density is a good global measure of the behavior audio waveforms. Since these are 20-millisecond windows, you can clearly see which segments are silent by just the behavior of the PSD plot - *a good alternative than looking through numpy arrays!* 😊

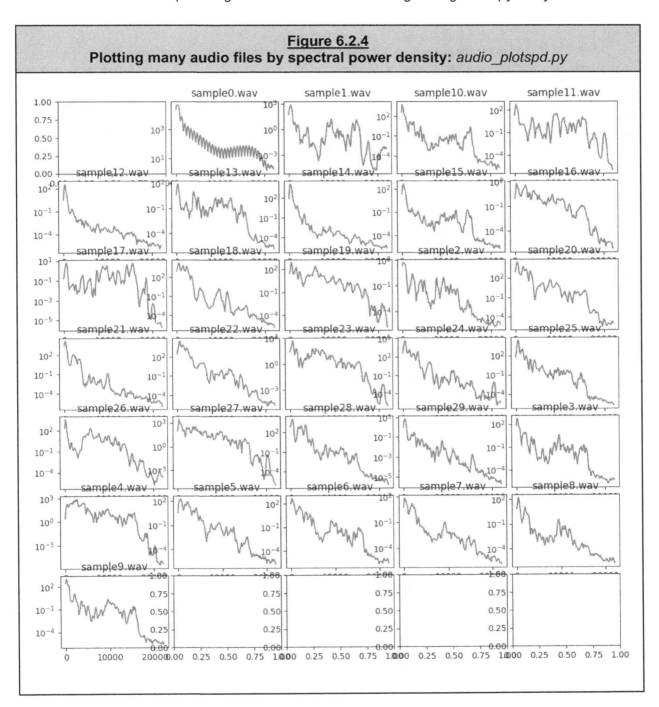

Figure 6.2.4
Plotting many audio files by spectral power density: *audio_plotspd.py*

You can also group samples over time with clustering techniques such as **k-means clustering**.[247] In this case, the root mean squared energy (RMSE) and MFCC coefficient 1 are used as features to separate the groups through a k-means clustering model (Figure 6.2.5). In this way, you can quickly visualize how classes are shifting throughout a time series array of audio samples.[248]

Figure 6.2.4
Clustering audio files with k-means clustering: *audio_cluster.py*

```python
import os, librosa
import scipy.io.wavfile as wav
from sklearn.cluster import KMeans
import matplotlib.pyplot as plt
import numpy as np


#######################################################################
##      MAIN CODE BASE                                               ##
#######################################################################

os.chdir('data/samples')
listdir=os.listdir()
wavfiles=list()
for i in range(len(listdir)):
    if listdir[i][-4:]=='.wav':
        wavfiles.append(listdir[i])
wavfiles=sorted(wavfiles)
samples=list()
for i in range(len(wavfiles)):
    y, sr = librosa.core.load(wavfiles[i])
    rmse=np.mean(librosa.feature.rmse(y)[0])
    mfcc=np.mean(librosa.feature.mfcc(y)[0])
    samples.append(np.array([rmse, mfcc]))

kmeans = KMeans(3, max_iter = 1000, n_init = 100)
kmeans.fit_transform(samples)
predictions = kmeans.predict(samples)

x=list()
y=list()
for i in range(len(predictions)):
    x.append(i)
    y.append(predictions[i])
```

---

[247] **Vector quantization** – Recall that vector quantization is also known as k-means clustering.
[248] **Dimensionality reduction techniques** - Note you could do this with any other sort of dimensionality reduction technique as well - like principal component analysis (PCA), as discussed in Chapter 3.

```python
x0=list()
x1=list()
x2=list()
y0=list()
y1=list()
y2=list()

for i in range(len(y)):
    if y[i] == 0:
        x0.append(x[i])
        y0.append(y[i])
    elif y[i] == 1:
        x1.append(x[i])
        y1.append(y[i])
    elif y[i] == 2:
        x2.append(x[i])
        y2.append(y[i])

plt.scatter(x0, y0, marker='o', c='black')
plt.scatter(x1, y1, marker='o', c='blue')
plt.scatter(x2, y2, marker='o', c='red')
plt.xlabel('sample number')
plt.ylabel('k means class')
plt.savefig('kmeans.png')
```

These six quick examples should give you some intuition as to how to visualize audio features. *Definitely try to tune these coding examples with different audio feature sets and models; you'll get the hang of it quickly!*

6.3 Visualizing text features

Recall that ***text features*** are features extracted from audio file transcripts. Similar to audio features, text features can be extracted in either a streaming or non-streaming manner.

To visualize ***streaming text features***, let's stream words on the screen that are spoken every second. Again, this is a super simple example of a visualization by just a text output on the screen, much like what we did with the bars to visualize streaming audio features.

Figure 6.3.1
Plotting words in real-time: *text_stream.py, recordings.json*

```python
import os, json, shutil
import speech_recognition as sr_audio
import sounddevice as sd
import soundfile as sf

def transcribe_pocket(filename):
    # transcribe the audio (note this is only done if a voice sample)
    r=sr_audio.Recognizer()
    with sr_audio.AudioFile(filename) as source:
        audio = r.record(source)
    text=r.recognize_sphinx(audio)

    return text

def sync_record(filename, duration, fs, channels):
    #print('recording')
    myrecording = sd.rec(int(duration * fs), samplerate=fs, channels=channels)
    sd.wait()
    sf.write(filename, myrecording, fs)
    #print('done recording')

# set recording params
duration=1
fs=44100
channels=1

try:
    os.mkdir('recordings')
    os.chdir(os.getcwd()+'/recordings')
except:
```

```
    shutil.rmtree('recordings')
    os.mkdir('recordings')
    os.chdir(os.getcwd()+'/recordings')

filenames=list()
transcripts=list()
for i in range(30):
    filename='%s.wav'%(str(i))
    sync_record(filename, duration, fs, channels)
    transcript=transcribe_pocket(filename)
    # print transcript on screen
    print(transcript)
    filenames.append(filename)
    transcripts.append(transcript)

data={
    'filenames':filenames,
    'transcripts':transcripts
    }

jsonfile=open('recordings.json','w')
json.dump(data,jsonfile)
jsonfile.close()
```

```
>> oh
>> it is gorgeous
>> testing on this
>> return to go
>> oh good and it's
>> …
>> where
>> it can be
>> ...
>> runny nose
>> ...
>> the
>> oh
>> the
>> we're then were
>> so good
>> ...
>> testing testing
>> deemed resting
>> …
```

We can plot **word count representations** over time with Matplotlib, much like we did for RMS power representations and audio files. This time, though, we can label the points with individual words of each second. In this way, you can quickly differentiate between speech segments and non-speech segments. You can also see how the content of conversations shifts over time (Figure 6.3.2).

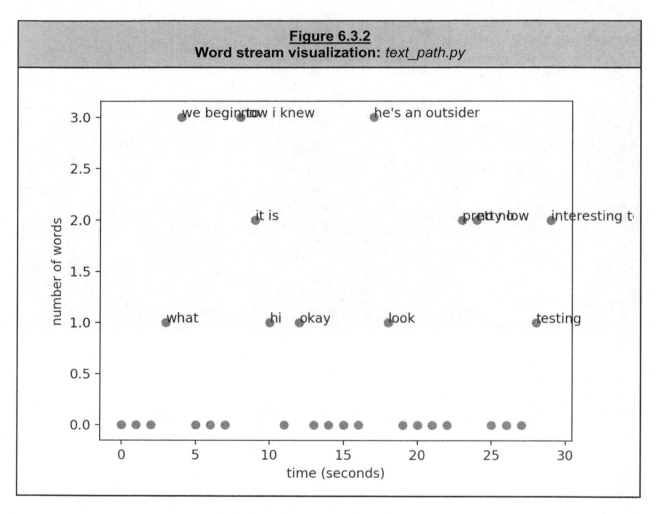

Figure 6.3.2
Word stream visualization: *text_path.py*

For recorded voice segments, we can transcribe a voice file with some third-party transcription engine (e.g. PocketSphinx) and then output some plots based on **word frequencies**. NLTK has a great package called FreqDist to do exactly this (Figure 6.3.3). You can also remove common words[249] like 'the' or 'this' with the stopwords package within NLTK. In this way, you quickly visualize sample vocabularies.

---

[249] **Stop words** – These words are known as stop words. Stop words are commonly removed as a part of filtering word frequencies to prepare visualizations, as they often are not very informative to describe voice sessions.

Figure 6.3.3
Word frequently plots: *text_freqplot.py, ./data/freqplot.wav, ./data/freqplot.png*

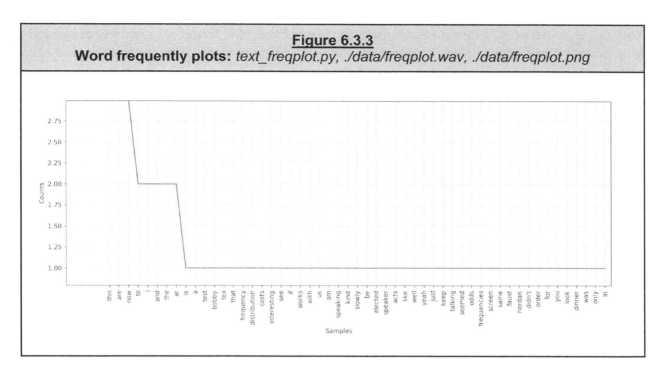

Another quick way to visualize text could be through a ***word cloud***. Python has a nifty module called **WordCloud** to generate cool visualizations based on word frequencies as an alternative to the Matplotlib / FreqDist() method laid out above. You can even output the wordcloud to shapes - like a Stormtrooper mask from Star Wars (Figure 6.3.4). In this way, you can have some more flexibility on how to visualize word frequencies and make the visualizations more engaging to end users.

Figure 6.3.4
Sample wordcloud shape:
https://amueller.github.io/word_cloud/auto_examples/a_new_hope.html

You can also use **spaCy** for visualizing ***parsed trees*** of text or in terms of their parts of speech (e.g. nouns). Dependency trees help to see the relationships of words with each other in sentences. These trees can be quite complicated, so it's best to break it up sentence-by-sentence so that they don't become too difficult to visualize (Figure 6.3.5). *Note that in order to see these images you need to pull up the web browser (usually https://localhost:5000).*

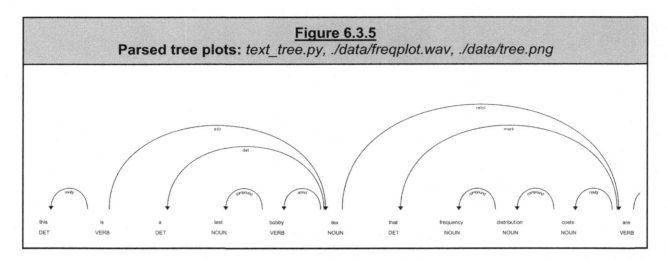

Figure 6.3.5
Parsed tree plots: *text_tree.py, ./data/freqplot.wav, ./data/tree.png*

SpaCy also comes with tools for highlighting ***named entities*** to make parsing through transcripts easier. Check out this visualization of the transcript from the *freqplot.wav* file recorded earlier (Figure 6.3.6). *Again, note that in order to see these images you need to pull up the web browser (usually https://localhost:3003).*

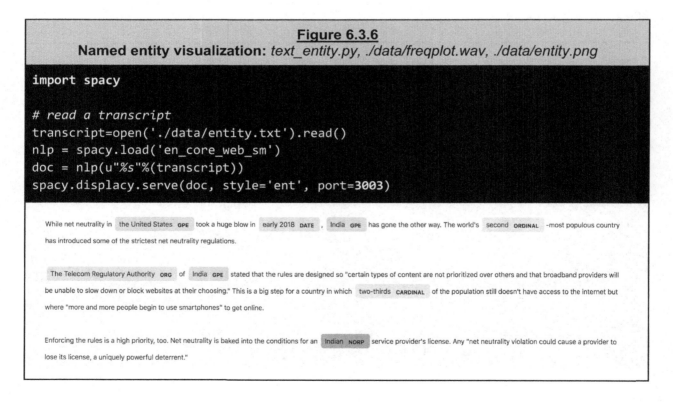

Figure 6.3.6
Named entity visualization: *text_entity.py, ./data/freqplot.wav, ./data/entity.png*

```
import spacy

# read a transcript
transcript=open('./data/entity.txt').read()
nlp = spacy.load('en_core_web_sm')
doc = nlp(u"%s"%(transcript))
spacy.displacy.serve(doc, style='ent', port=3003)
```

Also, **graph databases** can be used to visualize text data in terms of nodes and edges. The most commonly used graph library in Python is NetworkX. Below is a quick example on how to implement this library and plot out the number of unique words in terms of independent edges in a graph (Figure 6.3.7).[250] *Note there are also some good commercial graph databasel offerings which are better for production settings (e.g. GraphQL or Neo4j).*

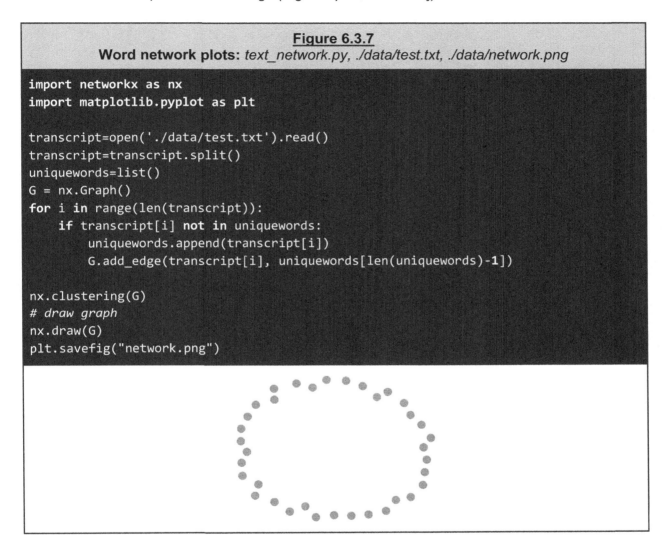

Figure 6.3.7
Word network plots: *text_network.py, ./data/test.txt, ./data/network.png*

```
import networkx as nx
import matplotlib.pyplot as plt

transcript=open('./data/test.txt').read()
transcript=transcript.split()
uniquewords=list()
G = nx.Graph()
for i in range(len(transcript)):
    if transcript[i] not in uniquewords:
        uniquewords.append(transcript[i])
        G.add_edge(transcript[i], uniquewords[len(uniquewords)-1])

nx.clustering(G)
# draw graph
nx.draw(G)
plt.savefig("network.png")
```

Moreover, you can use **gensim library** to plot ***Word2vec embeddings*** in two or three dimensions, depending on the size of the dataset (Figure 6.3.8). This is a compressed representation of word embeddings which simplifies the visualization of very large transcripts as a t-SNE plot. This should give you an idea as to how to apply dimensionality reduction techniques to text features (e.g. frequency distributions of vocabularities) to create neat visualizations.

---

[250] **You can many things with graph databases** - There are many other things you can do with graphs - including calculating nodes, add edges, and set graph types.

Figure 6.3.8
t-SNE plots: *text_tsne.py, ./data/test.txt, ./data/tsne_word.png*

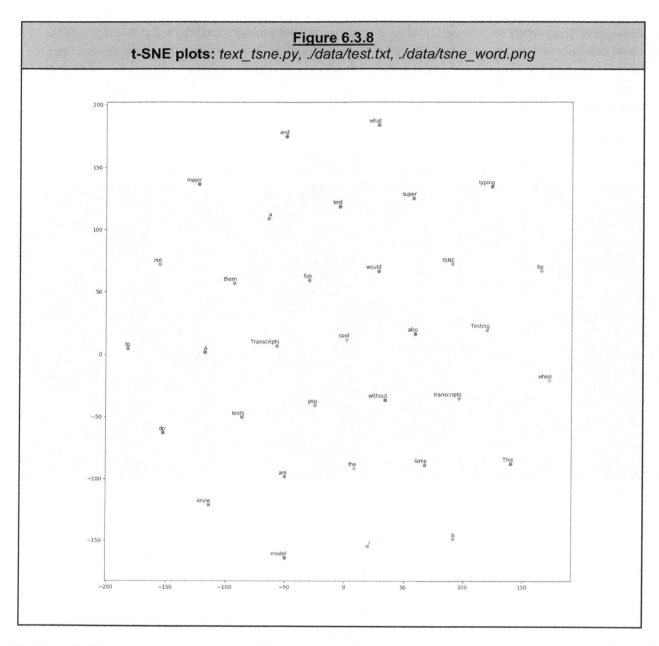

These t-SNE plots can be extended to many text files simultaneously; this allows for powerful visualizations to cross-compare transcripts (Figure 6.3.9). I prefer the t-SNE embedding plots when visualizing a lot of text files because I think it's one of the most compressed and elegant text feature representations. I also find that these plots can easily spot file duplicates based on the structure of the output word embeddings.[251] *Note that these plots can also be extended to any other dimensionality reduction technique - like PCA, LDA, or k-means cluster analysis - but t-SNE is typically a more standard technique for visualizing text data.*

---

[251] **Spotting duplicate files** – You can tell from the visualization in Figure 6.3.9 that there are only two unique files. This is often useful to use as a 'gut check' to see if there are duplicates and to guide you when first looking at text transcripts.

Figure 6.3.9
Plotting many t-SNE embeddings: *text_tsne_many.py, ./data/test.txt, ./data/plotmany_tsne.png*

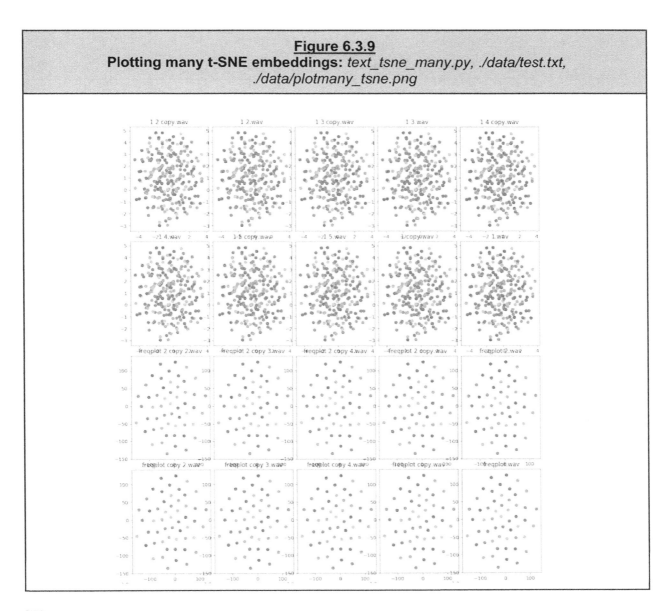

6.4 Visualizing mixed features

Mixed features are voice features that are composed of both auditory and text features. Mixed features can also be of streaming or non-streaming nature. Mixed features are a bit trickier to visualize, as they require superimposing text features on top of auditory features.

Let's jump right into some examples.

For streaming use cases, we can simply plot a bar chart with words every so often to get an idea of the power (as a sample feature) along with a text string (Figure 6.4.1). This is a very simple representation but can give you an idea of how various words relate to audio features.[252]

---

[252] **For example,** you can switch out these audio features with other ones like spectral rolloff or MFCC coefficients.

> **Figure 6.4.1**
> **Mixed features CLI plot:** *mixed_stream.py*
>
> ```
> >> ==.==.==.==.==.==.==.==.==.== as things were
> >> ==.==
> >> ==.==.==.==.==.==.==.==.==.== not sure who
> >> ==.==.==.==.==.== and it's all gone
> >> ==.==
> >> ==.==
> >> ==.== good
> >> ==.==.==.==.==.==.==.==.==.== exactly what
> >> ==.== air
> >> ==.== oh
> >> ==.==
> >> ==.==
> >> ==.==.==.==.==.==.==.==.==.==.== i was too good at all
> >> ==.==
> >> ==.==
> >> ==.==.==.==.==.==.==.==.== uh huh
> >> ==.==.==.==.==.==.==.==.==.== in the mud
> >> ==.==.==.==.==.==.==.==.== aren't you
> >> ==.==
> >> ==.==.==.==.==.==.==.==.==.== so
> >> ==.== mm
> >> ==.==
> >> ==.==
> >> ==.==
> >> ==.==.==.==.==.== this is
> >> ==.== oh
> >> ==.==
> >> ==.==.==.==.==.== oh
> >> ==.==
> >> ==.==
> >> minimum val: 0.05180590960662812
> >> max val: 39.191748946905136
> >> transcripts: ['as things were', '', 'not sure who', "and it's all gone", '', '', 'good', 'exactly what', 'air', 'oh', '', '', 'i was too good at all', '', '', 'uh huh', 'in the mud', "aren't you", '', 'so', 'mm', '', '', '', 'this is', 'oh', '', 'oh', '', '']
> ```

Alternatively, you can plot words on top of the auditory spectrogram in real-time (Figure 6.4.2). This makes it easy to see how vocabularies change throughout time, as well as how specific words may be emphasized. *Note that you can swap out any other audio feature here in the plot, such as the fundamental frequency to perhaps identify when speakers have changed in a session.*

Figure 6.4.2
Mixed features path plot: *mixed_path.py, ./data/mixedstream.py*

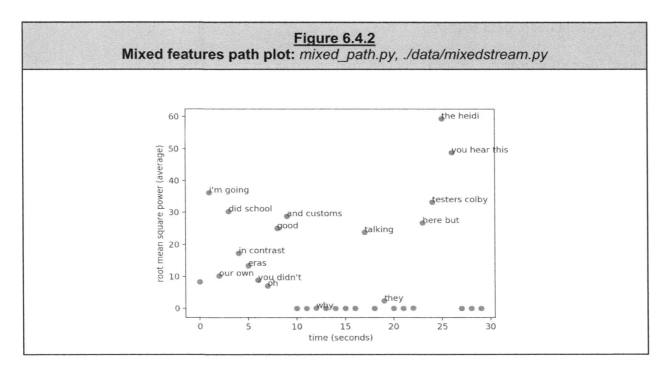

For non-streaming use cases, we can get a bit more creative and make videos superimposed with words over time. To do this, we need to break up individual audio files into windows (e.g. a 1-second window). We can then transcribe each of these windows and make images representations per second with an audio feature superimposed with a transcript. After making all these images, we can use the OpenCV library in Python to patch these images into a video, which updates every second (Figure 6.3.3). In the end, I find that videos like this allow for a powerful way to communicate mixed features in new, interesting ways to non-programmers.

Figure 6.4.3
Making videos of plots using opencv: *mixed_video.py, ./data/mixed_video.avi*

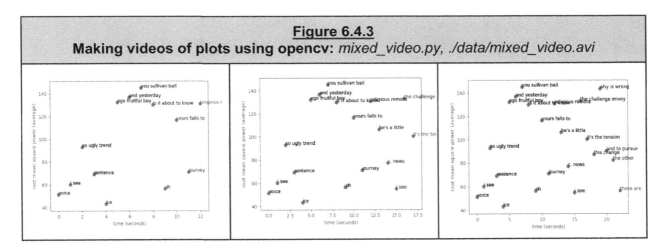

As you can see, there are many ways to visualize mixed features. These three quick examples should get you more comfortable making new visualizations that best fit your dataset the best.

225

6.5 Visualizing meta features

Lastly, **meta features** are features derived from pre-trained machine learning models. For example, we can detect the gender of the speaker by applying such machine learning models on audio, text, or mixed feature embeddings.[253] In this way, we automatically generate many labels for a given audio file.

*For **streaming use cases**,* we can apply a pre-trained machine learning model every second of recorded audio and propagate a graph on the screen from the model's output. The example below is a session of Jimmy Kimmel Live with various speakers; as you can see, the gender model works well at detecting genders shifts (1 - male, 0 - female). You can customize the meta_stream.py script to your needs. *Note, most of these models were trained on 20 seconds of audio so they may not perform well on 1 second intervals; however, gender is highly frequency-dependent so this may be an exception.*

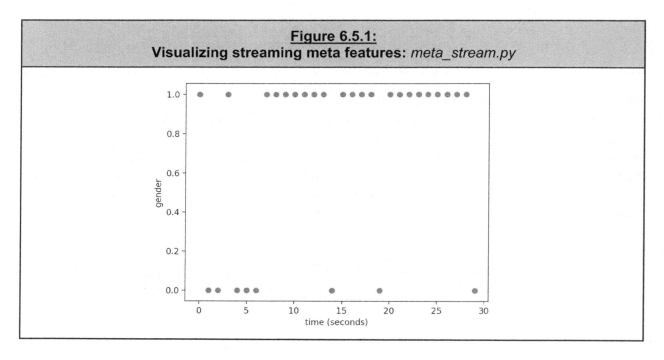

Figure 6.5.1:
Visualizing streaming meta features: *meta_stream.py*

We can also plot multiple charts in parallel to visualize how meta features change over time (Figure 6.5.2). In this example, we plot age (twenties vs. control) and gender (males/female) every second. Note you can extend this to N dimensional subplots. Feel free to experiment with these!

---

[253] **Meta model visualizations** - The list of visualizations is endless for applying machine learning models to time series audio data. However, I find these visualizations best in applications where there are multiple speakers or to get a glance of the data to determine who is speaking and at what times they are speaking. Meta model visualizations are also good at detecting net emotions in the conversation and when it shifts to be more angry, happy, or sad.

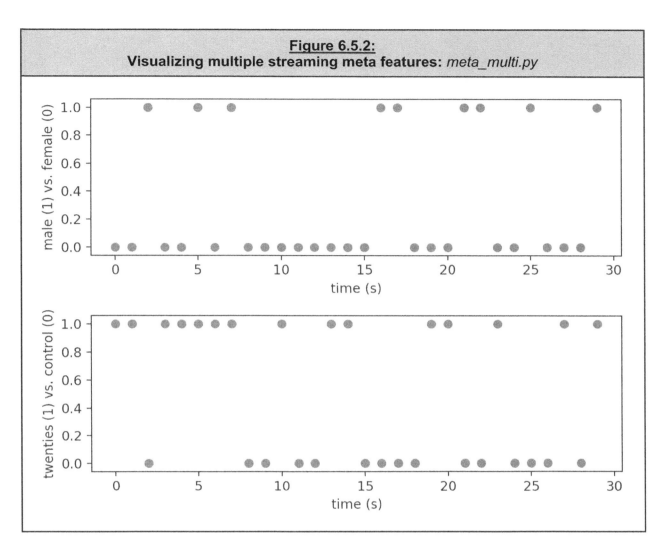

Figure 6.5.2:
Visualizing multiple streaming meta features: *meta_multi.py*

*For **non-streaming use cases**,* you can visualize meta features much like you would any other feature type in Matplotlib. In this case, we can just plot the frequency counts of each feature (71) over the entire length of the session and plot the results as a bar graph. The files are spliced in 20 second intervals (Figure 6.5.2). I find using bar charts horizontally like this is a good way to look at the data as a first-pass.

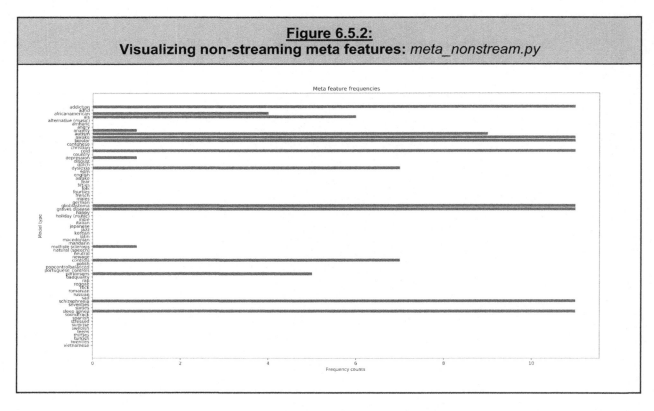

**Figure 6.5.2:
Visualizing non-streaming meta features:** *meta_nonstream.py*

There are many ways you can visualize meta features, but hopefully this gives you some inspiration to make new visualizations yourself. *I think meta features are perhaps the trickiest feature type to visualize as they often require manipulating time intervals and applying many machine learning models in parallel; however, with a bit of practice you can get the hang of it.*

6.6 Conclusion

👏 Congrats! You now know how to visualize audio, text, mixed, and meta features. Check out the following libraries and links for additional information:

- Visualization libraries
    - Matplotlib. https://matplotlib.org/tutorials/introductory/sample_plots.html
    - Seaborn. https://seaborn.pydata.org/
    - Ggplot. http://ggplot.yhathq.com/
    - Bokeh. https://bokeh.pydata.org/en/latest/
    - Pygal. http://pygal.org/en/stable/
    - Plotly Dash. https://plot.ly/
    - Geoplotlib. https://github.com/andrea-cuttone/geoplotlib
    - Gleam. https://github.com/dgrtwo/gleam
    - Missingno. https://github.com/ResidentMario/missingno
    - Leather. https://leather.readthedocs.io/en/0.3.3/

- Audio data
    - LibROSA. https://librosa.github.io/librosa/core.html
    - SoundFile. https://github.com/bastibe/SoundFile

- - Sounddevice. https://python-sounddevice.readthedocs.io/en/0.3.11/
- Text data
  - Sounddevice. https://python-sounddevice.readthedocs.io/en/0.3.11/
  - NLTK. https://www.nltk.org/
  - SpaCy. https://spacy.io/
  - NetworkX. https://networkx.github.io/
- Mixed data
  - Sounddevice. https://python-sounddevice.readthedocs.io/en/0.3.11/
  - OpenCV. https://opencv.org/
- Meta data
  - Keras. https://keras.io/
  - Scikit-learn. http://scikit-learn.org/stable/index.html

In the next chapter, we'll be discussing the how to design voice-computers from the ground up. In this way, you'll be able to customize the code you write to many forms of voice computing hardware and software.

Chapter 7:
Designing Voice Computers

"Siri, Cortana, Google Assistant, and Alexa ... are... clever but still first-generation clever."
-Ian Cohen
(CIO, Addison Lee)

Chapter Overview

It's an exciting time for voice computing. 1 in 4 searches on Google are now voice-enabled, Amazon Alexa just passed 10,000 skills, and 100 million calls are completed on WhatsApp daily. Transcription word error rates have gotten down to around 5% for state-of-the-art systems, which is right around the accuracy of human hearing. Over 40 million Amazon Echos have been sold, and there are over 1 billion voice-enabled devices in the USA.

The future for voice computing looks quite promising. 50% of all searches will be voice-enabled by 2020. Almost all the large tech companies are building voice interfaces to capture some of this market (e.g. Microsoft Cortana). It is very likely that voice computers will be ubiquitous across many forms of hardware and use cases - in cars, homes, laptops, refrigerators, dishwashers, and washing machines - tripling or quadrupling the number of voice-related IoT devices by 2020.[254][255]

Even with these trends, it is still unclear which voice computing platform will win in the long-run or which use cases will prove to be the most useful.[256] Many of the emerging voice computing devices (e.g. Amazon Echo) are still quite primitive, and new versions are being released roughly every 6 months. As a result, it's difficult to predict which forms of voice computing hardware and software consumers will adopt into the far future.

Therefore, this chapter takes you through the process of building a voice computer in terms of its hardware and software components. Then we'll learn how to build a voice assistant - Nala (yes, Nala from the Lion King) – on top of this hardware and software. In this way, you can iterate voice computer designs quickly around consumer demands.

Specifically, we'll go over:

- **7.1** - Defining voice computers
- **7.2** - Selecting hardware
- **7.3** - Building software
- **7.4** - Nala: a voice assistant

By the end of this chapter you'll be able to build "generation 2.0" voice computers, forging a future of ever-connected devices. :-)

---

[254] **Many home devices** have been enabled with Amazon Alexa by GE, such as dishwashers or ovens.

[255] **Most obviously,** these use cases are affecting the consumer market (homes); however, these use cases likely will become more business-to-business (B2B) and commercial-facing as we see productivity gains from adopting voice technology.

[256] **It seems like smart speakers** are much like early smartphones; we still don't know what the best interface will be. For this reason, expect much variation in the smark speaker market over the next few years, especially as Google Assistant makes up some of this market share in the future. Most people associate the word "voice computer" with Siri (on iPhone) or an Amazon Echo.

7.1 Defining voice computers

Recall the definition of a voice computer:

> A **voice computer** is any computerized system (assembled hardware and software) that can process voice inputs; This could include a personal computer (PC), voice assistant smart speaker (e.g. Amazon Echo), open source hardware devices (e.g. a Raspberry Pi device), and many other embodiments.[257][258]

From this definition, it's useful to think about some default configurations for voice computers in terms of their hardware and software components.

Some types of **default voice computing hardware** include desktop personal computers (PCs), laptops, Raspberry Pis, Arduinos, cell phones, and various smart speakers to name a few (Table 7.1.1). *Note that the most prolific voice computing hardware devices still are laptops and phones (>1B devices); however, there has been increased adoption of smart speakers over the past two years (>40M devices sold from 2017-2018).*

Table 7.1.1 Types of assembled voice computing hardware		
Voice hardware type	**Pros**	**Cons**
Desktop computers (iMac)	• Contains the greatest amount of computing power for household devices • More stable internet connection (if ethernet)	• Not portable; fixed location • Can be an invasive interface while working
Laptops (Macbook pro)	• High CPU power • Portable • Multi-purpose	• Can be an invasive interface while working
Raspberry Pi (Jasper, Mycroft)	• Portable • Simple assembly • Raspberry pi has a great community • Easy to modify • Many sensors can be paired with Raspberry Pi devices	• Restricted computational power (to run ML models)

---

[257] **Surprisingly, voice computing has really not had a formal definition** (at least on Wikipedia). It's often loosely used by the media to be associated with new voice interfaces, such as Amazon Alexa or Google Assistant. However, I believe it's necessary to more clearly define and coin this term for the purposes of this book.

[258] **Voice computers** can exhibit a screen or monitor, but this is not not necessary. This means that voice computing is quite different than hands-free computing.

Arduino (Arduino Uno)	• Great community; many tutorials to get started • Easy to modify (sensors, etc.) • Portable	• Less adoption in the voice computing community
Cell Phone (iPhone / Siri)	• 1B+ devices on market	• Often restricted by proprietary vendors (e.g. Apple / Google)
Smart speakers (Amazon Echo, Google Assistant, Apple HomePod)	• Increasing adoption of smart speakers by consumers	• Privacy, security, and legal risks (Chapter 9)

There are also many types of **default voice computing software** to load on top of the aforementioned voice computing hardware. Some examples of default voice computing software include the Alexa Voice Service (AVS), the Google Assistant SDK, the Cortana Skills Kit, the Jovo software framework, Jasper software, Mycroft AI, and Nala. *Note that some of these forms of software are tailored for certain forms of voice interfaces; for example, Jasper is more tailored for Raspberry Pi devices* (Table 7.1.2).

Table 7.1.2
Types of voice computing software

Voice software type	Pros	Cons
Alexa Voice Service (AVS)	• Compatible with Amazon Echo community • 20 million Alexa devices	• Commercial product coupled to AWS cloud provider
Google Assistant SDK	• Makes it seamless to interact with Google • Google assistant reaches 500 million devices	• Less support and documentation • Only Linux compatible
Cortana Skills Kit	• More compatible with PCs (Windows operating systems) • Documentation is getting better over time • 141 million active users of Cortana across Windows, Xbox, Androis, and iOS hardware	• Less adoption in the market

Jovo Framework	• Independent developer community • Quickly build skills published both on Google Assistant and Alexa	• Only Node.JS compatible
Jasper	• Optimized for raspberry-pi enabled • Completely open-source software	• Emerging developer community
Mycroft AI	• Optimized for PC or Raspberry Pi devices • Completely open-source software	• Great documentation • Growing community
Nala *You'll make her later in this chapter!*	• 100% open-source; lack of vendor lock-in • Can put on any hardware device • Great customizability • Python-first voice bot • Can customize for any purpose you'd like to • Keep queries for modeling later	• Intended to be local and not cloud-driven • Emerging developer community

Although there are these default configurations of voice hardware and software (and these configurations can be a good starting point to build voice assistants), it is important to know how to build voice computers from the ground-up. This is because your use case may require you to go beyond the hardware and software limitations of existing solutions.[259] Therefore, the rest of this chapter goes over how to build your own voice computer - both in terms of its hardware and software components.

If you'd prefer to not build your own voice computer - that's completely okay too. I'd suggest reading the links to the documentation for the default hardware and software listed in Table 7.1.1 and Table 7.1.2, as many of them (e.g. Amazon Alexa Voice Service) have detailed tutorials to get you up and running. You can just skip to Section 7.4 to build your own voice assistant.

---

[259] **For example,** you may need to have computationally intensive ML models loaded in the back-end of your voice computer. This cannot be done with existing smart speaker designs.

7.2 Selecting hardware

Voice computing hardware can include microphones, sound cards (with D/A and A/D converters), a motherboard, central processing units (CPUs), storage devices (e.g. hard disks), computer monitors, radio transmitters, WiFi transceivers, Bluetooth transceivers, speakers, and a power supply.

Selecting the right voice computing hardware depends on your end goal.[260] Some things to consider are unit costs, end user adoption curves, processing requirements, the average microphone distance between voice computers and end users, online / offline requirements, power requirements, storage requirements, and Bluetooth capabilities (Table 7.2.1).

\<center\>Table 7.2.1\<br\>Hardware considerations for voice computers\</center\>		
Consideration	**Question**	**Categories**
Unit costs[261]	What is your goal for the cost-per-device at scale?	**<$100** – Low-cost - Arduino microcontroller or Raspberry Pi pocket computer (Linux). **$100-300** – Moderate-cost - build a custom PC or desktop with a small form-factor motherboard. **>$300** – High-cost - motherboard + CPU + GPU + other components.
End user adoption curves[262]	What kinds of devices do your end users already have? What kind of devices will they buy? (Figure 8.2.1).	Devices to which U.S. internet users have given voice commands, by percentage of users: Smartphone 57% Tablet 29% Laptop 29% Desktop 29% Speaker 27% SOURCE PriceWaterhouseCooper George Petras/USA TODAY

---

[260] **Some example voice computer configurations / goals -** You can build your own computer with a high-quality microphone and sound card but skip a monitor. If you're building a personal project at home and coupling is not an issue, perhaps buying an Amazon Echo directly and programming an application could be a good fit for your needs. If you're trying to build a commercial product, I would suggest decoupling yourself from major vendors like Google, Amazon, etc. and use something like an Arduino or Raspberry Pi device.

[261] **Budget -** Make sure you set a budget and cost constraint per device; this will affect your margins later on if you build a commercial product and help you to define a supply chain that works for you.

[262] **Device adoption -** Make sure you are customizing hardware to what your end users will use. Don't over-engineer a hardware solution if users will not buy new hardware. If you're users are already using Mac computers, why not just build a Mac computer app?

Processing requirements[263]	Do you need any CPU- or GPU-intensive tasks on the device - like rendering videos, building ML models, and/or loading up specific software?	**Little processing** - likely can use Raspberry Pi default processor. **Moderate processing** - can use custom CPU with moderate thread count. **High processing** - requires custom CPU with high thread count (e.g. training ML models on chip).
Microphone distance[264]	How far away will the end user be from the device?	**Near** - electret or condenser microphones may be a good choice. **Mid-range** - directional microphones with beamforming may be a good choice. **Far** - wireless microphones may be a good choice.
Wifi-capability[265]	Does your device need to be connected to the Internet?	**No** - does not require a WiFi chip transceiver. **Yes** - requires a WiFi chip transceiver.
Power source[266]	Is your device portable or need to always be connected to the wall? If portable and requires a battery, how long of a life does the battery need?	**Plugged in** - no real battery requirements. **Battery** - battery consumption rate vs. capacity (e.g. low- vs. high-power).

---

[263] **Processing requirements** - Make sure you consider the processing requirements for your hardware. If you're doing a lot of machine learning, a PC or computer may be a better option than a Raspberry pi. If you are just collecting audio it may make sense to just go with the Raspberry Pi.
[264] **Microphone** - This helps determine the type of microphone to use.
[265] **Online mode** - Requires a WiFi card and/or ethernet connection.
[266] **Power** - This will define the type of power source you need for your device as well as the components (e.g. low vs. high-power modes).

Storage requirements[267]	How much storage do you need on the device?	**Little** - <2GB - could be find for a Raspberry Pi or Arduino. **Moderate** - <128 GB and > 10 GB - could do a SD card or similar device. **Large** - >1 TB - probably would be good to have a hard disk of some sort to store data.
Bluetooth chip capability	Does your device need to connect to other peripherals via Bluetooth?	**No** - do not need BT chip. **Yes** - need BT chip (Raspberry Pi and Arduino often have Bluetooth chips).

Functionally and cost-wise, it comes down to whether you'd like to start from a *microcontroller*[268] (e.g. Arduino) or a *fully-functioning pocket computer* (e.g. Raspberry Pi) or a *custom desktop computer* (Figure 7.2.1). Microcontrollers (e.g. *Arduino*) or fully-functioning pocket-computers (e.g. *Raspberry Pi*) are often more cost-efficient, but they lack the ability to process a lot of things on the circuit board. Desktops, on the other hand, are capable of adding custom CPUs and/or GPUs to do high-performance computing (e.g. if you need to do machine learning). Therefore, the best place to start is often whether or not you are building a small computer or a custom desktop computer (e.g. requires a custom motherboard form factor).

Once you have made up your mind, it's often useful to think about which microphone, sound card, CPU/RAM memory, graphics card, storage medium, monitor, WiFi chip, Bluetooth chip, speaker system, and power supply best fits your use case (Figure 7.2.1). Then, an outer housing can be built or selected to complete the hardware assembly process (Figure 7.2.1). Each of these components are discussed in greater detail in the sections that follow to help give more context as to how best to customize voice computing hardware to your needs.[269]

---

[267] **Storage** - If it is in TBs, you may want to have an external hard disk.

[268] **Microcontroller** - From Wikipedia: "A microcontroller (MCU for microcontroller unit, or UC for μ-controller) is a small computer on a single integrated circuit. In modern terminology, it is similar to, but less sophisticated than, a system on a chip or SoC; an SoC may include a microcontroller as one of its components. A microcontroller contains one or more CPUs (processor cores) along with memory and programmable input/output peripherals. Program memory in the form of ferroelectric RAM, NOR flash or OTP ROM is also often included on chip, as well as a small amount of RAM. Microcontrollers are designed for embedded applications, in contrast to the microprocessors used in personal computers or other general-purpose applications consisting of various discrete chips."

[269] **For example**, if you have a voice computer that is training lots of voice data and building custom machine learning models on device, a custom desktop computer with a USB condenser microphone and a sound card may make sense.

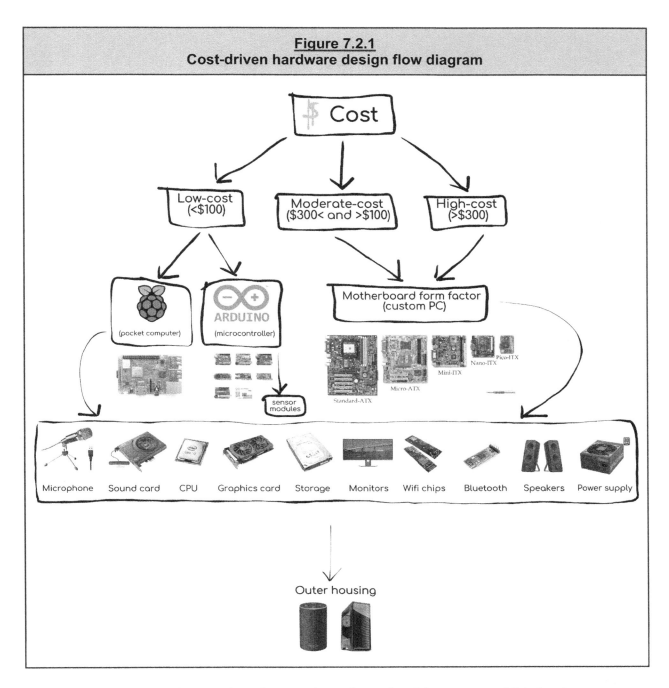

Figure 7.2.1
Cost-driven hardware design flow diagram

7.2.1 - Microphones - As mentioned many times throughout the course of this book, microphones are the instruments that transduce analog pressure into electrical signals, which are sent through wires to the sound card in a computer for further processing. Depending on the type of microphone, the method for transducing pressure may differ (Table 7.2.1.1). In general, the most cost-effective microphones tend to be electret microphones, which are the standard mic type in smartphones today. Also, USB-driven condenser microphones tend to be fairly high-performing microphones for their price range. *Note that any of these mics may be good for you, depending on your use case.*

Table 7.2.1.1
List of microphones, their utility, and cost

Microphone type	How they work	Utility	Cost
Condenser microphone	Uses two capacitor plates and a diaphragm to produce electric current. Capacitance and resistance allow for filtering of current in a way that produces an audio signal.	Wide variety of types; can get low-, moderate-, and high-quality microphones for home or commercial uses.	~$30-40/unit
Dynamic microphone	Uses induction coils attached to a diaphragm to produce sound via electromagnetic induction.	Can customize microphone to various parts of the audio spectrum (e.g. bases); useful for music performances or lecture halls.	~$20-70/unit
Ribbon microphone	Uses corrugated metal ribbon suspended in a magnetic field to produce sound via electromagnetic induction.	Useful for radio broadcasting applications.	$50-300/unit
Condenser MEMS microphone	A miniaturized version of the condenser microphone etched on silicon wafers.	Small size, high sound quality, reliable and affordable.	$0.79-$1.00/unit
Piezoelectric MEMS microphone	Uses a piezoelectric material to on a silicon wafer to produce electrical current when applied to mechanical stress.	Low-power and can be used in tough environments (waterproof, dustproof, particle-resistant, and shockproof). Quite high reliability.	N/A

Electret microphone	Uses a permanently charged material (e.g. PTFE plastic film) to produce voltage when subjected to pressure.	Useful for low-cost manufacturing in smartphones or personal computers.	~$0.30-0.50/unit
Noise-cancelling microphone	Many types, but a common type uses two ports as a condenser microphone to subtract noise out from the sample.	Useful to filter out noise in noisy environments and increase transcription accuracy.	$16-40/unit

Moreover, microphones can be put into arrays to achieve higher signal-to-noise (SNR) ratios through beamforming signal processing techniques (see Chapter 2: Collection). Although a bit more expensive, these arrays can perform a bit better in noisy environments and tend to be more reliable for recording samples (e.g. if one microphone channel fails, the others can still be used). If you can afford it, I'd highly recommend looking into starting out with a microphone array circuit board and then build a voice computer from there (Table 7.2.1.2).

<u>Table 7.2.1.2</u>
Types of microphone arrays

Microphone array	Specifications	Cost
UMA-8 Microphone Array	<ul><li>Circular USB microphone array</li><li>DSP processing for Beamforming</li><li>AEC</li><li>Noise reduction</li><li>2 channel and 8 channel mode.</li><li>Powered by XMOS XVF3000 new chipset.</li></ul>	$98/unit
Respeaker	<ul><li>Four microphones array / 12 programmable RGB LED indicators</li><li>Speech algorithms/features for voice activity detection (VAD)</li><li>Direction of arrival and noise suppression</li><li>De-reverberation/acoustic echo cancellation</li></ul>	$79/unit

Matrix creator	- 8 microphones with beamforming and echo cancellation - Contains temperature, pressure, UV, motion, and orientation sensors - Has Spartan-6 FPGA board - re-configurable for machine learning-on-a-chip and CPU-intensive tasks - Zigbee and Z-wave wireless device capability - Near-field communication (NFC) capability to interact with smartphones.	$99/unit
Blue Yeti microphone	- 3 condenser microphones - Can customize pattern selection - cardioid, bidirectional, omnidirectional & stereo - Gain control, mute button, zero-latency headphone output - Can be used for podcasting, voice-overs, interviews, and conference calls	$89/unit

7.2.2 - Sound cards - Recall that sound cards encode and decode audio data to and from analog and digital data formats (e.g. linear PCM data). Sound cards are equipped with codecs that can transform digital data into audio formats like .WAV (Chapter 1: Fundamentals). *The choice of sound card often determines the number of independent channels that can be recorded and combined on a voice computer, so keep this in mind when you're building one.*

If you're building on top of a Raspberry Pi, the sound emitted from the 3.5 mm output is often not that great, so it's often nice to update the default sound card (Table 7.2.2.1).

Table 7.2.2.1
List of [Raspberry Pi]-upgradable sound cards

Sound card	Pros	Cost
HiFiBerry DAC+ Standard	- Can be simply plugged onto your Raspberry Pi, it does not need any soldering	$28.90/unit

IQaudIO PiDAC+	• HAT compliant accessory; EEPROM, mounting holes • Full-HD audio – up to 24-bit/192kHz playback • Up to 2x35w of crystal clear amplification • No soldering required to your Raspberry Pi • Integrated hardware volume control (via ALSA) • Powers the Raspberry Pi from the Pi-DigiAMP+ power input • Linux driver support already delivered within Raspbian • AMP can be enabled / disabled via Raspberry Pi's GPIO22 • Advanced ESD protection • Uses the digital I2S audio signals to reduce CPU load over USB audio solutions • Fully built and tested Raspberry Pi accessory	$72.90/unit
JustBoom DAC Hat	• 2 x 55 Watt peak output at 8 ohms (2 x 30 Watt RMS) • High quality audio 192kHz/32bit • Includes both a DAC and power amplifier – simply connect your speakers! • Full driver support in Raspbian / NOOBS; Compatible with: OSMC / RuneAudio / Volumio / Moode / PiCorePlayer / PiMusicBox / OpenELEC and others • No soldering required; mounting hardware included. Compatible with Raspberry Pi A+, B+, 2B and 3B and Raspberry Pi Zero	$74.95/unit

Alternatively, if you are building a PC from a motherboard, you definitely need a sound card. Here are a few options of PC-enabled sound cards (Table 7.2.2.2).

<div align="center">**Table 7.2.2.2** **List of pc-enabled sound cards and their costs**</div>		
Sound card	**Description**	**Use case and cost**
Asus Xonar DSX PCIe 7.1	• Signal amplification capabilities to provide better sound quality • Xonar 192k/24 bit support minimizes signal-to-noise ratio (SNR ratio) • Upscaling sound quality	Movies, $98/unit

Asus Xonar GHX PCIe GX2.5	<ul><li>128 3D audio effects</li><li>Dolby Headphone 5.1 HD audio sound makes sounds feel immersive</li></ul>	VoIP, $37/unit
Creative Sound Blaster Audigy FX	<ul><li>5.1 surround sound</li><li>600 ohm microphone amp allows for good experience without needing an expensive mic</li><li>192KHz/24-bit stereo fidelity and a signal-to-noise ratio of 106dB</li></ul>	Podcasting, $39/unit
Creative Sound Blaster ZxR PCIe	<ul><li>Highest performing sound card on market</li><li>Tiny sound card</li><li>124 dB audio, sound gives 99.9% clarity (90% better than motherboard)</li><li>Outputs sound 24-bit and 192kHz, studio sound quality with 3D sound effects</li><li>600 ohm headphone amp</li></ul>	Gaming, $199.99/unit
Creative Sound Blaster Z	<ul><li>116 dB signal-to-noise ratio</li><li>600 ohm headphone amplifier</li><li>5 3.5 mm headphone jacks</li><li>Allows you to change presets and tweak microphone to middle frequencies</li></ul>	Gaming, $95/unit
Creative Sound Blaster Audigy PCIe RX	<ul><li>7.1-multi-channel audio</li><li>600-ohm headphone amp</li><li>Allows for customization of sound card - pitch, tone, and bass.</li><li>Allows for dual-microphone inputs to connect two mics at once</li></ul>	Multi-purpose (best value), $60/unit
Asus Essence STX II	<ul><li>124dB signal-to-noise ratio (SNR), 64x better performance than a standard new computer purchase.</li><li>7.1-channel sound card with headphone amplifier up to 600 ohms.</li><li>Swappable op-amp sockets to manipulate sound</li><li>Connects with Dolby Home Theater</li></ul>	Music production, $219/unit

7.2.3 - Motherboards - Motherboards ("mobos") are the main printed circuit boards for personal computers and microcomputers. It acts as the central unit for connecting CPUs, RAM memory, graphics cards, sound cards, hard drives, WiFi cards, and ports (e.g. USB ports) for peripheral devices. Thus, selecting the right motherboard is crucial to ensure you have a voice computer that can be assembled to meet your needs.[270]

The most important thing to know about motherboards is the form factor, or the size of the motherboard (Figure 7.2.3.1). If you're seeking smaller motherboards to build portable voice computers, you may want to check out the Nano-ITX or Pico-ITXI motherboard form factors (Figure 7.2.3.1).[271] If, on the other hand, you are trying to build a voice computer as more of a desktop or PC, you may want to start with buying a precompiled computer or make a more heavy desktop computer which uses gaming motherboards with standard-ATX motherboard designs (Figure 7.2.3.1 and Table 7.2.3.1). Regardless, you have a lot of freedom here and it's really up to you what motherboard makes the most sense for your use case.

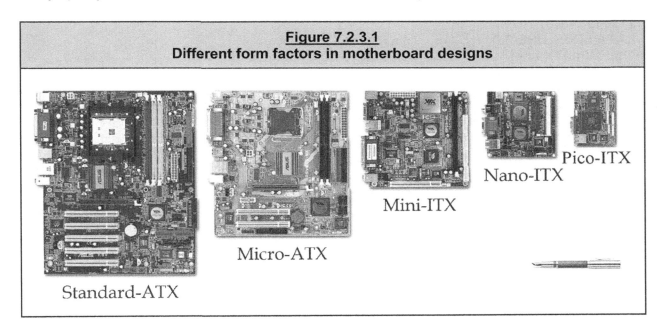

**Figure 7.2.3.1
Different form factors in motherboard designs**

---

[270] **Raspberry pis and Arduino motherboards** - Note that Raspberry Pis and Arduinos often come with fully assembled motherboards, so this section doesn't really apply to you if you're building from there (but instead of a CPU it uses a microprocessor).
[271] **Ultra small motherboards** - The emergence of ultra small form factor designs has come on market. Intel, for example, has released a 5x5 motherboard design, allowing for many more use cases for voice computers.

Table 7.2.3.1
List of desktop motherboards and costs (2018)

Motherboard	Use case (Specifications)	Cost
5x5 motherboard by intel	<ul><li>The 5x5 is 29 percent smaller than mini-ITX at 147x140mm (5.5x5.8 inches), making it the smallest socketed board available.</li><li>The 5x5 provides Celeron to Core processor scalability, supporting both 35W and 65W TDP CPUs. Intel says that despite the small size, it offers the same CPU upgradeability as a full-sized desktop.</li></ul>	N/A
ASUS Q87T/CSM LGA 1150 Intel Q87 HDMI SATA 6Gb/s USB 3.0 Thin Mini-ITX Intel Motherboard For AiO And Ultra Slim System	Portable computers (laptops)<ul><li>Thin Mini-ITX form factor</li><li>Corporate Stable Model (CSM)</li><li>USB 3.0 Boost</li><li>Onboard TPM (Infineon) and Intel vPro</li><li>Designed according to Intel thin mini-ITX</li></ul>	$127/unit
Gigabyte GA-H110M-A LGA1151 Intel H110 Micro ATX DDR4 Motherboard	Desktop PC<ul><li>LGA1151, Supports 7th/ 6th Generation Intel Core Processors</li><li>Dual Channel DDR4, 2 DIMMs</li><li>Audio Noise Guard with High Quality Audio Capacitors</li><li>HDMI 1.4 port for Full HD contents playback</li><li>Realtek GbE LAN with cFos Speed Internet Accelerator Software</li><li>All new GIGABYTE APP Center, simple and easy use. Support intel small business basics</li></ul>	$57.58/unit
MSI Pro Series Intel B250 LGA 1151 DDR4 HDMI USB 3.1 ATX Motherboard (B250 PC MATE)	Desktop PC<ul><li>Supports 7th/6th Gen Intel Core/Pentium/Celeron processors for LGA 1151 socket</li><li>Supports DDR4-2400 Memory;Memory Channel : Dual</li><li>Newer Memory requires Bios update</li><li>Easy Debug LED,Lightning USB</li></ul>	$84.88/unit

MSI ProSeries AMD Ryzen B350 DDR4 VR Ready HDMI USB 3 micro-ATX Motherboard (B350M PRO-VDH)	Desktop PC - 11.02 x 10.71 x 2.56 in - Gaming design with heatsinks, Ddr4 boost, PCI-E steel armor - DVI + VGA + HDMI port - Gaming LAN - Audio boost technology with premium audio jacks	$70.83/unit 

7.2.4 - Central processing units (CPUs) - Motherboards require the use of central *processing units* (e.g. desktop computers) and/or *microprocessors* (e.g. Arduinos) in order to process information. In general, CPUs perform basic arithmetic, logical, control, and input/output operations for computers. *Sockets* are CPUs with more than one core in a single chip; therefore, most modern CPUs are sockets.

Depending on your processing requirements, you may want a different configuration of a microprocessor or CPU. Here is a list of common microcontrollers (Table 7.2.4.1) and CPUs along with their technical specifications (Table 7.2.4.2).

<div align="center">**Table 7.2.4.2** **List of desktop CPUs and their costs (2018)**</div>		
CPU	**Specifications**	**Cost**
AMD Turion X2 Ultra ZM-84 TMZM84DAM23G G Mobile CPU Processor	- Turion X2 Ultra ZM-84 - Dual-Core - Clock speed: 2.3 GHz	$8.99/unit
Intel E6550 2.33 dual core 4mb 1333 mhz cpu - SLA9X	- Product Dimensions- 6 x 6 x 2 inches - Item Weight - 0.32 ounces	$12.20/unit

XCSOURCE ESP32S Development Board	<ul><li>ESP32 is already integrated antenna and RF balun, power amplifier, low-noise amplifiers, filters, and power management module.</li><li>2.4 GHz dual-mode Wi-Fi and BT chips by TSMC 40nm low power technology, best power and RF properties, which is safe, reliable, and scalable to a variety of applications.</li><li>Strong function with support LWIP protocol, Freertos.</li><li>Supporting three modes: AP, STA, and AP+STA.</li><li>Supporting Lua program, easily to develop.</li></ul>	$17.99/unit
Intel Celeron D 336 2.8GHz 533MHz 256K LGA775 EM64T CPU	<ul><li>Intel Celeron D 336 2.8 GHz 533 MHz 256 KB Socket 775 CPU General Features:</li><li>Intel Celeron D 336 processor 2.8 GHz clock speed 533 MHz System Bus 256 KB L2 Cache</li><li>1.25V-1.400V Socket 775</li></ul>	$29.95/unit
AMD FX-4300 Quad-Core Vishera Processor 3.8GHz	<ul><li>Frequency: 3.8/4.0GHZ (Base/Overdrive)</li><li>Cores: 4</li><li>Cache: 4/4MB (L2/L3)</li><li>Socket Type: AM3+</li></ul>	$60/unit
PENTIUM G4600	<ul><li>Socket LGA 1151</li><li>Intel 200/1001 Series Chipset Compatibility</li><li>Intel HD Graphics 630</li></ul>	$80/unit

CORE I5-8400	<ul><li>Intel UHD Graphics 630</li><li>Compatible only with Motherboards based on Intel 300 Series Chipsets</li><li>6 Cores / 12 Threads</li><li>2.80 GHz up to 4.00 GHz Max Turbo Frequency / 9 MB Cache</li><li>Intel Optane Memory Supported</li></ul>	$210/unit
Intel Computer CPU 1.7 8 BX80660E52609V4	<ul><li>Core Count: 8</li><li>Clock Speed: 1.7 GHz</li><li>Cache: 20 MB</li><li>Socket: LGA 2011-v3</li><li>Memory Type: DDR4-1866/1600</li></ul>	$350/unit
CORE I9-7900X	<ul><li>Socket LGA 2066</li><li>Compatibale with Intel X299 Chipset</li><li>10 Cores/20 Threads. Instruction Set Extensions: SSE4.1/4.2, AVX2, AVX-512</li><li>Intel Turbo Boost Max Technology 3.0</li><li>Intel Optane memory ready and support for Intel Optane SSDs</li></ul>	$960/unit

7.2.5 - RAM memory - If you're building a PC, you'll also need random-access (RAM) memory. RAM memory is like the short-term memory for computers; it is a fast type of computer memory that stores information the PC needs right now and in the near future. Increased RAM memory or faster RAM memory often helps speed up the time it takes to load applications. Here are some common RAM memory sizes, specifications, and relative unit costs (Figure 7.2.5.1).[272]

---

[272] **Amazon -** You can always find the most recent versions of RAM memory through a quick search on Amazon.

Figure 7.2.5.1
List of RAM memory and prices (2018)

RAM memory type	Specifications	Cost
A-tech micron 4GB RAM	<ul><li>4GB Module DIMM DDR3 ECC REGISTERED PC3-10600 1333MHz RAM memory</li><li>Genuine A-Tech memory</li><li>Lifetime warranty</li></ul>	$9.50/unit
Corsair 8GB RAM	<ul><li>Designed for high-performance overclocking</li><li>Designed for great looks. Compatibility : Intel 100 Series,Intel 200 Series,Intel 300 Series,Intel X299</li><li>Performance and Compatibility</li><li>Low-profile heat spreader design</li></ul>	$99.99/unit
Corsair 16GB RAM	<ul><li>Designed for high-performance overclocking</li><li>Designed for great looks</li><li>Performance and Compatibility</li><li>Low-profile heat spreader design</li><li>Compatibility: Intel 100 Series,Intel 200 Series,Intel 300 Series,Intel X299</li></ul>	$179.99/unit
Corsair 32GB RAM	<ul><li>Each Vengeance LPX module is built with a pure aluminum heat spreader for faster heat dissipation and cooler operation; and the eight-layer PCB helps manage heat and provides superior overclocking headroom.</li><li>Available in multiple colors to match your motherboard, your</li></ul>	$349.36/unit

		components, or just your style • Vengeance LPX is optimized and compatibility tested for the latest Intel 100 Series motherboards and offers higher frequencies, greater bandwidth, and lower power consumption. XMP 2.0 support for trouble-free automatic overclocking • The Vengeance LPX module height is carefully designed to fit smaller spaces. • Compatibility-Intel X99 and 100 Series platforms	

7.2.6 - Storage devices - Recall from Chapter 2 that it is important to keep the storage location of collected voice samples consistent. If you are using a Raspberry Pi and/or an Arduino with limited storage capacity, it may make sense to send all the samples to the cloud for processing so that the storage does not overflow quickly (e.g. store data in AWS S3 buckets). Alternatively, if you are collecting samples on a desktop computer it may make sense to just buy a hard disk, as they are quite affordable now on Amazon. Regardless, take this into consideration when designing a voice computer (Table 7.2.6.1).

Table 7.2.6.1 - List of storage mediums and cost (2018)		
Storage medium	**Storage capacity**	**Cost**
USB Flash drive	16GB - 256GB	$6.99-$61.99/unit[273]
SD Card	8GB - 512GB	$20.88-$299.99/unit[274]
Hard disk	500GB - 6TB	$44.50-173.99/unit[275]
FTP Server	Virtually unlimited	Varies[276]
Cloud provider	Virtually unlimited	$0.023/GB per month for AWS

---

[273] **Cost of USB Flash drive storage** - $61.99 (256GB), $27.99 (128GB), $13.99 (64GB), $7.99 (32GB), $6.99 (16GB).
[274] **Cost of SD card storage** - $299.99 (512GB), $124.99 (256GB), $58.95 (128GB), $34.50 (64GB), $20.88 (32GB)
[275] **Cost of hard disk storage** - $173.99 (6TB), $99.99 (4TB), $87.99 (3TB), $59.99 (2TB), $44.99 (1TB), $44.50 (500GB).
[276] **Cost of FTP server storage** - Depends on hosting service and plan. $11/mo for unlimited storage.

7.2.7 - Computer monitors - Note that voice computers can have a monitor. I find that adding a monitor helps to make voice computers more engaging; for example, you may want to add an avatar for a voice assistant with a projector. Also, if you plan to use the computer for more than voice purposes, monitors may be necessary (e.g. to use music editing software). Here are some typical computer monitors and their costs (Table 7.2.7.1).

<u>Table 7.2.7.1</u> List of monitors and costs (2018)		
Monitor type	**Description**	**Cost**
LCD or LED monitor	Projects images on screen and interacts with display by other means (e.g. mouses, etc.)	$80-200/unit
Touchscreen monitor	Can allow user to touch the screen and interact with display.	$150-500/unit
Projector	Can project images on walls and have a portable visualization interface.	$50-1,200/unit

7.2.8 - radiofrequency (RF) transceivers - There may be some use cases where you'd like to add a Radio Frequency (RF) transceiver to your voice computer. For example, you may want to broadcast a message to your voice computer from 30 miles away from your car (e.g. in the case of an emergency), which could then amplify that message throughout the house and/or local community through a specialized speaker system. If this seems cool to you, check out some of the transceivers in the following table (Table 7.2.8.1). Also, note that you must have an Amateur radio license in order to broadcast over specific bands (as required by the FCC), but some bands are unregulated if you are using low-power devices.[277][278]

---

[277] **Per the FCC website:** "Unlicensed operation on the AM and FM radio broadcast bands is permitted for some extremely low powered devices covered under Part 15 of the FCC's rules. On FM frequencies, these devices are limited to an effective service range of approximately 200 feet (61 meters). See 47 CFR (Code of Federal Regulations) Section 15.239, and the July 24, 1991 *Public Notice* Opens a New Window. (still in effect). On the AM broadcast band, these devices are limited to an effective service range of approximately 200 feet (61 meters). See 47 CFR Sections 15.207, 15.209, 15.219, and 15.221. These devices must accept any interference caused by any other operation, which may further limit the effective service range."

Table 7.2.8.1[279]
Types of radiofrequency transceivers compatible and costs (2018)

RF transceiver	Description	Cost
Hack RF-one SDR	<ul><li>1 MHz to 6 GHz operating frequency</li><li>Half-duplex transceiver</li><li>Up to 20 million samples per second</li><li>8-bit quadrature samples (8-bit I and 8-bit Q)</li><li>Compatible with GNU Radio, SDR#, and more</li><li>Software-configurable RX and TX gain and baseband filter</li><li>Software-controlled antenna port power (50 mA at 3.3 V)</li><li>SMA female antenna connector</li><li>SMA female clock input and output for synchronization</li><li>Convenient buttons for programming</li><li>Internal pin headers for expansion</li><li>Hi-speed USB 2.0</li><li>USB-powered</li><li>Open source hardware</li></ul>	$317/unit
Ubertooth One	<ul><li>2.4 GHz transmit and R\receive</li><li>Six indicator LEDs</li><li>Transmit power and receive sensitivity comparable to a Class 1 Bluetooth device</li><li>Standard cortex debug connector (10-pin 50-mil JTAG)</li><li>In-system programming (ISP) serial connector</li><li>Expansion connector intended for inter-Ubertooth communication or other future uses</li><li>2.4 GHz duck antenna included</li></ul>	$127/unit
Yarstick One USB transceiver	<ul><li>USB transceiver capable of transmitting and receiving most popular licence-free bands</li><li>Integrated receive amplifier and transmit amplifier</li><li>Integrated bias-tee to power antenna port accessories</li><li>Female SMA connector for connecting external antenna of your choice</li><li>A 915MHz SMA antenna is included</li></ul>	$123/unit

---

[278] **Amateur radio license** - It's quite easy to get an Amateur radio license; you just need to take a short test.

[279] **ARRL** – The ARRL website is a good place to get information on amteur radio is from https://www.ARRL.net. It is a 200,000 Ham radio member sponsored organization.

Seeedstudio Kiwi SDR 	<ul><li>SDR covers the 10 kHz to 30 MHz (VLF-HF) spectrum</li><li>Web interface based on OpenWebRX from András Retzler, HA7ILM</li><li>Demodulation modes: AM, AMN, LSB, USB, CW, CWN, NBFM</li><li>RF antenna connector: SMA and terminal block</li><li>GPS receives the Navstar system on L1 frequency 1575.42 MHz</li></ul>	$299/unit

7.2.9 - WiFi chips - WiFi chips allow for voice computers to access the Internet wirelessly without ethernet jacks. Typically, WiFi uses 2.4 GHz (12cm) and 5.8 GHz (5cm) ISM frequency bands and can be accessed within 30-60 feet of a router transmitting a wireless signal. The emergence of cheap WiFi chips has enabled a wide array of peripherals (e.g. refrigerators, dishwashers, etc.) to also connect to wireless networks, allowing voice computers to have control over home appliances (Figure 7.2.9.1). *Note that WiFi chips can be quite affordable and the pricing of the chips often reflects the speed at which the data can flow through the bands (Table 7.2.9.1).*

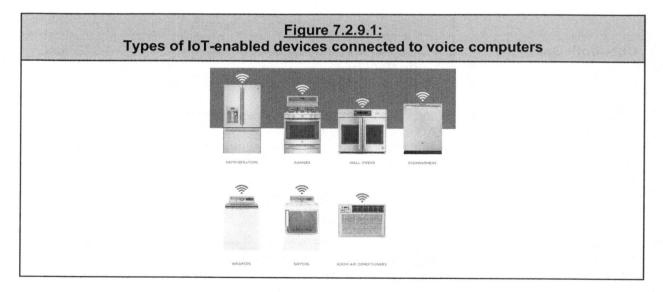

**Figure 7.2.9.1:
Types of IoT-enabled devices connected to voice computers**

Table 7.2.9.1 List of WiFi network adapters and costs (2018)		
WiFi Transceiver	Description	Cost
Plugable USB 2.0 Wireless N 802.11n 150 Mbps Nano WiFi Network Adapter	<ul><li>Add 802.11n wireless N network connectivity at up to 150 Mbps in an incredibly small package</li><li>Perfect to upgrade an old computer or bypass a broken wireless card. 2.4 GHz support only</li><li>Does not support 5 GHz Wi-Fi</li><li>Drivers provided for Windows 10, 8/8.1, 7, Vista, XP</li><li>Its Realtek RTL8188CUS chipset is Plug & Play with the Raspberry Pi and Pi2, Linux 2.6.38, 3.0.8 and later</li><li>Linux-based embedded platforms are also supported</li><li>Backwards compatible with Wireless G & B networks and USB 1.1 ports</li><li>Supports Ad-hoc and Infrastructure modes</li><li>We love our Plugable products and hope you will too. All of our products are backed with a 1-year limited parts and labor warranty and Seattle-based email support</li></ul>	$9.99/unit
TP-Link TL-WN881ND N300 PCI-E Wireless WiFi network Adapter card for pc	<ul><li>Wireless N speed up to 300Mbps makes it ideal for video streaming, online gaming and Internet calls</li><li>2T2R MIMOdelivers greater throughput at range versus conventional 1T1R</li><li>Supports 64/128 WEP, WPA /WPA2/WPA-PSK/WPA2-PSK(TKIP/AES), supports IEEE 802.1X</li><li>Supports Windows 7 32/64bit,??Windows XP 32/64bit, Vista 32/64bit</li><li>Supports ad-hoc and infrastructure mode</li><li>Bundled utility provides quick & hassle free installation</li><li>Seamlessly compatible with 802.11n/b/g products</li></ul>	$19.49/unit

Product	Features	Price
Feb Smart Wireless Dual Band N600 (2.4GHz 300Mbps or 5GHz 300Mbps) PCI Express (PCIe) Wi-Fi Adapter Network Card	<ul><li>The FS-N600 will add high speed 802.11 N Wi-Fi connectivity to a desktop computer through a PCI Express (PCIe 1X) slot</li><li>Allow desktop computer connect to wireless network at 2.4GHz 300Mbps or 5GHz 300Mbps</li><li>Build in Qualcomm Atheros chipset</li><li>Engineered 6dBi detachable external antenna</li><li>Improve wireless network reliability and performance. Provide high speed Wi-Fi connection for online gaming and HD video streaming</li><li>Seamless connect to wireless 802.11 ac/a/b/g/n device. Support 300Mbps max throughput on 2.4GHz band or 5GHz band. Comply with 64/128 WEP, WPA/WPA2,WPA-PSK/WPA2-PSK(TKIP/AES)security protocol</li><li>Compatible with Windows10, Windows8.1, Wondows8,Windows7, Windows XP,Windows Server(32/64bits)Works with PCI express X1,X4,X8,X16 slot. Low profile and standard profile bracket inside works with both mini and standard size PCs</li></ul>	$29.99/unit
ASUS Dual-Band Wireless-AC1900 PCI-E Adapter (PCE-AC68)	<ul><li>Provides an extensible design that enables Service prioritization for data</li><li>Design that delivers high availability, scalability, and for maximum flexibility and price/performance</li><li>The country of Origin is China. OS Support:Windows 8.1 (32bit/64bit), Windows 8 (32bit/64bit), Windows 7 (32bit/64bit), Windows Vista (32bit/64bit), Windows XP (32bit/64bit)</li><li>High-power design clears up dead zones with 150% greater coverage</li><li>Custom heatsink dissipates heat for more stable and reliable non-stop operation</li><li>5th generation 802.11ac chipset gives you dual-band,2.4GHz/5GHz for up to super-fast 1.30Gbps</li><li>Flexible extended antenna placement helps you pinpoint the best reception in your environment</li></ul>	$84.38/unit

7.2.10 - Bluetooth chips - Bluetooth chips allow for voice computers to connect to peripherals wirelessly through the ISM band from 2.4 to 2.485 GHz (Table 7.2.10). The range of Bluetooth receivers and transmitters depends on a lot of factors - like the antenna design, material, and battery conditions. Nonetheless, there are many wireless headsets (e.g. AirPods) and speakers (e.g. Sonos) that you can connect to via Bluetooth, so if this is a capability that you think is worthwhile you can add in a chip to your voice computer. *Note that Raspberry Pi Zeros already come with Bluetooth transceivers whereas there are specialized Arduino boards like the BLUNO ($24/unit) that allow for Bluetooth capability.*

<td colspan="3">**Table 7.2.10** **List of Bluetooth transceivers and costs (2018)**</td>		
Bluetooth transceiver	**Description**	**Cost**
Whitelabel Bluetooth 4.0 USB Dongle Adapter	• PLUG & PLAY on Win7, Win8, Win8.1 and Win10; Licensed and Latest IVT BlueSoliel driver compatible with 32 bit and 64 bit Windows XP/VISTA/7/8/10. • Latest Bluetooth 4.0 with low energy (BLE) technology and it is backward compatible with Bluetooth V3.0/2.1/2.0/1.1. • The Ultimate easy Solution for your Computer to Communicate With Bluetooth Enabled Devices Such As Mobiles, iPods, Bluetooth Headsets, Bluetooth Speakers, Printers, Mouse, Keyboard and More • USB Bluetooth Dongle Offers High Speed Up To 3mbps Wireless Transmitter Enables Long Range Connectivity Up to 50m	$5.00/unit
Gigabyte GC-WB867D-I REV Bluetooth 4.2/Wireless AC/B/G/N Band Dual Frequency 2.4Ghz/5.8Ghz Expansion Card	• Fully qualified Bluetooth 4.2 • IEEE 802.11ac standards compliant. Intel WiFi module supports Intel WIDI • Antenna to support WLAN 2Tx2R transmission • High speed wireless connection up to 867 Mbps • Bluetooth Enhanced Data Rate (EDR) support	$40.99/unit

Intel Dual Band Wireless-AC 7260 2x2 Network plus Bluetooth adapter (7260.HMWWB.R)	• Ultimate Wi-Fi performance more speed, coverage, larger capacity • Bluetooth 4.0 smart ready • Intel wireless display • Intel Smart Connect technology • Intel Wi-Fi HotSpot assistant • Business class wireless suite	$27.69/unit

7.2.11 - Speakers - To playback mono or stereo audio data, *a speaker* is necessary. Speakers operate in the reverse way as a microphone, where analog sound is transduced from an electrical signal (Table 7.2.11.1). First, the electrical signal is amplified with an **audio power amplifier** and sent to a speaker, which then makes a magnet move to produce pressure waves. Mono audio is played back as the same signal across all speakers, whereas stereo audio is played back on speakers independently in each channel (Figure Table 7.2.11.1). Like microphones, speakers can be **wireless** (e.g. Bluetooth-enabled) or **wired** depending on the needs of the end user.

<u>**Table 7.2.11.1:**</u>
Speaker types and their utility

Speaker type	Description	Utility
Headphones	Help to play sound to the ears while being muted in the exterior environment. Many types exist including in-ear, earphones, headsets, and noise-reduction headphones.	Allows for playback of sound without disturbing others around you.
Dynamic Speaker	Composed of a 1) magnet; 2) cooler; 3) voice coil; 4) suspension; and 5) membrane. A diaphragm moves back and forth to create pressure waves. The diaphragm is a cone for low and mid frequencies and a dome for high frequencies.	The most common type of loudspeaker. Can playback the entire audio frequency range. Typically in televisions, computer speakers, etc.

Piezoelectric speaker	Uses a piezoelectric material to generate sound.	Produce a high-frequency 'buzzing' sound (1-5kHz).
Electrostatic loudspeaker	Sound is generated by force exerted on membrane suspended in an electrostatic field.	Has a good frequency response, low distortion, and light weight; however, has a bad base response and sensitivity to humidity levels.
Loudspeaker	Composed of (1) mid-range driver; (2) a tweeter; and (3) woofers assembled together with an enclosure. Sometimes, (4) subwoofers are used for sounds in the lowest part of the audio spectrum (below 200 Hz). Drivers are sub-speakers and represent different parts of the audio spectrum.	Mid-range drivers reproduce middle frequencies of sound (250-2000 Hz); tweeters reproduce high audio frequencies (2000-20000 Hz); woofers reproduce low frequencies (40-500 Hz); and subwoofers reproduce ultra low frequencies (20-200 Hz).
Ribbon loudspeaker	Uses a thin diaphragm and a planar coil suspended in a magnetic field to produce sound; the reverse of the ribbon microphone configuration.	Ribbon tweeters are useful to produce high frequencies; often have directionality in the output speaker.

Speakers are an essential part of any voice computer if you desire to play back audio and voice content. Most voice computers today - like the Amazon Echo or the Google Assistant - have speakers embedded within them to play back text-to-speech files to the user in order to prompt queries (e.g. 'how can I help you?'). *I'd think about connecting wireless speakers with your voice computer, as Bluetooth speakers have become quite affordable (~$25/unit - Table 7.2.11.2).*

Table 7.2.11.2
List of speaker types and costs (2018)

Speaker	Specifications	Cost
ARVICKA Blue LED USB Speakers- Wired Laptop Speakers 2.0 Channel	<ul><li>Small and relatively portable for a USB speaker system</li><li>Clear sound</li><li>Simple operation</li><li>One knob control, LED switch available</li><li>Well-designed</li></ul>	$15.99/unit
DOSS Touch Wireless Bluetooth V4.0 Portable Speaker with HD Sound and Bass (Black)	<ul><li>Capacitive touch control</li><li>Wireless portable Bluetooth speaker</li><li>Bluetooth 4.0 technology</li><li>Superior sound quality</li><li>Long playtime</li></ul>	$27.99/unit
Anker Soundcore Bluetooth Speaker	<ul><li>Good sound</li><li>Long battery life (24 hours)</li><li>Great connectivity</li><li>Relatively portable</li></ul>	$26.99/unit

ION Audio Tailgater (iPA77) | Portable Bluetooth PA Speaker with Mic, AM/FM Radio, and USB Charge Port	<ul><li>Long battery life (50 hours of continuous use)</li><li>Dynamic, powerful speaker system with 50-hour rechargeable battery</li><li>Bluetooth connectivity plus iOS/Android app for expanded control. Robust woofer and wide-dispersion tweeter deliver high-quality sound</li><li>USB power bank to conveniently recharge your smartphone, tablet, and more</li><li>AM/FM radio with bright, clear display, and 1/8" auxiliary input; microphone and auxiliary cable included</li></ul>	$119/unit

7.2.12 - Power supplies / batteries - Power supplies and/or batteries are necessary to power your voice computer. There are a range of batteries to make Arduino- and/or [Raspberry Pi]-built voice computers portable (Table 7.2.12.1). In contrast, if these devices do not need to be portable they can be powered to USBs through host computers. PCs, on the other hand, need power supplies (Table 7.2.12.1). It often makes sense to use your voice computer for a while to test how much power it is consuming, and then get the appropriate battery if you'd like to make it portable (e.g. extrapolate energy use). Keep this in mind when selecting the right power supply and/or battery to fit your needs.

Table 7.2.12.1
List of power supply / battery types and costs (2018)

Power supply	Specifications	Cost
Kuman Lithium Battery Pack Expansion Board Power Supply	<ul><li>Specially designed for Raspberry Pi, which makes Raspberry Pi work up to 9 hours</li><li>Double USB output. One is for Raspberry Pi, the other can be connected with LCD screen</li><li>Easy to install, you can use provided fastening standoffs, screws and nuts to fasten your Raspberry pi board</li><li>It comes with 17cm micro USB cable</li><li>Battery capacity: 3800mAH Maximum; Output current: 1.8A</li></ul>	$14.98/unit

energyShield 2 Pro - Arduino Battery, Solar Powered, Eco Mode, Real Time Clock, and Fuel Gauge	<ul><li>Rechargeable Li-ION battery</li><li>Solar and USB charging</li><li>Power saving eco mode</li><li>Fuel gauge and real-time clock</li><li>Arduino shield form factor</li></ul>	$44.95/unit
Rosewill Gaming Power Supply, Arc Series 750 Watt (750W)	<ul><li>Reliable ARC Series power supplies</li><li>Silent operation</li><li>80+ Bronze Certified</li><li>3 year warranty</li><li>UL, FCC, CE Certificated</li><li>Active-PFC with auto AC-input voltage adjustment(100-240V)</li><li>Safety & EMI Approval: UL, FCC, CE, ROHS</li></ul>	$69.99/unit
NEXGADGET 42000mAh power	<ul><li>Portable power source</li><li>Small size and light</li><li>Prevents crashes of computers through pure sine wave</li><li>Fast charging</li><li>Safe</li></ul>	$199.99/unit

7.2.13 - Outer housing - Outer housings are the last thing to think about when building a voice computer. If you're building a Raspberry Pi and/or Arduino-based voice computer, there are many off-the-shelf outer housings that you use as a base for your designs (Table 7.2.13.1).[280] If you're building a PC-based voice computer, there are also many computer case housings you can use based on motherboard form factors (Table 7.2.13.1). *Although housings have little functional use, the housing appearance is a very important factor on consumer adoption.*

---

[280] **Raspberry pi / Arduino case designs** – See Table 7.2.13 different designs of housings for Arduinos and Raspberry Pis here.

Table 7.2.13.1
List of housing types and their costs (2018)

Type of housing	Specifications	Cost
Custom Raspberry Pi housing (various)		$6-25/unit
Custom Arduino housing (various)		$7-15/unit
DIYPC Skyline-06-WG	<ul><li>Steel ATX Full Tower</li><li>2 x USB3.0 + 2 x USB2.0</li><li>5 x 120mm Green Fans Pre-Installed</li><li>Hot Swap Docking (for 3.5" HDD or 2.5" SSD) on Top Panel</li></ul>	$78/unit
Thermaltake View 71 RGB	<ul><li>4-Sided 5mm thick Tempered Glass "Spaced" panels</li><li>Dual Swing 180 degree doors with full side panel windows</li><li>Vertical GPU Float bracket (Riser Cable Sold Separately)</li><li>Support up to 10x 2.5" SSD drives or 7x 3.5" HDD Drives</li><li>3-Way Radiator Mounting (Top, Front, Vertical Side) – Up to 420mm</li><li>Top/Front 45 degree mount I/O Panel with 2x USB 3.0/2x USB 2.0 with HD Audio</li></ul>	$169/unit

You can also design your own case. This may be necessary if you have a specific speaker and microphone configuration, as there may not be many types of cases that fit with your voice computer. In these scenarios, you have to do some material selection and assembly[281] and can build custom plastic frames using AutoCAD or SolidWorks. Generally, it's easier to 3D print

---

[281] **Wood frames** - For personal projects, I like to make stuff out of wood, as it's easier to cut wood and piece stuff like this together on wood frames.

custom dimensions nowadays and make plastic molds. The Apple HomePod is a great design of a custom voice computer frame around the elegantly compressed interior components, as shown in the figure below (Figure 7.2.13.1). *Make sure your housing can be mass-produced if you are building a voice computer for commercial use!*

**Figure 7.2.13.1
Outer housing of the Apple HomePod**

In general, I'd first check if there are any outer housings out there that fit you needs because making your own housing can be difficult, especially if you don't have an industrial design background. Who knows, if you really like the way Amazon designed their smart speaker it may make sense to develop on top of Amazon Alexa! 😊

7.3   Building software[282]

Now that we have assembled voice computing hardware, it's time to get back into programming some Python. In this section, we'll introduce some scripts that will help you to customize voice interfaces. Specifically, this section will overview how to detect wake words and build custom transcription models. In this way, you'll have the background knowledge necessary to build voice assistants from scratch!

---

[282] **Here are some things to consider** when building voice-enabled software (recall the MEMUPPS controls from Chapter 1). Make sure you keep this all constant when you record voice media, as it could lead to inconsistent operation of a voice assistant:

- **Microphone** - controls
- **Environment** - indoor vs. outdoor
- **Mode** - passive vs. active
- **User** - male vs. female vs. children vs. etc… mic distance
- **Processing** - models etc. (features)
- **Publishing** - local vs. online
- **Storage** - locally vs. in cloud

7.3.1. Bluetooth connection - If you built a custom voice computer, you may need to know how to connect to a Bluetooth device (e.g. a wireless headset). We can check for Bluetooth devices using the *PyBluez module* (Figure 7.3.1.1).[283]

Figure 7.3.1.1
Using PyBluez for Bluetooth data transmission: *bluetooth.py*

```
import bluetooth
from bluetooth.ble import DiscoveryService

# The MAC address of a Bluetooth adapter on the server.
# The server might have multiple Bluetooth adapters.
hostMACAddress = '00:1f:e1:dd:08:3d'
serverMACAddress = hostMACAddress
# 3 is an arbitrary choice. However, it must match the port used by the client.
port = 3

def get_devices():
    nearby_devices = bluetooth.discover_devices(lookup_names=True)
    print("found %d devices" % len(nearby_devices))
    for addr, name in nearby_devices:
        print("  %s - %s" % (addr, name))

    return nearby_devices

def bluetooth_send(serverMACAddress, port, data):
    s = bluetooth.BluetoothSocket(bluetooth.RFCOMM)
    s.connect((serverMACAddress, port))
    s.send(data)
    sock.close()

def bluetooth_receive(hostMACAddress, port):
    # receive data
    backlog = 1
    size = 1024
    s = bluetooth.BluetoothSocket(bluetooth.RFCOMM)
    s.bind((hostMACAddress, port))
    s.listen(backlog)
    try:
        client, clientInfo = s.accept()
        while 1:
            data = client.recv(size)
```

---

[283] **PyBluez vs. Python Sockets in Python 3** - Python sockets can now be used for Bluetooth communication (since Python 3.3). For a simple application, the code between PyBluez and Python sockets is almost identical. For some tasks, however, such as device discovery and Bluetooth service advertisements, it does not seem possible to carry them out using Python sockets. Consequently, PyBluez is better for functionality.

```
            if data:
                print(data)
                client.send(data) # Echo back to client
    except:
        print("Closing socket")
        client.close()
        s.close()
```

7.3.2. WiFi connection - Similarly, you may need to know how to automatically connect to a WiFi network if you have a chip on your laptop. If you're trying to connect to a network with WEP or WPA2 encryption, you can use the *wireless module*. I like the wireless module because it's fairly simple, though you can also use an alternative library called *wifi*, which has a bit more documentation and a greater community. Regardless, connecting to and from WiFi hotspots is quite easy in Python (Figure 7.3.2.1).

<u>**Figure 7.3.2.1**</u>
Using the wireless module to connect to WiFi network: *wifi.py*

```python
from wireless import Wireless

# connect to wireless network
wireless=Wireless()
ssid='I_am_cool'
password='password'
wireless.connect(ssid='ssid', password='password')

# various things you can get
print(wireless.current())
print(wireless.interfaces())
print(wireless.interface())
print(wireless.power())
print(wireless.driver())
```

7.3.3. Serial connections - You also may need to connect to serial ports to communicate with Arduino devices; for example, you may need to load up software on the COM3 port via a USB connection. The best module to do this is *PySerial*, which encapsulates the access for the serial port on your host machine. Let's go through a quick example of a simple command to open a port, write some data, then close a port (Figure 7.3.3.1). *Note that most computers nowadays do not have any serial ports by default, so this code will error if you don't have a serial port plugged in via USB.*

Figure 7.3.3.1
Connecting to Arduino devices through COM ports: *pyserial.py*

```python
import serial

# simple example of opening serial port and closing it
ser = serial.Serial()
ser.baudrate = 19200
ser.port = 'COM1'
print(ser)
ser.open()
print(ser.is_open)
# write some data
ser.write(b'hello')
ser.close()
print(ser.is_open) # False
```

7.3.4. Wake word detection - You may notice when you say 'Hey Siri' to a plugged in iPhone Siri responds to the query in a hands-free way. This 'Hey Siri' is known as a ***wake word***, or a voice utterance that provokes a response from a voice computer.

Let's first try building a wake word from things we already know how to do. We could look for hotwords every 3 seconds in a streaming way through a speech recognition system - like PocketSphinx (Figure 7.3.4.1). If done asynchronously, the hotword transcription detector could work as the samples are being recorded, and if the hotwords are detected multiple times in a section then it could break the loop and only provoke one response. In the example below, the computer responds 'hello' if you speak the hotwords 'test' or 'testing.'

Figure 7.3.4.1
Using transcription tools for wake words: *wake_transcribe.py*

```python
import soundfile as sf
import sounddevice as sd
import speech_recognition as sr_audio
import pyttsx3
import os, time

# transcribe with pocketsphinx (open-source)
def speak():
    engine = pyttsx3.init()
    engine.say("hello!!")
    engine.runAndWait()

def find_wake(transcript, hotwords):
    for i in range(len(hotwords)):
```

```python
##        print(transcript)
##        print(transcript.lower().find(hotwords[i]))
        if transcript.lower().find(hotwords[i])>=0:
            print('%s wakeword found!!'%(hotwords[i].upper()))
            speak()
            break

def transcribe_sphinx(file):
    try:
        r=sr_audio.Recognizer()
        with sr_audio.AudioFile(file) as source:
            audio = r.record(source)
        transcript=r.recognize_sphinx(audio)
        print('sphinx transcript: '+transcript)
    except:
        transcript=''
        print(transcript)
        
    return transcript

def async_record(hotwords, filename, filename2, duration, fs, channels):
    print('recording')
    myrecording = sd.rec(int(duration * fs), samplerate=fs, channels=channels)
    transcript=transcribe_sphinx(filename2)
    find_wake(transcript, hotwords)
    sd.wait()
    sf.write(filename, myrecording, fs)
    print('done recording')

# initial parameters
hotwords=['test', 'testing']
i=0
t=1
filename2='n/a'
# create infinite loop
while t>0:
    # record a mono file asynchronous, transcribe, and find wake word
    filename=str(i+1)+'.wav'
    async_record(hotwords, filename, filename2, 3, 16000, 1)
    filename2=filename
    i=i+1
    try:
        os.remove(str(i-2)+'.wav')
    except:
        pass
```

However, if you this code has a few issues:

- The PocketSphinx transcription model tends to transcribe words inaccurately - something you could fix with Google transcription but that would cost a lot of money ($0.006/query).
- You also may have a false positive where the word you spoke actually was not the wake word and then the computer executes the wake word unintentionally.
- It takes a bit of time for the wake word to be recognized and processed (e.g. every 3 seconds), leading to a bad user experience.

There's a much better way to recognize wake words - through **wake word engines** or **hotword detectors** (Figure 7.3.4.2). This strategy consumes much less power by processing streaming audio via a buffer (often 1024 bytes). Note that in general, the most accurate wake word detectors in Python tend to be Porcupine > Snowboy > PocketSphinx (Figure 7.3.4.2). We'll go through each of these wake word engines in the sections that follow.

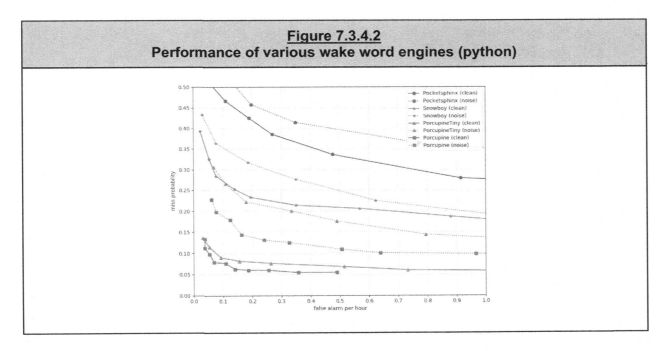

Figure 7.3.4.2
Performance of various wake word engines (python)

Let's start out building a **PocketSphinx-based hotword detector** (Figure 7.3.4.3). Now this code is much better at detecting wake words and stops after detecting the keyword ('test') once. Again, the computer responds by saying "hello" back with the pyttsx3 module. *Note that PocketSphinx has a restricted dictionary in its default model, so you may have a limit on the type of keyword that you use.*

Figure 7.3.4.3
Hotword detection with PocketSphinx: *wake_pocket.py*

```python
import os, pyaudio, pyttsx3
from pocketsphinx import *

def speak():
    engine = pyttsx3.init()
    engine.say("hello!!")
    engine.runAndWait()

def pocket_detect(key_phrase):

    modeldir = os.path.dirname(pocketsphinx.__file__)+'/model'
    # Create a decoder with certain model
    config = pocketsphinx.Decoder.default_config()
    # config.set_string('-hmm', os.path.join(modeldir, 'en-us/en-us'))
    config.set_string('-dict', modeldir+'/cmudict-en-us.dict')
    config.set_string('-hmm', os.path.join(modeldir, 'en-us'))
    config.set_string('-keyphrase', key_phrase)
    config.set_float('-kws_threshold', 1)
    # Start a pyaudio instance
    p = pyaudio.PyAudio()
    # Create an input stream with pyaudio
    stream = p.open(format=pyaudio.paInt16, channels=1, rate=16000, input=True, frames_per_buffer=1024)
    # Start the stream
    stream.start_stream()
    # Process audio chunk by chunk.
    decoder = pocketsphinx.Decoder(config)
    decoder.start_utt()
    # Loop forever
    while True:
        # Read 1024 samples from the buffer
        buf = stream.read(1024)
        # If data in the buffer, process using the sphinx decoder
        if buf:
            decoder.process_raw(buf, False, False)
        else:
            break
        # If the hypothesis is not none, the key phrase was recognized
        if decoder.hyp() is not None:
            keyphrase_function(keyword)
            # Stop and reinitialize the decoder
            decoder.end_utt()
```

```python
            decoder.start_utt()
            speak()
            break

def keyphrase_function(keyword):
    print("Keyword %s detected!"%(keyword))

keyword='test'
pocket_detect(keyword)
```

Next, we can implement a wake word detection model using **Snowboy**. First you need to train a wake word model on their website and download a *.pdml* model file (you can use "hey_nala.pdml" in '/data/' if you don't feel like doing this step). Then you can load it with the following script, which is executed in Python 3 (Figure 7.3.4.4). *Note you need to put the path to the pmdl file; in this case, it is in the current directory.*

Figure 7.3.4.4
Hotword detection with snowboy: *wake_snow.py*

```
cd ~
cd voicebook/chapter_7_design/snowboy
python3 hey_nala.pmdl
```

```
>> Listening... Press Ctrl+C to exit
>> INFO:snowboy:Keyword 1 detected at time: 2018-07-31 16:46:22
>> INFO:snowboy:Keyword 1 detected at time: 2018-07-31 16:46:27
```

Porcupine can be similarly implemented in Python3.[284][285] First, you need need to go to the *voicebook/chapter_7_design/porcupine* folder (Figure 7.3.4.5).[286] Now, we can run some code from the terminal to train a keyword with the Porcupine optimizer tool.

Figure 7.3.4.5
Training keywords with porcupine from CLI

```
cd ~
git clone https://github.com/Picovoice/Porcupine.git
cd porcupine
tools/optimizer/mac/x86_64/pv_porcupine_optimizer -r resources -w "hey test" -p mac
-o ~/voicebook/chapter_7_design/porcupine/
```

---

[284] **Porcupine Licensing** - Pretty much everything - from the code base to training new models - is licensed under an Apache 2.0 license. However, Porcupine makes you purchase a commercial license if you plan to develop on any other operating systems - so keep this in mind.
[285] **How it works** - Porcupine uses deep neural networks (DNNs) trained using MXNet.
[286] **Alternatively**, you can clone the repo and cd into that folder from the terminal.

Now we can run code to start a loop to detect the wake word "hey test" (Figure 7.3.4.6). *Note that Porcupine is the most accurate hotword detector, so I'd recommend using this one for production use cases.*

Figure 7.3.4.6
Hotword detection with porcupine: *wake_porcupine.py*

```
cd ~
cd voicebook/chapter_7_design/porcupine
python3 porcupine_demo.py --keyword_file_paths "hey test.ppn"

>> [2018-07-31 16:48:18.734792] detected keyword
>> [2018-07-31 16:48:20.680458] detected keyword
>> [2018-07-31 16:48:22.898576] detected keyword
```

7.3.5 - Custom transcription models – It's important to be able to build custom language models to determine intents of end users. In this way, you can achieve much higher transcription accuracies and make better experiences for end users.[287] [288]

We can easily build a custom language model with PocketSphinx. First, we need to create a text document with keywords to train the language model. These are the words that the transcription model will be trained to recognize. In general, the fewer the words in the master corpus the better transcription accuracy you'll achieve (Figure 7.3.5.1).

Figure 7.3.5.1
Building a keyword corpus for training a pocketsphinx language model:
/data/corpus.txt

```
one
two
three
four
five
six
seven
eight
nine
ten
```

---

[287] **Acoustic models -** Note that you can also build acoustic models, which represent phonemes in the voice. But these are much harder to build reliably without large datasets. I thus encourage you to restrict to building language models because it's simpler and often yields better results.

[288] **Amazon** does this through limiting the vocabulary to around 200-300 core words.

Now that we have our text training corpus, we can go to the **LMTool page** (http://www.speech.cs.cmu.edu/tools/lmtool-new.html). Simply click on the "Browse…" button, select the corpus.txt file you created, then click "COMPILE KNOWLEDGE BASE" and download all the files (Figure 7.3.5.2). In this case, there is a TAR4311.tgz file that I can download at the top easily into the downloads folder.

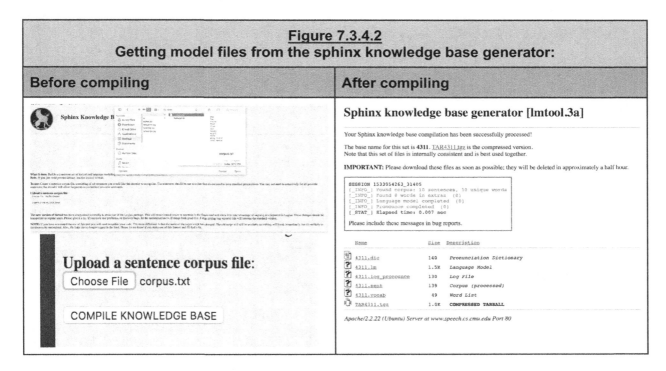

Figure 7.3.4.2
Getting model files from the sphinx knowledge base generator:

Now that we have all the required files, all we need to do is load them in PocketSphinx. You can use it for transcription! *Pretty easy, right?* (Figure 7.3.5.3).

Figure 7.3.5.3
Implementing a custom transcription model: *transcribe_custom.py (top), output (bottom)*

```python
import os, sys
from pocketsphinx.pocketsphinx import *
from sphinxbase.sphinxbase import *
import sounddevice as sd
import soundfile as sf

def sync_record(filename, duration, fs, channels):
    print('recording')
    myrecording = sd.rec(int(duration * fs), samplerate=fs, channels=channels)
    sd.wait()
    sf.write(filename, myrecording, fs)
    print('done recording')
```

```python
# Get all the directories right
def transcribe(sample):

    modeldir=os.getcwd()+'/data'
    # Create a decoder with certain model
    config = Decoder.default_config()
    config.set_string('-hmm', modeldir+'/en-us')
    config.set_string('-lm', modeldir+'/TAR4311/4311.lm')
    config.set_string('-dict', modeldir+'/TAR4311/4311.dic')
    decoder = Decoder(config)

    # Decode streaming data.
    decoder = Decoder(config)
    decoder.start_utt()
    stream = open(sample, 'rb')
    while True:
      buf = stream.read(1024)
      if buf:
        decoder.process_raw(buf, False, False)
      else:
        break
    decoder.end_utt()

    #print ('Best hypothesis segments: ', [seg.word for seg in decoder.seg()])
    output=[seg.word for seg in decoder.seg()]
    try:
        output.remove('<s>')
        output.remove('</s>')

        transcript = ''
        for i in range(len(output)):
            if output[i] == '<sil>':
                pass
            elif i == 0:
                transcript=transcript+output[i]
            else:
                transcript=transcript+' '+output[i]

        transcript=transcript.lower()
        print('transcript: '+transcript)
    except:
        transcript=''

    return transcript
```

```
t=1
i=0


while t>0:
    sync_record('test.wav',3,16000,1)
    transcribe('test.wav')
```

```
>> done recording
>> transcript: one [speech]
>> recording
>> done recording
>> transcript: two
>> recording
>> done recording
>> transcript: three
>> recording
>> done recording
>> transcript: four
>> recording...
```

We can now use custom transcription models for many purposes. ☺

7.4   Nala: a voice assistant

Now that we've built a voice computer in terms of its underlying software and hardware, it's time for us to build a voice assistant.

For the rest of the chapter we will be building a voice assistant named Nala. And yes, this is Nala from the Lion King! 🦁

7.4.1 - Initializing environment variables - We must first set up some environment variables: GOOGLE_APPLICATION_CREDENTIALS and SUDO_PASSWORD (Figure 7.4.1.1). *Note none of this data is shared on a 3rd party server; Nala is a completely local voice assistant for research, commercial, or personal use.*

Figure 7.4.1.1
Setting up environment variables: *terminal (top), .bash_profile (bottom)*

```
cd ~
open .bash_profile
```

```
export GOOGLE_APPLICATION_CREDENTIALS='application.json'
export SUDO_PASSWORD='sudo_password'
```

The **GOOGLE_APPLICATION_CREDENTIALS** is a path to a .json file for your credentials to use the Google Speech API. This must be in your environment variables. For example, it could be something like /Users/jimschwoebel/Desktop/appcreds/NLX-infrastructure-b9201d884ea5.json. *You only need this if you plan to use Google for transcription purposes.*

The **SUDO_PASSWORD** environment variable is the password to the root account. This is used for shutting down and restarting the computer. *If you don't care about these commands in your voice assistant, then don't worry about inserting it here.*

7.4.2 - Recording user queries - We can quickly write a function to allow for user queries to be recorded and subsequently processed and transcribed. This step is necessary to log and understand an intent from an end user. We can use the PyAudio module to record files (Figure 7.4.2.1). Although this is a bit messier than using the sounddevice and SoundFile modules, it still gets the job done.

Figure 7.4.2.1:
Recording user queries: *record.py*

```python
import pyaudio, os, wave

def record_to_file(path,filename,recordtime):

    # record 3 second voice file
    CHUNK = 1024
    FORMAT = pyaudio.paInt16 #paInt8
    CHANNELS = 1
    RATE = 16000 #sample rate
    RECORD_SECONDS = recordtime
    WAVE_OUTPUT_FILENAME = filename

    p = pyaudio.PyAudio()

    stream = p.open(format=FORMAT,
                    channels=CHANNELS,
                    rate=RATE,
                    input=True,
                    frames_per_buffer=CHUNK) #buffer

    print("* recording")

    frames = []

    for i in range(0, int(RATE / CHUNK * RECORD_SECONDS)):
        data = stream.read(CHUNK)
        frames.append(data) # 2 bytes(16 bits) per channel

    print("* done recording")

    stream.stop_stream()
    stream.close()
    p.terminate()

    wf = wave.open(WAVE_OUTPUT_FILENAME, 'wb')
    wf.setnchannels(CHANNELS)
    wf.setsampwidth(p.get_sample_size(FORMAT))
    wf.setframerate(RATE)
    wf.writeframes(b''.join(frames))
    wf.close()

# record 3 second file named 'test.wav'
record_to_file(os.getcwd(), 'test.wav',3)
```

7.4.3 - Transcription - We can now make a function to customize the type of transcription. Here you can specify transcription with PocketSphinx with "sphinx" (e.g. uses a custom model with a limited vocabulary) or "Google" (e.g. if you'd like to use Google's Speech-to-Text API). If the transcription process fails, an empty string is output from the function. *Note that if Google transcription fails the default PocketSphinx transcription model is used.*

Figure 7.4.3.1:
Function to transcribe audio: *transcribe.py*

```python
import speech_recognition as sr_audio
from nala.data.models import ps_transcribe as pst

def transcribe_audio(filename,hostdir,transcript_type):
    # transcribe the audio according to transcript type
    try:
        if transcript_type == 'sphinx':
            transcript=pst.transcribe(hostdir,filename)
            print('pocket: '+transcript)
        elif transcript_type == 'google':
            try:
                # try google if you can, otherwise use sphinx
                r=sr_audio.Recognizer()
                with sr_audio.AudioFile(filename) as source:
                    audio = r.record(source)
                transcript=r.recognize_google_cloud(audio)
                print('google: '+transcript)
            except:
                print('error')
                print('defaulting to pocketsphinx...')
                r=sr_audio.Recognizer()
                with sr_audio.AudioFile(filename) as source:
                    audio = r.record(source)
                transcript=r.recognize_sphinx(audio)
                print('sphinx (failed google): '+transcript)

        else:
            # default to sphinx if not sphinx or google inputs
            transcript=pst.transcribe(hostdir,filename)
            print('pocket: '+transcript)
    except:
        transcript=''

    return transcript
```

7.4.4 - Customizing wake word engine – It's quite easy to customize Nala's wake word engine. You can customize the wake word engine with the wakeup() function. This function goes into the *./data/models* directory and then initiates a wake word engine to listen for the desired wake word (e.g. 'Hey Nala'); after this, the loop is terminated and it moves on. In this way, we can use wake word engines as a trigger for Nala to be activated to then give some response.

Note, we can customize this hotword engine with the wake_type variable. The options are "sphinx" (PocketSphinx), "snowboy" (for Snowboy), and "porcupine" (for Porcupine). By default the setting is set to Porcupine, but the other options should work as well if you would prefer using them. In general, Porcupine is the most accurate and easiest to launch commercially without any additional licensing for Linux, Mac, and Windows platforms.

Figure 7.4.4.1:
Specifying wake word engines: *wakeup.py* (top), *terminal output* (bottom)

```python
import os

def wakeup(wake_type):
    if wake_type == 'porcupine':
        os.system('python3 wake_porcupine.py')
    elif wake_type == 'snowboy':
        os.system('python3 wake_snow.py')
    elif wake_type == 'sphinx':
        os.system('python3 wake_pocket.py')
    else:
        # default to porcupine if don't know
        os.system('python3 wake_porcupine.py')

os.chdir('nala/data/models')
wakeup('porcupine')
```

```
>> Jims-iMac:chapter_7_new jim$ python3 wakeup.py
>> [2018-08-02 12:10:55.401779] detected keyword
```

7.4.5 - Customizing text-to-speech (TTS) - You've already used text-to-speech (TTS) systems many times throughout this book using the *Pyttsx3 module*. Now we can apply this knowledge to customize the voice by the engine.setProperty function. Nala comes with a default voice (Fiona), which is a sweet Irish accent; however, you can change this to whatever you wish.

Note that we can use the argv() function with the sys module (e.g. sys.argv[0]) in Python to pass through text from the command line. We can also make sure every script uses the same voice by only modifying one master script (speak.py). In this way, it dramatically reduces the number of edits we need to make in our code base (Figure 7.4.5.1).

Figure 7.4.5.1
Customizing text-to-speech engine: *nala.py (top) | ./actions/speak.py (bottom)*

```python
import os

def speaktext(hostdir,text):
    # speak to user from a text sample (tts system)
    curdir=os.getcwd()
    os.chdir(hostdir+'/actions')
    os.system("python3 speak.py '%s'"%(str(text)))
    os.chdir(curdir)

speaktext(os.getcwd()+'/nala', 'hey this is awesome')
```

7.4.6 - Registering a new user - Before we can use Nala, we first need to register a new user account. We can do this through a function, register_user(), which we can call and modify later (Figure 7.4.6.1). This function takes in a variable action_list, which is a list of all the actions that Nala can do for users. The function also takes in the host directory where Nala is installed so it can properly make new folders and initialize databases.

Figure 7.4.6.1:
Registration process: *./voicebook/chapter_7_design/nala/nala.py*

```python
def register_user(action_list, hostdir):

    # hostdir
    os.chdir(hostdir)
    hostdir=os.getcwd()

    # assume default directory is hostdir
    # if any folders exist delete them
    try:
        os.mkdir(hostdir+'/data/wakewords')
    except:
        shutil.rmtree(hostdir+'/data/wakewords')
        os.mkdir(hostdir+'/data/wakewords')
    try:
        os.mkdir(hostdir+'/data/actions')
    except:
        shutil.rmtree(hostdir+'/data/actions')
        os.mkdir(hostdir+'/data/actions')
    try:
        os.mkdir(hostdir+'/data/queries')
    except:
        shutil.rmtree(hostdir+'/data/queries')
```

```python
        os.mkdir(hostdir+'/data/queries')
    try:
        os.mkdir(hostdir+'/data/baseline')
    except:
        shutil.rmtree(hostdir+'/data/baseline')
        os.mkdir(hostdir+'/data/baseline')

    os.chdir(hostdir+'/data/baseline')

    # get name from user profile name, if not record it
    speaktext(hostdir, 'To begin, you must register with us. I have a few quick questions for you. Please type in the answers to the following questions.')
    email=input('what is your email? \n')
    name=input('what is your name (leave blank for %s)? \n'%(getpass.getuser()))
    budget=input('what is the budget that you have to go out with friends? (e.g. 30) \n')
    genre=input('what is your favorite music genre? (e.g. rock) \n')

    # now get some wake words to authenticate the user's identity
    os.chdir(hostdir+'/data/wakewords')
    speaktext(hostdir, 'Okay, can you say Hey Nala for me?')
    playbackaudio(hostdir+'/data/tone.wav')
    record_to_file(os.getcwd(),'hey_nala_1.wav', 3)
    speaktext(hostdir, 'Can you say Hey Nala again?')
    playbackaudio(hostdir+'/data/tone.wav')
    record_to_file(os.getcwd(),'hey_nala_2.wav', 3)
    speaktext(hostdir, 'One more time.')
    playbackaudio(hostdir+'/data/tone.wav')
    record_to_file(os.getcwd(),'hey_nala_3.wav', 3)

    # go back to baseline directory to save databases
    os.chdir(hostdir+'/data/baseline')

    if name == '':
        name=getpass.getuser()

    speaktext(hostdir, 'Now give us a few seconds to make an account for you.')

    facenums=cut_faces(hostdir, name+'.avi')
    os.chdir(hostdir+'/data/baseline')

    jsonfile=open('settings.json','w')

    data = {
        'alarm': False,
        'alarm time': 8,
```

```python
        'greeting': True,
        'end': time.time(),
        'transcript type': 'sphinx',
        'wake type': 'porcupine',
        'query time':3,
        'multi query':True,
        'query save':True,
        'register face': True,
        'sleep time': 30,
        'query json': True,
        'budget': budget,
        'genre': genre,
}

jsonfile=open('settings.json','w')
json.dump(data,jsonfile)
jsonfile.close()

jsonfile=open('registration.json','w')
data = {
    'name': name,
    'email': email,
    'userID': 0,
    'hostdir': os.getcwd(),
    'location': curloc(),
    'rest time': 0.10,
    'facenums': facenums,
    'registration date': get_date(),
    'tts': 'com.apple.speech.synthesis.voice.fiona',
    }
json.dump(data,jsonfile)
jsonfile.close()
jsonfile=open('actions.json','w')
data = {
    'logins': [], # Login datetime
    'logouts': [], # logout datetime (last time before login)
    'active session': [],
    'sessions': [],
    'query count': 0,
    'queries': [],
    'noise': [],
    'action count': 0,
    'action log': [], #action, datetime, other stuff
    'loopnum': 0,
    'available actions': action_list,
}
```

```
# dump json data
json.dump(data, jsonfile)
jsonfile.close()

# store 2 copies in case of deletion
shutil.copy(os.getcwd()+'/registration.json', hostdir+'/registration.json')
shutil.copy(os.getcwd()+'/settings.json', hostdir+'/settings.json')
shutil.copy(os.getcwd()+'/actions.json', hostdir+'/actions.json')

# now respond to user and tell them they are registered
speaktext(hostdir, 'Thank you, you are now registered.')
```

As you can see, the registration process is straightforward and consists of 5 steps:

1. The user enters their name and email.
2. The user is prompted to say "Hey Nala" three times to store wake words later.
3. Various folders are made (wake words, actions, queries, and baseline).
4. The user's face is recognized and stored in ./baseline folder.
5. Databases are then made (registration.json, settings.json, and actions.json).

Note that you can modify many settings after the settings.json file is created. These settings control things like what transcription type you use, the wake word engine, how long each query takes (e.g. 3 seconds), and whether or not you save user queries in terms of .JSON files and/or .WAV files (Table 7.4.2.2). This architecture makes Nala highly customizable to your needs.

\multicolumn{3}{c}{**Table 7.4.2.2**}
\multicolumn{3}{c}{**Modifiable settings:** *settings.json*}
Variable	Options (**defaults**)[289]	**Description**
alarm	True | **False**	Whether the alarm is turned on or off at the designated time.
alarm_time	8	The time the alarm would go off at (in 24 hour time, 8 = 8AM, 13 = 1 PM) if the alarm action is turned on.
greeting	**True** | False	If True, then Nala will greet you every time you login and get the weather (default). If False, she will not do this.

---

[289] **Bolded** are default and recommended settings, but the settings may change depending on your use case.

transcription_type	**'sphinx'** | 'google'	The type of transcription. *Default is 'sphinx'*
wake_type	'sphinx' | 'snowboy' | **'porcupine'**	Wake word detector used to detect user queries. *Default is 'porcupine' as it is the most accurate wake word detector.*
query_time	**3** | any integer	Time in seconds of each query when Nala is activated. *The default query time is 2 seconds (from trial-and-error).*
multi_query	**True** | False	Multi-query capability allows you to separate queries with AND in the transcript, so it doesn't stop after one query. *Default is True.*
query_save	**True** | False	Ability to save queries once they have been propagated. Otherwise, they are deleted. This is useful if you want to cache query data or build a dataset. *Default is True.*
register_face	**True** | False	Store face when user registers to authenticate later with facial recognition. *Default is True.*
sleep_time	**30** | (any integer)	The time (in minutes) that Nala will sleep if you trigger the "Go to sleep" action query. Default is 30 minutes.
query_json	**True** | False	Save .json queries as well in the data/queries folder to match audio (e.g. sample.wav --> sample.json).
budget	**30** | (any integer)	Budget user has to go out with friends (for actions).
genre	**'classical'** | (string)	Type of music genre that user prefers (for actions).

7.4.7 - Loading databases – Now we need to load databases so that all the variables can be instantiated before the main event loop. This can be done by loading the .JSON database and naming the variables accordingly (Figure 7.4.7.1). *Note that Nala has inbuilt redundancy in the databases so if one database failed (e.g. actions.json), then it is restored from the ./data/baseline directory. Also note here that if a user is not registered (e.g. there is an error loading the database and the backup database) they then are registered.*

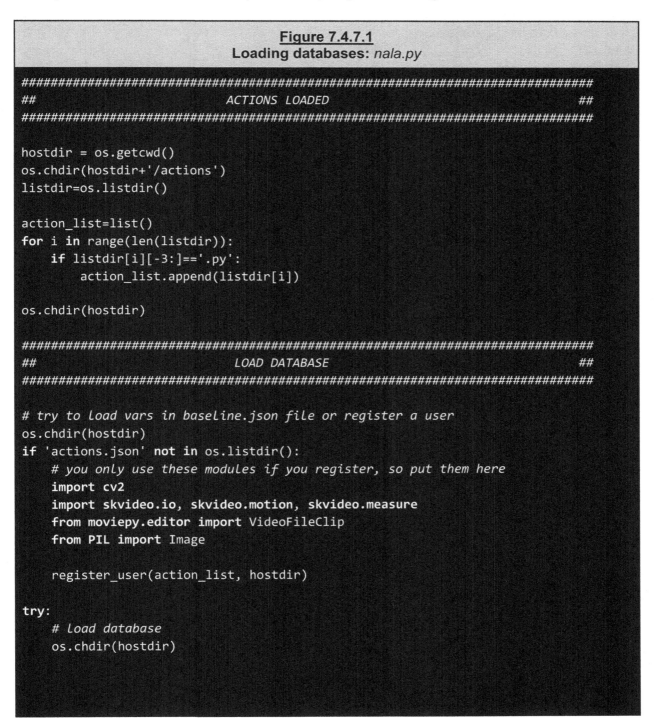

Figure 7.4.7.1
Loading databases: *nala.py*

```
################################################################################
##                           ACTIONS LOADED                                   ##
################################################################################

hostdir = os.getcwd()
os.chdir(hostdir+'/actions')
listdir=os.listdir()

action_list=list()
for i in range(len(listdir)):
    if listdir[i][-3:]=='.py':
        action_list.append(listdir[i])

os.chdir(hostdir)

################################################################################
##                           LOAD DATABASE                                    ##
################################################################################

# try to load vars in baseline.json file or register a user
os.chdir(hostdir)
if 'actions.json' not in os.listdir():
    # you only use these modules if you register, so put them here
    import cv2
    import skvideo.io, skvideo.motion, skvideo.measure
    from moviepy.editor import VideoFileClip
    from PIL import Image

    register_user(action_list, hostdir)

try:
    # load database
    os.chdir(hostdir)
```

```python
    # registration.json data
    try:
        database=json.load(open('registration.json'))
    except:
        # restore database if corrupted
        print('registration database corrupted, restoring...')
        os.chdir(hostdir+'/data/baseline/')
        database=json.load(open('registration.json'))
        os.chdir(hostdir)
        os.remove('registration.json')
shutil.copy(hostdir+'/data/baseline/registration.json',hostdir+'/registration.json')

    name=database['name']
    regdate=database['registration date']
    rest_time=database['rest time']

    # actions.json data
    try:
        database=json.load(open('actions.json'))
    except:
        # restore database if corrupted
        print('actions database corrupted, restoring...')
        os.chdir(hostdir+'/data/baseline/')
        database=json.load(open('actions.json'))
        os.chdir(hostdir)
        os.remove('actions.json')
        shutil.copy(hostdir+'/data/baseline/actions.json',hostdir+'/actions.json')

    logins=database['logins']
    logouts=database['logouts']
    session=database['active session']
    sessions=database['sessions']
    query_count=database['query count']
    queries=database['queries']
    noise=database['noise']
    action_count=database['action count']
    action_log=database['action log']
    loopnum=database['loopnum']
    avail_actions = database['available actions']
    #print(database)

    # settings.json data
    try:
        database=json.load(open('settings.json'))
```

```python
    except:
        # restore database if corrupted
        print('settings database corrupted, restoring...')
        os.chdir(hostdir+'/data/baseline/')
        database=json.load(open('settings.json'))
        os.chdir(hostdir)
        os.remove('settings.json')

shutil.copy(hostdir+'/data/baseline/settings.json',hostdir+'/settings.json')

    alarm=database['alarm']
    alarm_time=database['alarm time']
    greeting=database['greeting']
    end=database['end']
    transcript_type=database['transcript type']
    wake_type=database['wake type']
    query_time=database['query time']
    multi_query=database['multi query']
    query_save=database['query save']
    register_face=database['register face']
    sleep_time=database['sleep time']
    query_json=database['query json']

    # instantiate variables
    logins.append(get_date())
    t=1
    query_request=False
    turn_off = False
except:
    # register user if no user exists
    print('registering new user!')
    # you only use these modules if you register, so put them here
    import cv2
    import skvideo.io, skvideo.motion, skvideo.measure
    from moviepy.editor import VideoFileClip
    from PIL import Image
    register_user(action_list, hostdir)

    # load database
    os.chdir(hostdir)

    # registration data
    database=json.load(open('registration.json'))
    name=database['name']
    regdate=database['registration date']
    rest_time=database['rest time']
```

```python
# action data
database=json.load(open('actions.json'))
logins=database['logins']
logouts=database['logouts']
session=database['active session']
sessions=database['sessions']
query_count=database['query count']
queries=database['queries']
noise=database['noise']
action_count=database['action count']
action_log=database['action log']
loopnum=database['loopnum']
avail_actions = database['available actions']

# settings.json
alarm=database['alarm']
alarm_time=database['alarm time']
greeting=database['greeting']
end=database['end']
transcript_type=database['transcript type']
wake_type=database['wake type']
query_time=database['query time']
multi_query=database['multi query']
query_save=database['query save']
register_face=database['register face']
sleep_time=database['sleep time']
query_json=database['query json']

# instantiate variables
logins.append(get_date())
t=1
query_request=False
turn_off = False
```

7.4.8 - The intent loop - Now we need to understand the concept of the *intent loop*, or the process that occurs for Nala to understand a query from a user. First, a user states a wake word - (1) in this case, "Hey Nala" (2) - which then triggers a response from Nala - (3) in this case, "How can I help you?." Then, a user provides another query (usually after some beeping sound) such as (4) "I'd like the weather." Nala transcribes this query to understand it and then parses the query for keyword intents; for example, if the response is "I'd like the weather" the only word that really matters is "weather" and that would be used to provoke a response (5). Then, after this keyword maps onto an *action dictionary* (or a map of responses to keywords), the action is executed (6). The intent loop then repeats itself, looking for another wake word ("Hey Nala") before triggering another action (Figure 7.4.8.1).

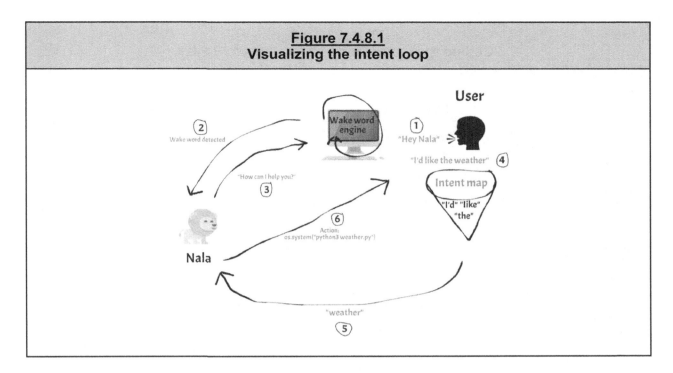

Figure 7.4.8.1
Visualizing the intent loop

Therefore, the intent loop is fundamental to understanding how machines parse through queries in voice assistants. Depending on how you design the ***intent map,*** the actions may differ. For example, if you built a chatbot based on questions and answers, this intent map could only look for queries based on similarity to a database and provoke a spoken response without really any external scripts (e.g. for example, an FAQ website, as talked about in Chapter 5).

Nala's intent map is quite simple yet powerful. The keyword intents map onto specific actions that are triggered with the os.system() module. In this way, all we need to do is pass through variables using the sys module in Python to trigger actions (e.g. sys.argv[]) - which are intended to eventually terminate and go back to the ***rest state.***

With this in mind, let us code a quick intent loop to start us off (Figure 7.4.8.2). We can start the loop with a while statement to see if Nala needs to be turned off or not. If she is on, then she continues. Then, she checks if an alarm is on or off and greets the user if necessary. After these initial steps, she then listens for a wake word ('Hey Nala') via a wake word engine from the *wake_type* variable (e.g. 'porcupine'); in most cases, this should be the Porcupine wake engine. Then, after Nala is woken up, Nala asks how she can help the user and a query is received from the user. This query is then transcribed according to the *transcript_type* variable (often 'sphinx'), and then saves in the ./data/queries folder if desired (e.g. if query_save is True). Lastly, the transcript is then broken up into word tokens and certain keywords are looked for - like 'weather' - which then triggers an action.

Figure 7.4.8.2
Coding the intent loop: *nala.py (lines 718-843)*

```python
while turn_off == False:
    # record a 3.0 second voice sample
    # use try statement to avoid errors
    try:

        # welcome user back if it's been over an hour since login
        start=time.time()

        # set alarm and make false after you trigger alarm
        if alarm == True and alarm_time == datetime.now().hour:
            os.chdir(hostdir+'/actions')
            os.system('python3 alarm.py %s'%(hostdir))
            alarm == False
            os.chdir(hostdir)


        if abs(end-start) > 60*60:

            end=time.time()

            if greeting == True:
                speaktext(hostdir,'welcome back, %s'%(name.split()[0]))
                os.chdir(hostdir+'/actions')
                os.system('python3 weather.py %s'%(hostdir))
                os.system('python3 news.py %s'%(hostdir))
                os.system('python3 events.py %s'%(hostdir))
                os.chdir(hostdir)

            # log session if the time of activity is greater than 60 minutes
            sessions.append(session)
            # start a new session
            session=list()

        # change to host directory
        os.chdir(hostdir)

        # wakeup according to wake_type then activate the query
        os.chdir(hostdir+'/data/models/')
        wakeup(wake_type)
        query_num=0
        query_request=False

        while query_request==False and query_num <= 3:
```

```python
            os.chdir(hostdir)
            if query_num==0:
                # if the first query, ask how you can help
                speaktext(hostdir,'how can I help you?')
                playbackaudio(hostdir+'/data/tone.wav')
            else:
                # the prior sample was noise, so we must add it as such
                message="Sorry, I didn't get that. How can I help?"
                query={
                    'date':get_date(),
                    'audio': unique_sample,
                    'transcript type': transcript_type,
                    'query transcript': query_transcript,
                    'transcript': transcript,
                    'response': [],
                    'meta': [message],
                }
                noise.append(query)
                session.append(query)
                # now ask user for another sample because previous sample was noise
                speaktext(hostdir,"Sorry, I did not get that. How can I help?")
                playbackaudio(hostdir+'/data/tone.wav')

            # record audio and initiate query
            time.sleep(0.50)
            unique_sample='sample'+str(loopnum)+'_'+str(query_num)+'.wav'
            record_to_file(os.getcwd(),unique_sample, query_time)

            # transcribe audio according to transcript_type (in settings.json)
            transcript=transcribe_audio(unique_sample, hostdir, transcript_type)

            # only save the query if you'd like to with query_save variable (in settings.json)
            if query_save == True:
                shutil.move(hostdir+'/'+unique_sample,hostdir+'/data/queries/'+unique_sample)
            else:
                os.remove(unique_sample)

            query_transcript=transcript.lower().split()

            # enable multiple queries if it is activated
            if multi_query == True:
                and_num = query_transcript.count('and')
            else:
                and_num = 0
```

```python
# break if it finds a query
for i in range(len(query_transcript)):

    # iterate through transcript
    os.chdir(hostdir+'/actions')
    print(query_transcript[i])

    if query_transcript[i] in ['weather', 'whether']:

        command='python3 weather.py %s'%(hostdir)
        os.system(command)

        query={
            'date':get_date(),
            'audio': unique_sample,
            'transcript type': transcript_type,
            'query transcript': query_transcript[i],
            'transcript': transcript,
            'response': command,
            'meta': list(),
        }

        # save query to json
        try:
            if query_json == True:
                save_query_json(unique_sample, query, hostdir)
        except:
            print('error')

        query_count=query_count+1
        queries.append(query)
        session.append(query)
        action_count=action_count+1
        query_request=True
        if and_num == 0:
            break
        else:
            and_num=and_num-1
```

The elif/then statements continue to the end of the script. If no intent is found, it then is treated as noise and another query is received from an end user (up to 3 queries). After executing an action and a query, the database is then updated with any variables that have been modified with the update_database() function (Figure 7.4.8.3). After this (if she is not in the process of logging out), Nala goes back to her rest state. Here, she listens again for the wake word 'Hey Nala' before doing anything else.

Figure 7.4.8.3
Closing the intent loop: *nala.py (lines 1801-1828)*

```
    # update database
    end=time.time()
    # can include this info in session, but I have left out because it can get a bit messy
    # session.append('updated database @ %s'%(get_date()))
    try:

update_database(hostdir,logins,logouts,session,sessions,query_count,queries,noise,action_count,loopnum, alarm, end)

    except:
        print('error updating database')

    # clean up wav files in host directory
    try:
        os.chdir(hostdir)
        wav_cleanup()
    except:
        pass

except:
    pass

    # sleep appropriately before each query to not harm the processor and suck battery
    time.sleep(rest_time)
    loopnum=loopnum+1

# say goodbye if loop breaks and is turned off
speaktext(hostdir,'Goodbye')
```

By using a *try statement,* Nala's intent loop architecture is fairly robust and does not fail easily. Nala can take many false queries and continue operating. These false queries can then be used to help tune action dictionary terms (e.g. "weather" == "what is the temperature?") to specific actions (e.g. "temperature" => "weather.py"). *Feel free to modify or play around with this intent loop before moving on.*

7.4.9 - Adding some simple actions - Actions are the way Nala responds to queries. If a query is given like "get the weather," Nala then goes through intent loop and selects the appropriate action from the query. All of these actions are stored in the .nala/actions/ folder. Therefore, all that is required to make a new action is to just code up an action, put it in the actions folder, add it into the event loop as an if/then statement with a keyword intent, and then update the PocketSphinx transcription model so that the queries can be understood. Nala handles the rest.

Let's go through an example to make a *makeajoke.py* action (Figure 7.4.9.1).

<u>**Figure 7.4.9.1:**</u>
Creating an action: *./nala/actions/makajoke.py*

```python
import random, os, sys, json, datetime

##########################################################################
##                          HELPER FUNCTIONS                            ##
##########################################################################


def get_date():
    return str(datetime.datetime.now())

def speaktext(hostdir,text):
    # speak to user from a text sample (tts system)
    curdir=os.getcwd()
    os.chdir(hostdir+'/actions')
    os.system("python3 speak.py '%s'"%(str(text)))
    os.chdir(curdir)


##########################################################################
##                            MAIN SCRIPT                               ##
##########################################################################


hostdir=sys.argv[1]
os.chdir(hostdir)

jokes=['What do you call a speeding french motorist? A speeding Monseiur.',
       'What do chemists' dogs do with their bones? They barium!',
       'What did the cat say when the mouse got away? You've got to be kitten me!',
       'What did the ocean\xa0say to the sailboat? Nothing, it just waved.',
       'What do you call a snowman in July? A puddle.',
       'What lies at the bottom of the ocean and twitches? A nervous wreck.',
       'What does a dolphin say when he's confused? Can you please be more Pacific?',
       'What is a Queens favorite kind of precipitation? Reign!',
       'What is the Mexican weather report? Chili today and hot tamale.',
       'What did the evaporating raindrop say? I'm going to pieces.',
```

```
            'What did the hail storm say to the roof? Hang onto your shingles, this will
be no ordinary sprinkles.',
            'What do you call a wet bear? A drizzly bear',
            'What do you call two straight days of rain in Seattle? A weekend.',
            'What goes up when the rain comes down? An Umbrella.',
            'What does it do before it rains candy? It sprinkles!',
            'What did one raindrop say to the other? Two's company, three's a cloud',
            'What's the difference between a horse and the weather? One is reined up and
the other rains down.',
            'What is a king's favorite kind of precipitation? Hail!',
            'What kind of music are balloons afraid of? Pop Music',
            'What is the musical part of a snake? The scales.',
            'What did Beethoven say to Johann Sebastian when he was helping him parallel
park? "Bach it up."',
            'What's an avocado's favorite music? Guac 'n' roll.',
            'What do you get when you drop a piano down a mineshaft? A-flat minor.',
            'What do you call a cow that can play a musical instrument? A moo-sician.',
            'What do you call a musician with problems? A trebled man.',
            'What was Beethoven's favorite fruit? BA-NA-NA-NAAAAAA.',
            'What did Jay-Z call his wife before they got married? Feyonce.',
            'What's a golf clubs favorite type of music? Swing.']

# tell a random joke
randomint=random.randint(0,len(jokes)-1)
joke = jokes[randomint]
speaktext(hostdir, joke)

# update database
database=json.load(open('actions.json'))
action_log=database['action log']

action={
    'action':'makeajoke.py',
    'date': get_date(),
    'meta': [joke],
}

action_log.append(action)
jsonfile=open('actions.json','w')
json.dump(database,jsonfile)
jsonfile.close()
```

There are a few key things here as general pointers. You almost always want to have these import statements and two functions to start off the actions, as you'll often need to speak to users and add the date when you get a new query (Figure 7.4.9.2):

Figure 7.4.9.2
Initializing import statements and help functions for actions: *makeajoke.py*

```python
import random, os, sys, json, datetime

def get_date():
    return str(datetime.datetime.now())

def speaktext(hostdir,text):
    # speak to user from a text sample (tts system)
    curdir=os.getcwd()
    os.chdir(hostdir+'/actions')
    os.system("python3 speak.py '%s'"%(str(text)))
    os.chdir(curdir)
```

Also, most actions make use of the sys.argv[] function to access variables from the command line (Figure 7.4.9.3). Specifically, when you look at the above section of code in Nala, you'll find that the *makeajoke.py* action is called with this command='python3 makeajoke.py %s'%(hostdir). In this way, we can pass the host directory to the action (which is the default directory where the *nala.py* script is executed), so you can reference where to store the data (in the actions.json file). Therefore, this snippet of code is extremely important for you to put into your code base.

Figure 7.4.9.3
Using sys.argv[1] to pass through directory information: *makeajoke.py*

```python
hostdir=sys.argv[1]
os.chdir(hostdir)
```

Then, after the main action is executed, you can terminate the action by updating the database (Figure 7.4.9.4). In general, this always has the 'action', 'date', and 'meta' fields. The action is the name of the script that is executed, the date is the current date/time, and the meta is anything useful that you'd like to pass along in the database in the form of a list - in this case, it's the joke itself that was played back to the user. In this way, you can cache action data in a well-structured database schema.

Figure 7.4.9.4
How to update databases while coding actions: *makeajoke.py*

```python
# update database
database=json.load(open('actions.json'))
action_log=database['action log']

action={
    'action':'makeajoke.py',
    'date': get_date(),
    'meta': [joke],
}

action_log.append(action)
jsonfile=open('actions.json','w')
json.dump(database,jsonfile)
jsonfile.close()
```

Below is a list of currently available actions for Nala (Table 7.4.8.1). If you'd like to make a new action, let me know by suggesting an enhancement on the Nala GitHub page!

Table 7.4.8.1 Action-intent pairs for Nala		
Action	**Description**	**Example query**
Alarm.py	Plays an alarm sound (e.g. to wake up in morning) based on the time of day you specified during user registration.	"Set alarm" "Stop alarm"
chillout.py	Plays music in the background to help you calm down.	"Chillout"
espn.py	Scrapes ESPN website to find any events going on later tonight. *This is a work-in-progress.*	"Get sports"
events.py	Scrape meetup.com for events in your local area.	"Find events"
generate_ poem.py	Generate a poem based on the generate poetry script we wrote a while back.	"Make a poem"
grateful.py	Helps you keep a gratitude journal by recording a sample of what you're grateful for today.	"Be grateful"
makeajoke.py	Plays back a joke from the database.	"Make a joke"
meditation.py	Guides you through a simple 60 second meditation.	"Meditate"
music.py	YouTube music links - based on a genre.	"Play music"

news.py	Searches some basic news sites related to computer science and machine learning (e.g. Hacker News).	"Grab the news"
nutrition.py	Searches for some healthy food nearby"	"Be healthy"
plan_trip.py	Schedules a trip in terms of AirBnB suggestions and flights.	"Plan trip"
reboot.py	Restarts the computer.	"Restart"
search.py	Search bing with a query.	First query: "Search" Second query: [search term]
shutdown.py	Shuts down the computer.	"Shut down"
sleep.py	Puts the computer to sleep for a designated time period.	'Go to sleep'
social.py	Alternative script to give you some suggestions based on your budget to go out later.	'Be social'
weather.py	Searches weather.com for the current weather at your location.	'Get the weather'
yelp.py	Based on the query, searches yelp for coffee, restaurants, food, nightlife, ice cream, or bars.	'Get me coffee', 'get me some food', 'nightlife', 'get ice cream', 'grab me some beer'

7.4.9 - 🎤🎤 **- Enabling multiple queries -** You may also want to enable multi-query capability. We can do this by adding an "AND" statement that helps to connect queries together. So instead of saying just "get the weather" we could say "get the weather AND sleep." First, the weather will be fetched via the *weather.py* script and then Nala will go to sleep (usually for 30 minutes). This allows for a rich array of possible queries.[290]

You can disable multi-query capability by setting it to FALSE in the settings.json file, per the instructions in section 7.4.1. However, I find this feature useful when I have many things to do in a short period of time.[291]

---

[290] **Query types -** 420 to be exact - 21P2
[291] **Feel free** to experiment with this; it's often a good way to test whether or not the transcription model is working.

7.4.10 - Piecing it all together - We can now piece everything together to form Nala, the world's first [Lion king]-inspired assistant! *Just for fun, I also opened up the Lion King soundtrack theme song before registering.*

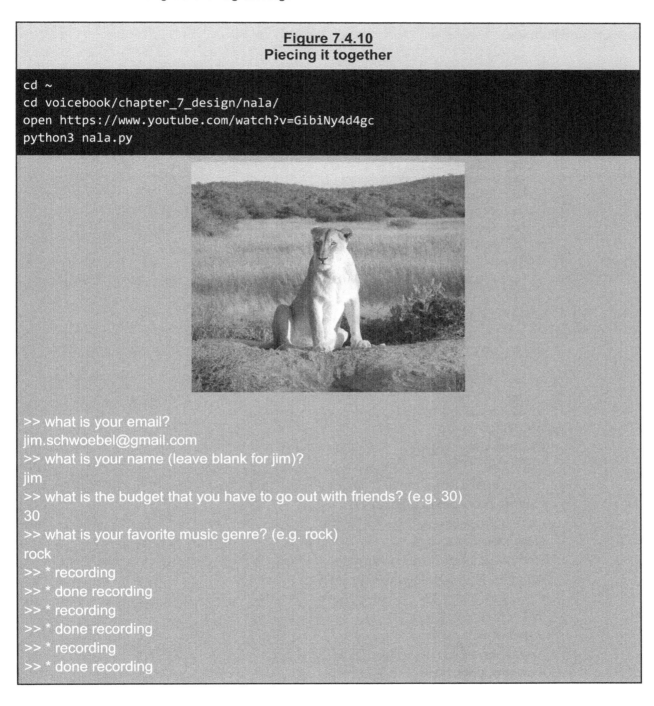

Figure 7.4.10
Piecing it together

7.5 Conclusion

👏 **WOOT!** Congratulations! You have just built a voice computer and voice assistant from scratch. If you want to go deeper on anything, check out the documentation for the following website and libraries:

- Defining a voice computer
    - Hardware
        - iMac. https://www.apple.com/imac/
        - Macbook pro. https://www.apple.com/macbook-pro/
        - Jasper. http://jasperproject.github.io/documentation/
        - Mycroft. https://mycroft.ai/
        - Arduino. https://www.arduino.cc/
        - iPhone / Siri. https://www.apple.com/ios/siri/
        - Amazon Echo. https://en.wikipedia.org/wiki/Amazon_Echo
        - Google Assistant. https://developers.google.com/actions/
        - Apple HomePod. https://www.apple.com/homepod
    - Software
        - Alexa voice service (AVS). https://developer.amazon.com/alexa-voice-service
        - Google Assistant SDK. https://developers.google.com/assistant/sdk/overview
        - Jovo software framework. https://github.com/jovotech/jovo-framework-nodejs
        - Jasper voice bot software. http://jasperproject.github.io/documentation/
        - Mycroft AI. https://mycroft.ai/
        - Nala. https://github.com/jim-schwoebel/nala
- Designing VC hardware
    - Microphone. https://en.wikipedia.org/wiki/Microphone
    - Sound card. https://en.wikipedia.org/wiki/Sound_card
    - Motherboard (form factor). https://en.wikipedia.org/wiki/Form_factor_(design)
    - Central processing unit (CPU). https://en.wikipedia.org/wiki/Central_processing_unit
    - Data storage device. https://en.wikipedia.org/wiki/Data_storage
    - Radiofrequency transceiver. https://en.wikipedia.org/wiki/RF_module
    - Amateur Radio Relay League (ARRL). https://en.wikipedia.org/wiki/American_Radio_Relay_League
    - WiFi chips. https://en.wikipedia.org/wiki/Wi-Fi
    - Bluetooth chips. https://en.wikipedia.org/wiki/Bluetooth
    - Speakers. https://en.wikipedia.org/wiki/Loudspeaker
    - Power supply. https://en.wikipedia.org/wiki/Power_supply
    - Battery. https://en.wikipedia.org/wiki/Electric_battery
    - Computer case. https://en.wikipedia.org/wiki/Computer_case
- Designing VC software
    - Bluetooth
        - Pybluez. https://github.com/pybluez/pybluez

- WiFi
  - Wireless. https://github.com/joshvillbrandt/wireless
  - Wifi. https://pypi.org/project/python-wifi/
- Serial connections
  - Pyserial. https://github.com/pyserial/pyserial
  - PyVISA. https://pyvisa.readthedocs.io/en/stable/getting.html
- Wake word detectors
  - PocketSphinx. https://cmusphinx.github.io/wiki/
  - Snowboy. http://docs.kitt.ai/snowboy/
  - Porcupine. https://github.com/Picovoice/Porcupine
- Transcription models
  - PocketSphinx Language models. https://cmusphinx.github.io/wiki/tutoriallm/
  - PyKaldi. https://github.com/pykaldi/pykaldi
  - LIUM diarization models. http://www-lium.univ-lemans.fr/diarization/doku.php/related_projects

- Nala: building voice assistants
  - Sys. https://docs.python.org/2/library/sys.html
  - Os. https://docs.python.org/3/library/os.html
  - Porcupine. https://github.com/Picovoice/Porcupine
  - Pyttsx3. https://pyttsx3.readthedocs.io/en/latest/
  - PocketSphinx. https://cmusphinx.github.io/wiki/tutoriallm/

The next chapter is all about how to build voice software for microservice server architectures. In this way, you can scale your software innovations to millions of users! 👥

302

Chapter 8:
Designing Server Architectures

"If bridge building were like programming, halfway through we'd find out that the far bank was now 50 meters farther out, that it was actually mud rather than granite, and that rather than building a footbridge we were instead building a road bridge."

-Sam Newman
(Technologist and Software Developer)

Chapter Overview

Building a server architecture is like building a bridge and finding out that you need to modify it halfway through construction. You may find that you need to re-route the bridge to another location or make it longer or shorter because you didn't calculate the distance of the bank properly.[292] It's quite a complicated web of people involved - ranging from the CEO to the CTO and individual developers to make and prioritize what needs to be built at what time.[293] At some point, the foundations become messy but everything works, leading to a substantial technical debt that must be addressed later.

Without the right foundations, major changes to server architectures can be costly and perhaps even kill companies.[294] Therefore, this chapter lays out a development philosophy and toolset to help you build enterprise-grade voice software.

Specifically, it covers:

- **8.1** - Server architectures
- **8.2** - Python web frameworks
- **8.3** - MongoDB databases
- **8.4** - Building Kafka microservices
- **8.5** - Minio as a wrapper for GCP/AWS
- **8.6** - Authentication with Auth0
- **8.7** - Working with Docker containers
- **8.8** - Unit test and integration tests
- **8.9** - Code deployment with GitHub/Heroku
- **8.10** - Code deployment with Kubernetes on GCP

In this way, you can build voice applications to reach the 3.2 billion users on the web.

> *Note that this is the only chapter that you will need to do some custom setup in order to get everything to work properly. This is mostly because you have to register on the MongoDB, Heroku, Postman, Robo 3T, and Docker websites to work through the provided examples.*

---

[292] **For example**, you may underestimate the costs and timeline for building your application or make false assumptions about users adopting your technology.
[293] **This political dynamic** makes building a server architecture incredibly tricky.
[294] **This idea is especially true** in voice computing, as there are many nuances to the way audio is collected and processed (on clients and servers).

8.1 Server architectures

To understand voice web architectures (V-Web architectures), you must first understand the *client-server model*. Specifically, clients **make requests** for certain types of information - for example, .HTML web pages, JavaScript code, images, etc. (Figure 8.1.1).[295] Servers **listen for these requests** and are programmed to **trigger responses** when a request is received (Figure 8.1.1). *User agents*, such as a web browser, establish the communication between the server and the client through standard protocols like **HTTP requests**[296] for web pages or **RTSP requests** for real-time voice applications. *In this way, clients and servers can communicate with each other in a seamless and uniform way.*

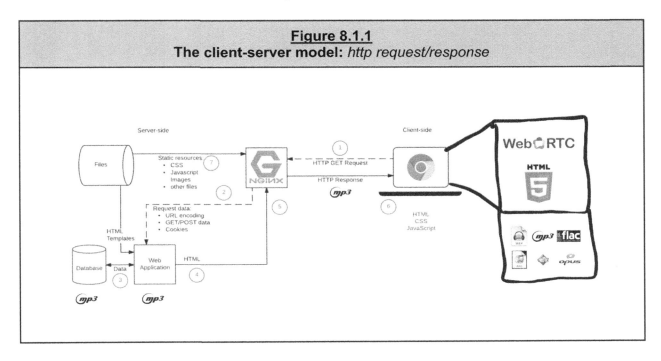

Figure 8.1.1
The client-server model: *http request/response*

There have been some major advancements over the years to allow for seamless audio file playback within *web browser clients*. Specifically, you can now use the <video> and <audio> tags to *playback video* and *audio media* in web browsers through the HTML5 markup language.[297] This has thus transformed how audio and video content can be served to clients through the client-server model and web browsers, as audio and video codecs are built directly within the web browsers themselves.

---

[295] **ReST-enabled architectures** - These clients are often personal computers making requests through web browsers operating via the http protocol but can also be representational state transfer (ReST-enabled) architectures that can handle other data formats such as XML, .JSON, or any other data resource.

[296] **Internet Protocol (IP) addresses**- Clients use IP addresses to use the Internet Protocol to ensure uniqueness. There can be multiple clients on the same IP address.

[297] **WebM** - These advancements led to Google creating WebM audiovisual media format. WebM can accommodate VP8/VP9 video and Vorbis/Opus compressed audio formats and has since become natively integrated into Mozilla Firefox, Opera, and Google Chrome. WebM is distributed under a BSD license.

Note that Google Chrome has the most flexibility for the <audio> tag and can cover almost all modern audio formats and codecs (Figure 8.1.2). Specifically, it can handle .WAV, .MP3, .MP4, .ADTS, .Vorbis, .OPUS, and .FLAC formats. Compared to other web browsers, it seems to be the most developer-friendly.

Figure 8.1.2
Web browsers that can play back audio media via HTML5 tag

Formats supported by different web browsers

Format	Container	MIME type	Chrome	Internet Explorer	Edge	Firefox	Opera	Safari
PCM	WAV	audio/wav	Yes	No	Yes	Yes, in v3.5	Yes, in v11.00	Yes, in v3.1
MP3	MP3	audio/mpeg	Yes[13]	Yes, in IE9	Yes	From OS[a]	Yes[13]	Yes, in v3.1
AAC	MP4	audio/mp4	Yes	Yes, in IE9	Yes	From OS[a]	Yes	Yes
AAC	ADTS[b]	audio/aac audio/aacp	Yes	No	Yes	From OS, in v45.0	Yes	Yes
Vorbis	Ogg	audio/ogg	Yes, in v9	No	with Web Media Extensions[16]	Yes, in v3.5	Yes, in v10.50	With Xiph QuickTime Components (macOS 10.11 and earlier)
Vorbis	WebM	audio/webm	Yes	No	with Web Media Extensions[16]	Yes, in v4.0	Yes, in v10.60	No
Opus	Ogg	audio/ogg	Yes, in v25 (in v31 for Windows)	No	with Web Media Extensions[16]	Yes, in v15.0	Yes, in v14	No
Opus	WebM	audio/webm	Yes	No	Only via MSE[17] Everywhere with Web Media Extensions[16]	Yes, in v28.0[18]	Yes	No
FLAC	FLAC	audio/flac	Yes, in v56[19]	No	Yes, in v16[20]	Yes, in v51[21]	Yes	Yes, in v11[22]
FLAC	Ogg	audio/ogg	Yes, in v56[19]	No	with Web Media Extensions[16]	Yes, in v51[21]	Yes	No

Similarly, advancements in web browsers led to the ability to directly **record content** in the browser through JavaScript code (e.g. <script> tag). **WebRTC** is the main JavaScript-based method for capturing the microphone and webcam in web pages.[298] Specifically, WebRTC works by allowing direct **peer-to-peer communication** without needing to install plugins or any third-party software.[299] This process is done via the WebRTC API, which is compatible with almost all modern web browsers (Figure 8.1.3). Peer-to-peer communication often requires a custom server architecture that uses a **relay server** and **NAT gateways** to ensure that data can be transmitted properly (Figure 8.1.3). *Therefore, it's likely that many streaming-based applications for voice computing in the browser require teams of engineers that know JavaScript to interface with your back-end Python code and specialized network topologies, two topics beyond the scope of this book.*

---

[298] **WebRTC Alternatives** include Mediastream Recording API and the Media Capture Streams API.
[299] **RTP -** This is known as the Real-time transport protocol (RTP), which is a network protocol for delivering audio and video over IP networks. This is used for implementing systems involving streaming media - e.g. VoIP.

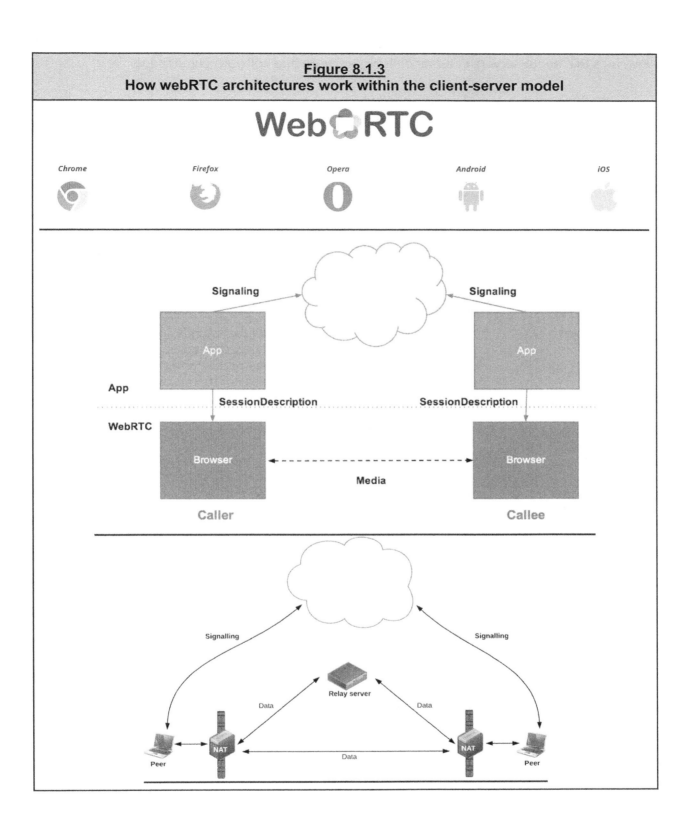
Figure 8.1.3
How webRTC architectures work within the client-server model

Now, let's talk about servers in terms of their hardware and software components.[300]

There are three main types of **server hardware**: tower servers, rack servers, and blade servers (Table 8.1.1). The most common type of server is likely a rack server, as they are most easily modifiable and expandable.[301] [302] [303] *Note that you don't really need to worry much about server hardware anymore because services like **Amazon Web Services (AWS)** and **Google Cloud Platform (GCP)** optimize server hardware for you depending on your needs. However, it's good to know this in case one day you want to build your own server.*

	Table 8.1.1 Types of servers	
Server type	**Server rack (image)**	**Description**
Tower server		<ul><li>Built in cabinet that stands alone</li><li>Like a Tower personal computer case</li><li>Allows for easier cooling and scalability</li><li>Bulkier and heavier than rack or blade server</li><li>Cabling can be complicated and noisy</li></ul>
Rack server		<ul><li>Designed to be installed on a rack</li><li>Rack contains mounting slots (bays) and is designed to hold a hardware unit with screws</li><li>Has low-profile enclosure</li><li>Can have multiple servers stacked on top of eachother, minimizing floor space</li><li>Needs special cooling systems</li></ul>
Blade server	(48 blade server)	<ul><li>Designed to minimize use of physical space and energy.</li><li>Uses blade enclosure (chassis) to hold multiple blade servers such as power, cooling, networking, and other things.</li><li>A blade and blade enclosure create a blade system</li></ul>

---

[300] **Server discussion** - We'll first talk about the types of server hardware and software. Then we'll talk about some common terms used in server-side computing, so you know what you are doing in the sections that follow. In this way, you'll have the foundational knowledge necessary to build V-Web architectures from scratch.

[301] **Supercomputers** - A supercomputer is when many servers are stacked and used together.

[302] **US DOE / IBM supercomputer** - The fastest supercomputer in the world is in the United States. With a peak performance of 200 petaflops, or 200,000 trillion calculations per second, Summit more than doubles the top speeds of TaihuLight, which can reach 93 petaflops. Summit is also capable of over 3 billion billion mixed precision calculations per second, or 3.3 exaops, and more than 10 petabytes of memory, which has allowed researchers to run the world's first exascale scientific calculation.

[303] **Google server count** - Google owns over 1 million servers as of 2011. They probably own many more now.

There are a number of types of **server software**; however, the two most common server types are **Apache-** or **NGINX-** based servers (Table 8.1.2). With Python, NGINX web servers are more common, as they are easily used with Docker containers.[304] In general, NGINX servers are more lightweight than Apache servers; however, Apache servers often have a richer set of modules (e.g. with cPanel) and can be more easily customized. Both of these server software types are powerful open source tools for web developers.

<div align="center">Table 8.1.2 Types of server software</div>		
Type of web server	Pros	Cons
Apache web server **(most popular)**	<ul><li>Open source</li><li>Flexible across operating systems</li><li>Modular and extremely flexible</li><li>Large community (most adopted web server type)</li></ul>	<ul><li>Can be a large learning curve</li><li>Process-based server</li><li>Modifying defaults can lead to common security vulnerabilities</li><li>Requires strict updating policy</li></ul>
NGINX web server (Engine-X) **(2nd most popular)**	<ul><li>Lightweight server that has high performance and stability</li><li>Relatively simple configuration</li><li>Scalable, event-driven architecture</li><li>Can be a proxy server, reverse proxy and load balancer</li></ul>	<ul><li>Less community support and documentation</li><li>Not as many modules/extensions as Apache</li><li>Not as well vetted as Apache (in terms of security)</li></ul>
LiteSpeed web server **(4th most popular)**	<ul><li>Replacement for Apache web server</li><li>Shares .htaccess and mod_security features with Apache</li><li>More secure</li><li>Reduce hardware costs</li></ul>	<ul><li>Less adoption globally</li><li>Proprietary solution / costs money</li></ul>

---

[304] **NGINX-Python servers** - I suggest using a NGINX server paired with Python to help with load-balancing and it's relative simplicity and compatibility with Docker containers.

Lighttpd 	<ul><li>Open source software</li><li>Secure and flexible</li><li>Can handle 10,000 connections in parallel on one server</li><li>Consumes less power</li><li>Compatible with multiple operating systems</li></ul>	<ul><li>Less adoption globally</li><li>Do not support sending large files from CGI, FastCGI, or proxies</li><li>No SPDY or HTTP/2 support</li></ul>

Servers almost always use *databases* in order to serve content to the client. A database can perform common *CRUD data operations*: specifically, it can **C**reate, **R**ead, **U**pdate, and **D**elete data from the database upon interacting with a request from a client.[305] Common databases for Python-based web applications include MongoDB,[306] Postgres, MySQL, or JSON databases.[307] *Each of these databases has their pros/cons, but I'd recommend MongoDB due to having built-in redundancy and better performance at scale (Table 8.1.3).*

Table 8.1.3 Common database types and their pros/cons		
Database type	**Pros**	**Cons**
MongoDB	<ul><li>Flexible schemas</li><li>Supports JSON and other NoSQL documents</li><li>Dynamic queries</li><li>Defined indexes</li><li>Good performance on big databases</li><li>Fastest development time</li></ul>	<ul><li>SQL not used as a query language</li><li>Costs money for enterprise packages</li><li>Sometimes requires significant time investment to train others on how to use it</li><li>Default settings are not secure</li></ul>
Postgres	<ul><li>Scalable database that can handle lots of data (TBs)</li><li>It supports JSON data</li><li>Many predefined useful functions</li><li>A number of interfaces are available</li></ul>	<ul><li>Documentation is okay; sometimes takes a bit to debug</li><li>Configuration can be confusing</li><li>Speed can suffer when doing bulk operations</li></ul>

---

[305] **ACID-compliant transactions** - Databases often support ACID transactions - Atomicity, Consistency, Isolation, and Durability.

[306] **MongoDB redundancy** – MongoDB has built-in redundancy to reduce risk for catastrophic failures and file loss.

[307] **SQL (relational) vs. NoSQL (non-relational) databases** - relational database management systems (SQL databases) are used in large enterprise scenarios except for MySQL, which is used for web apps. Note that SQL databases work with structured data and support ACID transactions (below) and limitless indexing, but do not scale out horizontally well and data is normalized affecting speed.

MySQL	<ul><li>Open-source and free</li><li>Can be used to work with other databases (e.g. DB2 and Oracle)</li><li>Variety of user interfaces that can be implemented with the database</li><li>Lots of functionality</li></ul>	<ul><li>Lots of effort to do simple tasks that other databases do automatically (e.g. automatic backups)</li><li>No built-in support for XML or OLAP</li><li>Support is available (for free version) but you need to pay for it</li></ul>
JSON	<ul><li>Compatible across pretty much every programming language</li><li>Quick prototyping</li></ul>	<ul><li>Slower performance on large queries</li><li>Not as powerful as XML</li></ul>

As servers scale-up, they need to use something called *load balancers* to help route client requests to server responses (Figure 8.1.4). This can be done through *horizontal scaling* by adding more machines to your pool of resources (e.g. adding more server racks) or *vertical scaling* by adding more CPU power to an existing machine.[308] Load balancers allow for horizontal or vertical scaling to be seamless with incoming requests so that you don't really have to do much to make sure each client request gets processed in the same way.

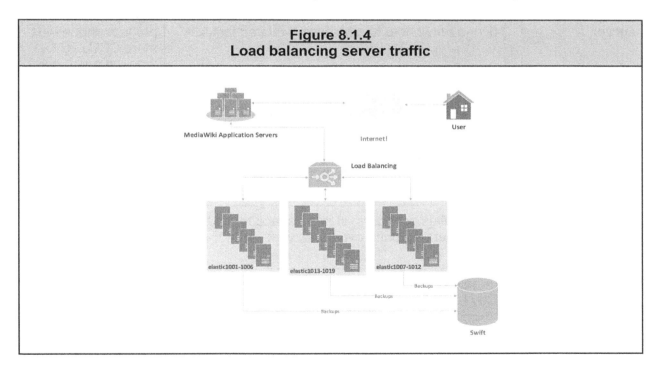

Figure 8.1.4
Load balancing server traffic

---

[308] **The most common way** to scale a server is through horizontal load balancing because it helps add redundancy to the server in case something goes wrong.

As you can imagine, **servers have many functions**. In fact, they are often classified in terms of their functions (Table 8.1.3). In general, servers exist primarily to share data/resources and distribute work.[309] *Any of these server types of servers could be useful to you.*

Table 8.1.3 Types of servers		
Server type	**Purpose**	**Clients**
Application server	Hosts web apps, or computer programs that run within a web browser, without needing to install a copy on the client.	Computers with a web browser.
Catalog server	Maintains an index or table of contents of information that can be found across a distributed network; directory and name servers are examples.	Any program that needs to find something on a network, such as a user lookup.
Communications server	Maintains an environment needed for one communication endpoint to find other endpoints and communicate with them.	Communication endpoints (users/devices).
Computing server	Shares computing resources (e.g. CPU/RAM) over a network to do processing-related tasks.	Any computer program that needs more CPU / RAM than the computer can afford.
Database server	Maintains and shares any form of a database over a network.	Any program that consumes data in large volumes.
Fax server	Shares one or more fax machines over a network, eliminating the need for physical access.	Any fax sender or recipient.
File server	Shares files or folders, storage space to hold files and folders, or both, over a network.	Networked computers or local programs.
Game server	Enables several computers or gaming devices to play multiplayer games.	PCs or gaming consoles.
Mail server	Makes email communication possible.	Senders / recipients of email.
Media server	Shares digital video and/or digital audio over a network through media streaming.	PCs with monitors and speakers.

---

[309] **Important server types** - the most important server types for voice computing likely are application servers, computing servers, sound servers, database servers, and web servers.

Print server	Shares one or more printers over a network.	PCs in need of printing something.
Sound server	Enables computer programs to play and/or record sound, individually or cooperatively.	Computer programs of the same computer and network clients.
Proxy server	Intermediary between a client and server to mask IP address and/or route traffic differently over a large and complex network.	Any networked computer.
Virtual server	Shares hardware and software resources with other virtual servers; exists within a hypervisor, leading to more efficient infrastructure.	Any networked computer.
Web server (most common)	Hosts web pages, making it possible for clients to reach web pages through web browsers.	Computers with a web browser.

There are two types of server architectures: **monolithic architectures** and **microservice-based architectures.** Monolithic approaches make one big master program to do the bulk of the work on the server. Microservice-based approaches, on the other hand, use a cluster of specialized programs to serve information to the client (Figure 8.1.3).

There are pros and cons to each of these approaches (Figure 8.1.3). For example, microservice-based server architectures allow for flexibility in having each microservice be maintained by a different group of developers; as a result, these architectures can be modified more easily. Monolithic approaches often can be programmed faster but are harder to modify later on (Table 8.1.3). *Often, the best server architectures are a mix of both of these architectural styles.*

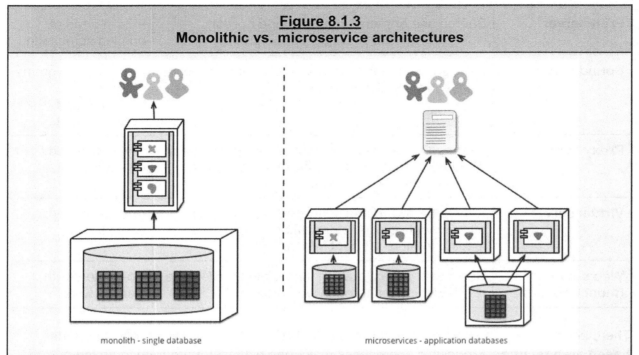

Figure 8.1.3
Monolithic vs. microservice architectures

monolith - single database   microservices - application databases

Architecture	Pros	Cons
Microservice approach	<ul><li>Easy to understand and develop</li><li>Generally more secure and reliable</li><li>Built for scale - horizontally and vertically</li><li>Can use multiple databases types and/or cloud providers</li><li>Faster adoption of new technologies</li><li>Flexible teams (e.g. can program in any language)</li></ul>	<ul><li>Large learning curve of 3rd party deployment services (e.g. Kafka, Docker, etc.)</li><li>Can get out of hand in terms of number of microservices</li><li>More complicated unit and integration tests</li><li>Operational complexity</li><li>Longer development cycles</li></ul>
Monolithic approach	<ul><li>Faster, simpler deployment cycle</li><li>Can have performance advantages</li><li>Whole system stored into one database</li><li>Simpler unit / integration tests</li></ul>	<ul><li>Harder to modify later on and contribute to the code base</li><li>Scaling one component requires entire application scaling</li><li>Slower adoption of new technologies</li><li>Poor reliability</li></ul>

When programming servers, it's often important to make sure the application will run consistently across any operating server environment. For example, sometimes a library will import properly on a Linux operating environment but not import properly on a Mac OSx environment.

To solve this problem, virtual machines and containers were invented (Figure 8.1.4). Originally, the concept of **virtual machines** (VMs) allowed for a host machine to create a complete operating system from a host machine, which is fairly resource-intensive. In contrast, **containers** are "lightweight, stand-alone, executable packages of software that includes everything needed to run it: code, runtime, system tools, system libraries, settings."[310] Simply, containers virtualize the underlying operating system whereas virtual machines virtualize the underlying hardware. *Containers are more commonly used to design server architectures, as they are more efficient, are highly editable, and scale better than VMs.*

Figure 8.1.4
Comparing virtual machines (VMs) and container environments

Virtualization technique	Pros	Cons
Virtual machines (VMs) vmware	<ul><li>Less physical hardware</li><li>Central location to manage assets</li><li>More eco-friendly</li><li>Faster disaster recovery</li><li>Easy to expand a new machine without buying new server rack</li><li>Supports legacy operating systems and can be forward-compatible</li></ul>	<ul><li>Large size, can host fewer instances on a server (3-10 GB)</li><li>Increased development time, testing, and deployment</li><li>Testing and bug tracking is more complicated</li></ul>

---

[310] **Container** - Definition of a container as defined on Docker's website.

Containers 	<ul><li>Compatible with microservice architectures</li><li>Small size can allow servers to host more containers (10-100 MB)</li><li>Less resource intensive than VMs</li><li>Easier to manage resource allocations</li><li>Decreased development time, testing, and deployment</li><li>Testing and bug tracking is less complicated because you can replicate the production environment locally</li><li>Cost-effective solution (less staff, less servers)</li></ul>	<ul><li>Security risks in sharing a kernel because of root access</li><li>Less flexibility in operating systems</li><li>Hard to deploy containers in isolated way without maintaining an adequate network connection</li></ul>

Thus, the trend nowadays is to go with a *microservices-first architecture,* often through *deploying containers* through *orchestration platforms*[311] that help to scale-up these architectures (Figure 8.1.5). Specifically, orchestration platforms deploy and scale containers through *clusters,* or groups of hosts (servers) that can balance web traffic appropriately for optimal performance.[312] There are many benefits around using orchestration platforms - mostly around automatic scaling of containers and allocating resources effectively to get the best performance from a server.[313]

*Note that the most widely used platforms are **Docker** (for containers), microservice platform is **Kafka** (for microservices), and **Kubernetes (k8s -** for orchestration). These are the tools that we will use in this book to build our own microservice architectures and to deploy our applications (Figure 8.1.5).*

---

[311] **Orchestration platforms** - In other words, orchestration platforms help manage containers when scaling up on server architectures.

[312] **From Wikipedia:** "A computer cluster is a set of loosely or tightly connected computers that work together so that, in many respects, they can be viewed as a single system. Unlike grid computers, computer clusters have each node set to perform the same task, controlled and scheduled by software."

[313] **The main benefits of using an orchestration platform** to manage your containers is that you can 1) orchestrate containers across multiple hosts; 2) better utilize hardware resources; 3) automate application deployments/updates; 4) add storage to run stateful apps (e.g. sessions); 5) scale applications horizontally on the fly; 6) declaratively manage services, which guarantees the deployed applications are always running how you deployed them; and 7) health checks to self-heal apps with autoplacement, autorestart, autoreplication, and autoscaling.

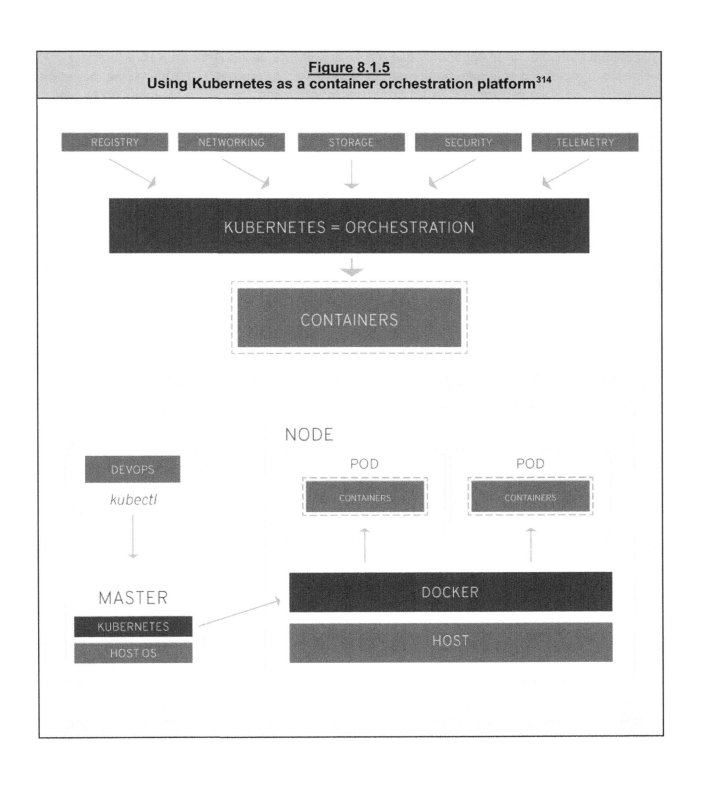

**Figure 8.1.5
Using Kubernetes as a container orchestration platform**[314]

---

[314] **Kubernetes**, or k8s (*k, 8 characters, s...get it?*), or "kube" if you're into brevity, is an open source platform that automates Linux container operations. It eliminates many of the manual processes involved in deploying and scaling containerized applications. In other words, you can cluster together groups of hosts running Linux containers, and Kubernetes helps you easily and efficiently manage those clusters. These clusters can span hosts across public, private, or hybrid clouds.

Microservice architectures commonly use a type of software called **Apache Kafka ('kafka')**[315] to help create a pipeline of jobs to be done from start to finish (Figure 8.1.6). Kafka uses **message topics**[316] to connect **producers**[317] and **consumers**[318] in a line of jobs. These jobs can thus be done asynchronously, and each task is stored in a message archive as they are completed. Kafka gives great flexibility for data pipelines to be fault-tolerant and scalable. When paired with Docker containers and Kubernetes (k8s), Kafka allows for a very powerful and robust server architecture. *In other words, Kafka can act as a **cluster** used by orchestration platforms like Kubernetes to scale applications.*

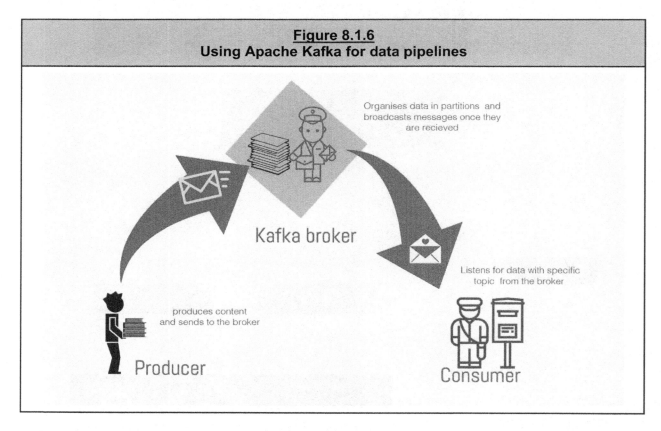

The last thing to think about in a server architecture is the choice of a cloud provider and third-party service dependencies. In general, it's best to try to be as **[cloud provider]-agnostic** as possible. For example, instead of adopting TensorFlow as the machine learning library of choice

---

[315] **How Kafka started** - Kafka started as a proprietary database format within LinkedIn for streaming applications and then was open sourced in 2011. The founders in 2014 created a company called Confluent to focus on Kafka support.

[316] **Message topic** - Just to put Kafka into perspective, think of the process of collecting an audio file from a browser which then needs to be processed. First, you may have a microservice that collects the audio file from the browser (e.g. via a collection microservice). After collecting the audio file and storing it in the database, the producer sends a message "COLLECTED_SAMPLE", which then triggers a consumer to pick up that message and then process the collected sample in some way - for example featurizing the audio sample with pyAudioAnalysis audio features. Therefore, a single microservice can act as a producer and a consumer and create a streaming line of pipelines until the data is stored into the database.

[317] **Producers** - make message topics and payloads.

[318] **Consumers** - consume message topics and payloads.

in Python, it may be better instead to choose Keras which can be connected to many other back-ends other than TensorFlow. This decouples you from Google Cloud as the only provider of back-end machine learning services. You also may find that AWS has a better encryption method and Google Cloud has a better k8s container management server and you can bridge these two gaps by using both Google Cloud and AWS in your server architecture. In contrast, if you don't think this way (e.g. use AWS's container management service instead of Docker), then such a move may be impossible.[319] *Therefore, keep this decoupled mindset in mind when making architectural decisions about choosing cloud providers and relying on third-party services.*

Let's quickly summarize what we just learned. Web servers communicate with clients via user agents, which can take the form of web browsers and/or robots (e.g. web crawlers). Specifically, clients send requests to servers, which then respond to these requests. There's been a lot of advancements in client-side computing to allow for audio recording and playback in the browser (e.g. Google Chrome). Similarly, advances in cloud computing have abstracted server hardware (e.g. rack servers) to allow for efficient horizontal load balancing based on user traffic or consumption. The trend now for servers is a NGINX-powered microservice-first architecture (e.g. Kafka) loaded with containers (e.g. Docker) managed by an orchestration platform (e.g. Kubernetes). Lastly, it's best to have a decoupled server architecture to avoid vendor lock-in, as it helps for server architectures to be more agile.

8.2 Python web frameworks

It's convenient to write client-server code using **web frameworks,** which are templates that make it easy to build code that solves client-server problems.[320] In Python, there are two main web frameworks: **Flask** and **Django**.[321] In general, Flask is a more minimalist web framework for quick deployments and Django is better for complex applications (e.g. due to its URL linking pattern). Both of these frameworks are useful to know depending on your use case.

Let's spin up a web server with the Flask framework (Figure 8.2.1).[322] As you can see, it's almost trivial to spin up a simple webpage locally. Flask is quite minimalistic; I think it's the best first web framework to learn because its simple syntax and clear documentation.

*Note that it's often useful to spin up Flask web servers in a virtual environment with the **virtualenv module** (or later in a Docker container) so that you can create an isolated Python environment that can be replicated on other computers (Figure 8.2.3).*

---

[319] **Difficulties in de-coupled architectures -** Sometimes it's very difficult to build a decoupled architecture, but if you think this way you will be able to span multiple cloud providers and scale out appropriately.
[320] **Web frameworks** — Web frameworks make it easy for us to write code to simplify deployments; however, can lead to common security vulnerabilities
[321] **Node.JS framework -** Note that if you are programming in Node.JS, the Express framework is common to use for voice-based applications.
[322] **Heroku -** While lightweight and easy to use, Flask's built-in server is not suitable for production as it doesn't scale well. One of the best and easiest ways to deploy Flask or a similar Python server is through Heroku, discussed later.

Figure 8.2.1
Spinning up a web server with the Flask framework:
flask_project.py (top) and *web page* (bottom)

```python
from flask import Flask
application = Flask(__name__)

@application.route("/")
def hello():
    return "<h1 style='color:blue'>Hello There!</h1>"

if __name__ == "__main__":
    application.run(host='0.0.0.0')
```

Hello There!

We can similarly spin up a server using the Django framework (Figure 8.2.2). This takes a few more steps than the Flask framework. First, you need to first run from the terminal the command *"django-admin startproject django_server."* This then creates a bunch of Django configuration files: *manage.py, .__init__.py, settings.py, urls.py, wsgi.py*. These files each have their own functions (taken from Django documentation). The Django web server is then simply launched with the *"python3 manage.py runserver"* command in the terminal (Figure 8.2.2).

Figure 8.2.2
Spinning up a web server with the Django framework:
django_server.py (top), *browser client* (bottom)

```python
import os

def dirtree(rootDir):
    list_dirs = os.walk(rootDir)
    for root, dirs, files in list_dirs:
        for d in dirs:
            print(os.path.join(root, d))
        for f in files:
            print(os.path.join(root, f))
```

```
# make a django project in the current directory
os.system('django-admin startproject django_server')[323]

print('CREATING FILES...')
print(dirtree(os.getcwd()+'/django_server'))

print('lauching server...')
os.chdir('django_server')
os.system('python3 manage.py runserver')
```

It worked!
Congratulations on your first Django-powered page.

Next, start your first app by running `python manage.py startapp [app_label]`.

You're seeing this message because you have DEBUG = True in your Django settings file and you haven't configured any URLs. Get to work!

Often, web frameworks don't scale well and are insecure for production environments; therefore, you need other web servers like **NGINX** (pronounced 'engine-X') to scale your application to a large number of users.[324] In the diagram below, a Python server fits into the **application server** block in the backend (Figure 8.2.3). In order for NGINX to know how to run Python, it needs a gateway to connect the application server to the web server via a NGINX server. Commonly, **Web Server Gateway Interface (WSGI) Servers** are used as this gateway. In Python, the **gunicorn, uwsgi, gevent,** and **twisted web** modules help with this task.

---

[323] **Django files:** After you run this command, these files should be created:
- **The outer django_server/ root directory** – This is just a container for your project. Its name doesn't matter to Django; you can rename it to anything you like.
- **Manage.py** - A command-line utility that lets you interact with this Django project in various ways. You can read all the details about manage.py in django-admin and manage.py.
- **The inner django_server/ directory** – This is the actual Python package for your project. Its name is the Python package name you'll need to use to import anything inside it (e.g. **django_server.urls**).
- **django_server/__init__.py** - An empty file that tells Python that this directory should be considered a Python package. If you're a Python beginner, read more about packages in the official Python docs.
- **django_server/settings.py** - Settings/configuration for this Django project. Django settings will tell you all about how settings work.
- **django_server/urls.py** - The URL declarations for this Django project; a "table of contents" of your Django-powered site. You can read more about URLs in URL dispatcher.
- **django_server/wsgi.py** - An entry-point for WSGI-compatible web servers to serve your project. See How to deploy with WSGI for more details.

[324] **10,000 user rule** - NGINX was built on the 10,000 user rule, meaning it was built to support 10k users at one time accessing it as a server and client.

Figure 8.2.3
How NGINX servers work with Python

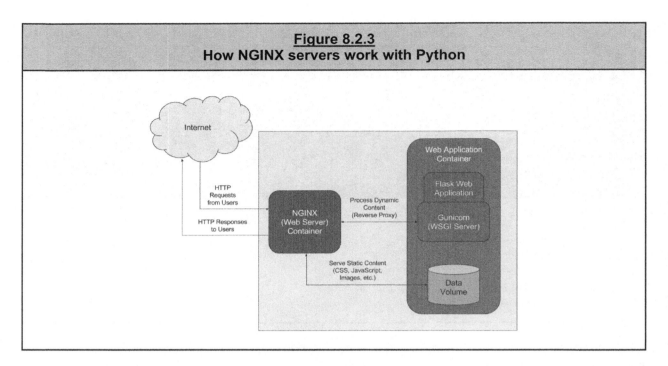

Now let's configure a NGINX server (Figure 8.2.2).[325] First, you need to install NGINX with Homebrew and then open up the NGINX configuration file (nginx.conf). The *nginx.conf* file tells the NGINX server what port to send data as a reverse proxy to a http-based WSGI web server (e.g. Gunicorn), which can then send data back/forth from Flask. You'll then notice a few sections here like http {} and server {}; the server{} part is the only part you really need to know for now.

Figure 8.2.4
Installing and configuring a NGINX-WSGI server with Flask:
terminal commands (top), web page (middle), nginx.conf (bottom)

```
brew install nginx
>> Updating Homebrew...
>> …
>> Error: nginx 1.15.2 is already installed
which nginx
>> /usr/local/bin/nginx
open http://0.0.0.0:8080
open /usr/local/etc/nginx/nginx.conf
```

---

[325] **Gunicorn** - for the sake of brevity, we will only use Gunicorn as the WSGI server to interface with our Python application. http://gunicorn.org/

> # Welcome to nginx!
>
> If you see this page, the nginx web server is successfully installed and working. Further configuration is required.
>
> For online documentation and support please refer to nginx.org. Commercial support is available at nginx.com.
>
> *Thank you for using nginx.*

```
...
http {
...
server {
   listen 80;
   server_name server_domain_or_IP;

   location / {
      include proxy_params;
      proxy_pass http://unix:/home/user/myproject/myproject.sock;
   }
}
...
```

We can now build a **NGINX-Gunicorn server** using a custom script to guide you along called *flask_virtual.py* that you can use as a guide. However, the tutorial is the best resource to boot up the server. I'm going to skip over this a bit because configuring NGINX-Gunicorn servers is a bit beyond the scope of this book; I just wanted to introduce these ideas to you so that they are not foreign when you work alongside teams that need you to build Python code compatible with these types of servers.[326]

Note that if you have a server up and running (e.g. *python3 flask_project.py*), you can also manually use a software package called **Postman** to test GET/POST requests onto a server. These requests can be saved to help debug code later. Note you can install Postman at this link (https://www.getpostman.com/apps) and then begin using it as soon as you create an account (Figure 8.2.5).

---

[326] **NGINX / Kubernetes / Kafka -** Later, we'll see that most microservice architectures use ingress and NGINX to build Kafka-based microservices on top of Kubernetes orchestration platforms.

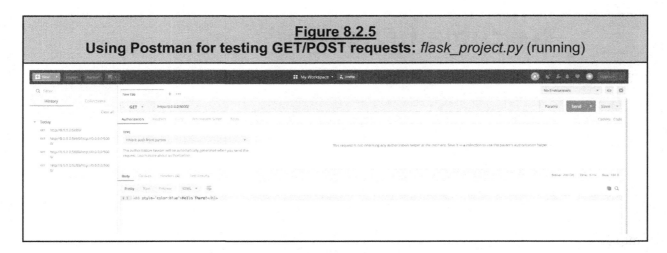

Figure 8.2.5
Using Postman for testing GET/POST requests: *flask_project.py* (running)

☺ Congrats! You can now setup and test NGINX-based servers with Flask and Postman, a huge first step in web server design.[327]

8.3   MongoDB databases

MongoDB is an open source, noSQL, and cross-platform database. MongoDB is a great database to use for enterprise applications because it's redundant and scalable with NGINX-based servers.

Before continuing, you need to install MongoDB on your machine. This is often done with *"brew install mongodb"* in the terminal.[328] After you you need to run *"mkdir -p /data/db"* in the terminal to make a database folder. Then, you need to run *"sudo chmod 777 /data/db"* to give this folder read/write privileges.[329] Now, you should be able to launch mongoDB by typing in *"mongod"* into the terminal.

Figure 8.3.1
Installing mongoDB from the terminal and launching it

```
brew install mongodb
mkdir -p /data/db
sudo chmod 777 /data/db
>> password: ****
mongod
```

---

[327] **If this feels a bit foreign** or uncomfortable to you; that's okay! It takes a bit of time getting used to all this. Most of the time a lot of this is abstracted for you in a production environment, but it's at least important to understand how things work to build server-side software.

[328] **Note -** you should have already done this if you have run the setup.py script at the beginning of this book, but if you haven't, be sure to download MongoDB or pymongo won't work properly.

[329] **A common issue** is IllegalOperation: Attempted to create a lock file on a read-only directory: /data/db, terminating. To get rid of this, you need to run 'sudo chmod 777 /data/db' to give the database a writing permission; otherwise you won't be able to setup a MongoDB server locally with the 'mongod' terminal command.

Now that you have MongoDB up and running, let's go through some common **PyMongo** commands (Table 8.3.1).[330] *Note that many of the MongoDB commands are conveniently formatted to be like a .JSON database schema so that you can quickly pick it up without much effort.*

<u>Table 8.3.1</u>
Common MongoDB commands in Python executed with the PyMongo module: *mongo_commands.py*

Command	Code
| Import library | ```
import pymongo, datetime
from pymongo import MongoClient
``` |
| Call up a mongoDB client | ```
client = MongoClient()
client = MongoClient('localhost', 27017)
# or client = MongoClient('mongodb://localhost:27017/')
``` |
| Access a database | ```
db = client.test_database
db = client['test-database']
``` |
| Making a document dictionary | ```
post = {"author": "Mike",
        "text": "My first blog post!",
        "tags": ["mongodb", "python", "pymongo"],
        "date": datetime.datetime.utcnow()}
``` |
| Insert a document into a database | ```
posts = db.posts
post_id = posts.insert_one(post).inserted_id
``` |
| Insert many documents in database | ```
posts = db.posts
post_id = posts.insert_one(post).inserted_id
print(post_id)
print(post)
new_posts = [{"author": "Mike",
              "text": "Another post!",
              "tags": ["bulk", "insert"],
              "date": datetime.datetime(2009, 11, 12, 11, 14)},
             {"author": "Eliot",
              "title": "MongoDB is fun",
              "text": "and pretty easy too!",
              "date": datetime.datetime(2009, 11, 10, 10, 45)}]
result=posts.insert_many(new_posts)
print(result.inserted_ids)
print(new_posts)
``` |

---

[330] **PyMongo** is the Python library that acts as a wrapper for MongoDB.

List all collections in a document	`db.collection_names(include_system_collections=False)`
Get a document in database	```# first document
print(posts.find_one())
# a specific request
posts.find_one({"author": "Eliot"})```
Find one by ID	```# note that
posts.find_one({"_id":str(post_id)})) will not work
posts.find_one({"_id":post_id})```
Converting a string to Object ID that's indexable	```from bson.objectid import ObjectId

def get(post_id):
    # Convert from string to ObjectId:
    document = client.db.collection.find_one({'_id': ObjectId(post_id)})``` |
| Counting items in a document | ```posts.count()
posts.find({"author":"Mike"}).count()``` |
| Querying date ranges | ```d = datetime.datetime(2009, 11, 12, 12)
for post in posts.find({"date": {"$lt": d}}).sort("author"):
    print(post)``` |
| Create databases that only accept unique values | ```result = db.profiles.create_index([('user_id', pymongo.ASCENDING)], unique=True)
sorted(list(db.profiles.index_information()))
user_profiles = [
    {'user_id': 211, 'name': 'Luke'},
    {'user_id': 212, 'name': 'Ziltoid'}]
result = db.profiles.insert_many(user_profiles)
new_profile = {'user_id': 213, 'name': 'Drew'}
duplicate_profile = {'user_id': 212, 'name': 'Tommy'}
# This is fine.
result = db.profiles.insert_one(new_profile)
# Results in error
result = db.profiles.insert_one(duplicate_profile)``` |

Conveniently, there is a tool called **Robo 3T** that you can use to visualize updates to MongoDB databases in real-time locally. Once you download/install the tool from their website (https://robomongo.org/download) you can use it as a sanity check during development. *Therefore, it's often useful to code in a Python client next to Robo 3T to quickly see if the code you are writing in Python is properly making changes to MongoDB databases* (Figure 8.8.3).

You may get this error when you install Robo 3T: "Robo 3T can't be opened because it is from an unidentified developer." To get rid of this message and allow for Robo 3T to be opened on your Mac, you can follow the steps below (Figure 8.3.1).

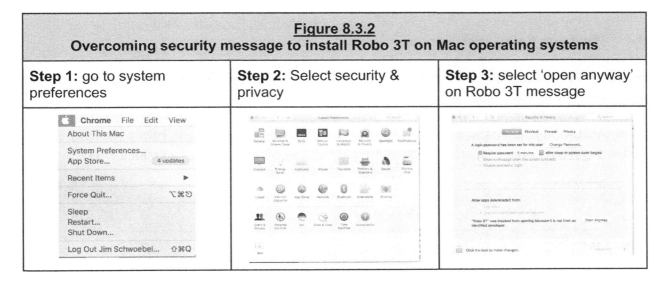

Figure 8.3.2
Overcoming security message to install Robo 3T on Mac operating systems

Step 1: go to system preferences	**Step 2:** Select security & privacy	**Step 3:** select 'open anyway' on Robo 3T message

We can now use Robo 3T to connect to local MongoDB databases on port 27017 or to MongoDB Atlas servers (Figure 8.3.3). *I encourage you to to do this now to comfortable with the interface.*

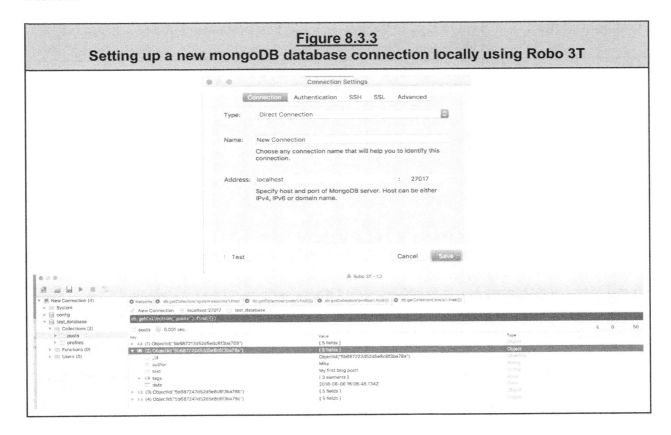

Figure 8.3.3
Setting up a new mongoDB database connection locally using Robo 3T

*Note there is a module called **flask-pymongo** that makes this easy to connect MongoDB with Flask servers. I won't elaborate upon this module here for the sake of keeping this chapter shorter. You can check out the flask-pymongo documentation on how to set up and configure these types of servers.*

8.4 Building Kafka microservices

As stated before, **Kafka** is used for building real-time data pipelines and streaming applications. Kafka has many use cases; in general, Kafka can be used to monitor activities, build microservices, aggregate log files, and manipulate data (Table 8.4.1). Kafka can even be used as an ACID-compliant database. In most cases, Kafka is most valuable to power microservices tied to streaming data (e.g. audio files in the case of voice-based server architectures).

Table 8.4.1 Some things that you can do with Kafka	
Concept	Description
Activity monitoring	Looking for trends in lots of streaming data. Could be audio files coming in and/or any data type.
Microservice Messaging	Can use messages to have producers and consumers trigger after each other in a "dumb pipe" - allowing for microservices.
Log aggregation	Store logs of the server for further processing and/or debugging later.
Data manipulation	Near real-time streaming allows for extract, transforming, and loading (ETL) - to transmit and store data in the proper format.
Database	You can use message topics and message payloads as databases in and of themselves.

Now let's install Kafka and start up the cluster. You can install the latest version of Kafka @ this link: https://www.apache.org/dyn/closer.cgi?path=/kafka/2.0.0/kafka_2.11-2.0.0.tgz.

Once you have it downloaded (kafka_2.11-2.0.0.tgz), untar the file and then cd into the folder (e.g. 'kafka_2.11-3.0.0 3'). Once you are in this folder, you can run the commands laid out below to launch a Kafka cluster from the command line (Figure 8.4.1). *Note you need to open up two terminal instances to run ZooKeeper and Kafka separately and in parallel.*[331]

---

[331] **Zookeeper** – From Apache's website: "ZooKeeper is a centralized service for maintaining configuration information, naming, providing distributed synchronization, and providing group services. All of these kinds of services are used in some form or another by distributed applications. Each time they are implemented there is a lot of work that goes into fixing the bugs and race conditions that are inevitable. Because of the difficulty of implementing these kinds of services, applications initially usually skimp on them, which make them brittle in the presence of change and difficult to manage. Even when done correctly, different implementations of these services lead to management complexity when the applications are deployed."

Figure 8.4.1
How to launch a Kafka cluster from the command line (port 9092)

```
cd ~
cd downloads
tar -xzf kafka_2.11-2.0.0.tgz
cd 'kafka_2.11-2.0.0'
bin/zookeeper-server-start.sh config/zookeeper.properties
```

```
# open up another terminal and run the commands below
cd ~
cd downloads/kafka_2.11-2.0.0
bin/kafka-server-start.sh config/server.properties
```

Command line Kafka commands	
Download link	https://www.apache.org/dyn/closer.cgi?path=/kafka/2.0.0/kafka_2.11-2.0.0.tgz
Create a new topic	bin/kafka-topics.sh --create --zookeeper localhost:2181 --replication-factor 1 --partitions 1 --topic test
Produce a message on topic	bin/kafka-console-producer.sh --broker-list localhost:9092 --topic test
Consume a message on topic	bin/kafka-console-consumer.sh --bootstrap-server localhost:9092 --topic test --from-beginning

Now that we have a Kafka cluster running, we can now make a **producer** to produce messages on the Kafka cluster (Figure 8.4.2). Python uses the **kafka-python** module to help with this. Note you need to listen on a certain port (e.g. 'localhost:9092') and a certain topic (e.g. 'test') for it to work and that you could also use the command line interface to produce and consume messages (Figure 8.4.1).

Figure 8.4.2
Making a Kafka producer: *kafka_producer.py*

```python
from kafka import KafkaProducer
import time

producer = KafkaProducer(bootstrap_servers='localhost:9092')
topic='test'

for i in range(30):
    print('sending message...%s'%(str(i)))
    producer.send(topic, b'test2')
    time.sleep(1)
```

Next, we need to make a **consumer** which consumes the messages of the producer (Figure 8.4.3). *Note that the consumer must listen to the same topic and port that the producer is on for things to work properly.*

Figure 8.4.3
Making a Kafka consumer: *kafka_consumer.py*

```python
from kafka import KafkaConsumer

topic='test'
consumer = KafkaConsumer(topic, bootstrap_servers='localhost:9092')
# creates a running loop to listen for messages
for msg in consumer:
    print(msg)
```

Now we just need to launch both the producer and consumer in parallel. When you do this, you should be able to see the messages propagated.[332] Pretty cool, right?

This should give you perspective on the power of Kafka. You can stream audio content near-instantaneously while having an audit log of the sessions as messages (e.g. when messages are consumed and produced). It's a powerful tool to build and optimize microservice architectures.

---

[332] **This assumes** ZooKeeper and Kafka are running with the message topic created. If you're getting errors, check the Kafka documentation.

8.5 Minio as a wrapper for GCP/AWS

If you're using Google Cloud Platform (GCP) or Amazon Web Services (AWS) for file storage, it's sometimes impractical to constantly reference online files (e.g. stored in S3) for testing your applications. Also, if you're using multiple storage platforms, it's often inefficient to use each third-party library to interact with your data.

To solve these problems, you can use a ***Minio storage server***. Specifically, Minio is a wrapper library for AWS S3/GCP Storage so that you can simulate these environments locally and offline. You can do mostly anything you would do in an online environment, such as create buckets and store data within these buckets. You can also make these servers compatible with these third-party services and use them as wrappers to store data into online buckets. *Thus, Minio is useful to develop locally before going to the production server and to make the data collection process from clients decoupled from any one vendor.* [333]

The only variables you need to setup a Minio client is an endpoint, access key, secret key, and secure value (Table 8.5.1).

<div align="center">Table 8.5.1 Variables needed to spin up a Minio client</div>	
Variables	**Description**
endpoint	URL to object storage service.
access_key	Access key is like user ID that uniquely identifies your account.
secret_key	Secret key is the password to your account.
secure	Set this value to 'True' to enable secure (HTTPS) access.

Once you have these things, it's quite easy to spin up a Minio client in Python (Figure 8.5.1).

---

[333] **Minio** - Selecting Minio as a storage solution fits into the decoupled philosophy mentioned in the first section of this chapter; you're not locked into one cloud vendor. Instead, you can pick from GCP, AWS, or Azure and/or mix them all. This is often useful when you have cloud credits as a startup.

Figure 8.5.1
Spinning up a Minio client in Python as an alternative to S3: *minio.py*

```python
# Import Minio library.
from minio import Minio
from minio.error import (ResponseError, BucketAlreadyOwnedByYou,
                         BucketAlreadyExists)

# Initialize minioClient with an endpoint and access/secret keys.
minioClient = Minio('play.minio.io:9000',
                    access_key='Q3AM3UQ867SPQQA43P2F',
                    secret_key='zuf+tfteSlswRu7BJ86wekitnifILbZam1KYY3TG',
                    secure=True)

# Make a bucket with the make_bucket API call.
try:
      minioClient.make_bucket("maylogs", location="us-east-1")
except BucketAlreadyOwnedByYou as err:
      pass
except BucketAlreadyExists as err:
      pass
except ResponseError as err:
      raise
else:
      # Put an object 'pumaserver_debug.log' with contents from
'pumaserver_debug.log'.
      try:
            minioClient.fput_object('maylogs', 'pumaserver_debug.log',
'/tmp/pumaserver_debug.log')
      except ResponseError as err:
            print(err)
```

This is a short introduction; if you're seeking more information check out Minio's documentation.

8.6   Authentication with Auth0

When you're building a web server you often need to authenticate user identities with third-parties to access certain information. For example, you may want to access a user's Google account to receive a user's email address and calendar data.

OAuth2 is the common protocol that most websites use to help with user authentication.[334] Specifically, an application requests authorization to get a resource from a user (Figure 8.6.1). The user then grants the application authorization to use those resources (often through a web

---

[334] Although you could get the username and password of a person and act on their behalf, this is inefficient and can lead to security vulnerabilities.

browser client), which then goes to the authorization server ('auth server') to grant access via an *authorization code*. Then the application uses the authorization code to request and receive an *access token* from the auth server. The application can then use these access tokens to get certain resources from the *resource server* (e.g. email address). *OAuth2 is the protocol that works behind the scenes to make this all happen seamlessly and securely.*

Before using OAuth2 with your application, you must register your application with the service - often through some sort of developer portal. This usually includes getting the application name, the application website, and the redirect URL that will be used by the user to confirm the authorization code and access token. Once your application is registered, the service will issue client credentials in the form of a *client identifier* and a *client secret*, which are then used to build the authorization URLs presented to users (client identifier) and for back-end access token requests (client secret).[335]

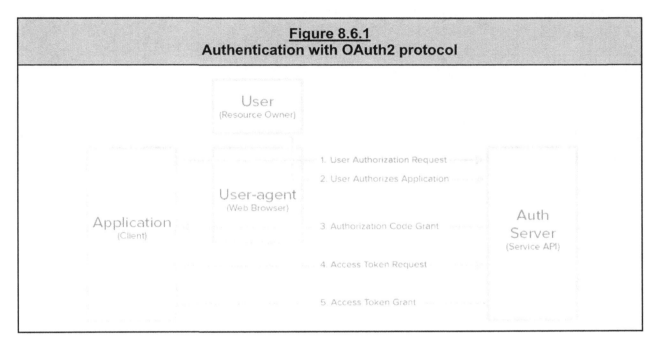

Figure 8.6.1
Authentication with OAuth2 protocol

To help with this, you can use a library called **Auth0** which implements the OAuth2 protocol automatically. Auth0 can connect to Google, Facebook, Microsoft Account, LinkedIn, GitHub, Twitter, Box, Salesforce, among others. To get started, all you need to do is solicit the client_ID and client_secret from a user and then you can get a token from the domain. In this way, you get back a management API token which can then be used to obtain user information (e.g. an email address). *Note that it's often a good practice to use authentication libraries like Auth0 that can easily integrate with many different types of third-party services (e.g. Facebook vs. Google); this makes server configurations more agile.*

---

[335] **Guard client secrets -** You should always guard your client secret from being exposed publicly. The client identifier is something that has to be exposed publicly in order for users to authorize requests.

Figure 8.6.2
How to use auth0 for user authentication: *auth0.py*

```python
from auth0.v3.authentication import GetToken
from auth0.v3.management import Auth0

# obtain a management token
domain = 'myaccount.auth0.com'
non_interactive_client_id = 'exampleid'
non_interactive_client_secret = 'examplesecret'

get_token = GetToken(domain)
token = get_token.client_credentials(non_interactive_client_id,
    non_interactive_client_secret, 'https://{}/api/v2/'.format(domain))
mgmt_api_token = token['access_token']

# use your management token
auth0 = Auth0(domain, mgmt_api_token)

#The Auth0() object is now ready to take orders! Let's see how we can use this to
get all available connections. (this action requires the token to have the
following scope: read:connections)
print(auth0.connections.all())
```

As a challenge, perhaps you would like to connect Auth0 with a Flask web server? Feel free to do this on your own to get comfortable with the Auth0 library.

8.7   Working with Docker containers

Docker[336] is by far the most widely used container management framework for shipping enterprise software.[337] Recall that containers are an alternative to virtual machines (VMs) and are much more efficient at repeated computations for servers. With containers your application is packaged together in a common shared format and deployed out to the cloud, so you don't have to worry about things like dependencies and operating environments.

Before continuing, make sure you install Docker community edition here: https://store.docker.com/editions/community/docker-ce-desktop-mac. You probably need to create an account for the download to start. Note ***you should not use "brew install docker"*** as this will not work with some of the commands that follow.

---

[336] **Created in March 2013,** Docker grew quickly originally as part of the Linux kernel. Now there is support for Docker across pretty much all operating systems.

[337] **As mentioned before, containers** are "lightweight, stand-alone, executable packages of software that includes everything needed to run it: code, runtime, system tools, system libraries, settings." Simply, containers virtualize the underlying operating system and make it easy to ship code.

The way Docker works is that you use a ***Dockerfile*** to build an ***image*** of an app (Table 8.7.1). This image includes all the system libraries (e.g. apt-get) as well as programming languages (e.g. python3) and any Python dependencies (e.g. Flask). Then, you can transform an image into a ***container*** which is a running instance of an image on a server. Each step of the build process generates an image of ***layered file system*** so that you don't have to rebuild things again the second time around; for example, if you built a Docker image with Ubuntu and Python already it can be loaded from the layered file system. *Note that you can use the **Docker Registry** to store or pull existing Docker images easily.*[338]

Table 8.7.1 Common Docker terms and definitions	
Term	**Description**
Layer	A read only snapshot of the filesystem.
Image	a read-only layer that is the base of your container.
Container	a runnable instance of the image, basically it is a process isolated by Docker that runs on top of the filesystem that an image provides
Registry / Hub	is the central place where all publicly published images live. You can search it, upload your images there and when you pull a Docker image, it comes the repository/hub.

Note there are three major types of Docker commands: *basic Docker commands, Docker compose commands, and Docker machine commands* (Table 8.7.2). **Basic Docker commands** allow you to build and remove Docker images. **Docker compose commands** allow you to build multiple containers together simultaneously. Lastly, **Docker machine commands** are useful in scenarios in provisioning and managing Docker hosts. Thus, you can build Docker images locally, publish Docker containers together, and/or edit Docker hosts.

Table 8.7.2: Useful docker commands	
Category	**CLI Command + Description**
Basic commands	***Basic Docker commands*** *allow you to build images, run images, look for log files, see what images are running, push Docker images to the cloud and/or pull Docker images from the cloud.*

---

[338] **To do this**, you need to use docker push/pull commands.

	`docker build ${image}`	builds an image
	`docker pull ${image}`	pull Docker image from Docker cloud
	`docker run ${image}`	creates a container and runs it
	`docker push ${image}`	push Docker image to Docker cloud
	`docker rmi ${IMAGE_ID}`	remove a Docker image
	`docker stop ${CID}`	stop a container
	`docker rm ${CID}`	remove a container
	`docker logs`	logs of files
	`docker ps`	see what images are running right now.
	`docker images`	list of installed images
	`docker rmi $(docker images -q)`	Get rid of all images.
	`docker rm $(docker ps -aq)`	Get rid of all containers.

Compose commands	*Docker compose commands* allow for you to launch many containers together simultaneously.	
	`docker-compose up`	starts all containers.
	`docker-compose build`	rebuilds all images.
	`docker-compose stop`	pauses the containers.
	`docker-compose down`	deletes all containers.

Machine commands	*Docker machine commands* are useful in scenarios when you are SSHing into servers. You can destroy or create multiple Kafka clusters this way.	
	`docker-machine create`	creates new Docker host
	`docker-machine ssh`	connects to host using SSH
	`docker-machine rm`	destroys host
	`docker-machine env`	sets env variables to connect to host

If you're stuck, definitely try navigating Docker's website documentation. There are also many Docker meetups and Slack channels that you can use to connect with other developers.

8.8 Unit and integration tests

There are many ways to test that your code operates as intended (Table 8.1.1). Generally, the most important tests are unit tests and integration tests. **Unit tests** are completely offline tests that just make sure the functions that you write do what they say they are doing; for example, making sure the function outputs a string when you call it. **Integration tests**, on the other hand, ensure that your code connects to other modules and/or services properly; for example, making sure you can download a file from Google Cloud Platform (GCP) in the proper bucket. As your product gets more mature, so do your automated tests. *There is a compromise on the number and type of automated tests and the overall costs of testing.*

Table 8.8.1 Common software testing techniques	
Test	**Definition**
Unit test	Test methods, functions, classes, and components of one specific piece of software; very easy to automate and cheap to do.
Integration test	Verify that different modules or services can work with each other - for example, can make sure you can connect to a database. Integration tests look for bugs in the system as a whole.
Functional tests	focus on business requirements; verify output of action and do not check for intermediate states of the systems.
End-to-end tests	replicates a user behavior with the software in a complete application environment; quite expensive.

Acceptance testing	Formal tests executed to verify if a system satisfies its business requirement.
Performance testing	Check the behaviors of the system when it is under a significant load; helps system administrators understand the reliability, stability, and availability of the platform (e.g. measuring response times with high number of requests).
Smoke testing	Basic quick tests that check basic functionality of the application; usually are done when you first install or build an application.

The easiest way to automate your unit and integration tests in Python is with the ***unittest()* module**.[339] This is good for things like testing whether or not two variables are equal to each other and/or just about anything to show that the code you have written works (Table 8.8.2).

Table 8.8.2
Useful unittest() comparison functions

Assertion	Command
Is a variable True?	`assertTrue(x, msg=None)`
Is a variable False?	`assertFalse(x, msg=None)`
Is a variable NoneType?	`assertIsNone(x, msg=None)`
Is a variable not a NoneType?	`assertIsNotNone(x, msg=None)`
Is variable A equal to variable B?	`assertEqual(a, b, msg=None)`
Is variable A not equal to variable B?	`assertNotEqual(a, b, msg=None)`
Is A in list B?	`assertIn(a, b, msg=None)`
Is A not in list B?	`assertNotIn(a, b, msg=None)`
Is an instance of A in list B?	`assertIsInstance(a, b, msg=None)`
Is not an instance of A in B?	`assertNotIsInstance(a, b, msg=None)`

---

[339] **Pytest** - As an alternative, you can also use pytest. I prefer using unittest() though because it seems like a more widely adopted and better documented library.

Just to show you the functionality of the unittest() module, let's go through a very simple example (Figure 8.8.1). Here all we're doing is seeing if a and b are equal to each other with the self.assert_equal() function (Table 8.8.2). Note that the output from the terminal shows the test being run and if it passes or fails.

Figure 8.8.1
Using the unittest module: *unit_test.py* (top), *terminal output* (bottom)

```python
import unittest

class SimplisticTest(unittest.TestCase):

    def test(self):
        a = 'a'
        b = 'a'
        self.assertEqual(a, b)

if __name__ == '__main__':
    unittest.main()
```

```
>> --------------------------------------------------------------
>> Ran 1 test in 0.000s
>>
>> OK
```

We can now put this in the Dockerfile to run tests during deployment by simply adding the command below (Figure 8.8.1). Then if you type in *"docker build ."* in the working directory (assuming you have the Docker daemon running) it should spin up the Docker image and have the same output as above.

Figure 8.8.2
Running automated tests in a Docker container: *./docker/Dockerfile*

```dockerfile
# get python-node base image
FROM combos/python_node:3_8

# set working directory
WORKDIR /usr/src/app
ADD . /usr/src/app

# run tests
RUN python unit_test.py
```

Going into advanced unit tests and integration tests is beyond the scope of this book. If these are new concepts for you, I'd encourage you to code a few examples yourself. Testing is extremely important when making code production-ready.

8.9 Code deployment with GitHub/Heroku

As you know, **GitHub** is a common tool for building and deploying code through **code repositories**.[340] GitHub allows you to track any changes you make to code repositories with the *Git version control system,* allowing for streamlined code base management (Table 8.9.1).[341] Through this software, you can create or clone new repositories, edit existing code bases through pull requests and branches, and create and fix bugs through the "Issues" tab. In this way, you can speed up the process of code deployment.

<div align="center">**Table 8.9.1** **Common GitHub terms and definitions**</div>	
Term	**Definition**
Code repository	This term is what is used to designate a collection of pieces of of code that you write. You can clone and/or collaborate on editing this repository through pull requests and branches.
Pull request ("PR")	Allows you to propose and collaborate on changes to a repository. Specifically, it allows you to make new branches (discussed below).
Branch	A spinoff code base from the main repository where you make some changes to merge later. The *master* branch is often the main code base currently being used and branches are only merged with master if it the branch meets a certain level of quality.
Fork	A copy of any repository; allows you to experiment with the code without affecting the original project. Typically, a repository is forked, then a fix i s made, and then a pull request is made to edit the main code and if the code owner likes the changes it can be merged with the master branch.
Readme.md	A readme is a short summary the repository are and how to setup the repository so it functions as intended. You need a Readme.md document to initialize a repository.
GitHub Command Line Interface (CLI)	The GitHub CLI allows for you to push changes to a repository directly from the terminal through commands that are overviewed in Table 8.9.2. You can always upload your code directly to the web too through GitHub's web uploading tool, but this is often looked down upon in the developer community ☺.

---

[340] **An alternative is GitLab**: https://gitlab.com/
[341] **Linus Torvalds** - From Wikipedia "Git was created by Linus Torvalds in 2005 for development of the Linux kernel, with other kernel developers contributing to its initial development.[12] Its current maintainer since 2005 is Junio Hamano."

GitHub Issues ("Issues")	Issues is a forum where you can track bugs, suggest enhancements, and/or provider support for users of code repositories. Its layout makes it much easier to respond to end users of a code repository.
GitHub Wiki ("Wiki")	GitHub also provides a 'wiki' tab in almost all of their repositories. Surprisingly, this wiki feature is only used some of the time. As the name implies, the wiki is an extension of the Readme to go further in depth about a particular repository. It usually discusses things like API calls and functions, database structures, and generally how best to utilize a repository.

The best place to learn how to use GitHub is through the ***GitHub Command Line Interface (CLI)***. Let's overview some common GitHub commands (Table 8.9.2). *I'm assuming you already have a GitHub account because you've cloned this book. If you haven't set up a GitHub account yet, set one up here:* https://github.com/join.

<u>**Table 8.9.2**</u>
Common GitHub CLI commands

Command	Description
`git init`	Create an empty git repo or reinitialize an existing one
`git clone [repo link]`	Clone a new repository.
`git checkout -b <new branch name>`	Change branches (often it's good to stay off the master branch when making changes to keep things clean).
`git status`	Sees what files have changed within the branch.
`git add .`	Adds changes to all the files (from the git status command).
`git add [Foo.js]`	Add only an individual file to change.
`git commit -m "{message}"`	This command commits the changes you made to the code with a message so others know what you did.
`git reset [file]`	Unstages the file but preserves its contents.
`git add -A && git commit -m "Your Message"`	Commit all changes in one line of code.
`git push`	Pushes the code and updates the GitHub repository with your comments.

One of the easiest ways to deploy live code through the GitHub CLI is through a nifty software tool called Heroku. **Heroku** is a cloud platform-as-a-service (PaaS) that lets you ship your GitHub code in practically 1-2 lines typed into the terminal.[342]

First, let's quickly install Heroku from the CLI with *"brew install heroku/brew/heroku."* Now, you need to go to the website and create an account. After you create an account, you can connect your Heroku account to the CLI by logging in (e.g. with *"heroku login"*).

Figure 8.9.1
Setting up the Heroku CLI

```
brew install heroku/brew/heroku
open https://www.heroku.com/
heroku login
>> heroku: Enter your login credentials
>> Email [example@gmail.com]: example@gmail.com
>> Password: **************************
```

Now that your Heroku account is tied to the terminal, we can ship code that we have built on GitHub with Heroku from the command line (Table 8.9.3).

Table 8.9.3
Common heroku CLI commands

Command	Description
cd ~/myapp heroku create	After going into proper directory, you can create a Heroku instance with the Heroku create command.
git push heroku master	Push master branch of existing GitHub repo to heroku.
heroku ps	See which heroku apps are deployed live.
heroku ps:scale web=1	Scale number of dynos that are running (to accommodate web traffic). Eventually this needs to upgrade to a paid plan.

---

[342] **Heroku's Utility** - I often find it as a good means to share prototypes with others. Note, however, if you are building production-level code it's probably better to do this through Google Cloud's container management software with Pods and everything.

| ```
git add -A
git commit -m "commit for deploy to heroku"
...
git push -f heroku
``` | General code to add a commit through GitHub and then push through to Heroku. |

Let's now use Heroku to deploy a Django server (Figure 8.9.2). This code deploys a web page at a temporary URL on Heroku (blooming-badlands-28947.herokuapp.com) which you can then change or forward to another domain.

Figure 8.9.2
Deploying code with Heroku

Heroku is by far the easiest tool I know to deploy a web server publicly. If you'd like to explore deployments with Heroku further, check out the documentation (which is tailored for Python developers who use Django framework).
```

8.10 Code deployment with GitHub/Kubernetes on GCP

When building a microservice architecture with Docker containers and Kafka, it's important to understand **Kubernetes (k8s)**, as it's the most widely used open source orchestration platform for microservices.[343] Its main purpose is to help automate the process of scaling containers across clusters of hosts.[344]

Table 8.10.1
Common Kubernetes terms and definitions

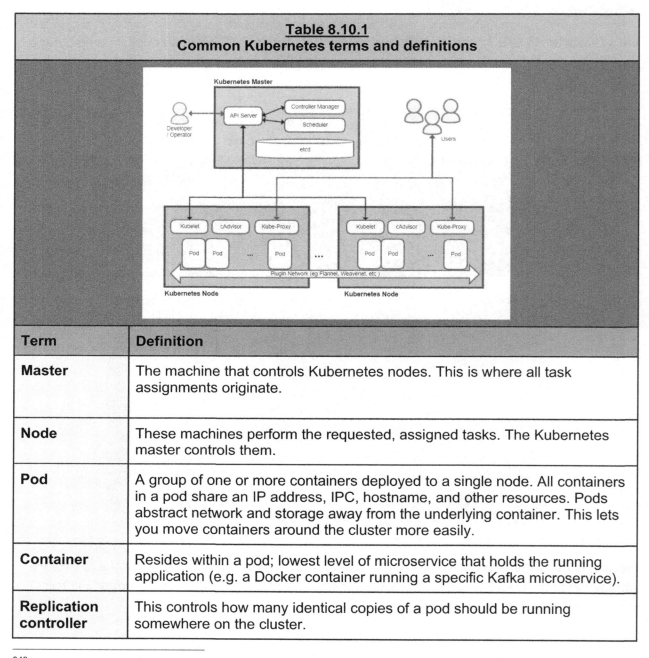

Term	Definition
Master	The machine that controls Kubernetes nodes. This is where all task assignments originate.
Node	These machines perform the requested, assigned tasks. The Kubernetes master controls them.
Pod	A group of one or more containers deployed to a single node. All containers in a pod share an IP address, IPC, hostname, and other resources. Pods abstract network and storage away from the underlying container. This lets you move containers around the cluster more easily.
Container	Resides within a pod; lowest level of microservice that holds the running application (e.g. a Docker container running a specific Kafka microservice).
Replication controller	This controls how many identical copies of a pod should be running somewhere on the cluster.

---

[343] **Docker Swarm vs. Kubernetes** - Kubernetes has become increasingly important the past year, as Docker has deprecated the Docker Swarm feature which allows you to manage containers through Docker Cloud. Therefore, it's really the only major offering right now that can support most needs for microservices.

[344] **Go** - Written by Google in the Go programming language (the same language that Docker is written in),

Service	This decouples work definitions from the pods. Kubernetes service proxies automatically get service requests to the right pod—no matter where it moves to in the cluster or even if it's been replaced.
Kubelet	This service runs on nodes and reads the container manifests and ensures the defined containers are started and running.
Kubectl	This is the command line configuration tool for Kubernetes.

Here are some useful commands for kubectl, the command line interface for Kubernetes (Table 8.10.2). Feel free to just type in *"kubectl"* into the terminal and many of these commands will be explained. If these commands do not work, you can install the Kubernetes CLI with Homebrew *("brew install kubernetes-cli")*.

<table>
<tr><td colspan="2" align="center">Table 8.10.2
Getting used to the kubectl CLI</td></tr>
<tr><td>CLI Command</td><td>Description</td></tr>
<tr><td><code>kubectl create</code></td><td>Create a resource from a file or from stdin.</td></tr>
<tr><td><code>kubectl expose</code></td><td>Take a replication controller, service, deployment or pod and expose it as a new Kubernetes Service.</td></tr>
<tr><td><code>kubectl run</code></td><td>Run a particular image on the cluster.</td></tr>
<tr><td><code>kubectl set</code></td><td>Set specific features on objects.</td></tr>
<tr><td><code>kubectl get</code></td><td>Display one or many resources.</td></tr>
<tr><td><code>kubectl explain</code></td><td>Documentation of resources.</td></tr>
<tr><td><code>kubectl edit</code></td><td>Edit a resource on the server.</td></tr>
<tr><td><code>kubectl delete</code></td><td>Delete resources by filenames, stdin, resources and names, or by resources and label selector.</td></tr>
</table>

Before you can run a Kubernetes cluster, you must connect the **Docker Hub** with the deployer that orchestrates the deployment through a webhook. Then Kubernetes is deployed on a cloud service (e.g. GCP Kubernetes engine). *The important takeaway here is that you need to connect Docker Hub with the Kubernetes Engine to enable automated container deployments.*

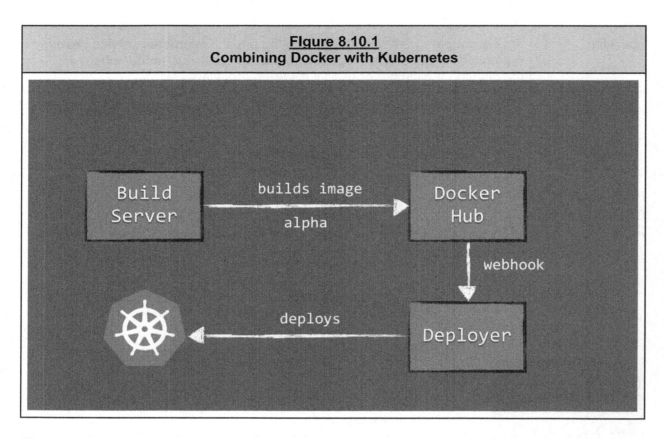

The only other thing you really need to know (as an introduction) is that you can configure Kubernetes with the **k8s-based code repository.** Specifically, each Kafka microservice and Kubernetes cluster that you build will need a **.yml configuration file** to be placed in this GitHub (or GitLab) repository for it to work properly. The example below shows how to build a NGINX server from the NGINX Docker image on port 80. Then, you can deploy this through adding build triggers in the GCP Kubernetes Engine with the cloudbuild.yml file.[345] *Note often you have a large collection of these .yml files - perhaps even hundreds - in a true microservice architecture at scale.*

---

[345] **20+ microservices** – At NeuroLex, we have about 20 right now in our current architecture with NeuroLex.

**Figure 8.10.2
Sample .yml file to load NGINX server:** *nginx.yml*

```yaml
apiVersion: v1
kind: Pod
metadata:
  name: nginx-apparmor
  # Note that the Pod does not need to be in the same namespace as the Loader.
  labels:
    app: nginx
  annotations:
    # Tell Kubernetes to apply the AppArmor profile "k8s-nginx".
    # Note that this is ignored if the Kubernetes node is not running version 1.4 or greater.
    container.apparmor.security.beta.kubernetes.io/nginx: localhost/k8s-nginx
spec:
  containers:
  - name: nginx
    image: nginx
    ports:
    - containerPort: 80
```

In closing, you can view Kubernetes deployments as a next step to deploy your Python applications at scale. You can setup Kubernetes by downloading the kubectl tool. You'll also need to install gcloud with "brew install gcloud." *For additional information, check out the GCP Kubernetes Engine documentation.*

8.11 Conclusion

👏 You rock! You now know a bit about server architectures, web frameworks, MongoDB databases, Kafka-based microservices, Minio as a wrapper for AWS, Auth0 for authentication, Docker containers, automated testing, and automated code deployments (with Heroku vs. the GCP Kubernetes engine).

I know, this is a lot. You're always learning when you are building web architectures. I don't know if you ever feel truly "comfortable." But these foundations should get you off to a good start, especially if you end up ever touching microservice architectures.

If you'd like to go deeper on anything, check out the following resources:

- Server architectures
  - Client-server architectures
    - Client-server model.
      https://en.wikipedia.org/wiki/Client%E2%80%93server_model

- Microservices vs. monoliths. https://martinfowler.com/articles/microservices.html
- Basics of web architecture. https://engineering.videoblocks.com/web-architecture-101-a3224e126947
    - Databases
        - MongoDB. https://realpython.com/introduction-to-mongodb-and-python/
        - Postgres. http://www.postgresqltutorial.com/postgresql-python/
        - MySQL. https://dev.mysql.com/doc/connector-python/en/
        - JSON. https://realpython.com/python-json/
    - Playing back media in browser
        - HTML5 audio tag. https://en.wikipedia.org/wiki/HTML5_audio
        - HTML5 video tag. https://en.wikipedia.org/wiki/HTML5_video
    - Recording media in browser
        - WebRTC API. https://developer.mozilla.org/en-US/docs/Web/API/WebRTC_API
        - Media Capture Streams API. https://developer.mozilla.org/en-US/docs/Web/API/Media_Streams_API
        - Mediastreams Recording API. https://developer.mozilla.org/en-US/docs/Web/API/MediaStream_Recording_API
    - Web server types
        - NGINX web server. https://www.fullstackpython.com/nginx.html
    - Containers / Orchestration
        - Difference between containers and virtual machines. https://medium.com/flow-ci/introduction-to-containers-concept-pros-and-cons-orchestration-docker-and-other-alternatives-9a2f1b61132c
        - VMware workstation pro. https://www.vmware.com/products/workstation-pro.html
        - Docker. https://www.docker.com/
        - Kubernetes. https://www.redhat.com/en/topics/containers/what-is-kubernetes
- Web frameworks
    - Flask. http://flask.pocoo.org/
    - Django. https://www.djangoproject.com/
    - NGINX. https://www.fullstackpython.com/nginx.html
    - Gunicorn. http://gunicorn.org/
    - UWSGI. https://uwsgi-docs.readthedocs.io/en/latest/WSGIquickstart.html
    - Virtualenv. https://virtualenv.pypa.io/en/stable/
    - Jinja (.HTML formatting). http://jinja.pocoo.org/docs/2.10/intro/#basic-api-usage
    - Postman (GET/POST requests). https://www.getpostman.com/docs/v6/
- Databases
    - Flask-pymongo. https://flask-pymongo.readthedocs.io/en/latest/
    - PyMongo (MongoDB). https://api.mongodb.com/python/current/
    - Pyycopg (postgres). http://initd.org/psycopg/
    - Sqlite3 (sqlite). https://docs.python.org/2/library/sqlite3.html

- o Json. https://developer.rhino3d.com/guides/rhinopython/python-xml-json/
  - o Robo 3T. https://robomongo.org/
- Kafka microservices
  - o Kafka-python. http://kafka-python.readthedocs.io/en/master/
- File storage
  - o Minio (offline). https://github.com/minio/minio-py
  - o AWS S3. https://docs.aws.amazon.com/AmazonS3/latest/gsg/CreatingABucket.html
  - o Google cloud storage. https://cloud.google.com/storage/
- Containers
  - o Docker. https://cloud.google.com/storage/
  - o Docker and python intro talk. https://www.youtube.com/watch?v=VhabrYF1nms
- Authentication
  - o Auth0. https://github.com/auth0/auth0-python
- Unit and integration tests
  - o Unittest() framework. https://docs.python.org/3/library/unittest.html
  - o Pytest. https://docs.pytest.org/en/latest/
- Deploying software applications
  - o Heroku. https://devcenter.heroku.com/articles/getting-started-with-python
  - o Kubernetes. https://github.com/kubernetes/kubernetes
  - o GCP Kubernetes Engine documentation. https://cloud.google.com/kubernetes-engine/docs/
  - o Github cheat sheet. https://education.github.com/git-cheat-sheet-education.pdf

The next chapter is all about building *secure software,* which is important given all the legal and privacy implications of voice computing. 🔒

Chapter 9:
Security, legal, and ethical considerations

"The Amazon Echo, despite being small, is a computer – it's a computer with microphones, speakers, and it's connected to the network. These are potential surveillance devices, and we have invited them further and further into our lives without examining how that could go wrong. And I think we are starting to see examples of that."

–Daniel Kahn Gillmor
(staff technologist for the ACLU's speech,
privacy, and technology project)

Chapter Overview

Your company's reputation is like a cup filled with water. If a dye is put inside this cup it can quickly pollute the water within seconds. Similarly, if a voice computer becomes breached by a malicious actor your company's reputation can be tarnished within minutes.[346][347]

Over 9.7 billion data records have been stolen since 2013. That's 198,304 records per hour, 4,759,304 every day, and 55 records per second.[348] It's clear that senior executives are still not grasping the importance of information security in today's world.[349]

Therefore, this chapter provides some frameworks on how to build secure software that complies with state, federal, and international laws (e.g. USA and Europe).[350][351] It ends in a discussion on how we, as the voice community, can come together to establish practical ethical frameworks to guide software development in voice computing.[352]

Specifically, we'll cover:

- **9.1** - Security considerations
- **9.2** - Legal considerations
- **9.3** - Ethical considerations

In this way, you can build secure, legally-compliant, and ethical voice software.[353]

---

[346] **For example,** through an unauthorized purchase.

[347] **Economy analogy -** As an economy, we're built on trust. When trust vanishes, markets act chaotically leading to lower wages, profit, and employment rates. When trust is strong, it leads to increased transaction volume and higher profits.

[348] **Breachlive index** - These statistics were taken from this website: https://breachlevelindex.com/

[349] **Talent shortage -** There's also a talent shortage; 51% of enterprises have a problematic shortage of cybersecurity skills.

[350] **Vulnerabilities -** There are all sorts of new security vulnerabilities for voice assistants. You can use a "DolphinAttack" to remotely activate voice assistants using ultrasonic waves, leading to unauthorized access. You can even store secret commands to send messages, make purchases, or wire money money. We still don't know the implications of these vulnerabilities and it's likely that they are greatly affecting. These vulnerabilities are discussed later on in this chapter.

[351] **Laws -** Legal definitions for voice privacy laws are blurry. For example, if you leave a voicemail on my phone you don't actually own the copyright to that voicemail; the voicemail owner does. I am free to publish that voicemail anywhere, or even sell this data to third parties. If I ran a machine learning model on that voicemail, I could determine things like risks for a depressive episode. New privacy regulations exist, and this chapter hopes to provide some overarching guidance here to build software that can comply with such laws.

[352] **Ethics guidelines** – These are necessary to ensure the public's trust in voice computing. We should try to minimize the risks posed to consumers.

[353] **Cost per breach -** The global average cost of a cyber breach is $3.6 million (or $141 per data record).

9.1 Security considerations

There are some simple things that you can do to secure user information. Specifically, you can build software 1) on premise or in the cloud; 2) with native encryption/decryption capabilities; 3) with physical security measures; 4) with 2-factor authentication; 5) that is certified (e.g. HIPAA-compliant); 6) that patches vulnerabilities from penetration tests; or 7) that fits into blockchain architectures. Together, this is known as the **Voice Security Framework** (Figure 9.1.1).

**Figure 9.1.1
The voice security framework (VSF)**

Voice security framework

1. only go in cloud if necessary

$\emptyset 1 \emptyset 1$ 2. encrypt data stores

3. apply physical security measures

 4. use 2-factor authentication

5. obtain security certifications

 6. hire a penetration tester

7. create a blockchain architecture

In this way, you can mitigate consumer risks when building voice computing server architectures.

9.1.1 - Cloud vs. on-prem considerations[354] - ***Cloud architectures*** connect and exchange data over the Internet whereas ***on-premise architectures*** are completely offline. *It's important to be capable as a developer to build both cloud-based and on-premise software.*[355]

When vetting cloud providers, the two most important things to consider are ***reliability*** and ***security***. Reliability is often measured through ***service-level agreements (SLAs)*** that guarantees compensation if the cloud provider does not meet certain requirements (e.g. 99.9% ***uptime***). Security, on the other hand, is usually vetted through the ***Cloud Security Alliance*** (CSA). The CSA certifies cloud providers who meet its security criteria, so you should only use cloud providers that are CSA certified.[356]

Figure 9.1.1.1
List of cloud providers by market share

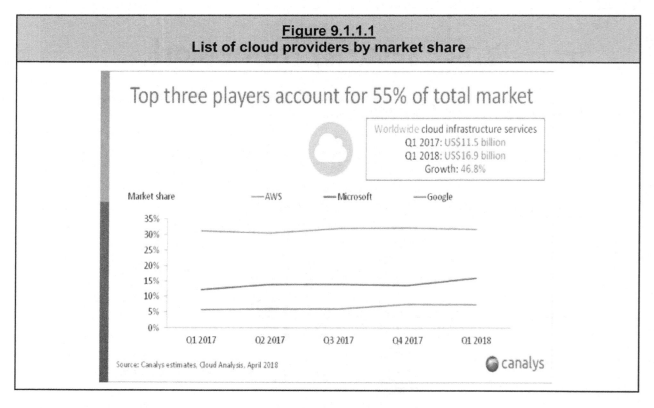

9.1.2 - Encrypting and decrypting data - Only 4% of breaches involve encrypted data. Therefore, a simple countermeasure you can take is to employ encryption on your server (and/or locally) so that your data remains secure.

---

[354] **For a long time**, large enterprises were afraid to connect with cloud-based providers because of the security risks involved. However, recent shifts in Washington DC (2018) have enabled for more trust in cloud-based providers. For example, the NSA and other government agencies have shifted over to adopt AWS for some of their back-end architectures, dramatically saving costs and improving efficiencies.

[355] **When you build an architecture** like we did in Chapter 8 (e.g. with Docker Containers / Minio, etc.), it allows for both *on-premise* and *cloud* capabilities. You should think about this when you design architectures, as some data is very sensitive and should not be transmitted over the Internet.

[356] **Note** that most major cloud providers are CSA certified, but it always is good to check to be absolutely sure.

There are three main types of encryption algorithms: *symmetric ciphers, asymmetric ciphers, and hybrid cyphers* (9.1.1.1). In general, all these encryption algorithms use **public keys** or **private keys** to encrypt or decrypt data; they just use these keys differently. The most common type of encryption method is a symmetric cipher (e.g. block cipher), where all parties use the same key for decrypting and encrypting data.[357] *Note that you should not try to make your own encryption algorithm. If you mess up, someone may be able to easily hack and access your data.*[358] [359]

Table 9.1.1.1 Types of ciphers for encrypting/decrypting data	
Type of cipher	**Description**
Symmetric ciphers	All parties use the same key, for both decrypting and encrypting data. Symmetric ciphers are typically very fast and can process very large amount of data.
Asymmetric ciphers	Senders and receivers use different keys. Senders encrypt with public keys (non-secret) whereas receivers decrypt with private keys (secret). Asymmetric ciphers are typically very slow and can process only very small payloads.
Hybrid ciphers	The two types of ciphers above can be combined in a construction that inherits the benefits of both. An asymmetric cipher is used to protect a short-lived symmetric key, and a symmetric cipher (under that key) encrypts the actual message.

To begin, we can generate a secure password string in 'utf-8' format with the **os module** and **urandom submodule** in under 15 lines of code (Figure 9.1.1.3).

Figure 9.1.1.2
How to generate a secure public key: *generate_password.py*

```python
from os import urandom
import random

def generate_password(length):
    char_set = 'abcdefghijklmnopqrstuvwxyz0123456789ABCDEFGHIJKLMNOPQRSTUVWXYZ^!\$%&/()=?{[]}+~#-_.:,;<>|\\'
    password=''
    for i in range(length):
```

---

[357] **Symmetric ciphers are commonly used** because they are really fast and suite enterprise applications well.
[358] **You could,** however, use things like cellular automata, as described by Stephen Wolfram.
[359] **RSA algorithms** have been broken for a number of years, so be sure to not use this type of encryption.

```
        password=password+random.choice(char_set)
    password=password.encode('utf-8')
    return password
```

We can now use the **pycryptodome module** to encrypt a file using a symmetric cipher with a generated public key (Figure 9.1.1.3). This script uses the Crypto.Cipher() module within pycryptodome to encrypt an input file ('piano2.wav') in the ./data directory. *Note that we can use pickled public keys (e.g. for storing keys locally) and different keys for every file to make the process of decrypting files more secure.*

Figure 9.1.1.3
How to encrypt an audio file: *encrypt_file.py*

```python
import hashlib, pickle
import os, random, struct
from Crypto.Cipher import AES
import generate_password as gp
from os import urandom

def encrypt_file(key, in_filename, out_filename=None, chunksize=64*1024):
    """ Encrypts a file using AES (CBC mode) with the
        given key.

        key:
            The encryption key - a string that must be
            either 16, 24 or 32 bytes long. Longer keys
            are more secure.

        in_filename:
            Name of the input file

        out_filename:
            If None, '<in_filename>.enc' will be used.

        chunksize:
            Sets the size of the chunk which the function
            uses to read and encrypt the file. Larger chunk
            sizes can be faster for some files and machines.
            chunksize must be divisible by 16.
    """
    if not out_filename:
        out_filename = in_filename + '.enc'

    iv = urandom(16)
```

```python
    encryptor = AES.new(key, AES.MODE_CBC, iv)
    filesize = os.path.getsize(in_filename)

    with open(in_filename, 'rb') as infile:
        with open(out_filename, 'wb') as outfile:
            outfile.write(struct.pack('<Q', filesize))
            outfile.write(iv)

            while True:
                print('hi2')
                chunk = infile.read(chunksize)
                if len(chunk) == 0:
                    break
                elif len(chunk) % 16 != 0:
                    chunk += ' '.encode('utf-8') * (16 - len(chunk) % 16)

                outfile.write(encryptor.encrypt(chunk))

    # make sure to output the key in pickle format
    picklefile=open(in_filename[0:-4]+'_key.pickle', 'wb')
    pickle.dump(key, picklefile)
    picklefile.close()

password = gp.generate_password(24)
key = hashlib.sha256(password).digest()
print(key)
encrypt_file(key, 'piano2.wav', out_filename=None, chunksize=64*1024)
```

We can similarly decrypt this file once it has been encrypted using the reverse process and same public key (Figure 9.1.1.4).[360]

Note that the most important part of the encryption process is secure management of encryption keys. There are cloud providers like AWS (e.g. AWS Key Management Service) that provide services for encryption key management with FIPS 140-2 validated hardware security modules. Key management services have an audit trail (e.g. AWS CloudTrail) to provide logs of all key usage to meet regulatory and compliance needs (e.g. HIPAA compliance). I recommend integrating your server with one of these key management platforms because of these benefits, as they often are not a huge cost relative to other cloud offerings.

---

[360] **Loading public keys as .PICKLE files** - Note that we can load the file keys directly from .PICKLE files (e.g. .JSON cannot be used because these keys are in the bytes format).

Figure 9.1.1.4
How to decrypt a file: *decrypt_file.py*

```python
import os, random, struct, json, pickle
from Crypto.Cipher import AES

def decrypt_file(in_filename, out_filename=None, chunksize=24*1024):
    """ Decrypts a file using AES (CBC mode) with the
        given key. Parameters are similar to encrypt_file,
        with one difference: out_filename, if not supplied
        will be in_filename without its last extension
        (i.e. if in_filename is 'aaa.zip.enc' then
        out_filename will be 'aaa.zip')
    """
    # Load public key from a pickle file
    keyfile=in_filename[0:-8]+'_key.pickle'
    try:
        key=pickle.load(open(keyfile,'rb'))
    except:
        print('please put %s in current directory'%(keyfile))
    if not out_filename:
        out_filename = os.path.splitext(in_filename)[0]
    with open(in_filename, 'rb') as infile:
        origsize = struct.unpack('<Q', infile.read(struct.calcsize('Q')))[0]
        iv = infile.read(16)
        decryptor = AES.new(key, AES.MODE_CBC, iv)

        with open(out_filename, 'wb') as outfile:
            while True:
                chunk = infile.read(chunksize)
                if len(chunk) == 0:
                    break
                outfile.write(decryptor.decrypt(chunk))

            outfile.truncate(origsize)

decrypt_file('piano2.wav.enc')
```

9.1.3 - Implement physical security measures - Most smart speaker designs are open-air with anyone being able to speak into them to initiate commands. If instead there was a physical security measure so that only certain people could enter the area and give a voice command, these devices could be more secure.

Specifically, I think of use cases where cars may be connected to the Internet and have voice commands; in this case, there is a physical security measure (e.g. a locked door) which prevents unauthorized access to the car's voice computer. In this way, you can prevent malicious actors from accessing voice software.

*Therefore, think of **physical security measures** whenever you design voice-enabled software - perhaps by adding locks and/or storing your voice assistants in secure locations. This will make it so that your voice computer cannot be accessed by unauthorized individuals.*

9.1.4 - Use two-factor authentication (2FA) - Many data breaches happen through hacked user credentials (e.g. username/password). Two-factor authentication (2FA) is useful to ensure that the user that has logged into an account is in fact the user that is using your application.[361] If you enable 2FA from the start user credentials are much less likely to be compromised.

Note that authentication is especially important for voice assistants. Many research groups have demonstrated that anyone within the household (or, for that matter, outside the household) can access an Alexa device in the home. There is usually no 2FA on these devices, which can lead to substantial security vulnerabilities.

The best way to implement 2FA in Python likely is with the **Auth0 library** (discussed in the prior chapter) or the **Duo Security API** (recently acquired by Oracle). Check out the documentation for these libraries for more information on how to implement 2FA into your code.

9.1.5 - Security certifications - As you pass through the vendor process as a startup company, you'll likely need certain security certifications like HIPAA, HITRUST, or PCI ESS (Table 9.1.5.1). When you go through these certification processes you often have to build internal policies for data access (e.g. data use agreements) and for enforcing security policies (e.g. all employees receive security awareness training). *In this way, certifications can help to prove to others that you take security seriously and allow you to be an approved vendor for Fortune 1000 enterprises.*

Table 9.1.5.1 Security certifications		
Certification	Description	Cost (time)
HIPAA Certification HHS.gov	A full HIPAA audit, when applied to technology vendors, assesses an organization against all the requirements in HIPAA Security Rule. It's a long list. It includes both technical settings and configurations as well as administrative requirements like training and business associate agreements. It will involve an auditor visit and will	$27k-$32k/year.

---

[361] **2FA definition -** Note that 2 factor authentication means that more than one method is being used. For example, you can use a wake word and a face to authenticate a login. Or, you may use a string password and a face to login. It can be any two factors which leads to a successful login.

		require documentation to support claims about security and compliance; this can include showing specific technology settings like password rules and guest access.	
HITRUST Certification HITRUST		HITRUST is a more complete, certifiable version of HIPAA. It was created by large healthcare enterprises to mirror PCI compliance. It is similar to a full HIPAA audit but goes into much more granular detail about the maturity of controls and compliance programs. There's now a standard web app that you use to enter information. Those entries are then validated by HITRUST approved assessor. Then HITRUST, the organization, reviews all the entries, typically asks for more evidence, and you hopefully get HITRUST CSF Certified at the end. The direct costs for this include both fees to HITRUST and to your auditor (approved assessor).	$44k-$59k/year
PCI DSS		The major players in the credit card business (Visa, MasterCard, American Express, Discover and JCB) have banded together to reduce credit card data loss. They created the Payment Card Industry Security Standards Council and that council established a standard for security of cardholder data and has released it as the PCI Data Security Standard (PCI DSS). All companies that accept, store, process or transmit credit card information are each required to report compliance with the Data Security Standard (DSS). If your company accepts cards or stores or transmits cardholder info, then it needs to meet the security requirements the card companies have set out in the DSS.	$60/mo to $50k/year depending on number of transactions.

9.1.6 - Penetration testing - Another way you can ensure that your software is safe is to hire a penetration tester or certified ethical hacker. These individuals are paid to break into your software and get past your security policies. Then, you can look back at the path they took to breach your software in order to patch bugs and make it less easy for future malicious actors to gain unauthorized access to your server.

Often, you can be your own penetration tester if you know universal or well-known vulnerabilities of your technology. If this interests you, here are some well-known vulnerabilities of voice-related software (Table 9.1.6.1).[362]

---

[362] **Cost of security audits / teams -** Note that hiring security teams internally can be quite costly, so it may make sense to just learn these vulnerabilities yourself and create your own patches.

Table 9.1.6.1
Voice security vulnerabilities

Vulnerability (date discovered)	Description
Voice squatting (UVA, June 2018)	Voice squatting is a method wherein a threat actor takes advantage or abuses the way a skill or action is invoked. For example, if a user says "Alexa, open Capital One" to run the Capital One skill, a threat actor can potentially create a malicious app with a similarly pronounced name, such as Capital Won. It's sort of like the way you can build phishing apps for voice purposes (e.g. emails that look real but are fake leading to malicious websites). This can lead to stolen identities and/or stealing credit card information.
Voice Masquerading (UVA, June 2018)	A method wherein a malicious skill impersonates a legitimate one to either trick users into giving out their personal information and account credentials or eavesdrop on conversations without user awareness. Researchers identified two ways this attack can be made: *in-communication skill switch* and *faking termination*. In communication skill switch takes advantage of the false assumption that smart assistants readily switch from one skill to another once users invoke a new one. Going back to our previous example, if Capital Won is already running and the user decides to ask "Alexa, what'll the weather be like today?", Capital Won then pretends to hand over control to the Weather skill in response to the invocation when, in fact, it is still Capital Won running but this time impersonating the Weather skill. Faking termination is when a skill says something like "Goodbye" when it is still executing code and/or doing things in the background without the user's consent.
Voice Adversarial Attack (UC Berkeley, May 2018)	Uses adversarial machine learning to transcribe a phrase to any phrase that choose with small perturbations in the audio. The researchers demonstrated that they could fool Mozilla DeepSpeech voice-to-text engine by hiding secret, inaudible commands within audio of a completely different phrase. Can also put rogue commands in music snippets. Could lead to more sophisticated attacks to send messages, make purchases, or wire money, etc.

Weak voice authentication / physical security (MSU, April 2018)	Demonstrated that the Alexa service weak single-factor authentication can be easily broken. Without a physical presence-based access control, the Alexa device accepts voice commands even when no persons are nearby. This security threat can easily propagate to the third-party voice services, which assume all the voice commands from the Alexa are benign. We then devise two proof-of-concept attacks to show that such security threat can cause Alexa users to experience a large financial loss.
DophinAttack (2017)	Inaudible ultrasonic transmissions can trigger voice assistants up to 25 feet away, leading to unauthorized access to Siri, Alexa, Cortana, and Google Assistant.

9.1.7 - Blockchain architectures - Blockchain architectures have been emerging over the past few years to help secure transactions over the Internet. Simply, you can think of a blockchain as a decentralized database that allows for data to be stored in blocks, which are then put together into a chain of blocks. This allows for data to be stored chronologically and publicly and for fully traceable transactions to occur between two or more people. These transactions are done through **tokens** that use many of the security encryption methods described earlier on in this chapter.

Blockchain architectures have created new ways to **monetize voice content** and **serve up voice infrastructure** (Table 9.1.7.1). Also, blockchain architectures have provided a way to raise alternative capital through initial coin offerings (ICOs). *However, note that ICOs are treated as capital investments and it's quite a barrier in terms of legal costs to get them done properly per SEC guidelines.*

Table 9.1.7.1
List of blockchain platforms relevant to voice computing

Blockchain name	Description
Voise	VOISE is a blockchain powered anonymous decentralized platform with personalized token based on Ethereum's smart contract ecosystem for transactions. VOISE is an innovative cryptocurrency powered solution for the music industry that allows artists to monetize their work in a collaborative P2P marketplace.
Video Coin	Raised $50MM. Video Infrastructure for the Blockchain-Enabled Internet.
CellTrust blockchain	Can help to capture incoming and outgoing calls, provide audio recordings, detailed reporting, traceability and archiving to name the least.
Langnet	Research platform to contribute speech and language data in exchange for tokens. Rob, their CEO, is based out of Korea but they have a great team across the world.
Snips AIR	Token sale is pending. Snips AIR is a network of devices collaborating to form a mesh of AI assistants. With this voice ecosystem you can now add a voice assistant to your entire home, while protecting your family's privacy.

9.2 Legal considerations

Laws pertaining to voice computing are complicated; they vary from country to country and even state-by-state (e.g. within the USA). At a high-level it's important to understand: 1) privacy laws; 2) enforcement of privacy laws; 3) copyright laws; 4) website terms of use provisions; and 5) patent laws. Together, these elements form the ***voice legal framework (VLF)*** (Figure 9.1.1).

Figure 9.2.1
The voice legal framework (VLF)

Voice Legal Framework

1. Privacy Laws

2. Law enforcement

3. Copyright laws

4. Terms of Service

5. Patent laws

Note that it is important to build software anticipating the future. Otherwise, you may be at risk getting sued as either an individual or company and/or shut down simply because the government decides to regulate the industry in a new way.

9.2.1 - Privacy Laws - The main privacy laws that pertain to voice computing include the Wiretap Act of 1968, the California Connected Television Statue, One-party/Two-party Consent Recording Laws (vary state-by-state), COPPA laws, the Computer Fraud and Abuse Act (CFAA), the General Data Protection Regulation (GDPR) and the Health Insurance Portability and Accountability Act (HIPAA). In general, these laws try to protect consumer privacy and critical voice infrastructure (Table 9.2.1.1).

Table 9.2.1.1
Important laws and their descriptions

Law	Description
Wiretap Act of 1968 (USA federal law)	According to the Wiretap Act of 1968 (18 U.S.C. § 2511.), it's illegal to secretly record any oral, telephonic, or electronic communication that is reasonably expected to be private. So, for example, recording a conversation with somebody in a bedroom, with the door shut, on private property, without them knowing is technically a federal crime in the loosest sense. There are, however, a few exceptions to this law that create some sizable loopholes. The biggest being the "one-party consent" rule that says you can record people secretly if at least one person in the conversation consents to the recording, or if the person recording is authorized by law to do it (like police with a warrant). There must also be a sign posted that clearly reveals that audio recording is taking place. Since audio recording is generally not legal, most people stick to video and picture evidence.
California Connected Televisions Statute (California, 2015)	California became the first state to regulate the collection and use of voice data through televisions. "A person or entity shall not provide the operation of a voice recognition feature within this state without prominently informing, during the initial setup or installation of a connected television, either the user or the person designated by the user to perform the initial setup or installation of the connected television." Given that the California statute is the first of its kind in effect in the United States, it provides a potential blueprint for future statutes or regulations in other jurisdictions and highlights topics that other legislators and regulators may wish to address.
One / two party consent laws (various states, USA)	In some states, such as Georgia (GA), you can record a conversation that you are speaking in without obtaining the other party's consent (known as a One-Party State). In other states, like Massachusetts (MA), you need the consent of both parties before you can record (known as a Two-Party consent state). Two-party consent states include: California, Connecticut, Florida, Hawaii, Illinois, Maryland, Massachusetts, Montana, Nevada, New Hampshire, Pennsylvania, and Washington. All other states are one-party consent states. Note that some states distinguish between electronic and in-person communication (e.g. Oregon is a one-party consent state for electronic communication but requires consent for in-person communication).

Child online privacy protection rule ("COPPA")	COPPA imposes certain requirements on operators of websites or online services directed to children under 13 years of age, and on operators of other websites or online services that have actual knowledge that they are collecting personal information online from a child under 13 years of age. This has been lessened so that children can use voice assistants, but the regulatory landscape of the future seems uncertain.
Computer Fraud and Abuse Act ("CFAA")	This act overviews much of the law related to web scraping. It's quite unclear how voice access to accounts is 'public' or 'private' web information. In traditional websites, passwords mark the boundary between public and private data. But with voice, it's a bit unclear.
General Data Protection Regulation (Europe)	A regulation in EU law on data protection and privacy for all individuals within the European Union (EU) and the European Economic Area (EEA). It addresses the export of personal data outside the EU and EEA areas. The GDPR aims primarily to give control to citizens and residents over their personal data and to simplify the regulatory environment for international business by unifying the regulation within the EU.
Health Insurance Portability and Accountability Act (HIPAA).	The uncertain regulatory climate of the future makes it important for you as a voice developer to know how to best protect and secure voice data. HIPAA violations can be costly - $100-$50,000 per record compromised, so it's important to ensure compliance through appropriate techniques and protocols.

The most important law in this list that has emerged recently is likely **General Data Protection Regulation (GDPR).** GDPR contains clauses for the **"right to be forgotten"** (or the "right of erasure") of citizens. This means that if a user wants to delete their account (either verbally or in writing) you must have an audit trail and be able to delete the user and all their interactions from the server that hosts the user's information within 30 days. *Note that this law only applies to European citizens; however, it's important to keep this in mind if you do intend to scale from the USA to Europe.*

Though you'll likely comply with the rest of the laws through obtaining a security certification (e.g. HIPAA), I'd check with a lawyer if you are unsure about anything – especially if you are in a legal gray area. Legal gray areas are common with voice-related projects.

9.2.2 - Law enforcement - Enforcement of these laws is quite complicated. According to the Council of Foreign Relations,

> *"While state attorneys general have an important role to play, the Federal Trade Commission (FTC) is the primary driver of enforcement of these laws. Generally, the FTC has the general power to prohibit "unfair and deceptive trade practices" under Section 5 of the FTC Act, and has attempted to establish a data-security baseline through over sixty different enforcement actions. However, companies have begun to aggressively push back against the FTC's legal authority to police data-security practices, and the FTC has limited jurisdiction over banks, insurance companies, nonprofit entities, and even some internet service providers...The Donald J. Trump administration appears to have little appetite for technology policy or legal regulation in general, and lawmakers' continuing failure to provide users with a set of privacy rights has also made the United States a global outlier."*

Meanwhile, the General Data Protection Regulation (GDPR) in Europe has become quite enforceable. For example, Google was recently fined over five billion dollars for GDPR noncompliance, resulting in a fine that resembles breaches in anti-trust laws (e.g. under the purview of the SEC in the USA). The message is clear; Tech companies that have global reach must comply with GDPR or there will be stiff penalties.

There has been a trend towards increasing privacy in the USA (Table 9.2.2.1). *As a startup, I'd err on the side of caution and build around GDPR so that you will be compliant in the future. For now, though, you should be okay because the United States seems to be taking a step back in regulating privacy laws.*

<u>Table 9.2.2.1</u>
Recent court cases and laws affecting consumer privacy

Court case	Result
Personal Data Notification and Protection Act	The bill requires that companies notify affected individuals within 30 days of the discovery of a breach of sensitive personal information and requires the Federal Trade Commission to help coordinate breach notification. Notification of the type of information stolen would need to be provided by mail, telephone or, in certain cases, email.
United States vs. Carpenter (Nov. 2017)	The Supreme Court ruled that the government needs a warrant to access a person's cell phone location history. The court found in a 5 to 4 decision that obtaining such information is a search under the Fourth Amendment and that a warrant from a judge based on probable cause is required.

9.2.3 - Copyright Law - US copyright law falls under the US Copyright Act of 1976. There are two main things that this act provisions: 1) the idea of **"fair use",** or the right to use copyrighted material without the permission of the copyright user; and 2) **"copyright"** is a legal right for how the original work may be used by others. In this way, all the code that you write is protected almost exclusively under copyright law.[363] Voice data is covered as a copyright as a "sound recording," which mostly was tailored to allow musicians to collect royalties from music recordings (Table 9.2.3.1).

<div align="center">**Table 9.2.3.1** **Rights you have for sound recordings under the US Copyright Act of 1976**</div>	
Right type	**Bulleted description**
Rights you have of a sound recording	<ul><li>Duplication or reproduction of a sound recording in a form that either directly or indirectly recaptures the actual sounds of the original sound recording</li><li>Preparing a derivative work in which the original sound recording is rearranged, remixed, or altered</li><li>Distributing any copies of the original sound recording, duplicates, or derivatives for a profit</li><li>Conducting a public performance through the use of digital audio transmissions for a profit</li></ul>
Rights you do not have under a sound recording	<ul><li>Duplication of another sound recording that imitates or simulates those of the copyrighted sound recording</li><li>Preparing a derivative work that imitates or simulates a copyrighted sound recording</li><li>Distributing any copies of an imitation or simulation of a copyrighted sound recording</li><li>Use by educational television or radio programs of a copyrighted sound recording</li></ul>

It's quite unclear if a machine learning model built from interaction with a service lends itself to copyright law. Companies like Lyrebird have the ability to create text-to-speech models with only a few samples of voice files. *There are currently no protections with the law under "derived models that can produce a simulated sound" or other such language.*

For example, if I use Google Hangout as a service and they collect about 5 hours of audio on my voice, they have an irrevocable license to the content that they recorded in the session. They could theoretically use this metadata to build a highly accurate voice model around my

---

[363] **Copyrights** extend up to 100 years after the death of the author.

own voice. If Google were to do this and package it under their text-to-speech (TTS) service, would I own that copyright or would Google own that copyright?[364]

Another *legal gray area* is that if you leave a voicemail on my phone I own the copyright to that voicemail legally. I can legally publish your voicemail on YouTube without your consent. Then, someone using YouTube could apply a machine learning model to detect whether or not you, the person calling me, is depressed or not. Health insurance companies could theoretically buy the data that routes back to you from a machine learning model that is depression and use this data to price your health plan, etc. *This is one use case, among many, which shows that copyright law has not caught up with potential litigation.*

How can we as a community come together to add some clarity on these issues?

I really don't know. I'm just providing some room for thought here. However, as a developer, you should keep up as laws are passed because this may change how you have to write and distribute your code base.

9.2.4 - Patent laws - Emerging patents can dramatically affect the future of voice computing. Patents can have severe consequences to what you can or cannot do as a voice developer (e.g. whether you can or cannot use certain libraries without risks of being sued).

Google recently submitted at least four patent applications for machine learning methods:

1. System and method for addressing overfitting in a neural network.[365]
2. Classifying data objects.
3. System and method for parallelizing convolutional neural networks.

Even if Google doesn't ever enforce these patents, it could create a culture where fundamental algorithms things in computing (and machine learning) are patentable. Big company employers may make filing patents like this the new status quo. These patents can then be transferred and/or enforced, leading to many lawsuits with small companies. Corporate patent trolls thus can dramatically thwart innovation now and into the future.[366]

In general, patent law and copyright law seem somewhat overlapping, and there likely will be some court proceeedings that will establish what is copyrightable versus what is patentable. There's a trend toward patents of machine learning algorithms as applied to certain use cases; however, when these algorithms become generative and emulate human consciousness, copyrightability seems questionable. *For the time being, the main intellectual property seems to be the training data, which is protected under copyright law.*

---

[364] **This is different** from using third party services like Google Speech API, which grant users of the service a copyright to the generated TTS file that was trained on hundreds of thousands of users.
[365] **This basically patents dropout,** a commonly used technique to reduce overfitting in neural networks.
[366] **Implications of patents in AutoML movement -** This topic something to watch in the near future as the AutoML movement reaches fruition.

As a result of these trends, I believe it is better to be unaware of patents when building software because eventually if you grow a large enough company you WILL be sued. If you knowingly infringe, it's 3X the damages. So not knowing is actually better than knowing. There have been so many patents awarded that a patent troll can always sue you over something.

9.2.5 - Terms of Service (TOS) provisions - Terms of service (ToS) nowadays are quite far-reaching. Let me use Google's Terms of Use as an example:

> "...When you upload, submit, store, send or receive content to or through our Services, you give Google (and those we work with) a worldwide license to use, host, store, reproduce, modify, create derivative works (such as those resulting from translations, adaptations or other changes we make so that your content works better with our Services), communicate, publish, publicly perform, publicly display and distribute such content. The rights you grant in this license are for the limited purpose of operating, promoting, and improving our Services, and to develop new ones. This license continues even if you stop using our Services (for example, for a business listing you have added to Google Maps). Some Services may offer you ways to access and remove content that has been provided to that Service. Also, in some of our Services, there are terms or settings that narrow the scope of our use of the content submitted in those Services. Make sure you have the necessary rights to grant us this license for any content that you submit to our Services…"

Wowsa. That means that Google can take my Google Maps data and correlate this with voice samples collected from my interactions with Google Assistant[367] as long as it helps them *"improve their services or develop new ones."* Theoretically, they build a biometric machine learning model (based on federated learning) to identify my voice to make it easier to log into Google into the future. This service may be sold to the federal government under some crazy data licensing deal, greatly affecting my privacy as a United States citizen.

I doubt Google is doing this as they have recently have stepped away from government contracts as a result of internal and external outcry from Project Maven. It's just a point here to show that it seems like they can do this with the wording of their Terms of Service.[368] [369]

---

[367] **Voice user registrations** – If I registered a new Google account with my voice, do the same Terms of Service (ToS) apply as their main website? I doubt that you could build a voice app to read the really long document to a user without them leaving suddenly. It would be quite hard to condense voice-based ToS so that a user fully understands what they sign up for.

[368] **From my own experiments,** you need roughly 30 samples of voice to authenticate users with roughly 80% accuracy. With over 100 samples, it goes up to 95% accuracy. Therefore, it is important to understand the implications of informed consent when using devices like Amazon Alexa or Google Assistant. These companies, in other words, may possess an irrevocable license to a model of your voice that can identify your voice with 95% accuracy and resell this data to third party providers (e.g. the NSA) according to their liberal Terms of Use. We need a broader conversation on how to reform Terms of Use according to ubiquitous voice interfaces to avoid such litigation.

[369] **Most already comply with COPPA** by making sure all users of websites are above 13 in the terms of use and they don't allow users under 13 to register accounts.

Therefore, I think it's important as a developer to make how you use and/or plan to use voice data explicitly clear in the Terms of Service (ToS). Having clear ToS can protect consumer privacy and maintain the trust of your end users. This can also help you avoid potential litigation and class-action lawsuits.

9.3 Ethical considerations[370]

We should not wait for lawsuits to happen to increase consumer protections. We have an obligation to make sure the public knows how the data collected about them can be used, hosted, stored, reproduced, modified, derived, communicated, published, publicly performed, publicly displayed and distributed. *Therefore, this section is entirely an opinion on how you can build voice software ethically.*

Overall, it seems as if the private sector must police itself when building voice computers. This creates various risks to end users, which can be mitigated by following the **voice ethics framework (VEF)**. Specifically, you should think about how you 1) collect data; 2) access data; 3) publish data; and 4) manipulate data (Figure 9.3.1).[371]

1. **Data collection** - Data can be collected in one of two ways: metadata (or features) or raw data (e.g. .WAV file). Obviously, collecting only metadata is less infringing than collecting raw data; however, you may be able to build your service with pure metadata. *In general, it's a best practice to collect as little data as possible from the user to reduce privacy risks.*

2. **Data access** - After data has been collected, it can be accessed locally or in the cloud. Often, this requires credentials (e.g. FTP credentials) to login and access the data. As mentioned before, only 4% of breaches use some sort of encryption. *Therefore, you should always encrypt user data (whether metadata or raw data) to ensure the security and integrity of your data and database.*

3. **Data publishing** - Data can also be published or manipulated on a server. In terms of being published through third-party services (e.g. YouTube), the data can be published privately and/or publicly. *It is better to assume data is private and have users change their settings to be public to minimize consumer privacy risks.*

4. **Data manipulation** - You can also manipulate user data in terms of data fusion (e.g. combining voice data with video data) or data modeling (e.g. apply a machine learning model to automatically label age and/or gender from the metadata). *It's important that users know how you plan to publish or manipulate their data in your Terms of Service (ToS) so they are not surprised and offended when such things occur.*

---

[370] **This section contains** many opinions of the author. Read with caution.
[371] **Note** that many of these things have already been discussed in the prior sections, but this schema can guide you when thinking about how to build ethical voice software.

Figure 9.3.1
The voice ethics framework (VEF)

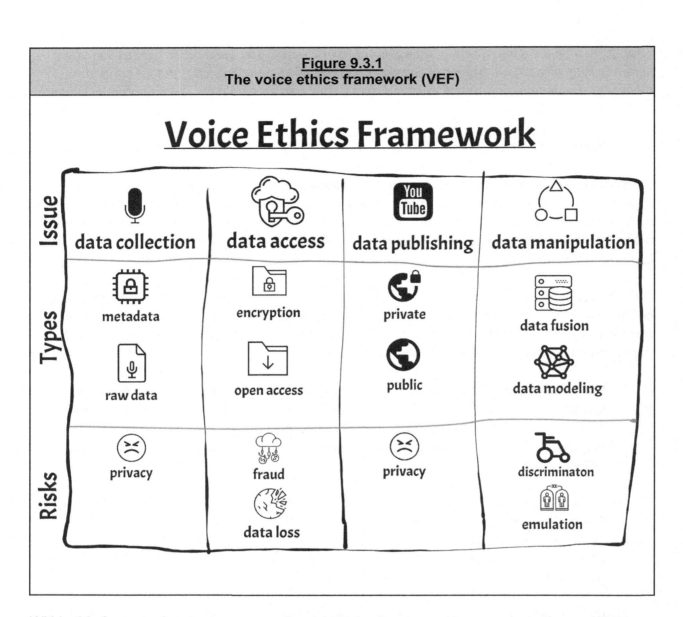

Within this framework, you can assess the risk that voice computers pose to end users (Table 9.3.1). Risks are stratified according to the underlying issue; for example, if someone is able to breach a voice computer and listens in on private conversations, that is a huge infringement in privacy.[372] You should thus keep in mind these risks when building your server architecture.

---

[372] **Emulation risks** – I believe the biggest risk is likely unauthorized emulation because cloning voices without explicit user consent can lead to larger risks - like confirming bank transactions over the phone or calling a loved one and telling them things that are not true; in other words, if unauthorized emulation is legalized it can emit doubt in almost all interactions we have virtually.

	Table 9.3.1 Risks voice computers pose to end users
Issue	**Risk Description**
Data collection	- **Privacy** - If you hack into a voice computer you could record voice data and send it to a third-party computer without a user's consent. This could contain sensitive data - like a conversation you recently had with your best friend that involved their father passing away. Therefore, software to collect voice data can lead to significant privacy risks.
Data access	- **Fraud** - I can use an adversarial network to train a model to transcribe speech into anything I'd like to, leading to unauthorized access to an Alexa device and purchase on a credit card (without 2FA). - **Data loss** - if someone hacks into a voice computer they can delete all prior information, which can lead to substantial data loss for an individual and/or a company.
Data publishing	- **Privacy** - Someone can record my voice on a phone call and publish this content on YouTube, which, if used with many other files published by others on YouTube (of my voice personally), could lead to models that then could be used by malicious actors (e.g. voice cloning above). This can all be done without my explicit consent if I lived in a one-party consent state like Georgia.
Data manipulation	- **Emulation** - I can also clone a user's voice with a text-to-speech WaveNet machine learning model and then use this model to unlock a bank account with a known social security number - leading to huge losses to the financial industry. - **Discrimination** - Employers could theoretically record interviewees to see if they have certain diseases from their voice (e.g. build a convex hull classification model to screen for psychosis risk). In this way, job discrimination can be invisible in today's world.[373]

---

[373] **Although much of this is legal today**, it's by no means ethical. Therefore, there should be some ethical guidance on how voice data should be manipulated.

There are a few actions that we could do as a larger community that can help mitigate these risks going into the future (Table 9.3.2). *These suggested solutions are by no means perfect; I hope the voice development community can come together to establish clearer ethics guidelines in the near future.*

	Table 9.3.2 Actions the larger voice community can take to reduce consumer risks
Risk	**Action**
Data collection	**1. Make voice datasets more accessible**[374] - Open source datasets like The Common Voice Project and AudioSet have transformed research in the voice computing space. For far too long we've had companies close off the world to voice training datasets; we need more datasets out there to know what can actually be done with such data. The reason why many voice datasets are collected in an unauthorized way is likely that there are too few open source datasets. **2. Make user interface guidelines to notify users when they are being recorded** - Google Chrome uses a red circular icon at the top of the browser to let the user know that a recording is happening. Apple uses a green light on the Macbook pro to know that a video recording is taking place. In a similar way, we need a larger discussion to be happening on how to best notify users when recordings are or are not happening within device hardware (e.g. Alexa devices) so that users know when unauthorized recordings are taking place.
Data access	**1. Create a closed-room security summit to disclose and patch security vulnerabilities on core platforms** - We need a forum to discuss voice-based security vulnerabilities. These vulnerabilities need to be discussed carefully to ensure that malicious actors do not use them to negatively affect the public. I think there needs to be a place in a closed room where individuals who have discovered these vulnerabilities can have a discussion and action plan on how to patch known bugs. I'm not sure how best to do this, but it would be great to start something like this soon.

---

[374] **We need to make the process publishing open source voice data easier,** and this can be done by groups like the Linguistic Data Consortiums or groups within large companies (e.g. Amazon Speech Understanding team).

	2. Require 2 factor authentication for payment transactions - This would make them more secure and reduce the risks associated with compromised credentials on voice computers. Apple has done this by default with mobile phones and the app store. Any company that commercializes voice assistants should implement 2FA as well. **3. Create standards for encrypting voice data at rest -** Make regulations so that devices that have audio or voice recording capability are encrypted by default, so even if unauthorized users gain access to such devices they cannot get access to the raw data through some public/private key pairing.
Data publishing	**1. Create new informed consent guidelines -** I believe much of the frustration that led to GDPR comes down to the process of *informed consent,* or, really knowing how data collected will be used. Leaving it vague and saying it can be used for any purposes as long as a service is improved blurs the line for end users to understand *how exactly this data will be used.* This blurriness creates the feeling that it can be used for anything for any purpose, which can lead to harm to end user and an uncertainty as to how long this data will be stored on the servers of corporations. We need some more clarity and transparency here. I'd suggest building some frameworks to help guide consent around voice data collection and distribution. **2. Make new Terms of Service (ToS) templates based on voice registrations -** We need some more templates for Terms of Service for voice-first applications. It's unclear what the best format for agreeing to terms is when you register with your voice. I think making some templates could greatly help developers comply with any state and federal laws. Specifically, there could be better clauses for informed consent on what you can or cannot do with voice data per the end user's request to comply with GDPR provisions and wiretapping laws of the USA.
Data manipulation	**1. Ensure that data is not used to persecute disabled individuals or individuals with health conditions -** The Americans with Disabilities act of 1990 prohibits discrimination based on disability. The Supreme Court decided under Title II of the ADA that mental illness is a form of disability and therefore covered under the ADA. However, there is no such mention of "screening for disabilities" by employers with built machine learning models or other such things that could be used for discrimination. There could

be a short working panel of people around these topics to help ensure protections to people who may have disabilities and/or be screened with disabilities through voice or language models.

2. Create ethics guidelines to build voice software - Create some guidelines as to how best to manipulate voice data. This could be through things like federated machine learning models (if you're tuning machine learning models to users) or restrict data for the sole purposes of transmitting data through voice infrastructure. There needs to be some uniformity of standards on how to most ethically interpret voice data. Right now, YouTube is a trove of voice data and it's not being regulated as to what exactly you can do with it. This goes back to some of the other things previously discussed, like voice emulation and publishing.

3. Draft new provisions in copyright law to reduce consumer emulation risks - I believe we need to figure out how best to modify the Copyright Act of 1976 to include "machine learning model derivatives" from "pooled data content." This is a larger discussion than just voice and can include any copyrightable work. Again, this needs to be done carefully with legislators and the private sector so that innovation is not dramatically affected. As a next step, it may be good to create a draft of goals for such changes via a legislator.

4. Draft new provisions in patent law to reduce consumer emulation risks [375] - A larger discussion needs to be had on what is patentable when it comes to software, specifically when it comes to emulation. I believe that any computerized text-to-speech system that emulates a specific individual's voice should not be patentable without their explicit consent. Right now patent laws are assessed in terms of their 1) novelty and 2) obviousness. But perhaps there is a third restricted class where they can be assessed in terms of their human emulating capabilities. As a next step, some of these ideas could be solidified as amendments to the US Patent Act.

---

[375] **Patent laws need edited to avoid sweeping claims**. The first-to-file provisions favors large companies to file as many patents as possible while leaving many sole inventors and small companies left behind. This has created classes and families of patents that dramatically affect the voice computing space; for example, transcription and text-to-speech models and the foundations of machine learning algorithms themselves. I believe the best way to go forward to open source many of these patents so that innovation can happen faster.

Hopefully this section has made you a bit more mindful of the risks for the voice computing field in general. By having more philosophical discussions about the ethics of voice data collection and publishing, I believe we can better create software and maintain the public's trust in voice computers.

9.4 Conclusion

👏 Congrats! Now you can build compliant, secure, and ethical voice software.

Check out the following resources if you'd like to go deeper on anything:

- Voice security framework (VSF)
    - Cloud vs. on premise considerations
        - Cloud Security Alliance. https://cloudsecurityalliance.org/
        - Amazon Web Services (AWS). https://aws.amazon.com/
        - Microsoft Azure. https://azure.microsoft.com/en-us/?v=18.27
        - Google Cloud Platform (GCP). https://cloud.google.com/
    - Encrypting/decrypting data
        - Pycryptodome. https://www.pycryptodome.org/en/latest/src/cipher/cipher.html
    - Physical security
        - Physical security. https://en.wikipedia.org/wiki/Physical_security
    - 2FA
        - Duo security. https://duo.com/docs/authapi-guide
        - Auth0. https://auth0.com/docs/quickstart/webapp/python/01-login
    - Security certifications
        - HIPAA. https://en.wikipedia.org/wiki/Health_Insurance_Portability_and_Accountability_Act
        - HITRUST. https://en.wikipedia.org/wiki/HITRUST
        - PCI DSS. https://en.wikipedia.org/wiki/Payment_Card_Industry_Data_Security_Standard
    - Penetration testing
        - Hacking. https://inventwithpython.com/hacking/chapter11.html
        - Voice squatting. https://blog.malwarebytes.com/cybercrime/2018/05/security-vulnerabilities-smart-assistants/
        - DophinAttack. https://www.cnet.com/news/security-researchers-warn-of-voice-vulnerabilities/
        - Adversarial network vulnerability. https://nicholas.carlini.com/code/audio_adversarial_examples/
        - Voice authentication threats. https://arxiv.org/pdf/1712.03327.pdf

- Blockchains
    - SEC guidance (on ICOs). https://www.sec.gov/ICO
    - Initial Coin Offering (ICO). https://en.wikipedia.org/wiki/Initial_coin_offering
    - Ethereum. https://www.ethereum.org/
    - Voise. https://www.voise.com/
    - Video Coin. https://videocoin.io/
    - Langnet. https://langnet.io/
    - Snips AIR. https://token.snips.ai/

- Voice legal framework (VLF)
    - Privacy Laws
        - Wiretap Act of 1968. https://lifehacker.com/what-you-need-to-know-when-recording-your-enemies-1795226719
        - Telephone recording laws. https://en.wikipedia.org/wiki/Telephone_recording_laws
        - California connected televisions statue. https://leginfo.legislature.ca.gov/faces/billTextClient.xhtml?bill_id=201520160AB1116
        - COPPA (FTC). https://www.ftc.gov/system/files/2012-31341.pdf
        - CFAA. https://en.wikipedia.org/wiki/Computer_Fraud_and_Abuse_Act
        - GDPR. https://en.wikipedia.org/wiki/General_Data_Protection_Regulation
        - HIPAA. https://en.wikipedia.org/wiki/Health_Insurance_Portability_and_Accountability_Act
    - Copyright Law
        - Copyright Act of 1976. https://en.wikipedia.org/wiki/Copyright_Act_of_1976
    - Terms of service provisions
        - Terms of Service. https://en.wikipedia.org/wiki/Terms_of_service
- Ethics
    - Laws
        - US patent act. https://www.law.cornell.edu/patent/patent.overview.html
        - Americans with Disability Act of 1990. https://en.wikipedia.org/wiki/Americans_with_Disabilities_Act_of_1990

The last chapter is all about how to get involved in the voice community. In this way, you can use the knowledge you have gained up to this point to positively impact the world.

Chapter 10:
Getting involved

"My work in the Tribe program has really benefited me and has opened up my eyes to [voice] research and working with a startup."

-Alice Romanov,
(Tribe 1 Innovation Fellow, NeuroLex)

Chapter Overview

By now you know a lot about voice computing; however, you may be looking for some practical experience. Therefore, this chapter is about how to become more engaged in the larger voice developer community.

Specifically, we'll cover:

- **10.1** - NeuroLex's story
- **10.2** - The Innovation Fellows Program
- **10.3** - Building open source software
- **10.4** - Conferences
- **10.5** - Graduate schools
- **10.6** - Finding a job
- **10.7** - Launching a startup
- **10.8** - Teaching voice computing

In this way, you can help the voice developer community grow and thrive!

10.1 NeuroLex's story

Eight years ago, I got a call from my crying mother saying that my brother was in the mental hospital with a severe psychotic episode. As you can imagine, this was a fairly traumatizing experience. He was not the person who I knew him to be (Figure 10.1.1).

**Figure 10.1.1
YouTube video of NeuroLex's story:** *Voicecamp demo day*

You can watch a video here: https://www.youtube.com/watch?v=oiCY3dcAbX0

Looking back, it was obvious something was off. He went to the primary care doctor 11 times complaining of the same vague symptoms - headaches, unclear thoughts, and anxiety. He even went to 6 different specialists, including a trained psychiatrist, who misdiagnosed him with an anxiety disorder. All this effort cost roughly $15,000 - all wasted money leading up to this hospitalization.[376]

The medical system failed my brother and is failing many other patients afflicted by schizophrenia. Many of these patients have family members abandon them and are left to be homeless on city streets.[377] I've reacted by embracing a deep empathy for such patients; I constantly seek ways to prevent this from happening to other families.

---

[376] **There is an 80% relapse rate** within 2 years in patients with schizophrenia.
[377] **554,000 people** are homeless in the USA and there is an 80% relapse rate within 2 years within a first psychotic episode for schizophrenia patients.

As trained biomedical engineer, I became more motivated on studying how to better diagnose and manage the disease. There didn't seem to be a good way to diagnose and track schizophrenia,[378] so I sought some alternative ways to characterize his symptoms. One data type that seemed interesting to examine was the voicemails he left on my phone. It seemed like over this 5-year period the voicemails leading up to his first episode seemed more disordered, as he used new words (neologisms) and wasn't making much sense.[379] Therefore, I wondered if there were some features[380] in the transcript from voicemails that could be used to reliably detect when my brother was progressing towards or away from psychotic episodes.[381]

Then, a paper was published in NPJ Schizophrenia that showed linguistic biomarkers could predict psychosis onset in high-risk youths.[382] In other words, you could predict who would or would not develop a psychotic episode from answering a very simple question like "how is your day today?"[383] This seemed quite remarkable and showed that some of the early ideas I had around early screening for psychosis were extensible to larger numbers of patients.[384]

A few weeks later I flew to New York City to meet with the authors of this study to see what could be done to translate this work to patients. As soon as I met with one of the authors, I felt as if my life calling were to commercialize this form of research. When I went there, I found out that voice biomarkers could characterize quite a few psychiatric and neurological conditions – from early-stage psychosis to depression and even Alzheimer's disease (Table 10.1.1).

Table 10.1.1 Summary of voice biomarker studies	
Disease	**Description**
Early-stage psychosis	100% accuracy to detect who will convert using linguistic features (frequency use of determiners, maximum phrase length, and the first-order semantic coherence) and convex hull classifier with leave-one-out analysis. This was a proof-of-concept study with 35 patients but has been followed on with 100+ patients at various sites (in talking with our collaborators).

---

[378] **Standard biomarkers do not work** - Blood, urine, and MRI images all were unreliable at diagnosing the disease.
[379] **Word salad** - The odd use of language associated with schizophrenia is known as 'word salad.'
[380] **Particularly features** that were a measure of disorder like lexical complexity and/or semantic coherence
[381] **It looked like** some of these features fed into anomaly detection methods (e.g. SVM models) could reliably predict when my brother was exhibiting more severe symptoms.
[382] **Features predicting psychosis** - the semantic coherence, the frequency use of determiners (e.g. 'this','that','whatever'), and the mean phrase length (e.g. length of each sentence)
[383] **After I saw this,** I immediately called Guillermo and flew to NYC to start NeuroLex to commercialize the technology - particularly, to build a universal voice test to screen for psychiatric and neurological symptoms early in primary care clinics much like Quest Diagnostics but for speech tests in the cloud.
[384] **Sample size** - the original sample size was very low (in the 30s), but now it's been tested on over 100 patients. The algorithm is roughly 80% accurate as measured by ROC curves.

Depression	a supervised learning support vector machine (SVM) approach was used to detect suicidal with mental illness, mental illness and not suicidal, and control (no mental illness) with 85% accuracy (N=379 patients).
Alzheimer's disease	The classification accuracy of automatic audio analyses were as follows: between HCs and those with MCI, 79% 6 5%; between HCs and those with AD, 87% 6 3%; and between those with MCI and those with AD, 80% 6 5%, demonstrating its assessment utility. Pause lengths in speech are most relevant here.
Parkinson's disease	Can classify PD patients or controls with 75% accuracy and could infer PD patients' level of motor impairment with 77% accuracy from semantic fields (via latent semantic analysis), grammatical choices (using part-of-speech tagging), and word-level repetitions (with graph embedding tools).

This led the creation of NeuroLex, a company that aims to commercialize a universal voice test to refer patients to specialists faster. You can think of our company kind of like a Quest Diagnostics but for speech tests in the cloud. In this way, patients like my brother could be diagnosed and treated earlier, leading to better outcomes (e.g. lower duration of untreated psychosis) and lower costs ($15k→ $3-5k) through more informed referrals (e.g. primary care physicians to psychiatrists).

However, since we started we've learned that healthcare is hard - *really hard.* It takes years of research to get new codes issues to reimburse new tests. During this journey, we built one of the largest voice computing labs in the world. Headquartered at the University of Washington under our Chief Medical Officer (Reza Hosseini Ghomi), we have grown our lab to include over 80 research collaborators across the world. As a result, we're 2-3 years from launching a commercial healthcare product that has a de novo 510k regulatory clearance indicated for depression.[385]

Since it will take a while for us to monetize our diagnostic tests, we've pivoted to build a new product, SurveyLex. This product lets users speak, as opposed to type or click, their responses (Figure 10.1.2). Using machine learning, we can auto-label responses with emotions (e.g. happy/sad), ages, genders, accents, and even races. In this way, we can dramatically reduce the number of questions on surveys up to 500% and decrease dropout rates by up to 50%, creating a better experience for the survey maker and the survey taker.[386]

---

[385] **Prospective studies for 510k clearance -** we are in the early planning phases of prospective studies to demonstrate cost savings to health plans and get payment for our tests (e.g. Optum/UHG).
[386] **Long-term vision -** we still haven't given up on our healthcare journey. We see that fit into the same architecture that we've built going into years 3-5 on our roadmap (Figure 10.1.2). We'll get there eventually (~2021), just through non-traditional means.

This strategy thus allows us to monetize a consumer product with the long-term vision to disrupt healthcare in mind years 3-5 on our roadmap (Figure 10.1.2).

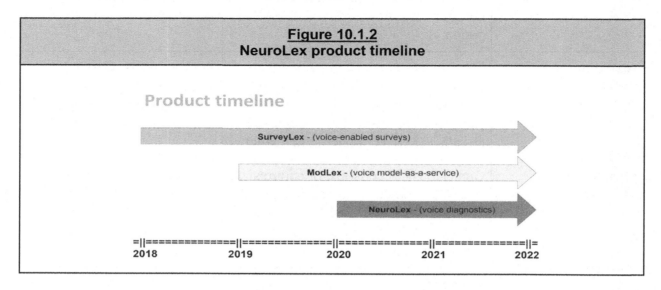

So why do I tell this story?

You may have an entrepreneurial itch. If you do, I highly encourage you to take the journey. *Nothing is more rewarding than building the future you want to live in and scaling that into the world.*

10.2   The Innovation Fellows Program

After telling NeuroLex's story many times, I kept running into many outstanding individuals that wanted to be involved in our vision. For a long time, I didn't really know how best to use our company to enable these individuals, as we obviously had limited resources as a startup company.[387] However, one day I woke up and wondered - "what if we could apply the Wikipedia model to startups, allowing for anyone to come into a startup company and contribute? What if someone could propose demo project - like proposing a new page or edit an existing page on Wikipedia – and execute these projects alongside our corporate structure?"

We thus invented the TRIBE model to engage outstanding individuals with our company in the form of a competition. These outstanding individuals apply (http://innovate.neurolex.co), and, if selected, pick a category to focus their demos (e.g. research, data science, or software). Fellows then are paired with mentors and propose and defend demo projects over the span of 6 months (Figure 10.2.1). The program culminates in a Demo Day where fellows present their work virtually to our team (at an internal corporate retreat).[388]

---

[387] **Specifically,** we had only raised $200,000 and had 10 part-time individuals contributing code to our architecture.

[388] **TRIBE program -** the winners (1st/2nd place) receive a small cash prize along and other perks (e.g. T-shirts).

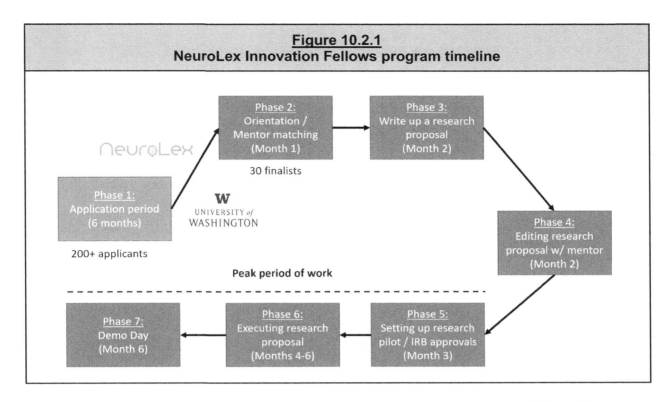

So far, the program has been incredibly successful. We have received over >200 applicants and over 60 fellows have gone through the program and have had over 30 completed demo projects. If you're interested, apply for the program @ http://innovate.neurolex.co.[389]

10.3 Building open source software

Another way that you can be involved in the voice community is to build open source datasets or software. There are three main ways that you can contribute here:

1. Publish new datasets
2. Contribute to an existing open source project
3. Create a new open source project

First, you can **publish open source datasets**. Although large companies have begun open sourcing their data (e.g. AudioSet / Google Research), there are still only a few large open source voice datasets accessible (Table 10.3.1).[390] By contributing data to these projects and/or making new datasets you can greatly help speed up voice research initiatives.[391] [392]

---

[389] **TRIBE contact** - Contact me @ js@neurolex.co with any questions.

[390] **Private datasets** - For a very long time, only a few companies have had training datasets for things like noise classification, text-to-speech models, and transcription models.

[391] **Kaggle** - Though there are multiple ways to publish your dataset, I'd highly recommend you to use Kaggle because I think it has the most robust community of data scientists to work with the data. I think you'd have much more impact there.

[392] **Project open data** - "In the United States, open and accessible data has been a standard since 2013. Three and a half years later, according to their open data dashboard, there are nearly 13,000 open datasets representing 20 US

Table 10.3.1
List of open source voice datasets

Dataset (link)	Description
Common Voice Dataset	150k recordings, open sourced by Mozilla Foundation. Useful for building models on age, accent, and gender.
Google AudioSet	2 million recordings over 600+ classes of audio (contains over 1 million speech samples). Some example classes include: music, speech, vehicle, and musical instrument.
Urban Sound dataset	1302 files of different urban related sounds. Specifically, each file is labeled with air_conditioner, car_horn, children_playing, dog_bark, drilling, enginge_idling, gun_shot, jackhammer, siren, and street_music.
NeuroLex Disease Dataset	This dataset contains over 500 YouTube samples labeled with addiction, adhd, als, anxiety, autism, cold, controls, depression, dyslexia, glioblastoma, graves disease, multiple_sclerosis, parkinsons, postpartum_depression, schizophrenia, sleep_apnea, and stressed. As of right now, it is the most diverse dataset for disease-related research across a range of diseases. We hope to expand it into the future.
NeuroLex Emotion Dataset	This dataset contains >2000 labeled emotions with 20 second voice files: happy, sad, neutral, angry, disgust, and fear. These were all extracted from YouTube videos.
Mivia audio events dataset.	6,000 recordings. Classes mostly include emergency related events like glass breaking, gunshots and screams. The 6000 events are divided into a training set (composed of 4200 events) and a test set (composed of 1800 events).
Karoldvl	2000 recordings of various animals sounds including dogs, rooster, pigs, cows, and frogs.

Note that NeuroLex is actively building datasets related to tagging various diseases with voice data through the train_diseases repository on GitHub. If this is of interest to you, let us know and we can get you involved.

---

agencies. Along this journey, they have done an excellent job of outlining general principles of open data which you should expect to find anywhere open data lives. The principles, which you can find referenced at Project Open Data, include the following:

1. Open
2. Accessible
3. Described
4. Reusable
5. Complete
6. Timely
7. Managed post-release"

Next, you can contribute to an existing open source project. Here are some open source projects currently in development (Table 10.3.2). Of course, this is a very limited list. You can do your own searches on GitHub and clone repos / make branches as necessary to improve existing repositories and distribute them as new packages.

Table 10.3.2 **List of some open source voice projects**	
Library	**Description**
LibROSA	LibROSA is a Python package for music and audio analysis. It provides the building blocks necessary to create music information retrieval systems.
PyAudioAnalysis	PyAudioAnalysis is a Python library covering a wide range of audio analysis tasks. With pyAudioAnalysis you can: • Extract audio features and representations (e.g. MFCCs, spectrogram, chromagram) • Classify unknown sounds • Train, parameter tune and evaluate classifiers of audio segments • Detect audio events and exclude silence periods from long recordings • Perform supervised segmentation (joint segmentation - classification) • Perform unsupervised segmentation (e.g. speaker diarization) • Extract audio thumbnails • Train and use audio regression models (example application: emotion recognition) • Apply dimensionality reduction to visualize audio data and content similarities
SoundFile	SoundFile can read and write sound files. File reading/writing is supported through libsndfile, which is a free, cross-platform, open-source (LGPL) library for reading and writing many different sampled sound file formats that runs on many platforms including Windows, OS X, and Unix. It is accessed through CFFI, which is a foreign function interface for Python calling C code. CFFI is supported for CPython 2.6+, 3.x and PyPy 2.0+. SoundFile represents audio data as NumPy arrays.
Sounddevice	This Python module provides bindings for the PortAudio library and a few convenience functions to play and record NumPy arrays containing audio signals.

SpeechRecognition	Library for performing speech recognition, with support for several engines and APIs, online and offline including: • CMU Sphinx (works offline) • Google Speech Recognition • Google Cloud Speech API • Wit.ai • Microsoft Bing Voice Recognition • Houndify API • IBM Speech to Text • Snowboy Hotword Detection (works offline)
PocketSphinx	Pocketsphinx is a part of the CMU Sphinx Open Source Toolkit For Speech Recognition. This package provides a Python interface to CMU Sphinxbase and Pocketsphinx libraries created with SWIG and Setuptools.
SIDEKIT	SIDEKIT is an open source package for Speaker and Language recognition. The aim of SIDEKIT is to provide an educational and efficient toolkit for speaker/language recognition including the whole chain of treatment that goes from the audio data to the analysis of the system performance.

Lastly, you can even make a new open source project. It is fun to take two or more open source projects and put them together in a new way. *If you do build an open source project I encourage you to release your code under an Apache 2.0 license to have the most impact and portability; otherwise, adding more restrictions may limit the use of the code by others.*

10.4 Conferences

Another way to get involved in the voice community is to attend a conference. The most well-attended conference in voice computing is the VOICE summit. There are also vertical-specific conferences like the Voice of Healthcare Summit in Boston (Table 10.4.1).[393] In general, most of these conferences seem to be how to build applications on top of smart speakers (e.g. Amazon Alexa) as opposed to voice computing generally – mostly as a result of their sponsors (e.g. Amazon is a diamond sponsor of the VOICE summit).

---

[393] **I'm still trying to navigate** through all these conferences, but it's often a good way to see all the innovation going on in the voice computing space.

Table 10.4.1
Voice computing conferences

Conference	Location	Dates
Smart Voice Summit	Paris	February 1–2, 2018
Conversational Interaction Conference	San Jose, California	February 5–6, 2018
Bottish	Your Computer – free!	February 22 and April 26, 2018
Superbot	San Francisco	April 3, 2018
SpeechTEK	Washington, D.C.	April 9–11, 2018
Voice & Beyond	Berlin	Spring 2018
Conversational Commerce Conference	London	May 8–9, 2018
Business of Bots	San Francisco	May 15–17, 2018
Voicecon	New York City	May 22, 2018
Connections: Connected Home Conference	San Francisco	May 22–24, 2018
Voice Summit	Newark	July 24–26, 2018
ML Conf	Atlanta, SF, NYC, Seattle	November 14th, 2018
The Voice of Healthcare Summit	Boston	August 7, 2018
Conversational Commerce Conference	San Francisco	September 1, 2018
VoiceCon Canada	Toronto	September 2018
All About Voice	Munich	October 12, 2018
AWS re:INVENT	Las Vegas	November 26–30, 2018

Voice Conference	Berlin	December 5–7, 2018
CES	Las Vegas	January 8–11, 2019
The Alexa Conference	Chattanooga, Tennessee	January 15–17, 2019
Lingofest	Ogden, Utah	2019

10.5 Graduate schools

It's a bit unclear to me which universities provide the best training for voice computing. Generally, graduate schools with degrees in computational linguistics (MS/PhDs) tend to prepare you well for [voice computing]-related jobs. Here's a short list of 8 schools that are known for their speech processing and linguistics programs which can provide strong foundations for voice computing:

1. Stanford University (MS/PhD in linguistics)
2. Carnegie Mellon University (MS/PhD in Language / Information Technology)
3. Johns Hopkins University[394] (MA, PhD)
4. Georgia Tech (MS/PhD in machine learning/signals)
5. University of Pennsylvania (MS, PhD in linguistics)[395]
6. Massachusetts Institute of Technology (MS in machine learning, PhD in linguistics)
7. University of Washington (MS, PhD in computational linguistics)
8. UC Berkeley (MS, PhD in signal processing)

The field of voice computing seems to be emerging, with few universities actually carving out training for the field. Your best bet seems like you should take classes related to affective computing, machine learning, and/or linguistics and then get involved in independent research projects that involve voice data of some kind.

If you are in grad school currently doing research related to voice computing, there are a few conferences to present your work (Table 10.4.1). The most important voice-related research conferences tend to be ICASSP, AVEC, and Interspeech each year.

---

[394] **Johns Hopkins University's Whiting School of Engineering** is home to the Center for Language and Speech Processing (CLSP). The CLSP is one of the most well-known language research groups in the world

[395] **Mark Liberman** directs the Linguistic Data Consortium, a well-known group that publishes speech datasets.

	Table 10.4.1 List of voice-related research conferences			
Event date	Event name	Location	Deadline	Camera Ready
Apr 22-27, 2018	ICASSP2018 Int'l Conf. on Acoustics	Seoul	Oct 27, 2017	Feb 9, 2018
Aug 20-24, 2018	ICPR2018 24rd Int'l Conf. on Pattern Recognition	Beijing	Nov 5, 2017	May 20, 2018
Sep 2-6, 2018	Interspeech2018 19th Int'l Conf. on Speech Communication and Technology	Hyderabad	Mar 23, 2018	Jun 17, 2018
Oct 22-26, 2018	AVEC2018 8th Audio/Visual Emotion Challenge and Workshop	Seoul	Jun 30, 2018	Aug 14, 2018
Nov 5 - Dec 8, 2018	IVA2018 18th Int'l Conf. on Intelligent Virtual Agents	Sydney	May 15, 2018	Aug 2018
May 12-17, 2019	ICASSP2019 Int'l Conf. on Acoustics	Brighton	Nov 26, 2018	Mar 18, 2019
May 14-18, 2019	FG2019 14th IEEE Int'l Conf. on Automatic Face and Gesture Recognition	Lille	Sep 21, 2018	Feb 15, 2019
Aug 4-10, 2019	ICPhS2019 9th Int'l Congress of Phonetic Sciences	Melbourne	Feb 2019	May 2019
Sep 2019	ACII2019 The 8th Int'l Conf. on Affective Computing and Intelligent Interaction	Cambridge	May 2019	Aug 2019
Sep 15-19, 2019	Interspeech2019 20th Int'l Conf. on Speech Communication and Technology	Graz	Mar 2019	May 2019
Sep 22-25, 2019	ICDAR2019 15th Int'l Conf. on Document Analysys and Recognition	Brisbane	Mar 15, 2019	N/A
Apr 4-9, 2020	ICASSP2020 Int'l Conf. on Acoustics	Barcelona	Nov 2019	Mar 2019
May 25-29, 2020	Eurographics 2020 The 41th annual Conf. of the European Association for Computer Graphics	Norrköping	Oct 2019	Feb 2020
Sep 8-10, 2020	ICFHR-2020 17th Int'l Conf. on Frontiers in Handwriting Recognition	Dortmund	Mar 2020	Jun 2020

Sep 14-18, 2020	Interspeech2020 21st Int'l Conf. on Speech Communication and Technology	Shanghai	Mar 2020	May 2020
Apr 25-30, 2021	ICASSP2021 Int'l Conf. on Acoustics	Toronto	Nov 2020	Mar 2020
Apr 24-28, 2022	ICASSP2022 Int'l Conf. on Acoustics	Singapore	Nov 2021	Mar 2022

10.6 Finding a job

If you have gotten this far, perhaps you feel proficient enough to interview for an entry-level or mid-level job at a technology company that builds [voice computing]-related applications. *Note that many of these companies require that you have at least a Master's (MS) or PhD degree to do data science, though there are jobs for entry-level developers.*

The voice tech landscape can help guide you when applying for jobs in the voice computing industry (Figure 10.6.1). In general, voice companies are separated into **verticals**,[396] **horizontals**,[397] and/or **infrastructure**.[398] Often, companies have different teams and divisions based on these categories. For example, some teams are more product-driven and others are more research driven. *Keep this in mind when finding and applying for your ideal job.*

If you're looking for a job within a larger company, you can check out any of the large tech companies as well. In general, the two most active companies in the voice computing space seem to be Amazon and Google because of their recent market dominance with smart speakers (e.g. Amazon Alexa and Google Assitant). *Boston and New York City also seem to be emerging hubs for voice computing because larger companies are scaling up product and research teams in these locations.*

- Amazon Alexa
- Facebook
- Google Assistant
- Microsoft Cortana
- IBM Watson
- Sonos
- Bose
- Twilio

---

[396] **Vertical categories** - healthcare, e-commerce, finance, manufacturing/supply chain, and real-estate
[397] **Horizontal categories** - business intelligence, customer support, marketing/sales, coaching, recruiting, productivity
[398] **Infrastructure categories** - cloud platforms, speech-to-text, text-to-speech, core platforms, NLP/conversational AI, CPAAS, Emotion detection, prototyping voice apps, voice data monetization, and analytics

**Figure 10.6.1
The voice tech landscape**

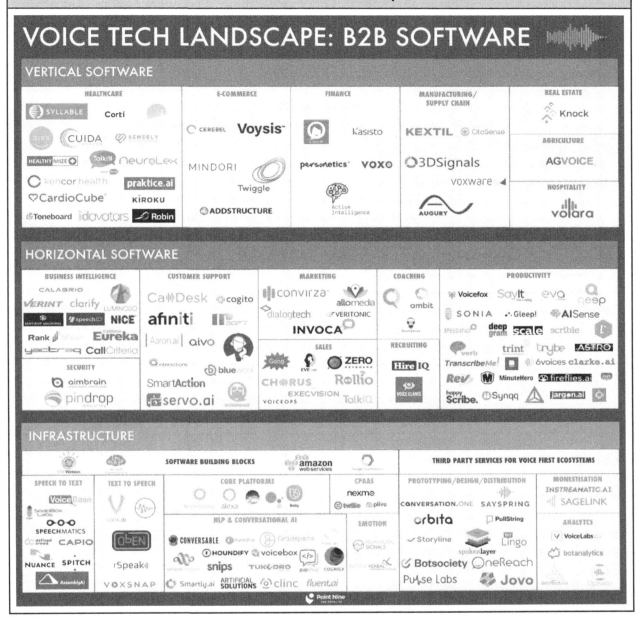

10.7 Launching a startup

If you've built a voice application that seems monetizable, there is no better time to start a company. Here are some early-stage accelerator funds that can help get you off the ground, often investing roughly $100k for 7% equity in the form of SAFE notes or convertible debt (Table 10.7.1).[399]

Table 10.7.1 List of accelerators to launch your voice startup[400]	
Accelerator	**Description**
Y-Combinator	The most well-known accelerator that has funded over 900 startups. YC has explicitly stated in their Requests for Startups page that they are excited to invest in the voice computing space.
Techstars	Techstars has various accelerators across the USA. They have a strong interest to invest in machine learning and [voice computing]-related startups.
Betaworks	Betaworks is a great leader in the voice computing space. They were one of the first VCs to explicitly host a voice-based accelerator program called VoiceCamp (NYC, NY).
Alexa Accelerator	The Amazon Alexa Fund (Accelerator) exists to invest in voice-based startups out of Seattle, WA. They're mostly interested in startups that make use of the Alexa Voice Service (AVS).

10.8 Teaching opportunities

Last but not least, you can teach voice computing to others! *I find teaching is the best way to learn something. You always learn something when you teach because students provide a fresh perspective and look on problems you are currently facing; it helps you become an agile developer that can communicate complicated concepts to others in a simple way.*

As a way to get more tangibly involved, I have thought about creating a Udacity course to teach voice computing to more people. If this is something that interests you, please reach out and we can find a way to work together ☺.

---

[399] **Accelerator definition** - If you are unfamiliar with the term 'accelerator' it's just an investing group that invests in your company in exchange for equity, often through SAFE notes or convertible debt. They often help you for a constrained period of time (3-6 months) before moving onto a new batch. During the time they help you they often connect you to many mentors and customers to help speed up your growth.

[400] **Investors** - If you're looking to finance a company, I highly recommend you connect with other VCs in this space to build a thesis.

10.9 Conclusion

Congrats! You now know how to get involved in the voice computing community. Check out any of the following links for additional information:

- NeuroLex
    - NeuroLex's story (video). https://www.youtube.com/watch?v=oiCY3dcAbX0
    - The Innovation Fellows Program. https://innovate.neurolex.co
- Open source software
    - LibROSA. https://librosa.github.io/librosa/
    - PyAudioAnalysis. https://github.com/tyiannak/pyAudioAnalysis
    - SoundFile. https://github.com/bastibe/SoundFile
    - Sounddevice. https://python-sounddevice.readthedocs.io/en/0.3.11/
    - SpeechRecognition. https://pypi.org/project/SpeechRecognition/
    - PocketSphinx. https://github.com/cmusphinx/pocketsphinx-python
    - SIDEKIT. http://www-lium.univ-lemans.fr/sidekit/install.html
- Conferences
    - Smart Voice Summit. http://smartvoicesummit.com/
    - Conversational Interaction Conference. http://www.conversationalinteraction.com/
    - Bottish. http://www.bottish.co/
    - Superbot. http://sb2018.dashbot.io/
    - SpeechTEK. http://www.speechtek.com/2018/
    - Voice & Beyond. https://www.jovo.tech/conference
    - Conversational Commerce Conference. http://opusresearch.net/wordpress/2017/10/19/announcing-the-2018-conversational-commerce-conference-global-series/
    - Business of Bots. https://businessofbots.com/san-francisco-2018/
    - Voicecon. http://voicecon.co/
    - Connections: Connected Home Conference. http://www.parksassociates.com/events/connections-us
    - Voice Summit. https://www.voicesummit.ai/
    - ML Conf. https://mlconf.com/
    - The Voice of Healthcare Summit. https://www.vohsummit.com/
    - Conversational Commerce Conference. http://opusresearch.net/wordpress/2017/10/19/announcing-the-2018-conversational-commerce-conference-global-series/
    - All About Voice. https://www.allaboutvoice.io/
    - Voice Conference. https://voicecon.net/
    - AWS re:INVENT. https://reinvent.awsevents.com/
    - CES. https://www.ces.tech/
    - The Alexa Conference. https://www.alexaconference.com/
    - Lingofest. https://www.lingofest2018.com/

- Graduate schools
    - Stanford University. https://linguistics.stanford.edu/research/computational-linguistics
    - Carnegie Mellon University. https://www.lti.cs.cmu.edu/
    - Johns Hopkins University (Center for Speech Language Technology). https://www.cs.jhu.edu/research/language-speech-processing/
    - Georgia Tech. https://www.omscs.gatech.edu/specialization-machine-learning
    - University of Pennsylvania. https://www.ling.upenn.edu/graduate/
    - Massachusetts Institute of Technology (EECS). https://www.eecs.mit.edu/academics-admissions/graduate-program
    - University of Washington. https://www.cs.washington.edu/research/ml
    - UC Berkeley (Computational Linguistics). https://lx.berkeley.edu/research/computational-and-experimental-methods
- Corporate jobs
    - Voice tech landscape. https://medium.com/point-nine-news/voice-tech-landscape-150-startups-mapped-and-analysed-82c5adaf710
    - Amazon Alexa. https://amazon.jobs/en/business_categories/alexa
    - Google Assistant. https://careers.google.com/teams/people/
    - Microsoft Cortana. https://www.microsoft.com/en-us/research/group/cortana-research/
    - IBM Watson. https://www.ibm.com/talent-management/hr-solutions/recruiting-software
    - Sonos. https://www.sonos.com/en-us/life-at-sonos
    - Bose. https://www.bose.com/en_us/careers.html
    - Twilio. https://www.twilio.com/company/jobs
- Investment
    - Y-Combinator. https://www.ycombinator.com/rfs/#voice
    - Techstars. https://www.techstars.com/
    - Betaworks Voicecamp. https://betaworks.com/voicecamp/
    - Alexa Accelerator. https://www.techstars.com/programs/alexa-program/

Thanks for taking this journey with me.

It's time to celebrate! 🎉

If I can help you with anything, please reach out to me @ js@neurolex.co.

Copyright permissions

For a complete list of copyright permissions please visit https://github.com/jim-schwoebel/voicebook/blob/master/references/Copyright.pdf

Please contact me at jim.schwoebel@gmail.com if you have any concerns and I will fix these issues promptly.

References

For a complete list of references, please visit https://github.com/jim-schwoebel/voicebook/blob/master/references/References.pdf

A URL is provided here to save trees :)

Index

A

Actions (Nala)........294-298
Adaboost (algorithm)........162
Affective computing........15
Algorithms........143, 151, 161-162, 167-168
Analog period (history)........17
Apache (web server)........309
Apple HomePod........19, 35, 234, 264
Audio coding format........45-46
Audio channels........47, 51, 56, 74, 88
Audio features........111-121
Audioset embedding........119-120
Auth0 (module)........332-334
Auto-keras (module)........184
Automated machine learning...153, 180-185
ARD regression........168

B

Backpropagation (deep learning)........173
Batch size (deep learning)........172
Blockchain architectures........362-363
Bluetooth chips........257-258
Bluetooth (software)........265-266
Bokeh (module)........206
Brunet's index (feature)........122

C

Canonical correlation analysis........140
Cleaning audio files........84-90
Character frequency (feature)........122
Chatbots........195-197, 199-201
Chatterbot (module)........195-196
Central processing unit (CPU)........247-249
Changing volume.........85-86
Classification........151, 161-167
Client-server model........305
Codec........45
Combining audio files........86-87
Computer monitors........252-254
Computing (definition)........15
Condenser microphone........24, 43-44, 71
Condenser MEMS microphone........44, 72
Conferences (voice)........388-390

Containers........316, 334
Copyright law........368-369
Cross-validation........109, 152
CRUD operations (databases)........310

D

Databases (definition)........310-311
Databases (Nala)........285-288
Data labeling (definition)........109, 157-160
DataRobot (company)........184
Decision trees (algorithm)........161
Decryption........357-358
Deep learning model(s)........153, 172-179
Devol (module)........184
Dimensionality reduction........139-143
Digital period (history)........18
Distance (from microphone)........72-73
Django (framework)........320-321
Docker........316, 334-337
Dolphin attack........362
Downloading (training data)........159
Drivers (speaker)........47
Dynamic microphone........24, 27, 44
Dynamic speaker........48

E

Encryption........354-358
Elastic net (regression)........168
Electret microphone........26, 43-44
Electrostatic loudspeaker........49
Environment variables........63, 66, 276
Epoch (deep learning)........172
Ethical considerations........371-377

F

False positive........109, 136, 269
Features (definition)........109, 151
Feature selection........143-147
File duration (feature)........112
Flask (framework)........319-321
Formant frequencies (features)........112
Fundamental frequency (feature)........112
Ffmpy (module)........58, 87

FFmpeg (software)........30, 18, 59, 154
.FLAC (audio format)........46, 51, 60, 93
FTP server (uploading)........96-98

G
Gensim (module)........130-133, 221-223
Geoplotlib (module)........206
Ggplot (module)........205
GitHub (software)........340-342
Gleam (module)........206
Google Duplex........189
Google (machine learning)........185
Google (speech-to-text)........63-64
Google (text-to-speech)........66-67
Google (storage).........98
Gradient boosting (algorithm)........162
Graduate schools (voice)........390-392

H
Hardware........15, 236-237
Hard voting (algorithm)........162
Hands-free computing........15
Headphones........17, 24, 48
Heroku (software)........342-343
HIPAA certification........359-360
HITRUST certification........360
Huber regression........169
H20.ai (company)........184

I
Independent component analysis........139
Innovation Fellows Program.........384-385
Intent loop (Nala)........288-293
Internet period (history)..................18-19
Investors (voice startups).............394

J
Jitter (feature)........112
Jobs (voice computing)........392-393
JSON (database)........311

K
Kafka (software)........316, 318-319, 328-330
Keyword frequency (feature)........122
Keras (module)........173-174, 178-179
Kubernetes (k8s)........316-317, 344-347
K-means clustering........140
K-nearest neighbors (algorithm).....161, 214

L
Labels (machine learning)........157-160
Language period (history)........16
LARS lasso (regression)........168
Lasso (regression)........167
Layers (deep learning)........172
Least angle regression (LARS)........168
Leather (module)........207
LibROSA (module)........34, 51-52, 114-116
LiteSpeed (web server)........304
Lighttpd (web server)........309
Load balancer (server)........311
Logistic regression.........168
Loss functions (deep learning)........153, 173
Loudspeaker........24, 48-49
Linear discriminant analysis........140

M
Machine-generated audio data........197-199
Machine-generated mixed data.......199-201
Machine-generated text data........190-197
Machine-generated voice data........189-190
Machine learning........37, 109, 151-153
Manifold learning........140
Matplotlib (module)........205
Meta features........135-138, 226-228
Missingno (module)........206
MFCC (features)........112
MFCC delta coefficients (features)........112
MEMUPPS voice controls........103-105
Microphone........17, 21, 43-45, 71-72
Microphone arrays........74-75
Microservices (servers)........313-316
Microsoft Azure........185
Minio (module)........331-332

Mixed features........134-135, 223-225
Mixers........77
MongoDB (database)........310, 324-328
Monolith (servers)........313-314
Morphological features........122, 130
Motherboard........245-247
Motherboard (form factor)........245
Multi-task elastic net (regression)........168
Multi-task lasso (regression)........167
Music computing........15
Music period (history)........16-17
MySQL (database)........310-311

N
Nala........276-299
Naive bayes (algorithm)........161
Named entity recognition (features)........123
NAT gateways (networking)........306-307
NetworkX (module)........221
Neural networks (algorithm)....172-176
NeuroLex (story)........381-384
Neuron (neural network)........172
NGINX (web server)........309, 321-323
NLTK (module)........126-130
Noise-cancelling microphone........45, 72
Noise reduction (cleaning)........84-85
Numpy (module)........110-111

O
Onset strength (feature)........113
OpenSMILE embedding........119-120
Open source software........56-57, 385-388
Open source dataset........155-156
OpenCV (module)........225
.OPUS (audio format)........18, 33, 46, 94-96
Ordinary least squares (regression)........167
OMP regression........168
Outer housing 262-264
Overfitting........109

P
Parsed tree plot........220
Part-of-speech tags (features)........122

Partial least squares regression........140
Passive aggressive (regression)........168
Patent laws........369-370
Path plotting........209-210
PCI DSS certification........360
Penetration testing........360-362
Perceptron (regression)........168
Physical security........358-359
Piezoelectric MEMS microphone........44, 72
Piezoelectric speaker........49
Play back audio........54-55
Plotly dash (module)........206
PocketSphinx (module).......30, 61-62, 123
PockSphinx (wake word) 269-271
Polynomial regression........169
Porcupine (wake word) 271-272
Postgres (database)........310
Power supply........261-262
Principal component analysis........139
Privacy laws........364-366
Private keys (encryption)........355
Proprietary software........61
Proprietary dataset........156
Public keys (encryption)........355
Publishing (voice content)........99-102
PyAudioAnalysis (module)........34, 116
Pybluez (module)........265
Pydub (module)........50-54
Pygal (module)........206
Pygame (module)........54
Pyserial (module)........266-267
Pysox (module)........52
Pyttsx3 (module)........65-66

R
Random forest (algorithm)........161
RAM memory........249-251
RANSAC (regression)........168
Recording environments........73, 103
Recording modes........78-84
Regression (models)........151, 167-171
Regularization (deep learning)........173
RF transceivers........252-254
Ribbon microphone........25, 44, 71

Ribbon loudspeaker........49, 259
Ridge regression........167
Robo 3T (software)........326-327
Robustness regression........168
Root mean squared (RMS) energy........113

S
Sample rate........87-88
Scientific period (history)........17
SciPy (module)........50-52
Seaborn (module)........205
Sentiment polarity (feature)........122
Security (voice apps)........353-363
Security certifications........359-360
Serial connections........266-267
Server hardware........308
Server software........309-310
Shimmer (feature)........112
Silence removal........89
Snowboy (wake word)........271
Sound computing........15
Software (voice)........15
Soft voting (algorithm)........162
Sound card(s)........46-47, 242-244
Sounddevice (module)........55-58, 387
Soundfile (module)........51, 387
SoX (filtering)........18, 30, 52-54, 84-90
SoX (feature extraction)........117-118
SpaCy (module)........130, 220
Speaker diarization........90-92
Speakers........47-49, 77, 258-261
Spectral centroid (feature)........113
Spectral flatness (feature)........113
Spectral flux (feature)........113
Spectral rolloff (feature)........113
Spectrograms........211
Stochastic gradient descent........168
Storage devices........251
Storing voice files........93-98
String manipulation........124-125
Subwoofer (speaker)........48
Supervised dictionary learning........140
Supervised learning........152, 161
Support vector machines........161

Syntactic features........122

T
Teaching opportunities........394
Terms of service........370, 375
Testing set........109, 151
TextgenRNN (module)........192-195
Text features........122-134, 216-223
Text-to-speech engines........18, 65-67, 168
Theil-Sen estimator (regression)........169
TPOT (module)........180-183
Training set........109, 151
T-SNE embeddings........221-223
Transcription (default)........60-64, 123-124
Transcription (custom)........272-275, 278
Transcoding audio........45, 58-60, 87
Trimming audio files........86
Tweeters (speaker)........47
Two-factor authentication........359-360

U
Ubiquitous computing........15
Unit testing........337-339
Unittest (module)........338-339
Unsupervised learning....139, 141, 152, 161
User registration (Nala)........280-284

V
Validation data........152
Variational autoencoders........140
Visualization........203-230
Vector quantization........140
Virtual machines (VMs)........315
VGGish embedding........119
Voice adversarial attack........361
Voice assistants........33, 35, 37, 276-299
Voice cleaning software.........89-90
Voice computer (definition)........15, 233
Voice computing (timeline)........20-35
Voice ethics framework........371-372
Voice hardware........15, 236-264
Voice features........109
Voice-first period (history)........19

Voice legal framework........363-364
Voice masquerading........361
Voice security framework........353
Voice squatting........361
Voice software........15, 234-235

W
Wake word(s)........78, 267-272, 279
Wave (module)........50-51
Web frameworks........319-321
WebRTC........306-307
Weights (deep learning)........153, 172
WiFi chips........254-256
WiFi (software)........266
Windows (signal processing)........111
Wireless (module)........266
Woofers (speaker)........47-48
Word frequencies (visualization)......218-219
WordCloud (module)........219
Word2vec embeddings........218

Z
Zero-crossing rate (feature)........113, 116

About the author

Jim Schwoebel is the founding CEO of NeuroLex Labs, a company with the goal to make voice computing accessible to everyone. In less than one year (2017-2018), NeuroLex has grown to over 11 core team members, raised >$200k of investment, launched 13 pilots, and has completed 4 accelerator programs: Voicecamp (New York City), Mass Challenge (Boston), TMCx (Houston), and the Bridge Community (Atlanta). Previously, Jim was a founding partner of CyberLaunch, an accelerator fund which invested in and grew over 22 companies in the neuroscience, machine learning, and cybersecurity verticals.

Jim is passionate about training others to begin careers in voice computing through demo projects. In this capacity, he created the Innovation Fellows Program to help outstanding developers grow in their careers. Since its inception, the Innovation Fellows Program has trained over 60 individuals through 20 demo projects. This book emerged as a way to scale the scope of this program to others across the world.

Jim's work has been covered by the Atlantic, the American Psychiatric Association, the Atlanta Business Chronicle, Venture Atlanta, and Hypepotamus. In 2014, Jim was awarded the Alvin M. Ferst Leadership and Entrepreneurship Award. He holds a B.S. in Biomedical Engineering from Georgia Tech.

Contact information

- jim.schwoebel@gmail.com
- https://github.com/jim-schwoebel/
- https://twitter.com/jim_schwoebel
- https://www.linkedin.com/in/jimschwoebel/

Made in the USA
Monee, IL
02 September 2019